W9-CEJ-266

AIR TRAFFIC CONTROL
Career Prep

**CD ROM ENCLOSED. $5.00
CHARGE IF NOT RETURNED**

AIR TRAFFIC CONTROL
Career Prep

By Dr. Patrick R. Mattson, CTO

Aviation Supplies & Academics, Inc.
Newcastle, WA 98059

Air Traffic Control Career Prep
Text by Patrick Mattson

Aviation Supplies & Academics, Inc.
7005 132nd Place SE
Newcastle, Washington 98059-3153
Email: asa@asa2fly.com
Website: www.asa2fly.com

ASA-ATC-2
ISBN 1-56027-614-2
  978-1-56027-614-2

Printed in the United States of America

2010 2009 2008 2007 2006 9 8 7 6 5 4 3 2 1

Library of Congress Cataloging-in-Publication Data:
Mattson, Patrick R.
  Air traffic control career prep : a comprehensive guide to one of the best-paying federal government careers, including test preparation for the initial air traffic control exams / Patrick R. Mattson.
    p. cm.
  Includes bibliographical references.
  ISBN-13: 978-1-56027-614-2 (pbk. : alk. paper)
  ISBN-10: 1-56027-614-2 (pbk. : alk. paper)
  1. Air traffic control—Vocational guidance. 2. Air traffic controllers. I. Title.
  TL725.3.T7M38 2006
  387.7'4042602373—dc22
       2006021778

Table of Contents

Introduction _____

Welcome to the *Air Traffic Control Career Prep.* This book was written with two purposes in mind. First, to introduce the reader to the aviation industry, the role of the FAA, and what to expect as one pursues a career in air traffic control. Secondly, to discuss the general format of the Air Traffic Selection and Training aptitude test (AT-SAT) and give readers ample practice sets to study, in preparation for that test. The author's goal is to provide pertinent information related to an air traffic control career, designed to help readers improve their chances of earning a high score on the test and becoming a candidate for an air traffic control position.

The Big Picture

The following is a bird's-eye view of hiring and training for this career—there are several tests involved in the process of becoming an air traffic controller. The first one to pass is the aptitude-checking test called the AT-SAT, which is the test covered in this book. Your first goal is to achieve a high score on the AT-SAT exam, and once you qualify, then you are eligible to compete for an appointment to the FAA's Oklahoma City Academy.

If you are offered what is called a "temporary excepted appointment" to the Academy you may have to take other tests as part of your training, including the "Basics of ATC" test. This test covers the material CTI students learn in college. Additionally, those students who are Academy "off the street" applicants would receive five weeks of basic training at Oklahoma City. Usually, ex-military controllers are exempted from this, as they have ATC training, previous ratings and experience. A person selected for a control tower position would also need to take and pass the Control Tower Operator (CTO) and Tower Visibility tests.

Some further good sources of background and study materials are as follows (check for the most current versions for the FAA Orders at www.faa.gov/atpubs/):

- Air Traffic Control (FAA Order 7110.65)

- Facility Operation and Administration (FAA Order 7210.3U)

- Air Traffic Technical Training (FAA Order 3120.4)

- Aeronautical Information Manual

- Air Traffic Control System: A Commonsense Guide, by Milovan S. Brenlove (originally published 2003 by Iowa State Press, latest edition published by ASA, ISBN 1560276355)

- Fundamentals of Air Traffic Control, by Michael S. Nolan, 4th Edition (Brooks Cole, 2003), ISBN 0534393888

- ATCsimulator®2 provides a re-creation of approach-departure control (TRACON) for the MS-Windows platform. http://www.atcsimulator.com

Good luck in your ATC endeavors!

Chapter One
Your Air Traffic Control Career

General Overview

For over 100 years, the aviation industry has played a leading role in the economy of the United States and has fostered a variety of technological advances. From the beginning, major airline companies have used the emerging technology to reshape the face of cargo and passenger travel. Keeping in step with the growth of aviation, the U.S. has had a variety of federal agencies that promote air safety and enable users of the National Airspace System (NAS) to enjoy a safe, orderly, and expeditious flight. General aviation, the airlines, and the military services have generated a large volume of air traffic in the past; it is predicted that these segments of the industry will continue to grow rapidly in the 21st century and beyond.

Today, the job of aviation safety is the responsibility of the Federal Aviation Administration (FAA). The role of the FAA is to ensure air safety and improve and coordinate the effectiveness of the NAS to meet the ever-growing demand caused by the increase in aviation operations.

While all parts of the FAA's operation are important, the crucial link in the efficiency of the system is the air traffic controller. The controller is the point of contact between users of the aviation system and their ultimate safe and expeditious journey through national airspace. Air traffic controllers are the least visible element of the aviation system, but form an integral part of air safety. The role of an air traffic controller is not an easy one; nor is the job attained without a great deal of effort, dedication, and discipline on the part of anyone who desires to enter this demanding occupation. For the person who enjoys a definite challenge and does not mind hard work, being an air traffic controller represents an exciting, rewarding, and high-paying career.

The FAA Air Traffic Control System

The United States has had a federal air traffic control (ATC) system since 1935. Today's FAA is the result of many citizens, pilots, legislators, airline companies, military services, and government agencies seeking way to best serve this country's aviation interests and needs. The FAA is not an independent agency; it is part of the Department of Transportation (DOT). The DOT is managed by the Secretary of Transportation, a cabinet-level position, secured by direct presidential appointment and confirmed by the Congress. The NAS consists of air traffic control, airports, airmen, aircraft, and airways. (Think of them as highways in the sky.) The FAA employs over 45,000 people to keep the airways and airspace safe and ensure the efficient use of the NAS, 24 hours a day, 365 days a year.

Airway Facilities

The U.S. air traffic control system is the most advanced in the world. The FAA relies on its Airway Facilities (AF) branch to keep the complex system running smoothly. The AF is involved in the maintenance, support, and administrative sections, employing over 9,000 dedicated and highly-trained personnel. They are directly responsible for the maintenance of the navigational aids, radar, computer, and communication systems located throughout the country. AF personnel are not air traffic controllers, but they must be experts in their field and maintain an in-depth knowledge of the air traffic control system and its needs.

ATC Facilities

Work Roles

This information is adapted from the FAA's Air Traffic Control Specialist (ATCS) employment information pamphlets webpage at the ATCS job series webpage (http://www.faa.gov/careers/employment/atc.htm). An air traffic control specialist is responsible for the safe, orderly, and expeditious flow of air traffic. It is their function to direct air traffic so it flows smoothly, efficiently and above all, safely—both on the ground and in the air. There are three specializations:

- **Terminal (Tower)**

  Terminal controllers control air traffic at airports and give pilots taxiing and takeoff instructions, air traffic clearances, and advice based on their own observations and information from the National Weather Service, air route traffic control centers (ARTCC), flight service stations, pilots, and other sources. They provide separation between landing and departing aircraft. They transfer control of aircraft to the ARTCC controller when the aircraft leaves their airspace, and they receive control of aircraft coming into their airspace from controllers at adjacent facilities. Air traffic controllers must be familiar with the aircraft identification and positions of the aircraft under their control, aircraft types and speeds, and the location of navigational aids and landmarks in the area.

- **Enroute Center**

  Air traffic control specialists at ARTCCs give aircraft instructions, air traffic clearances, and advice regarding flight conditions while enroute between airports. They provide separation between aircraft flying along the federal airways or operating into or out of airports not served by a terminal facility. Center controllers use radar, or in some cases, manual procedures to track the progress of all instrument flights within the center's airspace. Where radar coverage is available and their workload permits, enroute controllers also provide radar service to pilots who are not on instrument flight plans, alerting them to potential traffic conflicts. Enroute controllers transfer control of aircraft to controllers in adjacent centers, or approach control, or terminal, when the aircraft enters that facility's airspace.

- **Flight Service Station Specialist**

  (Contracted to Lockheed-Martin as of February 2005.)

Air traffic control specialists at FAA automated flight service stations (AFSS) provide preflight, in-flight and emergency assistance to all pilots on request. They work with some pilots face-to-face at their facilities and also communicate with pilots by phone and radio. They provide information about weather conditions for specific flights; receive and forward pilots' flight plans; relay air traffic control instructions; assist pilots in emergency situations; provide airport advisory service, and initiate searches for missing or overdue aircraft.

Regardless of where a controller works or the facility is located, the goal of the air traffic control system remains the same: ensure the safety of flight, meet the country's aviation needs, and provide for the efficient use of the National Airspace System. All air traffic controllers have a huge responsibility and take great pride in their profession. As civil servants, they provide a vital service to the aviation industry, its users, and the nation. The job requires quick, correct decision-making skills; employment in this field is not for everyone. Those who become fully-certified professional controllers are true professionals, dedicated to the mission of safe air travel in the U.S. and abroad.

ATC Facility Visits

It is often a rewarding experience for the applicant to visit an FAA air traffic control facility before or during the application process. FAA ATC facilities welcome visitors (with prior approval), especially those persons who are considering employment in the field. One should call first for an appointment during regular business hours and inform the facility representative of his/her interest in the FAA and air traffic control. Most facilities have career information on hand; see Pages 8-10 for a map (Figure 1-1), and list of phone numbers.

An ATC Career

This section is adapted from the 2004-05 Occupational Outlook Handbook webpage (http://stats.bls.gov/oco/pdf/ocos108.pdf). Keep in mind these significant points regarding an ATC career:

- Nearly all air traffic controllers are employed by the FAA.

- Large numbers of air traffic controllers will be eligible to retire over the next decade, potentially creating many job openings.

- Aircraft controllers earn high pay and good benefits.

The air traffic control system is a vast network of people and equipment that ensures the safe operation of commercial and private aircraft. Air traffic controllers coordinate the movement of air traffic to make certain that planes stay a safe distance apart. Their immediate concern is safety, but controllers also must direct planes efficiently to minimize delays. Some regulate airport traffic; others regulate flights between airports.

Although airport tower or terminal controllers watch over all planes traveling through the airport's airspace, their main responsibility is to organize the flow of aircraft into and out of the airport. Relying on radar and visual observation, they closely monitor each plane to ensure a safe distance between all aircraft and to guide pilots between the hangar or ramp and the end of the airport's air-space. In addition, controllers keep pilots informed about changes in weather conditions such as wind shear—a sudden change in the velocity or direction of the wind that can cause the pilot to lose control of the aircraft.

During arrival or departure, several controllers direct each plane. As a plane approaches an airport, the pilot radios ahead to inform the terminal of the plane's presence. The controller in the radar room, just beneath the control tower, has a copy of the plane's flight plan and has already observed the plane on radar. If the path is clear, the controller directs the pilot to a runway; if not, the plane is directed into the traffic pattern along with other aircraft waiting to land. As the plane nears the runway, the pilot is asked to contact the tower. There, another controller, who is also watching the plane on radar, monitors the aircraft the last mile or so to the runway, delaying any departures that would interfere with the plane's landing. Once the plane has landed, a ground controller in the tower directs it along the taxiways to its assigned gate. The ground controller usually works entirely by sight, but may use radar if visibility is poor.

The procedure is reversed for departures. The ground controller directs the plane to the proper runway. The local controller then informs the pilot about conditions at the airport, such as weather, speed and direction of wind, and visibility. The local controller also issues runway clearance for the pilot to take off. Once in the air, the plane is guided out of the airport's airspace by the departure controller.

After each plane departs, airport tower controllers notify Enroute controllers who will next take charge. There are 21 air route traffic control centers located around the country, each employing 300 to 700 controllers, with more than 150 on duty during peak hours at the busier facilities. Airplanes usually fly along designated routes; each center is assigned a certain airspace containing many different routes. Enroute controllers work in teams of up to three members, depending on how heavy traffic is; each team is responsible for a section of the center's airspace. A team, for example, might be responsible for all planes 30 to 100 miles north of an airport and flying at an altitude between 6,000 and 18,000 feet.

To prepare for planes about to enter the team's airspace, the radar associate controller organizes flight plans coming off a printer. If two planes are scheduled to enter the team's airspace at nearly the same time, location, and altitude, this controller may arrange with the preceding control unit for one plane to change its flight path. The previous unit may have been another team at the same or an adjacent center, or a departure controller at a neighboring terminal. As a plane approaches a team's airspace, the radar controller accepts responsibility for the plane from the previous controlling unit. The controller also delegates responsibility for the plane to the next controlling unit when the plane leaves the team's airspace.

The radar controller, who is the senior team member, observes on radar the planes in the team's airspace and communicates with the pilots when necessary. Radar controllers warn pilots about nearby planes, bad weather conditions, and other potential hazards. Two planes on a collision course will be directed around each other. If a pilot wants to change altitude in search of better flying conditions, the controller will make sure no other planes will be along the proposed path. As the flight progresses, the team responsible for the aircraft notifies the next team in charge of the airspace ahead. Through team coordination, the plane arrives safely at its destination.

Both airport tower and enroute controllers usually control several planes at a time; often they have to make quick decisions about completely different activities. For example, a controller might direct a plane on its landing approach and at the same time, provide pilots entering the airport's airspace with information about conditions at the airport. While instructing these pilots, the controller would also observe other planes in the vicinity, such as those in a holding pattern waiting for permission to land, to ensure that they remain well separated.

In addition to airport towers and enroute centers, air traffic controllers also work in flight service stations operated at more than 100 locations. These flight service specialists provide pilots with information on the station's particular area, including terrain, pre-flight and in-flight weather information, suggested routes, and other information important to the safety of a flight. Flight service station specialists help pilots in emergency situations and initiate and coordinate searches for missing or overdue aircraft. They are not, however, involved in actively managing air traffic.

Some air traffic controllers work at the FAA Air Traffic Control Systems Command Center in Herndon, Virginia, where they oversee the entire system. They look for situations that will create bottlenecks or other problems in the system, then respond with a management plan for traffic into and out of the troubled sector. The objective is to keep traffic levels in the trouble spots manageable for the controllers working at enroute centers.

Working Conditions
Controllers work a basic 40-hour week; however, they may work additional hours for which they receive overtime pay or equal time off. Most controllers rotate night and weekend shifts because all centers, and most large control towers, operate 24/7.

During busy times, controllers must work quickly and efficiently. Total concentration is required to keep track of several planes at the same time and to ensure all pilots receive correct instructions. The mental stress of being responsible for the safety of several aircraft and their passengers can be exhausting for some people.

Air traffic controllers held about 26,000 jobs in 2004. The vast majority were employed by the FAA. Air traffic controllers work at airports—in towers and flight service stations—and in air route traffic control centers. Some professional controllers conduct research at the FAA's national experimental center near Atlantic City, New Jersey. Others serve as instructors at the FAA Academy in Oklahoma City, Oklahoma. A small number of civilian controllers work for the U.S. Department of Defense. In addition to controllers employed by the federal government, some work for private air traffic control companies providing service to contracted non-FAA towers. These towers must follow the same rules as their FAA counterparts.

Training, Other Qualifications, and Advancement
To become an air traffic controller, a person must pass a pre-employment test that measures his or her ability to learn the controller's duties in order to qualify for job openings. The Collegiate Training Initiative (CTI) program is one of several methods used by the FAA to recruit and hire controller applicants; the others include military veterans, military retirees (Phoenix-20 program), FAA reinstatements (PATCO), Flight Service employees, AT-SAT direct hire, and Academy applications. Although hiring started in the spring of 2005, it will be at least mid-2006 before the FAA offers employment to those not in the CTI pipeline. As of July 2006 the pre-employment test is currently offered only to students in the CTI program. In addition, applicants must have 3 years of full-time work experience or 4 years of college, or a combination of both. In combining education and experience, 1 year of undergraduate study (30 semester or 45 quarter hours) is equivalent to 9 months of work experience.

Upon successful completion of the CTI program, individuals who receive school recommendation and meet the basic qualification requirements, including age limit and a qualifying score on the FAA authorized pre-employment test, become eligible for employment as an air traffic controller. Candidates also must pass a medical exam, drug screening, and security clearance before they can be hired. After selection, employees attend the FAA Academy in Oklahoma City for 12 weeks of training, during which they learn the fundamentals of the airway system, FAA regulations, controller equipment, and aircraft performance characteristics, as well as more specialized tasks.

After graduation, it takes several years of progressively more responsible work experience, interspersed with considerable classroom instruction and independent study, to become a fully qualified controller. Controllers who fail to complete either the Academy or the on-the-job portion of the training are usually dismissed. Controllers must pass a physical examination each year and a job performance examination twice each year. Failure to become certified in any position at a facility within a specified time may also result in dismissal. Controllers are also subject to drug screening as a condition of continuing employment.

Air traffic controllers must be articulate, because pilots must be given directions quickly and clearly. Intelligence, a basic math aptitude, and a good memory are also important because controllers constantly receive information that they must immediately grasp, interpret, and remember. Decisiveness is also required because controllers have to make quick decisions. The ability to concentrate is crucial because controllers must make decisions in the midst of noise and other distractions.

At airports, new controllers begin by supplying pilots with basic flight data and airport information. They then advance to the position of ground controller, then local controller, departure controller, and finally, arrival controller. At an air route traffic control center, new controllers first deliver printed flight plans to teams, gradually advancing to radar associate controller and then radar controller.

If approved, controllers can transfer to jobs at different locations, advance to supervisory positions such as management or staff jobs in air traffic control, or to top administrative jobs in the FAA. However, there are only limited opportunities for a controller to switch from a position in an enroute center to a tower.

Job Outlook

Employment of air traffic controllers through 2015 is expected to grow significantly, as nearly 70 percent of FAA controllers are eligible to retire. Increasing air traffic will require more controllers to handle the additional work. The increasing automation of the air traffic control system and federal budget constraints may limit future employment growth; however, this growth is not expected to keep pace with growth in the number of aircraft flying. New computerized systems will help controllers make routine decisions, which will allow them to handle more traffic, thus increasing their productivity.

Although the majority of today's air traffic controllers will be eligible to retire over the next decade, not all are expected to do so. Replacement needs will nevertheless be substantial and will result in about 1,000 to 1,250 annual job opportunities for those graduating from the FAA training programs. Despite the increasing number of jobs coming open, competition to get into the FAA training programs is expected to remain keen, as there generally are many more applicants than there are openings. But those who graduate have good prospects of getting a job as a controller. Air traffic controllers who continue to meet the proficiency and medical requirements enjoy more job security than do most workers. The demand for air travel and the workloads of air traffic controllers decline during recessions, but controllers are seldom laid off.

Pay and Benefits

As of May 1, 2005 the initial salary was $16,016 for 15 weeks while in training at the FAA's Oklahoma City Academy. The salary range for new controller candidates successfully completing the Academy is $36,928 to $46,075 depending on the facility of assignment. Most control towers pay less than enroute centers, with major international airport towers and Tracons paying near or more than the enroute center scale. Academy Graduates (AG) are placed in a developmental status until they make CPC (fully rated in their area of facility assignment). Developmental status has three stages. After acquiring appropriate ratings, a controller can earn from $95,745 (journeymen) to $134,043 (certified professional controller) plus locality pay; this does not include premium pay and/or benefits.*

The 2005 range of controller compensation, including salary, premium pay, and benefits, was $136,000 to $205,000 with the median at approximately $165,000. Both the job responsibilities and complexity of the particular facility determine a controller's pay. For example, controllers who work at the FAA's busiest air traffic control facilities earn higher pay. Depending on length of service and or military time, air traffic controllers receive 13 to 26 days of paid vacation and 13 days of paid sick leave each year, life insurance, and health benefits. In addition, controllers can retire at an earlier age and with fewer years of service than other federal employees. Air traffic controllers are eligible to retire at age 50 with 20 years of service as an active air traffic controller, or after 25 years of active service at any age. There is a mandatory retirement age of 56 for active FAA controllers who manage air traffic, but they can seek other jobs (traffic management, administration, etc) with the FAA in order to remain in a salaried status. Federal law also provides for exemptions to the mandatory age of 56, up to age 61, for controllers who have exceptional skills and experience. For more information see the Denver Center webpage, "FAA ATC Hiring" (see Appendix 6 for the web address).

Certified Professional Controllers (CPC)

A CPC is one who holds all of the appropriate ratings for their facility of assignment. Each air traffic control facility has its own criteria for certification. This is due to the type of air traffic service each facility provides and the amount of traffic handled on an annual basis. To determine CPC grades, the facilities are first grouped by the type of air traffic service they provide: Flight Service Station (FSS), Airport Traffic Control Tower (ATCT), or Air Route Traffic Control Center (ARTCC). Then each group is divided into levels of activity representing the volume of air traffic services provided. ARTCCs are divided into three levels while ATCTs are divided into five. Level I is the lowest volume of air traffic related services provided. Heavier traffic greatly increases the controller's workload, thus the higher pay at busier facilities. Each facility keeps a careful record of its aviation related services so it will be classified correctly and staffed appropriately. A rural airport may have only a dozen or less controllers, whereas at a very busy airport, the large international tower may employ as many as 125 controllers and the enroute center over 300.

---

*Note from the author: The above information regarding controller pay was correct at the time of my research. Readers should check with the FAA for official information regarding salary and benefits (which varies for each facility) at the time of application.

ARTCC Locations and Offices

The current Air Traffic Organization (ATO) regions consolidated nine regions into three (Western, Central, and Eastern), directed by the Congress under Presidential Executive Order 13180 in December 2000. See Figure 1-1. The FAA began designing the ATO in 2001 and implemented it in 2003-04. In March 2006, the FAA announced that all regional air traffic Terminal and Enroute/Oceanic service units would be located at the same offices.

ATO Regional Offices
WESTERN:

Renton, WA (425) 227-2542 (was Alaska, Northwest Mountain, and Western Pacific)

ARTCCs — Anchorage (ZAN), Albuquerque (ZAB), Denver (ZDV), Guam (ZUA), Honolulu (ZHN), Los Angeles (ZLA), Oakland (ZOA), Salt Lake City (ZLC), Seattle (ZSE)

CENTRAL:

Fort Worth, TX (817) 222-5599 (was Central, Southwest, and Great Lakes regions)

ARTCCs — Chicago (ZAU), Cleveland (ZOB), Fort Worth (ZFW), Houston (ZHU), Indianapolis (ZID), Kansas City (ZKC), Minneapolis (ZMP)

EASTERN:

Atlanta, GA (404) 305-5630 (was Eastern, New England, and Southern regions)

ARTCCs — Atlanta (ZTL), Boston (ZBW), Jacksonville (ZJX), Memphis (ZME), Miami (ZMA), New York (ZNY), San Juan (ZSU), Washington DC (ZDC)

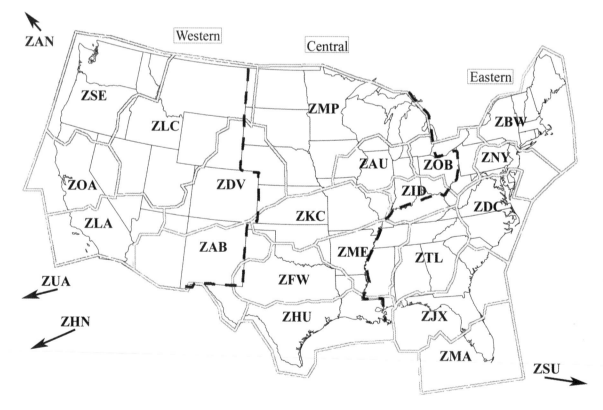

Figure 1-1. FAA regions with ARTCCs listed

ARTCC, Tracon and Airport Telephone Numbers

Current as of January 31, 2006

ARTCC	BUSINESS HOURS	BUS. PHONE
Albuquerque	7:30 a.m. - 4:00 p.m.	505-856-4300
Anchorage	7:30 a.m. - 4:00 p.m.	907-269-1137
Atlanta	7:30 a.m. - 5:00 p.m.	770-210-7601
Boston	7:30 a.m. - 4:00 p.m.	603-879-6633
Chicago	8:00 a.m. - 4:00 p.m.	630-906-8221
Cleveland	8:00 a.m. - 4:00 p.m.	440-774-0310
Denver	7:30 a.m. - 4:00 p.m.	303-651-4100
Ft. Worth	7:30 a.m. - 4:00 p.m.	817-858-7300
Houston	7:30 a.m. - 4:00 p.m.	723-230-5300
Indianapolis	8:00 a.m. - 4:00 p.m.	317-247-2231
Jacksonville	8:00 a.m. - 4:30 p.m.	904-549-1501
Kansas City	7:30 a.m. - 4:00 p.m.	913-254-8500
Los Angeles	7:30 a.m. - 4:00 p.m.	661-265-8200
Memphis	7:30 a.m. - 4:00 p.m.	901-368-8103
Miami	7:30 a.m. - 3:30 p.m.	305-716-1500
Minneapolis	8:00 a.m. - 4:00 p.m.	612-463-5510
New York	8:00 a.m. - 4:40 p.m.	516-468-1001
Oakland	7:30 a.m. - 4:00 p.m.	510-745-3301
Salt Lake City	7:30 a.m. - 4:00 p.m.	801-320-2500
Seattle	7:30 a.m. - 4:00 p.m.	253-351-3500
Washington	8:00 a.m. - 4:30 p.m.	703-771-3401
TRACON NAME	**BUSINESS HOURS**	**BUS. PHONE**
Atlanta	7:30 a.m. - 3:30 p.m.	404-669-1200
Chicago	8:00 a.m. - 4:00 p.m.	847-608-5509
Dallas/Ft. Worth	7:30 a.m. - 4:00 p.m.	972-615-2500
Denver	7:30 a.m. - 4:00 p.m.	303-342-1500
Houston	7:30 a.m. - 4:00 p.m.	713-230-8400
New York	8:00 a.m. - 4:30 p.m.	516-683-2901
Oakland Bay	7:30 a.m. - 4:00 p.m.	510-273-6005
Southern CA	7:30 a.m. - 4:00 p.m.	858-537-5800

Continued...

AIRPORT NAME	BUSINESS HOURS	BUS. PHONE
Albuquerque Intl, NM	8:00 a.m. - 5:00 p.m.	505-842-4366
Andrews AFB, MD	8:00 a.m. - 4:30 p.m.	301-735-2380
Atlanta Hartsfield Intl, GA	7:00 a.m. - 3:30 p.m.	404-669-1200
Baltimore-Washington Intl, MD	8:00 a.m. - 4:30 p.m.	410-962-3555
Boston Logan Intl, MA	7:30 a.m. - 4:00 p.m.	617-561-5901
Bradley Intl, CT	7:30 a.m. - 4:00 p.m.	203-627-3428
Charlotte Douglas Intl, NC	8:00 a.m. - 4:30 p.m.	704-344-6487
Chicago Midway, IL	8:00 a.m. - 4:00 p.m.	773-884-3670
Chicago O'Hare Intl, IL	8:00 a.m. - 4:00 p.m.	773-601-7600
Cleveland Hopkins Intl, OH	8:00 a.m. - 4:00 p.m.	216-898-2020
Covington/Cincinnati, OH	8:00 a.m. - 4:30 p.m.	606-767-1006
Dallas/Ft. Worth Intl, TX	8:30 a.m. - 5:00 p.m.	972-615-2531
Dayton Cox Intl, OH	7:30 a.m. - 4:00 p.m.	937-454-7300
Denver Intl, CO	7:30 a.m. - 4:00 p.m.	303-342-1600
Detroit Metro, MI	8:00 a.m. - 4:00 p.m.	734-955-5000
Fairbanks Intl, AK	7:30 a.m. - 4:00 p.m.	907-474-0050
Fort Lauderdale Intl, FL	7:00 a.m. - 3:30 p.m.	305-356-7932
Intercontinental Houston, TX	7:30 a.m. - 4:00 p.m.	713-230-8400
Honolulu Intl, HI	7:30 a.m. - 4:00 p.m.	808-836-1761
Houston Hobby, TX	8:00 a.m. - 5:00 p.m.	713-847-1400
Indianapolis Intl, IN	8:00 a.m. - 4:00 p.m.	317-484-6600
Kahului/Maui, HI	7:30 a.m. - 4:00 p.m.	808-877-0725
Kansas City Intl, MO	7:30 a.m. - 4:00 p.m.	816-243-2700
Las Vegas McCarran, NV	7:30 a.m. - 4:00 p.m.	702-262-5978
Los Angeles Intl, CA	7:00 a.m. - 3:30 p.m.	310-342-4900
Memphis Intl, TN	7:30 a.m. - 4:00 p.m.	901-345-3235
Miami Intl, FL	7:00 a.m. - 4:00 p.m.	305-869-5400
Minneapolis/St. Paul, MN	8:00 a.m. - 4:00 p.m.	612-713-4000
Nashville Intl, TN	7:00 a.m. - 3:30 p.m.	615-781-5460
New Orleans Intl, LA	7:00 a.m. - 4:30 p.m.	504-471-4300
New York Kennedy Intl, NY	8:00 a.m. - 4:30 p.m.	718-656-0335
New York La Guardia, NY	8:00 a.m. - 4:30 p.m.	718-335-5461
Newark Intl, NJ	8:00 a.m. - 4:30 p.m.	973-645-3103
Ontario Intl, CA	7:30 a.m. - 4:00 p.m.	909-983-7518
Orlando Intl. FL	7:30 a.m. - 5:00 p.m.	407-850-7000
Philadelphia Intl, PA	8:00 a.m. - 4:30 p.m.	215-492-4100
Phoenix Sky Harbor Intl, AZ	7:30 a.m. - 4:00 p.m.	602-379-4226
Pittsburgh Intl, PA	8:00 a.m. - 4:30 p.m.	412-269-9237
Portland Intl, OR	7:30 a.m. - 4:00 p.m.	503-493-7500
Raleigh-Durham, NC	8:00 a.m. - 4:30 p.m.	919-840-5544
Reagan Washington National, DC	8:00 a.m. - 4:30 p.m.	703-413-1535
Salt Lake City, UT	7:30 a.m. - 4:00 p.m.	801-325-9600
San Antonio Intl, TX	8:00 a.m. - 4:30 p.m.	210-805-5507
San Diego Lindbergh Intl, CA	8:00 a.m. - 4:30 p.m.	619-299-0677
San Francisco Intl, CA	7:00 a.m. - 3:30 p.m.	650-876-2883
San Jose Intl, CA	7:30 a.m. - 4:00 p.m.	408-982-0750
San Juan Intl, PR	7:30 a.m. - 5:00 p.m.	809-253-8663
Seattle-Tacoma Intl, WA	7:30 a.m. - 4:00 p.m.	206-768-2900
St. Louis Lambert, MO	7:30 a.m. - 4:00 p.m.	314-890-1000
Tampa Intl, FL	7:30 a.m. - 4:00 p.m.	813-371-7700
Ted Stevens Anchorage Intl, AK	7:30 a.m. - 4:00 p.m.	907-271-2700
Teterboro, NJ	8:00 a.m. - 4:30 p.m.	201-288-1889
Washington Dulles Intl, DC	8:00 a.m. - 4:30 p.m.	703-661-6031
West Palm Beach, FL	8:00 a.m. - 4:30 p.m.	407-683-1867
Westchester Co, NY	8:00 a.m. - 4:30 p.m.	914-948-6520

Chapter Two

The Entry Level ATC Position

Qualifications and Training

During the next 10 years, 73 percent of the FAA's 15,000 controllers will be eligible to retire. Most have said they will do so. This means the agency will need to hire about 11,000 new controllers. "A Plan for the Future: The FAA's 10-Year Strategy for the Air Traffic Control Workforce" was released in December of 2004 and is the agency's primary planning document for hiring and training new controllers. The FAA will update the plan annually and make adjustments accordingly.

This chapter provides the reader with insight into the hiring process, the Oklahoma City Academy experience, and finally a look at what training is like in an enroute center. Several Internet links are listed in Appendix 6 along with a list of forms needed for employment processing. If selected as an air traffic control candidate, you will be sent a packet of materials that include the necessary forms.

Initial Training Requirements for ATC Specialists

To qualify for entry-level air traffic control specialist positions, applicants must achieve a qualifying score on the current FAA authorized pre-employment test. (Source: FAA Order 3120.4L, 6/22/05 Section 3.)

Most individuals the FAA currently considers for ATC employment are those who have completed a two- or four-year degree from an approved CTI (College Training Initiative) college. After selection they must complete the FAA Academy part-task training and skills-building sessions at Oklahoma City.

The CTI program is only one of several methods the FAA uses to recruit applicants. Military veterans, military retirees (Phoenix-20 program), FAA reinstatements (PATCO), Flight Service employees, and the AT-SAT direct hire (limited as of September, 2005) program are also methods used for recruiting. Hiring started in May 2005 and will continue, possibly peaking about 2011; normal hiring to adjust for attrition will be ongoing after that date. Significant direct hire candidate selection will probably not happen until later in 2006 or beyond.

The FAA hopes to increase hiring efficiency by improving the screening process. The old nine-week screen was reduced to an eight-hour test (called AT-SAT) and saves the FAA about

---

Pages 1 to 5 adapted http://www.faa.gov/careers/employment/atc-quals.htm and a briefing to the National Hispanic Coalition of Federal Aviation Employees (NHCFAE) by T. P. Williams. (2005, May). 2005-2014 Air Traffic Controller Workforce Plan Enroute

$10,000 per candidate. Today, it costs the agency about $800 per candidate to administer the AT-SAT test. The old style air traffic control training academy experienced a 57 percent pass rate; early numbers from new classes in the summer of 2005 indicate a 95 to 97 percent pass rate. Hopefully this will not result in a higher failure rate in the facilities.

The reader should note that all training is pass-fail, and depending on if and where the trainee fails, that person could be out of a job and on the street. One key item to remember is that once a federal employee passes his/her probationary period (usually the first three to five years) they are considered permanent employees and are treated differently regarding separation. In the past, employees who failed at certain points in the training were offered employment at less complex facilities. For example, a trainee who fails enroute ARTCC might be placed in a low level VFR tower, Automated Flight Service Station, or midsize approach-departure control facility. This may not be the case in the future because the less busy, less complex ATC facilities have been privatized.

Although the FAA Academy is no longer a screening program, it does train students in the following:

- Air Traffic Academics: principles of flight, federal aviation regulations (FAR), meteorology, and aircraft performance, characteristics, and procedures.

- Part-Task Training: applying basic controller skills, significant non-radar section.

- Skills Building: radar familiarization, radar associate training (closely mirrors actual control room environments).

- Performance Verification (Student Evaluations): current operational supervisors are brought in from the field to perform the final evaluations. (Williams, 2005, n.p.)

See the "ATCCTI" webpage for an explanation of this process (internet addresses and sources are listed by chapter in Appendix 6 at the back of the book). Figure 2-1 and Table 2-1 (see page 14) outline the initial training requirements based on hiring source.

General Work Experience

General work experience is defined as any progressively responsible work. For example, a person working full-time (40 hours per week) for three years would meet the three-year general work experience requirement. A person who works part-time (20 hours per week) for six years would also meet the three-year general work experience requirement.

Education Requirements

A qualifying education is defined as the successful completion of study in any field leading to a bachelor's or higher degree at an accredited college or university. In combining education and experience, one year of undergraduate study (30 semester or 45 quarter hours) is equivalent to nine months of general experience. Thus, if you had 60 semester hours or 90 quarter hours of college study, that would equal 18 months of general experience. You would need an additional 18 months of general work experience to meet the three-year work requirement. Students who will complete the amount of education needed to qualify within nine months of the test date may apply and be selected, but they must complete their studies before they begin work.

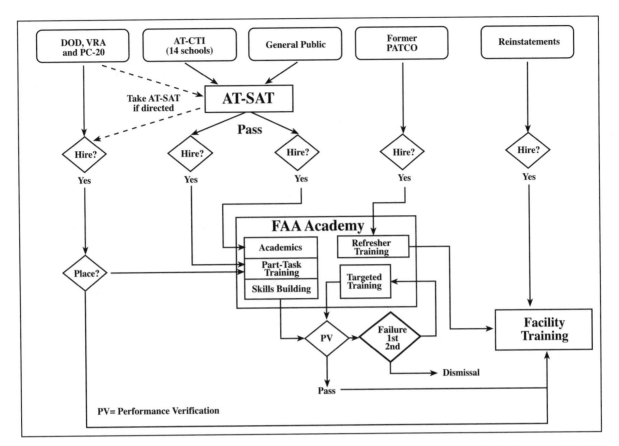

Figure 2-1. FAA ATC hiring and training path. (Adapted from FAA "A Plan for the Future," p.51.)

Age Limitation

For most new hires, the maximum entry age is 31. The maximum retirement age from actively working traffic is 56. See FAA policy websites listed in Appendix 6 for more information regarding age limitations.

Citizenship Requirements

In accordance with Presidential intent (as contained in Executive Order 11935) and congressional intent (as contained in the Treasury, Postal Service, and General Government Appropriations Act), initial appointments made after April 30, 1998 to positions in the Federal Aviation Service will be restricted to U.S. citizens and nationals (residents of American Samoa and Guam) unless, as determined by the selecting official, there is an insufficient number of well-qualified applicants; or, for a brief period, in an emergency.

Interview Requirement

Applicants must successfully complete an interview that demonstrates their ability to read, write, and understand the English language and speak it rapidly without accent or impediment of speech that would interfere with two-way radio conversation.

HIRING SOURCE	INITIAL TRAINING REQUIREMENT
General Public (off-the-street) at the FAA	Air Traffic Basics and Initial Qualification Course (AT Basics) conducted Academy for the appropriate option.
Collegiate Training Initiative (CTI)	Initial Qualification Course conducted at the FAA Academy for the appropriate option.Not required to attend AT Basics.
Veterans Recruitment Appointment (VRA) military controllers	Terminal Option: No Academy tower initial qualification training required. Enter appropriate stage of field training determined by receiving facility. NOTE: VRA hires assigned to radar approach control facilities shall attend Course 50034, Terminal Basic Radar Training at the FAA Academy's Radar Training Facility (RTF) En Route Option: En Route Initial Qualification Course conducted at the FAA Academy. Not required to attend AT Basics
Retired military controllers (PC-20 program)	No Academy tower initial qualification training required. Enter appropriate stage of field training determined by receiving facility. NOTE: Individuals assigned to radar approach control facilities shall attend Course 50034, Terminal Basic Radar Training at the FAA Academy's Radar Training Facility (RTF)
Department of Defense (DOD) civilian controllers	Terminal Option: No Academy tower initial qualification training required. Enter appropriate stage of field training determined by receiving facility. Those assigned to radar approach control facilities attend Course 50034, Terminal Basic Radar Training at the FAA Academy; En Route Option: En Route Initial Qualification Course conducted at the FAA Academy. Not required to attend AT Basics.
Alaskan Flight Service Training Initiative (AFTI)	No Academy initial training required. Enter appropriate stage of field training at an Alaskan Service station only.
Former Professional Air Traffic Control Organization (PATCO)	Academy training for the appropriate option specifically developed for former PATCO controllers.

Table 2-1

Medical Examination

Applicants for ATCS employment in an enroute center or a terminal must pass a rigid medical exam that includes:

Vision Standards—Applicants must have distant and near vision of 20/20 or better in each eye separately, without correction, or have lenses that correct distance and near vision to 20/20, each eye separately. Applicants for a flight service station specialist position must have distance and near vision of 20/20 or better in at least one eye, without correction, or have lenses that correct distance and near vision to 20/20, in at least one eye.

Color Vision Standards—Applicants must have normal color vision.

Hearing Standards—Applicants must have no hearing loss in either ear of more than 25 db at 500, 1000 and 2000 Hz, and no more than a 20 db loss in the better ear by audiometry, using ANSI (1969) standards.

Cardiovascular Standards—Applicants must have no medical history of any form of heart disease. A history of high blood pressure requiring medication will be subject to special review.

Neurological Standards—Applicants must have no medical history or clinical diagnosis of a convulsive disorder, or a disturbance of consciousness, without satisfactory medical explanation of the cause. They must not be under any treatment, including preventive, for any condition of the nervous system.

Psychiatric Standards—Any medical history or clinical diagnosis of a psychosis, or other severe mental disorder, is disqualifying.

Diabetes—A medical history or diagnosis of diabetes mellitus will require special review.

Substance Abuse/Dependency—A history of substance abuse/dependency, including alcohol, narcotic, non-narcotic drugs, and other substances will be investigated.

Psychological Exam—Individuals must take and pass a psychological exam (called the "16PF").

General Medical—All other medical conditions will be evaluated on an individual basis. All applicants' medical histories and current examinations will be carefully reviewed. This includes past medical records and, if applicable, a review of military medical records.

Suitability Determination and Security Investigation (SF-86)

In this U.S. government standard form #SF86 suitability adjudications will be made in accordance with applicable agency guidelines. Applicants must pass a rigid security and background investigation to qualify for Secret Security Clearance. The following issues are reviewed as part of the background and security check: general or dishonorable military discharge; government loyalty; evidence of dishonesty in an application or examination process (e.g., falsification of application); drug-related offenses; felony offenses; firearms or explosives offenses; alcohol-related incidents; willful disregard of financial obligations; derogatory employment terminations; and/or patterns and/or combinations of incidents that lead to questions about the applicant's behavior and intent.

Collegiate Training Initiative (CTI)

The CTI education and training program for air traffic control, developed to FAA standards, provides a pool of potential qualified applicants the FAA can consider for future air traffic control positions and increased employment opportunities for participating students. The list of schools with CTI programs in Table 2-2 is for informational purposes only. Inclusion on the list does not constitute an endorsement of any particular institution or program. See Table 2-2 on page 17.

A light blue state in Figure 2-2 means it has two-and four-year schools that have an agreement with the FAA, which established the CTI program in 1990. Graduates who meet ATCS basic qualification requirements may then be considered for employment in towers and enroute centers.

CTI Qualification Process

CTI schools submit names of students enrolled in their program to the FAA, Aviation Careers, AMH-300. Names are maintained in the CTI database for tracking purposes until graduation and recommendation.

The FAA authorized pre-employment test is given just after enrollment in a CTI program. The purpose of the test is to determine whether an applicant has the aptitude to become an air traffic control specialist. Prior to testing, applicants complete and submit a citizenship paper stating that they are U.S citizens. Those who are not U.S. citizens will not be allowed to test. After achieving a qualifying score on the FAA authorized pre-employment test, applicants are notified of the results. If an individual achieves a qualifying score, he or she is asked to complete several forms, which include a geographic preference sheet and a self identify veterans' preference sheet.

Upon successful completion of an FAA approved CTI program, individuals who receive school recommendation, and who meet basic qualification requirements, are included in the CTI database for employment consideration. Candidates who do not receive recommendation

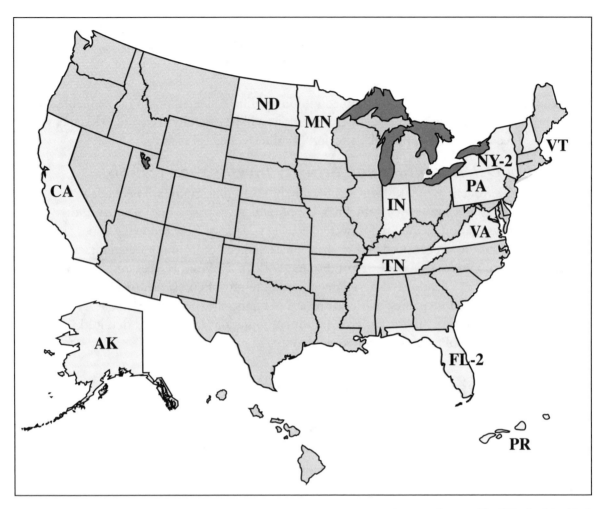

Figure 2-2. States with air traffic CTI school (in blue).

will not be considered for employment under this program and will not be included in the CTI database. Applicants have one chance for recommendation by school officials.

When it has been determined that ATCS vacancies can be filled from the CTI database, a region contacts the Aviation Careers Division for a list of eligible graduates for that geographic location. Referral lists are issued based on the graduates' primary geographic preference, and graduates are referred by GPA, with veterans' preference rules applied. Note that second and third geographic preferences are only used if a shortage exists in that location.

Candidates being considered for employment by the hiring region will begin the pre-employment process, i.e., suitability, medical, and security clearances. If hired by the agency, they then attend the FAA Academy in Oklahoma City for training. Candidates who were referred but not selected are returned to the database for future referral until their eligibility expires, or they reach age 31, or they decline a position, or they are selected, whichever comes first. However, they must renew annually. Candidates may not reapply through this program if they fail to meet any qualification requirements or do not receive recommendation from school officials.

Air Traffic Collegiate Training Initiative (CTI) program schools
(as of October 15, 2005)

ALASKA
University of Alaska Anchorage
Department of Aviation Technology
2811 Merrill Field Drive
Anchorage, AK 99501
(907) 264-7415
http://www.uaa.alaska.edu/

CALIFORNIA
Mt. San Antonio College
Aeronautics & Transportation
1100 North Grand Avenue
Walnut, CA 91789
(909) 594-5611
http://www.mtsac.edu/

FLORIDA
Embry-Riddle Aeronautical University
Aeronautical Science
600 South Clyde Morris Blvd.
Daytona Beach, FL 32114-3900
(904) 226-6448
http://www.db.erau.edu/

Miami-Dade Community College
500 College Terrace
Homestead, FL 33030
(305) 237-5132
http://www.mdcc.edu/

INDIANA
Purdue University
Department of Aviation Technology
1 Purdue Airport
West Lafayette, IN 47906-3398
(765) 494-9962
http://www.purdue.edu/

MINNESOTA
Minneapolis Community & Technical College
10100 flying Cloud drive
Eden prairie, MN 55347
(800) 475-2828
http://minneapolis.edu/airTraffic/

NEW HAMPSHIRE
Daniel Webster College
Twenty University Drive
Nashua, NH 03063-1699
(603) 577-6452
http://www.dwc.edu/

NEW YORK
Vaughn College of Aeronautics
LaGuardia Airport
Flushing, NY 11371
(866) 682-8446
http://www.vaughn.edu/

Dowling College
School of Aviation
Brookhaven, Long Island, NY 11967
(631) 244-1331
http://www.dowling.edu/

NORTH DAKOTA
University of North Dakota
4201 University Ave
Grand Forks, ND 58202-9023
(800) 258-1525
http://www.und.nodak.edu/

PENNSYLVANIA
Community College of Beaver County
125 Cessna Drive
Beaver Falls, PA 15010-1060
(724) 847-7000
http://www.ccbc.edu/

PUERTO RICO
Bayamon Campus
Inter American University of Puerto Rico
School of Aeronautics
Carr. 830 Num 500
Cerro Gordo
Bayamon, PR 00957
(787) 725-1912
http://bc.inter.edu/

TENNESSEE
Middle Tennessee State University
Aerospace Department
Box 67, MTSU
Murfreesboro, TN 37132
(615) 898-2788
http://www.mtsu.edu/

VIRGINIA
Hampton University
Department of Aviation
Hampton, VA 23668
(757) 727-5418
http://www.hamptonu.edu

Table 2-2

CTI Graduate Advice

Mr. Michael Lees, a recent CTI graduate and now a developmental controller at Atlanta Center (ZTL), offers some advice about the training process. This is a very basic description of how the CTI Program works. Please keep in mind that individual experiences will vary.

1. Complete all of the required classes for your degree and the CTI program.

2. Take the federal test being offered (AT-SAT).

3. Upon graduation from the CTI school and program, a notification will be sent to the CTI program director informing them that you completed the requirements (recommendation).

4. A service area will request a list of eligible candidates from the director. Your name will be on that list.

5. The FAA service area will mail you a packet of information and ask you to fill it out and send it back.

6. You will be scheduled for your psychological and medical tests. If qualified, your security clearance will be, "adjudicated in the positive," meaning that you have passed the security clearance. Your medical will be cleared as well.

7. Print your SF86 form and fill it out *early!* (It took me several months to complete.) You will also need to obtain your Selective Service Number for the SF-86 form.

8. Obtain a copy of all three of your credit reports: Experian, TransUnion, and Equifax. Each of these credit agencies has slightly different reporting policies, so it is not safe to assume that one report will be all you need. Check each report for accuracy of information, and correct any errors with all three agencies.

9. Start a list of past residences and the dates you lived in each one. Do the same thing for previous employers so you have accurate and current information. Go to the Clerk of Court in your county and ask for a Lifetime Driving Record. This will detail all your tickets and fines, which is information you need when filling out the SF86.

Training Perspective

Oklahoma City Academy Training

The following pages 19 to 34 are reprinted by permission from Michael Lees, who attended and successfully completed the FAA's Oklahoma City air traffic control training program during the summer of 2005. This journal is informational only and is not meant to be reflective of anyone else's experience.

Travel Day

You are officially on the clock beginning today and can use this travel time to prepare for the Academy. After arrival, I met other trainees for dinner, unpacked, and got ready for my first day of training.

You also need to fill out a packet of paperwork sent to you in advance. This packet contains maps, your travel voucher, and other pertinent items for your first day at work. There are several forms in the packet, many of which are a repeat of the SF 86 form. You will have to fill those out again noting any changes since your original application. They ask you to fill them out in advance, which most of us did; however, they give you plenty of time to do it there.

Day One

We found out that the north entrance to the Mike Monroney Aeronautical Center (MMAC) is the one that you want to use when you first get there. All visitors, including us, must stop at a nearby building to get the proper credentialing. At this point, they also give you a parking permit to display on your dash whenever you are on the property.

We had several people talk to us today to welcome us to the MMAC. We heard from Human Resources, the FAA Credit Union, Student Services, our instructors, Sick and Annual Leave, and a few other departments.

Some "highlights" of the day:

- Filled out lots of HR paperwork.

- Were sworn in as government employees and had to read the affidavit out loud and raise our right hands.

- Got our official MMAC identification badges.

- Took the CTI pre-hire test, which included some simple questions (IMO) about aviation and ATC, and some other questions whose answers I think we were just too tired to remember.

- Took five or so ten-minute breaks.

- Got a welcome packet with the new 7110.65 and all the updates.

- Received our aero map and lesson plans for the first chapter, and talked about some things we should concentrate on over the weekend.

- Talked about the layout of the MMAC campus with the security division.

Day Two

Today we went over the full lesson plan for the AeroCenter Map and had time to study and ask questions. We were also allowed some personal time to take care of anything we needed to take care of during business hours (all FAA or government related). Afterwards, we had a presentation on the Employee Assistance Program (EAP) and talked about the restrictions and confidentiality issues associated with seeking the help of the EAP.

Next, the medical department (CAMI) came over and spoke to us about the battery of tests and research that they use to track students over the years. To determine what qualities are most common in ATCSs, CAMI gave us a battery of psychological tests this morning that cannot be used against us and can remain anonymous if we so choose. We had the option to not take the exams, but all of us decided to take them. These tests included:

Minnesota Multiphasic Personality Inventory-2 (MMPI-2). This test contained 567 true or false questions. The answers were recorded on a scantron (which took a long time) and then submitted. This test most resembled the Cattell 16-PF exam that we all had to take to get hired in the first place.

Armstrong Laboratory Aviation Personality Survey (ALAPS). This test had 240 true or false questions. This exam was similar to the first one, except you could mark your answers on the page itself. This was a quick test to take.

Biographical Questionnaire. This test had 195 multiple choice questions asking about your biographical information. Very easy to fill out.

Applicant Background Assessment. This test had 142 multiple choice questions about education and background. Very easy to complete as well.

That is about all we did today. The battery of tests above took about 3.5 to 4.0 hours to complete.

Day Three

Today started out with a question and answer period (as has every day so far) to make sure there was nothing we were confused about or needed clarification on.

We met the program manager for the ATC program and he welcomed us to the MMAC and Oklahoma City. He then asked for volunteers to take the AT-SAT test for research and statistical purposes only.

We had the option to either take the test today, or remain behind and study our map for the entire day. If I am not mistaken, the entire class decided their time would be better spent studying and learning the map. Since it was an option, there were no consequences associated with either choice.

Day Four

Believe it or not, I don't think we met anyone new! We spent the first half of the day working on very basic phraseology and radio and interphone procedures. This was basic 7110.65 stuff. Some people looked up the things we were talking about in the 7110 that was provided to each of us, and others just took notes and listened. We discussed hear-back and read-back errors and did some audio examples of each. After this session, we had more time to study and learn our maps, as that test is coming up next week.

After lunch, we started flight strip notations and the fundamentals of non-radar dictation on strips. We went through each box of the strip and determined which piece of information belonged there and who would update it. We then got a cheat sheet for figuring out how many miles per minute aircraft travel so we can determine how long it takes for each aircraft to get to each fix. We did several examples of this in class, and then some people headed up to the boards for problem-solving.

Another 2.5 hours on strips and markings tomorrow!

Day Five

We spent the entire day working on how to post a flight strip and flight strip markings. We covered two pages of different markings including the exact place of each marking on the actual flight strips. There are approximately 30 specific areas on a flight strip where information is placed. We have to know the exact placement location for each type of information.

We then discussed how to figure the distance and speed aircraft travel and started to learn non-radar procedures. We talked about clearances and fixes and determined how far each aircraft can travel in a given amount of time based on their true airspeed.

Everything we learned today was to prepare us for the non-radar environment. We began learning the degree divergence table found in the 7110.65, and determined how to use these tables in conjunction with our airspace.

Day Six

Today we began with a very depressing and anti-motivating briefing from an ATO representative. These are the people who will grade us on the performance evaluation ("PV") at the end of the course. They are the ones who will determine if we continue to our facility, or pack our bags and head home.

One of the ATO's responsibilities was to tell us that this is going to be very difficult for the next few weeks, and that we will most likely have a few more people drop out or fail. (We actually had one person drop out after the first day. Maybe this person's heart wasn't in it. Not exactly the most uplifting thing, however, for 0700 on a Monday morning.)

After that, we continued with our flight strip marking briefing and finished the remaining symbology that we will use on those strips while we are here at the Academy.

Our breaks appear to be getting shorter and shorter lately.

After lunch, we continued with interphone procedures for flight progress strips and learned how to communicate with each other, and other facilities, for most matters that relate to flight planning. We discussed passing inbounds, route changes, altitude changes, proper phraseology for those, and several other things.

We finished out our day with eight minutes of map study time (we are not able to leave until work is done at 1530). We will continue tomorrow on the flight strip posting, and will have our map test on Tuesday, which happens to be our first paycheck, a mere 20 days after we began our time here in OKC.

Oh yeah.... plan ahead.... save money.... you may just need some when you get here!

Day Seven

Today we continued posting flight strips and practicing the various calls that go along with the posting and coordinating of flights through your airspace.

After lunch, we started non-radar procedures for flights through our airspace and delved into the 7110.65 to find information that was pertinent to today's briefing. We discussed some basic

7110.65 items and then headed upstairs to the non-radar lab where we looked at a non-radar problem and determined how to set up our boards for good management of the board.

We ended the day trying to run a very basic non-radar problem where we were all seriously behind the ball in both understanding and comprehension. With that said, tomorrow is a new day and holds lots of promise for us to start getting this stuff ironed out.

Tomorrow we will also take our preliminary map test to see where we are with the map and what else we need to study.

Day Eight

We started today with the continuation of non-radar board management techniques and learned how to organize and "see" traffic in a non-radar environment. We continued to delve into the letters of agreement (LOA) and SOPs that govern the decisions we make, and continued to look to the 7110.65 and rules of engagement for making decisions. After this, we all stepped outside for a class picture, which, I assume will be made available later.

We then did a map review session where each of us was called up to the front of the room and asked questions about the map. We practiced identifying the items and giving the distances between each of the fixes and airways overall. After this session, we started looking at IFR clearances and how to deliver them appropriately to FSS, pilots, and other recipients. We ended the day taking an in-depth look at a departure clearance and determining the items necessary for proper clearance. We will continue on this in the morning!

Day Nine

We finished covering departure procedures and did some practice exercises on giving clearances and departure instructions to aircraft. We also looked at how to protect holding airspace and strip marking that is associated with both of these. We also did some board management work in relation to this. We then started (and completed) altimeter and altitude lessons that deal with the 7110.65 and what it has to say about issuing altitudes and altimeter settings at different points in the NAS. We discussed where and when it is appropriate to give information on the altimeter and what the book says about proper issuance of information throughout your facility and sector. We then practiced the strip marking and phraseology associated with altimeter and altitude assignments, and then finished the day with map study time for our test in a few days.

Day Ten

Today the focus was on holding procedures. This dealt with a lot of IFR type information about holds, clearing aircraft to fixes, routing concerns, DME / RNAV fixes, standard and non-standard holding patterns and the phraseology that accompanies each. We then talked about delays into airports and how to stack and manage your holding pattern effectively.

After this, we talked about enroute arrival and approach procedures. These included strip marking and interphone procedures for calling facilities and FSS, relaying the proper information to each, published vs. non-published routing clearances, and the phraseology that accompanies these.

We then started to learn the LOAs that directly affect the AeroCenter airspace and talked our way through several tasks we may be required to do in a non-radar and radar environment. We will have our first block exam in Day 11 and our 330 question map test on Day 12.

Day Eleven

Today was quite easy. We started by finishing all of the LOAs for the airspace that we will work and learned the radar and non-radar procedures that accompany the airspace. There are a few different fixes and procedures for when the radar and FDEP are working properly versus when they are out of service.

We then reviewed for our Block One Test. We had a question and answer period followed by the computerized test. We had an hour to complete the timed test, but most people finished in 20 to 30 minutes. This was a cumulative test on the first twelve lessons and required a little time to prepare.

We then completed an overview of Block 2, which starts tomorrow, and spent the rest of the day in personal map study time preparing for our 300 question map test at 0700 on Day 12.

Day Twelve

We started the day with our complete map test of all the airspace. Every detail is accounted for and graded. After this exam, we studied the non-radar vertical separation and applied the techniques to some strip marking and phraseology.

We then broke for lunch and, as coincidence would have it, there was a press conference about the FAA-NATCA contract negotiations being held in the MMAC building. It was interesting to see this happen right in front of us. However, there was no information given that was not covered in the other 21 press conferences that the FAA held today.

We ended the day with longitudinal separation as it applies to our airspace and non-radar procedures. We discussed some of the rules and regulations that apply to our airspace and began working on exercises to help solidify the concepts we have talked about.

Day Thirteen

We finished lateral separation techniques and ran several non-radar problems to solidify the concepts we discussed. We ran a non-radar problem, extremely slowly, explaining every move to everyone in the class. This is called a walk-through. Although there were only about 10 aircraft in the scenario, it took us several hours to walk through and coordinate everything that needs coordination. This is all we did today.

Day Fourteen

We did another walk-through on a non-radar problem to review Day 13. This problem had several other concepts we had yet to encounter in a non-radar situation, so this also took a while to complete.

We then had a lesson on longitudinal separation. At the conclusion of this lesson, we had several individual examples that we then discussed corporately. There are several different ways to solve non-radar problems, and we discussed a few of them. We also discussed the flight strip markings associated with longitudinal separation and learned all the rules for each.

We ended the day with another non-radar problem that was timed. There was a little more pressure involved here, and several people felt overwhelmed. Despite that, we are all looking forward to continuing the classes.

Day Fifteen

We looked at the minimum divergence angles that can be used to minimize the standard separation for arrivals and departures. This includes multiple arrivals and departures and a mixture of the two. There are several rules a controller can use to minimize the separation standards to keep aircraft moving and get them off the ground or on the ground as requested. We also talked about the effectiveness of paper stops (non-radar) and how to use them effectively. We then prepped a scenario for us to study over the weekend and discussed a few more tips on how to figure out and solve non-radar problems.

Day Sixteen

We had several more walk-throughs of non-radar problems. If memory serves me, we ran three or four problems as an entire class. We all planned our approach to the problem, and then people were called on at random to give clearances and restrictions as necessary, based on the time in the scenario. It is becoming crucial that we know our mileages and boundary markings at this stage. We are seeing that there is little time to refer to the map, and we need to commit these items to memory.

Lastly, we began to look at the remote pilot (pseudo-pilot / pilot) position and some of the responsibilities associated with it. The remote pilot serves as the pilot for all aircraft and also serves as the approach control facilities, FSS, Class D towers, ZFW, ZHU and the AeroCenter sectors surrounding our area. The remote must keep track of everything in the scenario and make the appropriate calls at the correct times. The remote pilot is also responsible for determining exact locations of the aircraft at any given time based on the last reported fix and speed.

Day Seventeen

Today we looked at the remote pilot in detail. All of the scenarios (six in total) were geared toward teaching the remote pilot how to operate and properly serve as a remote pilot. Today was the first day we had one teacher for every two people. In each scenario, one person would act as the controller and issue as many clearances as they could, and the other would act as the remote pilot under the direction and watchful eye of the instructor. We ran five or six scenarios, each taking slightly over one hour to complete from the pre-planning stage until the end of the last aircraft. Again, while one person was serving as the controller, the focus was not on what the controller was saying, but rather on the remote pilot. The idea was to teach us how to be a good remote. While the remote pilot position is not a graded position, all strips and phraseology must be accurate at all times.

We were issued our official, rented headsets today, which we must return at the end of the course. These headsets are used in the classroom during the scenarios for practice in issuing control instructions over the radio. Even though your remote pilot is sitting next to you, using the headsets help build confidence and coordination when issuing control instructions.

Day Eighteen

We ran three more problems today. We controlled three and were the remote pilot for the same three so that all of us could run the scenario, as a controller, one time through. We ran two full scenarios before lunch and one after. We then broke and de-briefed for 30 or 45 minutes before heading home. All of the scenarios you are controlling for are graded by a teacher who is sitting right behind you and offering help from time to time. When I say graded in this case, I mean that the teacher comments on things you did well and things you did poorly. The scenarios run about 30 minutes with 15 minutes to prepare and 10 to 15 minutes to debrief the controller afterwards. During the de-briefing, you and the teacher go through all the comments and sign them. The controller gets a copy, and the other copy is placed in your MMAC file.

We will continue doing this same process for the next two weeks. More tomorrow!

Day Nineteen

As with yesterday, we completed three scenarios for each person in class to control. I failed to mention earlier that the instructors are anticipating high death tolls this first week and well into next week. This week alone, I collided enough aircraft to wipe out a small country. But that's the point! While all these problems are slightly out of the reach and comprehension of students, they force us to learn and push forward. They build on one another, so to speak. The first few scenarios were more geared toward the slight lateral separation needed to complete successfully. Most of us, however, did not successfully complete that task. The next few scenarios added departures and arrivals to the various airports and required holding for most airports. Most of us were not successful in these scenarios either, but we were now successful at the lateral separation asked for in the first few scenarios.

Today we were working with head-on situations and solving "down in front, up in back" scenarios. We also introduced holding at DME fixes instead of intersections or NAVAIDs, and added more departures and arrivals at the same time. Although we were only mildly successful at those, we are now starting to get the lateral, vertical, and longitudinal separation, and were even able to put aircraft into holding at different airports.

It appears the training is geared to keep you moving in a forward direction and pushing you to learn the previous material. This is all a push until you almost choke... then let off a bit... then push until you turn blue... then let off a bit... then push until you stop breathing... resuscitate you... then let off a bit.... I think you get the idea. I hope that puts a new perspective on this training thing we are doing out here.

Day Twenty

Today we completed four more non-radar problems before lunch and two after lunch. We started the day asking if anyone had questions and then ended the day with a review. The scenarios dealt with simultaneous departures and arrivals into most airports in the sector and several instances where re-routing must be done on the alternate airways to keep the aircraft separated.

We have been working towards a "skills check" day for all controllers. We will not be helped on anything. The teachers will merely sit back and record all violations we have. Nothing more, nothing less. From what I understand, it is used as a tool to judge our strengths and weaknesses and identify where we are in relation to where we should be. I think the majority of us are now feeling better about this non-radar beast that we are slowly starting to tame. We still have a full week of running problems before the final performance verification.

It ought to be a very interesting day tomorrow!

Day Twenty-one

We ran two scenarios each in the morning and then had our skills check scenario after lunch. Before you think it or ask... no, we cannot keep our strips for the skills check. They dispose of them immediately after the scenario. The skills check was like any other scenario with a more thorough report by the instructor on the controller's performance. The main difference was that the instructors were not allowed to speak at all until the end of the scenario, and therefore did not offer any help to us during the pre-planning stages or the scenario itself. Afterwards, we had a chalk-talk session about the days events, then headed home.

More of the same planned for tomorrow!

Day Twenty-two

More of the same today. Four scenarios in the morning, and two in the afternoon. Today we were pushed a bit further. We had multiple holding patterns happening at one time, simultaneous requests for departures, and multiple arrivals into multiple airports. Although the complexity of the problems has increased, there are only so many events they can throw at us before we have seen every situation. For example, ours today focused on using the rules for longitudinal separation (or aircraft in trail). The complexity of the scenarios just reflects the amount of tools we have in our tool box. The body counts are still high on average, but starting to subside. Instead of crashing 10 aircraft with 10 separate restrictions, most of us are killing four aircraft in one restriction. You will learn more about that later, but suffice it to say that if we fix the one bad restriction, everyone lives! Until tomorrow.

Day Twenty-three

Today we reviewed for our Block II test and took it first thing in the morning. The test covered all of the non-radar separation requirements in the 7110.65 to include lateral, longitudinal, vertical, and visual. After the test, we ran two more problems each of non-radar. We were all at about our non-radar threshold this morning. The week has been pretty long and mentally exhausting. After a quick review of the days events and an overview of the items that were missed on the test, we were dismissed an entire 4 minutes early in honor of the weekend! We only have a few more days of non-radar, a final exam and evaluation on non-radar, and then we start the radar portion of the class.

Day Twenty-four

We are slowly starting to wind-down the non-radar portion of the training. We ran three more problems today. They continue to increase in complexity and busy-ness as time goes on. We have two more days of practice and then have the non-radar performance verification written test and practical test on Thursday. That will be a long day!

Tomorrow we have two more problems, and then get to choose the problem or type of problem that we would like to work on for the last scenario of the day. We will continue to work on problems on Wednesday, and then be done on Thursday!

Day Twenty-five

Today we ran two more scenarios that were new, and then had the opportunity to run a scenario of our choice to prepare for the PV.

The scenarios were more difficult today than in the past. They appear to be getting more complicated and faster paced as time goes on. We have our final scenarios tomorrow. The two today focused more on longitudinal separation and less on the other forms of separation. They changed several things throughout the problems, requiring us to do even more work.

Tomorrow holds the final three scenarios. They are, in theory, going to be the most complicated. It is like putting together a moving puzzle that is constantly changing. Interesting some say... frustrating as all get-out, others say.

Some classmates are rethinking their desire to be controllers as it seems like the pressure will never let up. Others think this is a big game and enjoy every minute of it. It just depends on the person.

Day Twenty-six

Today was more of the same. We ran three non-radar problems and continued to work with our teachers that come in to help us. The problems are getting increasingly more difficult. We just have a few more days to do this and we are done!

Things move fast here, but that is good because the days go by very quickly. More of the same tomorrow.

Day Twenty-seven

More of exactly the same thing we did yesterday. Nothing more than that. Sorry for the boring update.

Day Twenty-eight

Today was the performance evaluation (PV) written test, which we took at 0700. We showed up, they asked us if we had any questions, and we signed onto the computer to take our 50-question multiple-choice test, which was a combination of the other tests we have taken. After this exam, which we all passed, we began the non-radar practical performance verification. We had two groups of five and one group of four (to account for all 14 of us) going the first two runs. The scenarios were all different, so no one had an advantage over the other person.

Although slightly intimidating (at least for me), the evaluations went quite well, and all of us were asked to continue our training. That is a good thing! The biggest thing of all is that we are completely done with non-radar at the Academy. We have gotten through this part and are moving on to radar starting tomorrow. We ended the day with a briefing from the Traffic Management Unit (TMU) about how the TMU can help controllers in the field and the role that TMU plays in keeping traffic moving.

The PV non-radar practical will be taken in two groups of five and one group of four. If you are not a remote pilot or a person serving as a controller, you will be sent out of the room and on break until you are needed back in the room. All scenarios will be different tomorrow.

Day Twenty-nine

Finally, we started radar today! We began with a briefing on the radar airspace, which is slightly different from the non-radar airspace. We then talked about all the sectors, which own the airspace above those depicted on the maps, and how we do a few things in the radar room. We then reviewed all LOAs again and focused on the radar portion of them. After that, we jumped right into the DSR radar display and how things appear on the scope. We talked in depth about the full and limited data blocks and information in each. We looked at the different lists that can be moved around the screen and learned how to toggle things on and off on the radar scope.

We then moved onto beacon code assignments and talked about the requirements for assigning them and how to do that in a live environment. We briefly covered emergency situations including radio failure and hijacking. There were a few more things discussed here, but you will have to experience it in person.

Day Thirty

We started with radar identification procedures and how to determine what is an appropriate and air-tight way of identifying aircraft. We talked about the beacon code and non-beacon code identifications and how to carry them out. We looked at the different symbols shown on a radar scope, discussed the information they show, and where the information comes from. We then began looking at radar handoffs and point-outs in an automated and non-automated world. We discussed this for quite a while as there is a very important difference between the two, and this particular topic appears to be one that is a hot button with the ATO for our final PV check. After discussing the phraseology and procedural issues associated with both, we ran a very easy scenario using monitors at each station to serve as our radar scope. We then did all of our point-outs and handoffs for the scenario to acquaint us with how things are done in our sector.

Day Thirty-one

Today we continued with the radar portion of the class, particularly safety alerts, conflict alerts, mode C intruders, and E-MSAW alerts on the DSR screens and systems. We discussed radar vectoring for noise abatement, traffic, weather, and other situations that would require us to move aircraft off their requested or present routes. We talked about issuing altitude restrictions and no-gyro vectors, and finished with the MEAs and MIAs related to our airspace. We discussed radar departures and arrivals and how the approach gate, final approach fix, and final approach all come together to get the aircraft into the intended airport for landing. We learned about intercepting the ILS and how we do that in relation to the approach gate. The day ended discussion of visual approach clearances and special VFR activity and how they both relate. Lastly, we talked about contact approaches, who can issue and request them, and how they are completed.

Day Thirty-two

Today we started speed adjustments and emergencies in the enroute environment. We talked about several different scenarios where we must give speed adjustments to sequence aircraft throughout our airspace. There are certain altitudes where no speed adjustments can be made and certain aircraft that are restricted to minimum and maximum speeds, depending on altitudes. We then applied the LOAs we have learned and determined how to best meet the them with our current traffic flows. We ended this section with an instructor-led radar exercise.

In the emergencies section, we learned about a plethora of emergency situations and how the controller can be of assistance. In short, controllers just try to give any and all assistance to an aircraft in distress, and notify as many people as needed to help with the situation. We discussed VFR weather emergencies and military emergencies where additional workload is required to forward the information to the appropriate authorities. We covered unusual situations, radar and communication loss, and procedures to handle overdue aircraft.

Day Thirty-three

Today we looked at additional services and military operations. We spent quite a bit of time on issuing traffic advisories, how to effectively deal with merging targets and manage a holding stack and pattern, and information on weather, including HIWAS, FLIGHTWATCH, AWOS, ASOS, and PIREPs. The section ended with a discussion of bird advisories and the rules and regulations for those. We learned that additional services are not an optional part of the job, but mandatory if we can manage and handle the additional requests.

Next was military operations and the ins and outs of aerial re-fueling, minimums for special use airspace and ATC assigned airspace, ALTRV, military training routes, formation flights, special military flights and operations, and code names for special military operations. There are many items that need to be forwarded to different agencies when a military aircraft alters its course, so those items were also discussed in some detail. Although this section was lengthy, it was interesting.

We ended the day with a review for our Block 3 test and an overview of Block 4. We take the Block 3 test first thing in the morning.

Day Thirty-four

We began our day with the Block 3 test, and we all did relatively well. After this, we started on the position relief briefing that we will receive and give for each radar problem. We discussed all items in the briefing and listened to a few examples of a good one. Once this was done, we took a tour of the radar lab and the ghost and remote pilot labs to get a better idea of what happens in the radar room. We observed a class working on problems, so that allowed us to see a real scenario and how it all works.

After this, we discussed the PILOT system for controlling the aircraft and ran some scenarios where we were able to play around with the system and figure things out. We then went over all of the rules, regulations, and guidelines for being in the radar lab and discussed how things will run when we start there next week.

Day Thirty-five

We covered the first part of computer entry for the DSR radar units. We were in the classroom for the first part of the day going through the briefing, and then we went downstairs to practice for the first time in the radar lab.

We entered several flight plans, then practiced making changes and amendments to all the aircraft in the scenario. We only had one hour in the lab to work on the scenario, so it was a quick trip, to say the least.

After this, we were briefed on the benefit packages available to us on the last day of the Academy. We will be able to choose all of our health and federal benefits before we leave for our specific facilities. We were given this information now so we can look through it over the next three weeks and turn in our paperwork right before we leave. Our benefits will start shortly thereafter.

Day Thirty-six

We studied the voice switching and communication system (VSCS) used in conjunction with the DSR equipment at the Academy. We learned how to make and accept phone calls, holler lines, and other means of communication using the VSCS. We also continued our practice on DSR computer entries to help set the foundation for the upcoming scenarios that start in two days. We learned a few short cuts today for entering flight plans and amending them, and learned how to manipulate the data on the radar scope. I must say that it is becoming more exciting as this is the stuff we will be doing at our facilities in just a few more weeks. All new lab instructors are joining us on the radar problems, so it is exciting to meet them and talk about their experiences.

Day Thirty-seven

We practiced entering flight plans into the D side Computer Readout Display (CDR) and making changes to active aircraft and amendments and for non-active aircraft. Then we started the first of nine-part tasking problems to get us familiar with the procedure we need to follow in certain situations. When problems are run at the Academy, we have an instructor serving as the radar controller, a student acting as a D-side controller, another student acting as a facility remote (in another room), and a Oklahoma University person acting as the pilot of the scenario (in the same room as the facility remote). As a general rule, the R-side and the pilot communicate, and the D-side and the facility remote communicate on a regular basis. We had a slight learning curve to being a facility remote, but we overcame it quickly.

The next few problems are geared toward allowing us to practice certain things at the same time. We will start again tomorrow.

Day Thirty-eight

We ran three problems that dealt with specific tasks we are supposed to learn. Similar to the non-radar portion of the class, we have one student act as the D-side, and we run the scenario again with that person acting as the facility remote. One of our problems had several departures as the main focus. We had to make sure there was no active traffic for the aircraft we were about to depart. This included several point-outs that needed to be done to allow the aircraft to get where it wanted to go. One of the scenarios dealt with manual handoffs to all facilities. We were simulating a computer failure at the different facilities we deal with. We then had to perform manual handoffs to each of these facilities.

Day Thirty-nine

We ran three more part-task radar problems today. We had a scenario with several IFR and VFR pop-ups that asked for flight plans and flight-following in all different areas of the scope. This accounted for two scenarios. This scenario was built on to the manual handoffs and point-outs we learned previously. The other scenario dealt with increasing our speed on scanning for traffic and point-outs, and more importantly, entering the information into the computer in a timely fashion. There were a few instances where we had to coordinate some departures in advance of releasing them because their flight time to the boundary was less than five minutes.

With that said, we only have about 13 working days left to get us up to speed for the performance evaluation on the last day. Hopefully we can all get this down by then!

Day Forty

We continued with our part-task exercises. We had to get through three more before the skills check, which is scheduled for tomorrow. As I said earlier, the part-task exercises are geared toward helping us learn a specific task in combination with what we already know and understand. Once we learn something new, we are off and running on changes to that knowledge or a new concept all together. These exercises are still one-on-one instruction with the radar controller who is an instructor. There is a lot of interaction between the student and the instructor at this stage of the game, and we constantly communication about the aircraft on the scope and the flight strips.

Day Forty-one

Today we ran a targeted training exercise that allows us to work on the areas that we and the instructors feel are our weakest points. Once we got through these exercises, we did a skills check where a radar controller (instructor) talked to the aircraft but was not providing instruction to us. At the same time, we had an instructor who was grading us on the problem. The skills check comes before you even start running the problems, so that the instructor and student can determine which strengths and weaknesses should be addressed before the real radar problems begin. Once they do, we will have an instructor plugged in for teaching, and one on the scope to control traffic, making the experience a bit more realistic.

Day Forty-two

We ran our first three radar problems. There are two instructors per student. One acts as the radar controller and talks to the aircraft, and the other one teaches and monitors the student. There is also a paid remote pilot in the other lab that controls the movement of the aircraft and a student to serve as the other facilities. All in all, there are at least four people to help you run your problem.

Today's problems were a big step up from what we were used to in the part-task exercises, but they appeared manageable. Each problem builds on the previous one and attempts to keep comprehension just-out-of-reach of most students. This can be extremely frustrating, but it is perfectly normal. Three more tomorrow!

Day Forty-three

Same format today as yesterday. We ran two problems before lunch and one after lunch for each person. The problems are most definitely increasing in workload and complexity. Most of us are still able to keep up, but are at the brink of our speed and understanding of this whole concept. If you type fast, you are going to be a step ahead. If you cannot type fast, it is not a big deal, but it will mean that you have to be most accurate in your entries so that you do not have to go back and correct them later. Oh yeah... one thing that is messing us up a bit here. The keyboards we use in the enroute environment are different from the QWERTY and ARTS III keyboards you may have used in the past. Thankfully, the letters on the DSR keyboard are in the same place as the QWERTY keyboard, but a few of the other keys have been moved around. Not a huge big deal, but get this: The number pad, which is the only place where numbers exist on the keyboard, are just the opposite of a regular keyboard where the number 1 2 3 are on the bottom row, and the 7 8 9 are on the top row. The DSR keyboard is set up like a telephone keypad with 1 2 3 on the top and 7 8 9 on the bottom.

If you are someone who touch-types, this can really mess with your head when you get out here. You will try to enter N129SP and end up typing in a flight plan for N783SP instead. Once this is entered, you have to remove the old flight plan (with the incorrect information) and re-enter a new one (with the correct information). Anyhow, it is not a big deal, these things are easy to do, just a pain in the backside to have to go back and change it when you are already behind!

Day Forty-four

Today was the same as the past two days. We all ran three problems and then went home. All problems from now on will be graded and kept in a file. We will have a total of four graded problems that will be sent to our respective facilities for their official records. No big deal! We will just keep pushing forward and focus on the immediate future. We only have seven more working days left, and then we have our final performance evaluation. We are all starting to get a bit nervous about this. LOL! We ran three problems today that started out busy and got busier as the scenario went along. According to our instructor, the last problem we ran today is a simulation of an actual work day in the center. We are constantly moving and barely able to keep up. Hopefully, in the next seven days, our speed and accuracy will continue to improve in preparation for the PV!

Day Forty-five

To help us get back into the swing of things after a long weekend, we started with Targeted Training, which is an easier problem. After we ran this scenario for all classmates, we completed a graded skills check problem to see where we were in relation to where they think we should be. The 4 to 5 graded skills checks are sent to our center as part of our Academy packet. Depending on the center that it is sent to, rumor has it there is little done with them once they arrive.

After we completed the skills check, we completed another DSR problem. This problem appeared to be easier than the previous problems, but it could just be that we are getting a bit better than we were last week. Afterwards, we had a lengthy de-briefing session with our lead instructor and talked about anything and everything that is still somewhat confusing. This helped clarify several things for us. Here's to just a few more days!

Day Forty-six

Today we were back into the full swing of things. We had, as usual, three more scenarios that increased in complexity and number of aircraft. Nothing out of the ordinary happened, though; just the same schedule as we have always had. Once again, it can be a bit frustrating to always feel behind in the problem and then hear your instructors tell you all the things you did wrong; however, it is just a phase we have to go through to get to the final performance evaluation. Nothing new to report today.

Day Forty-seven

We completed three more scenarios and talked about some of the things that we have collectively been doing wrong. We also finalized the PV schedule for Day 53, so we all know what time we are scheduled, who our radar person is going to be, and who our evaluator will be. Not that any of this helps us much (except knowing who our radar person will be). We were able to choose which instructor we wanted for our performance verification. Armed with this knowledge, we are now scheduling the scenarios carefully so that we can maximize the amount of time we have left to work with our radar person in the next three days of scenarios. For example, instead of having two random instructors for our teachers for the next few days, we will attempt to work with our PV radar person as much as possible. This way, we can iron out all of our movements and such before the actual PV.

Day Forty-eight

This morning we completed one more scenario, which had a TON of departures off every airport. This proved to be challenging for those of us who are struggling to give out clearances and listen to the radar person at the same time. Since we are on the phone so much giving departure clearances and coordinating, we are not able to listen to the radar person as much and continuously mark the strips. After this, we did another skills check problem that proved to be the most difficult one so far. This was yet another graded problem that lists our strengths and weaknesses and will be sent to our center when the time comes. Afterwards, we did a targeted training exercise with no grader behind us. The team was just us and the radar person. This was the most realistic experience thus far. We were forced to communicate well with only the radar person because there was no one else there to communicate with, i.e., the grading instructor. Our next three days will be composed of three scenarios per day as they get us ready for our final performance verification on Day 53.

Day Forty-nine

Today we ran three more scenarios that add significant workload to our daily routine. The focus appears to be building our speed on computer entries and getting it right the first time. When you have to go back and correct things, it becomes increasingly more time consuming, and you miss that much more of what is happening real time. Other than that, there was nothing too exciting that happened today.

Day Fifty

We continued doing radar problems. As usual, the complexity level is increasing, as is the importance of getting things done the first time. We are near the end of the radar problems, however, so most people are listening very carefully to instructors as they try to prepare us for the PV. You can feel the tension in the air as people begin preparing mentally for the final performance evaluation. We have multiple chalk talks to discuss the items that appear to be causing the majority of us problems. We have gotten extremely nit-picky with everything now. Even the smallest of things are being called on the carpet in hopes of teaching us how to do this in the real world. Only one more day of problems!

Day Fifty-one

Today we ran our last DSR problem. It was, without a doubt, one of the toughest and busiest problems we have had so far. We started it at 0700 and it was non-stop. This was the ultimate test to see if we could keep up! Afterwards, we ran a skills check problem as a final graded problem. This was a step down from the one we ran in the morning, but was still busy. This skills check was a final brush up before the PV tomorrow. Lastly, we ran one targeted training problem, which was not graded. There was no instructor sitting behind us; it was just for our benefit. This is how it will be for the PV, with the exception of the evaluator standing behind us, watching our every move and taking notes.

Most of us are running clearances in our heads, thinking about the restricted and MOA areas, deciphering what we are going to be doing with aircraft at the same altitude, and trying to calm our nerves. More tomorrow. Keep your fingers crossed!

Day Fifty-two...The Determining Factor

Holy cow! Although we were the first all-CTI class to pass the first time under the new system, it was not without a struggle. I have to say that the final PV was extremely fair, extremely even as far as traffic flow across the different scenarios, and well done.

Four of us ran the scenario at one time. The evaluator would come out of the radar room and call a name. You would meet him or her for the first time and have a brief conversation to help calm you down (doesn't help much IMO). Then an ATO person would come into the hall and verify that all of the pilots and ghosts in the lab were ready to go and plugged in. They would then check with all the students and make sure they were ready to go and waiting by the door. They would then head into the radar lab and make sure all of the instructors serving as our radar people and all of the evaluators, ATO, and FAA people who were there observing, were ready as well. When the green light was given, we were invited into the room with the scenario already running.

As I said before, all four people in the room were running different scenarios, so there was no need, or desire, to listen to others in hopes of catching something you may have missed. Likewise, although the scenarios were different, they were very much the same in the amount of work and calls that need to be completed.

It would not do me, or you, any good to walk you through the types of things that I saw in the scenario as they are constantly changing and being updated. With that said, I can tell you that you will run into approximately one of everything you did in class, but instead of everything happening all at one time, you will have a more steady and consistent pace that you can work at. Some problems from last week are an all-out race to try to get things done in a timely fashion and help you improve your speed. This is not the case on the PV. Things are more relaxed (as far as the timing in the scenarios). They are very reasonable.

Let me throw in one more thing here that is very important. I think some of the pomp and circumstance that went along with PV day could be a major contributor to someone not passing on the first try. For example, they will put paper up over all the windows so that you cannot see inside; you are not allowed to stand in the hallway by the radar room when scenarios are being done; the scenarios are started and stopped by the "head radar person" so there can be no unfair timing of scenarios; most evaluators do not tell you if you passed or failed until after you are sent out of the room and then called back in moments later; the ghosts and remotes are not allowed to converse with the students while the PVs are in session; however, we did see each other in the hall and expressed our mutual thanks and congratulations. The whole day looks really official with suits and ties walking around everywhere, but in reality, it is just you, your radar controller, and the evaluator that matter. The other people are for show only. I think this is what gets to people on PV day. It got to me!

I think it is best to just find your center and relax. I even suggest not being in the building when you are not running the scenario. This will help get your mind away from all the hustle and bustle that is happening behind the scenes. Our class came back together right before everyone was done with the PV to offer support and congratulate each other; however, we scattered as soon as the doors closed.

All in all, the Academy was a fast-paced experience that really brought a lot of us closer together. As with anything of this intensity, it was bitter-sweet to say our good-byes to the teachers who invested so much in our training.

P.S. If you get instructors named Buck, Gale, or Joe (JD), consider yourself extremely lucky. They will all do whatever it takes to make sure you are the most successful person you can be, both at the Academy and in your facilities. The three of them will be missed by everyone in our class. (I can only speak to these teachers because they were the ones assigned to our class. I have heard of other exceptional teachers, but did not have the privilege of working with them.)

I hope you were able to learn something from this journal. I just want people to know that it is a very personal and intense experience, and feelings of frustration, anger, hurt, and joy should be expected!

Best of luck to all of you,
Michael

Facility Training (Enroute Option)

There are three main positions in the enroute center: A-side (assistant), D-side (non-radar associate or radar developmental), and R-side (radar controller). The main duty of the A-side position is to ensure that the printed flight progress strips are placed into the plastic strip holders and put into the proper sector; at times they may be asked to answer phone calls from other sectors and/or facilities. The implementation of the User Request Evaluation Tool (URET), which displays an electronic form of flight progress strips on a computer monitor, will make this position obsolete.

The D-side position is next to the R-side and assists with point-outs, resolves traffic conflicts, initiates aircraft reroutes, coordinates with other sectors and facilities via landlines and phones, and inputs revised flight information into the computer. URET allows this controller to update and reroute via a point-and-click function rather than typing on a keyboard; flight progress strips will be automatically updated with the new information.

The R-side functions as the main controller on this team and uses the radio to communicate with pilots, giving control instructions and safety alerts. He or she has overall responsibility for everything that happens in a sector, or when combined, two or more sectors (during low traffic periods or midnight to early AM work shifts). See this NASA Web site for an excellent ATC tutorial: http://virtualskies.arc.nasa.gov/.

The following pages 35 to 61 are reprinted by permission from Chip Jones, a certified professional controller at Atlanta Center (ZTL). This material is meant as informational only and is not meant to be reflective of anyone else's experience.

So you are through with the Academy and Stage I, and you are reporting to Atlanta Center as ordered. You will find ZTL about 25 miles south of Atlanta, on U.S. 19-41 in the rolling hills of the Georgia Piedmont. Your first few days will be spent in-processing. You will be officially assigned to ZTL-520, which is the training department. Your first day will probably begin at 0800 and end at 1630 (4:30 PM). Administrative hours at ZTL are Monday through Friday 0800-1630. That is an 8 hour day with weekends off. Watch-standing personnel like controllers and AF techs work an 8-hour shift and rotate their schedule around the 24-hour clock, 7 days in the week. However, as long as you are assigned to the administrative side of ZTL, you work administrative hours.

There is plenty of security here, so one of your first priorities will be to get a control room badge. You will also get a facility decal issued for your car(s). There is also an interview with the Chief, an interview with the NATCA facility representative, a visit to the personnel office, a visit to T&A, and a tour of the facility to accomplish. Also, I highly recommend you join NATCA as soon as possible; in my opinion it is the best move you can make for your job security.

You will get briefings on paperwork by the Human Resource clerks, and then you will fill out a bunch of forms like FEGLI, health insurance, and emergency Point of Contact (POC). Much like the military, as a controller you are always on call, so ZTL will need your phone numbers. Your business is their business. If you fail to show up for work one day and they cannot reach you by phone, they will actually send the police out looking for you.

You will be issued a locker and headset, and you will select your unique operating initials from a list of those available; a popular combination is the first letter of your first and last name, i.e., Peter Jenkins (PJ) or Jessica Simpson (JS). It might take you the first three days to accomplish these basic tasks. The rest of the time you will spend just absorbing the environment and getting used to your new workplace. Enjoy the down time.

At some point during these first few days, ZTL-520 will tell you which area of specialty you have been assigned to. The process of area assignment is transparent to you and will likely have occurred before you graduated from OKC. Basically at ZTL, at the pleasure of our Chief Controller, NATCA still has a major say in what areas newbies are assigned. They consider your background (CTI, MARC, ex-terminal, VRA, FSS, etc.) your seniority and your arrival date. NATCA suggests, and the Chief disposes.

Once you find out what area you are going to, you can start to dial into your training focus. FAA will too. Your training will be in accordance with FAA Order 3120.4, which you can find online at the FAA's "Air Traffic Publications" website (www.faa.gov/ATpubs). It is being modified, so things might change a bit while you are at OKC, but the components of the training program have not changed for years and probably will not in the future. There is also a ZTL training order that supplements the national order. The ZTL order specifies the target hours you get per position, in other words how much time FAA will give you to train on a scope or a D-side. You have four stages or phases of training. In my day, we called them phases, and there were a few more of them to reflect OJTI. The four stages are:

1. FAA Academy Training (Course 50132). Prepares the individual to enter facility training.

2. Assistant Controller (Flight Data) (Course 55053). Prepares the individual for assistant controller position qualification and certification. Includes OJT for qualification and certification on assistant controller positions.

3. Non-Radar/Radar-Associate Controller (Courses 55054 and 55056). Prepares the individual for position qualification and certification on all non-radar/radar-associate positions. Includes OJT on non-radar/radar-associate positions.

4. Radar Controller (Courses 55055 and 55057). Prepares the individual for qualification and radar certification on all radar positions. Includes OJT on the full range of controller duties.

Now that you have completed Stage I training out at OKC, you will enter Stage II training as soon as you have been in-processed. This is the part where you draw your map, obtain your area of specialization rating, and begin your tribal initiation as a controller. I will delve into Stage II in the next part.

Having been in-processed and having spent a few days checking boxes in the training department, you are now chomping at the bit to begin training. Before we go any further, I am going to take a minute and describe how ZTL is laid out, both administratively and operationally. After that, I am going to assign you to my own area (Area 7), and we will start Stage II training together. By placing you in the Fighting Seventh with the rest of us, the "Battling Bastards of Burne," I will be able to give you a snapshot of how a real ARTCC area of specialization works and how you will train in one.

I hope you like acronyms. I am also going to ramble on from time to time with my spin on things. Please take my spin with a grain of salt—it's the way I see things through my own experience. For those of you not ZTL bound, this part may be too detailed with ZTL minutiae.

Life at ZTL

ZTL is home to almost 1,000 people broken into a few camps. Besides air traffic (AT) people, there are also Airways and Facilities (AF) people, contractors, and a whole bunch of people who work in the NADIN facility, which is co-located on the grounds. Do not ask me about NADIN, because I have no answers. All I know is they do their own thing and take up lots of spots in our parking lot. The two main tribes of employees at ZTL are AT and AF people. There are two Chiefs here; one is the Air Traffic Manager who runs the whole shebang, and the other is the Airways Facilities Sector Chief who hangs his shingle out at ZTL, and if you ask him, runs the whole shebang too. Since you are an Air Traffic employee, we will skip the organization of AF. Their main job is to keep our system up and running, and they are having to do it with less and less resources, just like everyone else in the field. Something breaks, from a light bulb to a super computer, and AF fixes it, somehow.

Other offices include the Admin shop, where we have three or four Human Resources clerks. They know all there is to know about FAA personnel paperwork, TSP, FEGLI, GHI, etc. There is the T&A office, where one harried clerk and her assistant keep up with everyone's pay and leave.

And then there is the Quality Assurance office. QA has a Manager level slot at its head, the QA Manager. Four or five people work for him at ZTL. Whenever you screw up—and you will—QA launches a huge investigation into the minutiae surrounding your misfortune.

ZTL-520 is the training department. All these shops have ZTL-5XX designators but I cannot remember them all. By now, you have come to know the training department pretty well, having spent a week there one day. There is a manager for training. Ours is a touchy-feely type who is genuinely concerned with your success at ZTL. Under her are a couple of walking wounded controllers in temporary training staff jobs helping her with the mountains of paperwork produced by training enroute developmentals. The training department also works closely with the contract instructors who will do your classroom and DYSIM lab instruction. These guys are all ex-ZTL controllers who have retired and are back as teachers. They work for the Washington Consulting Group, and there are probably 15 to 20 of them plus a secretary, boss, etc. ZTL-520 also maintains the CBI lab, which stands for Computer Based Instruction. You will spend a lot of time in the CBI lab.

Other staff offices include ZTL-530, which is the Airspace and Procedures office. They handle airspace issues, rewrite LOAs, work with Terminal Instrument Procedures (TERPs) on Instrument Approach Procedures (IAPs), etc. There is a Military Liaison office that coordinates all the secret and not-so-secret military stuff you will be doing. There is also an automation office that handles computer issues (sort of a hybrid between AT and AF, and some contractors).

The Seven Areas of Operation

Operationally, ZTL is divided into seven areas of specialization plus a Traffic Management Unit (TMU). Each area has an operations manager (OM) who will be your boss. Because of management politics, these people are in a constant state of flux, so if you do not like your boss, hang in there as he or she will not be there long. Under each OM is a team of supervisors (SATCS). Each area nominally has seven SATCSs—one per crew or team (here at ZTL we call them teams) of controllers (ATCS) on the line. The idea is that the SATCS is your boss of record, and the OM is their boss of record, but your boss as well. Controller teams are organized to provide 24-7-365 watch standing capability.

In each area, there are seven teams, one team for each set of regular scheduled days off (RDO). Team 1 has Sunday through Monday RDOs; Team 2 has Monday through Tuesday RDOs; Team 3 has Tuesday through Wednesday and so forth. CPCs bid every year on these teams based on seniority, and here in the bargaining unit, seniority is winner-take-all. That is just the way it is. In addition to being your boss of record (meaning in your chain of command for discipline, etc.), the SATCS also provide first level supervision to the area. At ZTL, from about 0630 until 2330, there is an SATCS on duty in each area, watching the controllers work and trying not to get in the way.

Each of the seven areas is an operational division of ZTL airspace. Each area consists of six or seven sectors. Each sector has a Display System Replacement Plan View Display (DSR PVD), aka a radar scope. Each sector has strip bays to the left or right of the PVD. In between the scopes is a thermal strip printer that spits out flight progress strips. Although ZTL still uses strips, URET is scheduled for deployment in August 2005. However, the FAA is not going to get around to training us on it right away because there is no money. The jury is out on what will happen with URET at ZTL. My money says that when you arrive at ZTL in the fall of '05, we will still be using flight strips.

Each sector is designed to be operated by two to three controllers, aka a radar team. At ZTL, like at other ARTCCs, this team is often a team of one (even when it shouldn't be). The R-side controller (or radar or radio controller, your choice) works the radio and uses the radar to separate traffic. The R-side is the captain of the sector and outranks everyone except God himself. Not even the SATCS outranks the R-side on the sector as far as the other radar team members are concerned. The SATCS can order the R-side to do something, but such orders are so rare as to be almost unheard of. The airspace belongs to the R-side, and his tactics rule while he is plugged in.

The D-side, or data controller, or radar associate controller, uses the flight strips and the landlines to separate traffic. At least, the D-side does this in theory. There was a time in the very early 1990s when it was possible to actually use the strips to separate almost all conflictions at a sector. This was pure manual non-radar type stuff, even though you were operating in a pure radar environment. Now however, traffic is up so high that the D-side is mainly a strip shuffler, phone caller, and coordinator for the R-side. Also, a quick mention that ZTL does things differently than most other ARTCCs when it come to D-side. Here at ZTL, the D-side makes and takes point-outs, makes and takes handoffs, and makes and takes radar separation calls on traffic. Almost all landline calls come in to the D-side. This makes D-side training at ZTL a real challenge, because you will be doing all kinds of stuff that other centers (Zs) don't load their D-sides with. More on this in the Stage III description.

When things get really hairy at a sector, and if staffing permits, a third controller will be brought in to act as a coordinator and another set of eyes on the scope. At ZTL, we call this position "the tracker." Other Zs may call them coordinator or handoff controller.

Finally, in support of the various radar teams, a controller will be assigned to work the A-Side. Because we still use strips to control airplanes, every strip that comes off the printer must be pulled, culled through, and probably posted. Most areas have three or four printers that are printing continuously. ZTL is surrounded by URET-equipped ARTCCs, and they reroute and update the daylights out of flight plans, causing hundreds of extra strips per hour to flood the ZTL printers. We call this killing trees because of all the wasted paper. The A-side has to sort through this mess and deliver the necessary strips to the radar team working at the sector. When we are busy, you literally might run out of places to post the strip at the sector. Each full-sized strip bay holds 18 strips. You can imagine how busy you are when five full bays are filled with active strips and more printing out every minute. The A-side is usually staffed almost continuously from about 0700 to 2300.

Areas 1 Through 7

Area 1 works the NE side of the center, mainly over the mountains of North Carolina, East Tennessee and part of Virginia. It has seven sectors and butts up against ZID and ZDC. Area 1 has a couple of nasty high sectors where they blend Charlotte, NC arrivals and departures with enroute traffic. They feed the main arrival bang into the Charlotte Class B, so they hold and sequence daily. They also work a lot of low airspace with plenty of non-radar and provide approach control service up in the mountains between Knoxville and Bristol TN, north of Charlotte, NC and Pulaski, VA. Area 1 currently seems to be a happy ship at ZTL with 57 or so people.

Area 2 is traditionally the busiest area by volume in ZTL. It lies between Atlanta and Charlotte, NC, and much of its airspace is concerned with the southern part of Charlotte terminal airspace. Area 2 has seven sectors and shares a boundary with ZDC and ZJX. Like Area 1, Area 2 works CLT arrivals and departures into and out of the CLT terminal area. It does not do non-radar, and they own very little low altitude airspace except on the midnight shift, when they assume the Greeneville-Spartanburg, SC terminal airspace. This area is busy and often gets no notice holding (aircraft are stopped without advance notice) from ZDC when ZNY shuts off ZDC on New York and East Coast traffic. Area 2 has about 55 controllers.

Area 3 is almost completely surrounded by other ZTL areas, and its primary focus is on serving the busy Atlanta Terminal Area (ATL). It works the ATL east departures and also has two low/ultra low sectors NE of Atlanta that have something like 27 or so IAPs into these airports. However, Area 3's primary focus is on Atlanta arrival traffic headed inbound to ATL via the Macey arrival corridor. This is no-joke Atlanta arrival traffic. For a look-see, follow this URL which is spying on the Area 3 controllers working the Logen sector (http://atcmonitor.com/). It will be really busy on Wednesday, Thursday, and Friday PM. Area 3 has six sectors and 40 CPCs. They are hurting for bodies. They are not happy.

Area 4 works the SE side of ZTL. They butt up against ZJX. Area 4 has one of the easiest workloads at ZTL, yet when we recently did a traffic study we discovered that Area 4 was the busiest area at ZTL that week. Who'd have thunk it? They have the lightest ATL arrival stream and own almost no airspace down to the ground. The staffing crisis has only recently started to impact Area 4. They have about 54 mostly happy controllers working seven sectors.

Area 5 is the easiest (a relative term in ATC business and one that Area 5 controllers would fight me about) and happiest Area in ZTL. They work the SW side of ZTL, butting up against ZJX and ZHU and maybe ZME (I cannot remember). Area 5 also works ATL arrivals, and primarily overlies Alabama and a part of Mississippi. They have a lot of not quite as busy airspace. Area 5 controllers are still living in that magic time when everyone had staffing. It has about 58 shiny, happy people working seven sectors.

Area 6 is another difficult area. It lies NW and W of ATL, butting up against ZME, overlying BHM and RMG. They work some very complicated traffic flows, including having an ATL arrival stream that is almost as busy as Macey, but which has the added complexity of a routine tailwind and gobs of traffic crossing the arrival corridor that these arrivals have to get through. In addition, they have a lot of low altitude airspace and major morale problems. Area 6 has 43 controllers working six sectors.

Since this is the airspace you and I will be training on as we progress through these parts, Area 7 will be our home at ZTL. It has seven sectors, but one of them (ultra low) has only been opened five times in the last 10 years and stays combined on another position. Area 7 runs from ATL up to and over Chattanooga to east of Nashville to west of Knoxville and back south along the west slope of the Blue Ridge. We have North Departure, Crossville, the world famous Burne Sector, Blue Ridge, Alatuna, and Hinch Mountain.

North and Hinch are low sectors owning at or below FL230. We provide approach control service to seven airports with IAPs, including an ILS at CSV, plus a wad of small VFR type airfields. Mainly we are concerned with traffic emerging from the Atlanta terminal monster. North Departure is the busiest of all Atlanta departure sectors, and because the sector owns to the ground, it gets bogged down with transient puddle jumpers as well. Crossville and Burne own from FL240 to FL340. Blueridge and Alatuna own from FL350 to FL600. When combined, we call this airspace the Blue Tuna. Burne is the monster in Area 7. It's the sector that will make you or break you. I'll describe it in detail when we get to Phase IV.

Stage II Training at ZTL and You

You have now completed your ARTCC in-processing and are familiar enough with the building layout to find the control room, cafeteria, and bathrooms. You may feel like a fish out of water and get the feeling that everyone is looking at you as new meat. They probably are. The first couple of days at ZTL are pretty lonely.

Finally, someone from ZTL-520 (training) has told you of your assignment to Area 7, which will be your home until you either check out as a CPC or wash out as an enroute training failure (ETF). Now begins your true ATC training. This is the stuff that your hard work, and money spent, on your CTI degree and training at the OKC non-radar program has been preparing you for. Believe me when I tell you that this will be the biggest challenge you have ever undertaken, and that the reward at the end of the road is well worth the hard travel. You, being highly motivated, chasing your dream, and like Cortez in Mexico having already burned all of your boats and marched on Montezuma, you ain't gonna be a stinkin' ETF. Not you. Maybe the other poor bastards, but not you.

From here on out, you will be working shoulder to shoulder with some very smart and talented people, none of whom want to see you fail. There will be many times when you laugh, some times when you feel like crying, and plenty of times when you will be so mad that you will want to hit someone. On the road, you will encounter brilliance, mediocrity, professionalism, administrative incompetence, operational stupidity, delay, and paradox. Hold on to your headsets, it will be a wild ride.

The following Stage II program is specific to ZTL. Other facilities may have waivers, not use strips, not have A-sides, etc. If you are not bound for ZTL, your Stage II experience will undoubtedly be a little different, but I would wager not much different.

In Stage II, you will be assigned to ZTL-520 as an Area 7 developmental controller. This means that you work Monday through Friday 0800-1630 and have weekends off. Stage II training is where you learn your airspace, learn your airspace, and learn your airspace again. You will also learn the basics of how ZTL works operationally, how your area fits into the NAS, and how to pull strips in the area. At the end of Stage II, you will qualify as an assistant controller in Area 7. To the CPCs in the area, that means you will be an apprentice controller. The CPCs also fervently believe that any controller's five-year-old child could pass Stage II training, so your accomplishment does not mean beans to them. Keep that in mind while you are drawing your airspace map for the 50th time, or wading through the 30-plus page multiple-appendix ZTL-Atlanta Approach LOA, or trying to make sense of the Dobbins Dump. These are baby steps.

At ZTL, the National Training Order FAAO 3120.4 is supplemented by ZTL Order 7210.1B, Facility Administration, Chapter 9. The official objective of Stage II training at ZTL is to prepare you for assistant controller qualification and certification, i.e., to mint a new Area 7 A-side controller. Stage II training includes OJT for qualification and certification on A-side positions of operation in the area of specialization. In other words, someone will show you how to pull and post strips in Area 7, after which they will check the box and say that you are certified to do so.

Other far more important things (especially to you) will also be happening during Stage II. You will get 80 hours of classroom time for map and area study. That is two weeks in a classroom preparing to pass your map tests. Officially, you are expected to be able to draw the ZTL High Altitude Map, the ZTL Low Altitude Map, and your Area of Specialization Map. At the beginning of the class, a Washington Consulting Group (WCG) contract training instructor or two will take you under their wing and give you a list of required items that must be included on the map tests. At the end of the 80 hours, you will be expected to take a blank ZTL-Hi chart, a blank ZTL-Lo Chart, and an Area 7 chart, and draw in all of the required lines, airways, radials, NAVAIDs, etc. The Hi and Lo maps won't be as hard to draw as your Area map, because on this map, you will have to draw every minor detail, which adds airports, sector boundaries, intersections, mileages, MTRs, ARs, MOAs, alert areas, etc. You must pass the map test with a score of at least 70 percent to pass the classroom portion of Stage II. The map phase is pass/fail.

After this phase, you will have some classroom and Dynamic Simulation (DYSIM) lab training, such as basic instruction on computer keyboard entries that you will be required to do as an A-side. You will also learn the basics of the VSCS communication equipment, so that you know how to place and answer landline calls on the control room floor. You will learn how to type in flight plans, copy flight plans, and you will get a course in ZTL's peculiar form of archaic strip marking.

A quick word here on ZTL strip marking. We have strip marking for everything. It is partially codified in the 7110.65P, but ZTL goes way beyond the 7110 in detail. We have symbology for control actions that the 7110 does not even consider. You can find basic FAA strip marking online at http://www.faa.gov/ATpubs/ATC/Chp2/atc0203.html#2-3-9. We use all of that, and then some. ZTL has its own strip marking order, and we actually mark our strips, constantly writing as we talk to airplanes. It is possible for two ZTL air traffic controllers to work a sector, one at the R-side and one at the D-side, and they never have to say a word to each other, instead communicating purely through strips and strip marking. (Well, it used to be possible, that is, back before everyone else got URET and went crazy with the flight plan updates, which flood us with strips.

Getting back to the strip marking arcane, when you see ZTL strip marking you will likely be amazed. Then again, URET may be here before you get to really use it.

In the DYSIM lab, you will run 10 instructional exercises on computer entries and practical application of what you learned in the classroom. The problems will run 30-60 minutes each and are not evaluated for pass/fail. Once you finish the classroom and DYSIM, which I think takes a week or so, you will report to your area for A-side On-the-Job Training (OJT). By now, you have been at ZTL for three or four weeks. You have someone, probably a WCG instructor, to lead you by the hand to your area where you will be turned over to the supervisor on duty in that area. Remember, at ZTL there are seven areas so there are seven supes on duty, working under an Operations Manager who is managing the entire control room. The supe in your area will be one of the guys in your chain of command. We have five others too, with one slot vacant, for a total of six supes. You may not have ever laid eyes on this supe before, but over the next couple of months you will come to know him or her well.

The supervisor (Operational Supervisor in Charge) will start your OJT on the A-side. Officially, you are allowed 10 target hours of OJTI to learn how to be an A-side in Area 7. However, you are allowed to certify at 20 percent of the target hours on the A-side at ZTL, which means that you have to have at least two hours of OJT before the supervisor can sign you off. Believe me, you will get signed off in two hours. It's not rocket science. Later, we will return to all the personal stuff that will be happening to you while you get this A-side OJTI, but right now I just want to lay out the official basics of Stage II.

All evaluations in Stage II are pass/fail. Such evaluations include the map tests, whatever classroom tests they may give for the flight data stuff, and your OJTI down on the control room floor learning how to be an A-side in the area. If you fail to achieve a passing grade of 70 percent or greater on any evaluation in Stage II training, and the training manager feels additional training is warranted, you can receive up to eight additional hours of training, including the time for a re-evaluation. This training can be in the classroom, or lab, or both. If the developmental fails to meet requirements, he or she will be withdrawn from training and "processed in accordance with agency directives." This is a fancy way of saying "You're fired." The good thing is that very, very, very few people wash out of Stage II, because getting through it is not hard. But just know that it can happen, and take it seriously.

About the OJT A-side training, and Stage II in general: When you come down to the floor for the first time, you are going to be nervous. This is the Big Show you've worked so long to break into. It will be noisy, and the place will be humming with adrenaline and energy, airplanes probably all over the scopes. You and the supervisor will walk into the area together. Suddenly, a lot of heads will turn your way. Everyone—and I mean everyone—is going to be sizing you up. Get used to it. You will be struck by the easy camaraderie between the controllers you are watching. Here's a tip: The people you are watching have been controlling planes in this area for at least 10 to 15 years together. They know each other extremely well, so if it looks like a family, it's because it is. They make it look easy, but it isn't until you have done it awhile. I can look at any controller in Area 7 and instantly recall their strengths and weaknesses. They can do the same to me or anyone else. You are the new unknown, and every move from here to CPC will build on or detract from your reputation in the eyes of your new workmates. If your new area looks like an exclusive club, that's because it is, and not just any exclusive club, but the world's most exclusive club. Your goal is to become a member. It is very important to say here that you do not have to be a CPC to join the club. What you have to do is become a reliable member of the team. Most people do not pull this off before making CPC, but I have seen a few do it.

Stage II is completed— at this point, you are now an officially certified A-side. You will now be reassigned from ZTL-520 and assigned to an Area 7 controller team. That team will nominally consist of a supervisor, five to eight CPCs, and a developmental or two. You will rotate your 0800-1630 shifts and weekends off into something more like the shifts other controllers work. For the purpose of this description, you will be assigned to Area 7 Team 3, so we can be on the same team. Tuesdays and Wednesdays will be your weekend, and your work week will begin Thursdays at 1600 and end on Mondays at 1500. You will not work mids (midnight to early AM). Since you are qualified on the A-side, you may begin to work credit hours at the pleasure of the agency, and you will also be eligible for overtime, subject to the local rules governing overtime and A-side controllers. People in the area, especially on your team, will start to get to know you, and you will slowly assimilate into the fabric of the area like a new pair of shoes on old feet. You will work as an A-side between two weeks and eight months while the training department tries to slide you into a Stage III class.

So, What is Stage III Training Anyway?

The FAA's description of Stage III training can be found online at the FAA Air Traffic Publications website. Regardless of which ARTCC you are headed for, FAA Order 3120.4J, Technical Training, Appendix 4, is the governing document. The 3120 will be modified or supplemented by a local, facility-specific Facility Order or Training Addendum, because each ARTCC has slightly different training needs. In the Atlanta ARTCC, the 3120 is modified by ZTL Order 7210.1, Facility Administration, Chapter 9.

Stage III training is designed to prepare developmentals to perform independently (under general supervision) all duties of a non-radar and a radar-associate controller on all sectors within the assigned area of specialization and to attain certification on those sectors (Course 55054). For Area 7, this means seven sectors, although we really only open six, so you can forget independent training on the never-opened Nello sector. Once you pass Stage III, you will be able to work all of the D-sides in your assigned area, plus all of the A-sides. Essentially, you will have graduated from an apprentice controller to a one-armer, as we like to call them. By general supervision, the FAA means you will be doing your own thing in the area, working the position (A or D) that you have been assigned, while the supervisor does his or her thing and watches over the whole area without paying much attention to what you are doing.

Nationally, Stage III is subdivided into three types of training: classroom/situational, simulation (i.e., DYSIM lab), and on-the-job training on the floor with live traffic. Pass/fail criteria applies in this stage. When you enter Stage III training, you will be transferred administratively back from ZTL-540-7 (Operations, Area 7) to ZTL-520 (Training). You will give up your 8-hour shift and return to an 8.5-hour shift. You will give up your wacky controller schedule (Tuesdays and Wednesday off), and go back to having Saturdays and Sundays off. The idea is to totally immerse you in Stage III training upstairs and in the lab for the DYSIM.

While you are assigned to Stage III classroom and lab, you will not be eligible to work credit; nor will you be eligible to work overtime, because you will not be working with live traffic. The only exceptions at ZTL are cut holidays, which are July Fourth, Thanksgiving, Christmas and New Year's Day. On these days, you might be allowed to work on the floor for holiday pay, because doing so will help a CPC get holiday leave.

At ZTL, Stage III training is conducted under the direction of ZTL-520. The training consists of classroom instruction and the administration of facility-developmental, area-specific non-radar and radar-associate control problems. You will run these problems in the DYSIM lab. The control problems will be based on one sector in your Area of Specialization, which will be a low altitude-ultra low altitude sector, because the high sectors are too high speed and complex to run non-radar. In Area 7, you will be running the Stage III control problems on the Hinch Mountain Sector (aka ZTL-41). You will get classroom instruction and OJT in the DYSIM lab, and your instructors will be WCG contract teachers, all ex-ZTL controllers who have retired from active duty.

The first phase consists of up to 80 hours of map/area study. You will be working from 0800-1630, weekends off. You will draw your Area of Specialization map again, just like in Stage II, but you will not have to draw the ZTL High and Low Maps this time. Again, your map will be pass/fail. You will be given a list of items that must be drawn on the map, and the map will be graded in accordance with (IOW) the IPG contained in FAA order 3120.4, Appendix 4. You will also study for your Area Rating during this portion of Stage III. This is where you study and memorize your LOAs, procedures, approach plates, IR routes, AR routes, etc. At the end of this phase, you will head to the CBI lab, where you will take an Area 7 Area Rating test on the computer. You must pass it with a 70 percent or better. You will then draw your Area Map and must make at least a 70 percent to pass.

After passing your map and acquiring your area rating, you will head into the classroom for 40 hours of non-radar instruction. This phase is also pass/fail. The goal here is to sharpen your non-radar skills, teach you how non-radar works (or is supposed to work) at ZTL, and to prepare you to pass the non-radar lab. As CTIs, you will most likely breeze through the academics here. The tests are probably still multiple choice and not very difficult. Your 40 hours in the classroom could be working 0800-1630, if no other Stage III or IV inputs are being taught. On the other hand, if there is a Stage IV or another Stage III class also going on, then you might be working a "day" rotation and the other class an "evening" rotation. Also, some instructors will allow your class to vote on either dayshifts or evening shifts, with majority rule. A sample evening shift class is working strait 1430-2300 with weekends off. Most of the WCGs are older men who like day shifts, but you never know. The possibility of working evening shifts will carry throughout the rest of your ZTL-520 time in Stage III, including the non-radar lab, the radar-associate classroom and the radar-associate DYSIM training.

The non-radar lab consists of 10 non-radar simulation scenarios. You will run one problem per day, so this phase will take you about two weeks. All non-radar scenarios except for problems 1, 8 and 10 are administered as instructional problems. Problem 1 is a familiarization problem so that you can get your feet wet. Problem 8 is a practice evaluation. Problem 10 is a pass/fail evaluation scenario. If you fail Problem 10, your career as a developmental might be very short.

Problems will run for 60 minutes but may end early if the instructor sees that as beneficial. Basically, during the non-radar problems, you will start out at about 50 percent complexity for Problem 1 and slowly increase to a 60 percent complexity by Problem 10. The idea is to teach you non-radar as it applies to your area, not to wash you out. It is presumed non-radar screening already occurred at OKC. Nevertheless, you can wash out right here in the non-radar lab. Thus, it greatly behooves you to work your tail off in the classroom, especially on your area map and your area rating. Do not think that knowing your map well enough to make a 70 on the map test will allow you to pass non-radar Problem 10. I couldn't have. Take this phase very seriously. Your instructors certainly will.

Once you have shed the bugaboo of non-radar, you will probably breathe a little bit easier. You will see non-radar on the floor with live traffic, depending on which area you are headed for as well as other factors. Area 1 at ZTL does the most real life non-radar, by the way. You will find some routine non-radar situations in Areas 3 and 7. Remember that Areas 1, 3 and 7 all share airspace in or near the Appalachian Mountains, so terrain often masks the radar line of sight. The good thing is, out on the floor with live traffic, the CPCs in your area will teach you how we really do non-radar at ZTL. You will find that a good dose of common sense goes a long way. The non-radar lab is harder than live non-radar, in my opinion.

You passed. Take a breath. You've earned it.

After the non-radar lab, it is back to the classroom for radar associate instruction. You will learn the role of the D-side in the ZTL radar team. You will become intimately acquainted with ZTL's archaic strip marking symbology. You will cover a lot of stuff that might be familiar to you (like aircraft equipment suffixes and MIA versus MVA) and stuff that might not be (like the difference between flat track, free track and coast track data blocks, temporary versus hard altitude key board entries, etc.). This part is also pass/fail, but it is Simple-Simon stuff. A CTI grad with college skills will find the FAA's multiple choice academics to be very easy. However, pay attention because many of you may not have a clue how the D-side works to begin with, and the ZTL D-sides are taught and expected to do more than most other ARTCC D-sides are allowed to do. So ask questions.

Once the classroom instruction is over (takes a week or so), you will be headed back down to the DYSIM lab to run D-side problems. Now is as good a time as any to describe the DYSIM lab at ZTL. Here at ZTL, like other ARTCCs, we have a massive computer running the place. This computer is down in the bowels of ZTL, and it is called the host computer. The host drives all sectors and the DYSIM lab at ZTL. The lab is located in its own room, away from the actual control room. This room is set up like a mini-ARTCC, including DSR scopes, strip bays, mock-VSCS, and thermal printers, just like the Real McCoy. In fact, the DSR sectors in the DYSIM lab have unique sector numbers that do not duplicate the real ones out on the floor. The lab is where ZTL conducts all of its hands-on training including annual refresher, remedial, and skill enhancement training. It has slots for up to six training positions plus other support PVDs, where remote pilots control airplanes and talk to the personnel being trained on the supported scope. Because the DYSIM lab has a limited capacity for supported control positions, lab time is a precious commodity.

At ZTL, Stage III and Stage IV classes are limited to eight developmentals per class due to room size. Only two people per class can run problems at the same time. In Stage III, person number one will be taking the problem, and persons two through four will be supporting that person. Person number five will be taking the problem, and persons number six through eight will be in support. In support means they act as remote pilots and help make the problem work. Generally, there will be a cadre of four to six WCG instructors assigned to each Stage III or IV class. Likely, they will be assigned to the class based on their own experience with the Areas of Specialization the class hails from. If there are Area 7 developmentals in a Stage III class, then WCG will do its best to have one of its retired Area 7 instructors in the class.

In the lab, an instructor will act as the R-side and work the radios, communicating with the pilots (remotes, your classmates) flying through the sector. You will sit on the D-side and take instruction from another WCG instructor while the problem runs. You will find, much to your chagrin, that the guy working the R-side will not do a thing to help you. All he will do is work the radio. You will be doing all of the separation, strip marking, non-radar, departure clearances, landline calls, etc. The goal is to teach you that at ZTL, the D-side is a controller who actually separates traffic.

The radar-associate lab portion of your Stage III training consists of four familiarization (fam) problems and twenty instructional control problems. You will be working the same sector as you did in the non-radar lab, which for us in Area 7 will still be Hinch Mountain. Problems 1, 2, 3, and 4 are FAM problems, so you can get your feet wet. Problems 5 thru 14 are instructional scenarios. You will work the D-side and the instructor will teach. Problem 15 is a practice evaluation. Problems 16 and 17 are instructional. Problem 18 is a pass/fail evaluation problem. Problems 19 and 20 are instructional. Problem 21 is a pass/fail eval. Problems 22 and 23 are instructional, and problem 24 is a pass/fail eval. Problems will run for 60 minutes. After the problem, you will swap places with your classmates. They will climb into the hot seat, and you will move into a supporting role as a remote pilot or observer. Expect to run one problem per day over a minimum of four weeks. As the problems progress from 1 to 24, the volume and complexity of the control problem will slowly increase. Problem 1 starts at 70 percent. Eval problem 18 is at 90 percent. Eval Problem 21 is at 95 percent, and eval problem 24 is at 100 percent.

The problems are designed to mimic the real life sector as much as possible. At Hinch Mountain, for example, we have a precision approach into CSV and non-precision approaches into RKW and JAU. RKW and JAU require coordination with Knoxville Tracon. We have landlines to Nashville AFSS (who will be wearing you out for departure clearances). We have a military IR route, and an AR route, a Class E Surface Area, semi-mountainous terrain with variable MIAs. ZTL-41 airspace butts up against and overlies two approach controls, and shares boundaries with both ZID and ZME. During the problems, expect the instructors to throw all kinds of stuff at you, such as non-radar departure clearances, IR routes, emergencies, VFR flight following, military change of destination, deviations, and wired aircraft that require you to intervene on the landlines to provide separation or positive separation. You will be busy and feel stressed, especially before the eval problems. But you will probably be too busy to feel stressed during the actual problems. That's pretty realistic. Did I mention it helps if you know your airspace like the back of your hand?

You must satisfactorily complete all evaluation control problems. The pass/fail criteria are not arbitrary and are codified in Appendix 2 of FAAO 3120.4J. After each unsuccessful eval, ZTL-520 will determine whether or not you get a re-take. If they decide to give you one, you can get up to two additional instructional problems at the same complexity/volume level, followed by a retake of the eval, which will not be the same control problem. If you have still not met the requirements for a passing score, or if ZTL-520 decides a retake is not warranted, then you will be informed, in writing, of the reasons why. You will then be withdrawn from training and processed in accordance with appropriate agency directives. Wash out of the D-school, and your FAA air traffic career is over.

When you pass the radar associate lab, your upstairs portion of Stage III training is nearly over. You have been eating, sleeping, and dreaming radar associate training for almost three months. Now it is time to return to your operational Area of Specialty for OJTI with live traffic.

Stage III, Part 2

Before we begin the OJTI portion of your Stage III training, we should talk briefly about how things will work administratively during this phase.

You have already met your OJT training team, which consists of two OJTIs, a supervisor and you. Remember there are seven teams of controllers in each area. In theory, each team belongs to a single supervisor called the Supervisor of Record. Supervisors are administratively responsible for the members of their team. They document OJT training, conduct routine checkups on your progress, and certify you on the position. Only your supervisor can certify you. More about this later.

One of the supervisors in Area 7 will be wearing two hats. In addition to running a controller team, he or she is the Training Liaison Supervisor (TLS). The TLS will be the cheese in the area about training for all area developmentals. The TLS acts as a go-between for Area 7 and the training department, provides peer-to-peer training guidance for other area supes, reports to the area manager about training issues, and tracks all training paperwork.

Generally, there are developmentals on every team of controllers at ZTL. Each area assigns developmentals to controller teams based on several factors, the main one being where management feels you can get the best training. The idea is to even out the load of developmentals and spread the training opportunities across the work week. In Area 7, we will have anywhere between five and ten developmentals when you get here. We will try to follow national and facility guidelines to get you trained, but due to staffing problems, we will fail to meet every letter of the law. The actual training process is arbitrary and capricious for a myriad of reasons, but I will simplify it here.

For illustrative purposes, we will pretend there are 14 developmentals in Area 7, which will give us two developmentals for each of the seven teams. You will be one of those developmentals. There will also be seven CPCs and one supervisor on each team. Thus, for our purposes here, each controller team in Area 7 has 1 SATCS, 7 CPCs and 2 developmentals. Remember this is a fantasy team, which I will use again to illustrate Stage IV training, which follows later.

When you come down to Area 7 from the training department to begin your D-side OJTI training, four people will have decided which controller team you will train on. These four folks are the TLS, the scheduling supervisor, the lead supervisor and the Area NATCA rep. There is a very good chance you will have no say as to which controller team you are assigned. There is also a very good chance you will get not so hot days off. This is because developmentals (like CPCs) get to select regular days off (RDO) once a year by seniority. AT ZTL, this selection occurs in September and is effective the following year. It is likely that this selection will occur before you get here or before you know when Stage III training will kick off. The developmentals, who came on the floor before you, will bid RDOs and will likely suck up the good days off, like Fri-Sat or Sat-Sun. Welcome back to team three Tuesday-Wednesday weekends.

Out of the 49 CPCs in Area 7, there are going to be, for our purposes, three OJTIs per team, for an area total of 21. These 21 make up the area OJTI cadre. Note this is an optimistic figure. The National Training Order specifies that each developmental shall have a primary and secondary OJTI. In real life, we do not always come close. Currently we have 14 OJTIs on our area cadre.

On Team 3, we have two developmentals, you and Joe. Joe is training on the R-side, which means he is in Stage IV. You are training on the D-side. You and Joe will be sharing the three

OJTIs on controller Team 3. CPC Sue will be training Joe. I will be training you. CPC Debbie will be the secondary OJTI for both you and Joe. When I am not here to train you, Debbie will do it. Sue will be tied up with Joe. When Debbie and I are not available, you will probably pull strips instead of train, because you already know how to do the A-side, and you are not yet certified on any D-side. It is possible for someone else on the OJTI cadre to train you, but probably not because they will be busy training someone on their own team.

Our supervisor of record will be SATCS Jane. Jane "owns" Team 3. Jane is our boss, and she is a part of your training team. As long as you are on Team 3, SATCS Jane is the only person in the FAA who can certify you on a position.

So What is an OJT Instructor?

At ZTL, an OJTI is someone who has met the following minimum requirements: They have been certified for at least six months on the position involved. For D-sides, in theory you could have a non-CPC radar associate train you on the D-side. In practice, however, only CPCs are considered for OJTI certification at ZTL.

The OJTI must be current on the position involved. Currency requirements are met monthly. At ZTL, a controller remains current by working at least 16 hours on the boards and at least one minute per sector per calendar month. Supervisors only maintain currency at one or two positions in the entire area, usually at one sector. (They have to work live traffic at least eight hours per month. Strangely enough, in Area 7 they are all checked out at the easier sectors. No supervisors are certified at Burne or North Departure because the work is too hard and high-speed for them to handle a routine push at only eight hours per month. Enroute ATC is not like riding a bicycle.)

They also must be recommended by the Supervisor of Record (their immediate supervisor). The Area TLS and NATCA rep make OJTI selection recommendations to the area manager, who selects CPCs to become OJTIs. He is supposed to consider human relations skills, communication skills, motivation and attitude, and objectivity and credibility. In real life, we have good OJTIs, bad OJTIs and everything in between.

OJTIs must successfully complete the approved FAA Air Traffic OJTI Course or local OJTI Cadre Course. They must be certified by a SATCS to perform OJT based on an OJTI Checkride. Basically, a supervisor plugs in with the OJTI on his or her first training session and documents the certification. OJTIs shall be evaluated by the supervisors within 30 days of assignment to OJTI duties and at least every six months thereafter. These evals are also documented.

During Stage III training, your goal is to certify on every D-side in Area 7. Your OJTI is essentially a mentor who will give you one-on-one instruction as you work live traffic at an operational control position. They are responsible for helping you acquire the knowledge and skills necessary to certify on that control position and for ensuring the training process includes preferred methods of teaching through a combination of instruction, demonstration, and practical application. They issue guidance on control judgment and make sure alternative techniques are demonstrated. The OJTI is supposed to document OJT results on an FAA form in accordance with the National Training Order, with at least one report per training session.

When you come down to the floor to begin the OJTI phase of your D-side training, the TLS will have created a formal training plan for you. This document will read like military marching orders. It will identify your training team members by name and will spell out to the letter which positions you will be taking your training on first. It will specify how many target hours of training you are allowed for certification. You, your two instructors, and your supervisor will discuss this plan in your first meeting with them. Your supervisor will then lay out his vision of what you are expected to do, what the team responsibilities are, what to do if you have personality problems with your OJTIs, and what your target hours are. He will also address any individual training needs you have. After the supervisor's spiel, the primary OJTI will discuss what he expects of you during OJTI. It is most important that you pay attention here, because usually the primary OJTI will go over ground rules for day-to-day training. (Details to follow.) Anyway, the training plan can be modified at any time by an addendum if something comes up that needs to be tweaked.

In Area 7, you will be training on 2 D-side positions at a time. You will be expected to certify on them within the target hours allotted. When you certify on the first two, you will be "seasoned" for a few weeks during which you will work those two positions. Then another training plan will be written, another training team meeting will be held, and you will start OJTI on the next two D-sides. Upon certification on the second two, the seasoning process will be repeated. Finally, another training plan will assign you to OJTI on the last 2 D-sides in the area. Once you certify on them, Stage III will be over and you will be a certified radar associate controller, aka D-side.

Target hours are the hours of OJTI you are allotted and within which you are expected to certify. In Area 7, the target hours are as follows (other areas will be similar): For the first two sectors, you get 130 hours per position. For the second two sectors, 110 hours per position. For the remaining sectors, 90 per position. For the Burne Sector, target hours are 130 hours per position, regardless of the sequence in training. Minimum certification hours are 20 percent of the allotted hours.

You also get 10 hours of on-the-job familiarization (OJF). OJF is tracked but not graded. During OJF, you simply plug in and shadow someone, usually your OJTI, and watch them work the position. The idea is that you get to watch the position for a couple of hours before you have to jump in and start working it.

After the training team meeting, the scheduling supervisor will try to schedule you to work the same shifts I work, as your primary OJTI (or Debbie, as your secondary). You will go back to Tuesday/Wednesday weekends and that wacky ATC watch schedule. If I have a 1600 shift, then you will have a 1600 shift. If I have leave, then you will probably be assigned to work Debbie's shift. If both Debbie and I are unavailable, then any other area OJTI will train you. However, chances are that on those days when neither your primary nor secondary are at work, you will be assigned to work currency. Since you are only qualified to pull strips at this point, currency means you do the A-side.

Alright, let's get to work, shall we? For your first two D-side positions, area management has assigned you to train at Sector 38, North Departure, and Sector 41, Hinch Mountain. You get 130 target hours to learn North and 130 to learn Hinch. You are eligible for certification at 20 percent of those target hours, so you need at least 26 hours of instruction before you can be signed off. In actual practice, you will need to get at least 80 hours at each sector before the supervisor will consider signing you off, no matter how much of a superstar you are. No one gets checked out at minimum hours on their first two D-sides because there is no advantage to doing so. When you get signed off at North, you will be magically certified to work the never-opened

Nello ultra-low sector. Nello underlies North Departure and has opened only five times since 1996, so you get no training on it.

Before we plug in, I lay out my ground rules for you. They are simple. Just like an airplane, a control position can have only one person actually "flying" it at a time. The way OJTI works is you will work the position and I will ride herd on you. There are four headset jacks at each D-side position. You will plug in to one jack. I will plug in to an adjacent jack with an override capability. My job is to listen to everything you say, watch everything you do, and to teach, monitor and correct you as you work. I can override you, literally cutting your voice out by pressing my microphone push-to-talk. There will be times, trust me, when I have to intervene. If you hear me say "I got it," then you shut up until I tell you "OK, you've got it." There are no exceptions to this rule. One of the most confusing things you can hear on an ATC tape is when a trainee and instructor get into a pickle, and both of them try to simultaneously work the traffic. You get two voices on the landlines or radios, maybe two different traffic solutions, and mass confusion every time. That is not going to happen to us. It it's either your airplane or it's my airplane, and it's my call.

When we sit down on a D-side, we will receive a briefing from the outgoing D-side (whom we are relieving) or from the R-side if there is no D-side there. The basic briefing checklist is status, equipment, weather, and traffic. Once we have a grip on what is going on in the sector, we assume the position. Using the D-side keyboard, you will log us in via a SISO keystroke. (SISO stands for sign-in, sign-out.) Basically, you will type my initials and your initials into the computer. This way, if anything goes wrong at the sector, the people in QA know who to blame.

A quick word about blame. Here at ZTL, there are only two kinds of controllers. Those who have had operational errors (called a deal), and those who will. Like I said in an earlier section, at ZTL you face a 25-30 percent chance each year of having a deal. Unlike some other facilities that are slower and less complex, we get slammed with lots of traffic every day. We run well over three million operations a year here, and average over 10,000 a day on most weekdays. That's a boat load of traffic, and ours is usually stuffed to beyond bursting. The only way you can absolutely avoid personal risk here is to run screaming from the control room as soon as possible and into a management, staff, or flow control job. To survive training at ZTL, you have to completely blow off any notions of fear. When you have a deal at ZTL (or ZDC, ZNY, ZAU, ZOB, etc.), it's just another day at work. You will have one. As far as I know, I am the only person at ZTL with over fourteen years on the boards who has never had a deal. While I am very good, more importantly I'm the luckiest man in air traffic control. I have the war stories to prove it, but you will have to get here to hear them. In short, I would rather be lucky than good. I am still due for a deal soon, and I know it. It keeps me on my toes.

While we are training, any mistakes you make will be my fault. A developmental cannot be charged with an operational error at ZTL. Anything that QA has to say about one of our training sessions, they will be saying to me. This is one reason a lot of very good certified controllers never become OJTIs. The OJTI is on the hook for all the mistakes the developmental makes. Since January, we have had 11 operational errors where a developmental screwed up, separation was lost, and the OJTI bought the deal. In every case, the OJTI had no excuse, regardless of the circumstances. That is one of the hassles of being an OJTI and is why when I say "I've got it," you make yourself small until I give it back.

A daily OJTI session in a perfect world will see us working D-38 or D-41 for a couple of hours, taking a short break, getting back into training, doing lunch, training again and then calling it a day. Your target hours are counted for time you are actually plugged in with me and receiving training. During an 8-hour shift, you might average 4.5 hours of OJTI. Depending on things, we could get over 5.5 or less than 2 in any given shift. Every time we sign on, we generate a SISO record. When we sign off, the printer kicks out a strip with our session time on it. As the developmental, one of your tasks is to get your hands on that strip and save it. At the end of the day, you will tally your total time for the day. (More on this later.)

If we can get 4.5 hours of OJTI a day, it might take you 10-12 weeks to get certified on your first two D-sides. Remember you are training on two D-sides at a time, so we have to split the time between two sectors when we train. That is, we may get 4.5 hours at Sector 38 for a day, and zero on Sector 41.

At the end of each day of training, I have to fill out paperwork on the session, documenting your progress and identifying deficiencies. Say our shift started at 0800 and ends at 1600. At around 1500, we will want to knock off the OJTI and debrief. You and I will get your training folder and head for a quiet room to discuss the day's session. This training folder will contain your training plan, a log in which you track your OJTI hours at D38 and D41, and all your daily training paperwork. You will be responsible for maintaining the tracking log and keeping the folder up to date. To keep you honest, the supervisor will peek in the folder from time to see how you are doing with the upkeep.

You and I will go over what I saw during the day, and then we will have a session about what happened and what you did right and what you did wrong. You ask questions, and I answer them. Finally, I fill out the paperwork for that day's session using a standard FAA form called an Instruction/Evaluation Report, FAA Form 3120-25 (see Appendix 2, page 131). This is a detailed form with lots of boxes in lots of categories and lots of room on the back for explanations and summary of the day's session. You are required to have at least of one these forms filled out per session.

The first time you head down to the floor with your headset in hand and me in tow, you are likely to be nervous. I know I was. There is nothing you can do about these opening day jitters except to ignore them and press on. The first few minutes I was plugged in for OJTI, I was lost, mentally lost. There were butterflies in my stomach, my ears were ringing, and I had a touch of panic vertigo. The radio guy started talking to airplanes and all I heard was "Nowes123lantroggoodal22995" or "Wampwampwamprogerblather." I had no comprehension whatsoever. This is one reason we have instituted on-the-job familiarization, so that the "Charlie Brown's Teacher" radio syndrome is conquered before you start OJTI. Every CPC that I know has told me they had the same problems on the first session—nerves, mike fight and a general incomprehension of the "flick." So don't worry. It goes away very quickly.

Here at ZTL, the D-side's primary job is to manage the strip board. At Sector 38, you will have a hundred or so departure strips in your suspense bay, and you will have a wad of active overflight strips in your active bay. As the A-side delivers strips, you will be expected to post them correctly at the sector. You will be doing stuff like looking for duplicate strips, recognizing wrong for direction, spotting aircraft filed below the MIA or MEA, writing altitude updates on strips, etc. You will also be responsible for monitoring the radar scope; making and taking radar point-outs; making and taking radar handoffs; making and taking APREQ calls; entering control information in the radar data blocks; moving data blocks to keep them from overlapping;

dropping data blocks that have left the sector; issuing departure clearances through FSS; coordinating speeds, vectors and altitudes with adjacent sectors; resolving non-radar conflictions; forwarding PIREPs to weather and international departure times to flight data, etc. One of the hardest things you learn to do is to write as you talk, because strip marking is so important at ZTL. The symbology will also take getting used to.

ZTL D-sides do it all, and ZTL D-side training IMO is harder than R-side training in many ways. Almost all landline calls, including radar calls like handoffs and point-outs, come in to the D-side. You will find yourself constantly behind when the sector gets busy. When you are not actively doing something, you should be looking for stuff to do. At moderate or greater traffic levels, there will almost always be something that you can do, either on the boards or on the scope. Remember, the first person at a ZTL sector who is supposed to go down the tubes is the D-side. You should sink first so the R-side can stand on your shoulders with his head above the waves while he works the radio. When he sinks, then we will hopefully have the staffing to toss a tracker into the position.

As your OJTI, I will be discovering which training techniques work best with you. In my bag of tricks, I have the coach technique, the brother technique, the father technique, the drill instructor technique, etc. Some trainees respond to gentle prodding. Some respond to simple mentoring techniques. Others respond to sarcasm or anger. There is no way I can know, right off the bat, what will work for you. I start out easy going, and as time goes on, I tweak my style until I find the best way to get through to you. It is all about how you learn as an individual, and I eventually find a way to connect with you. I am responsible for documenting all of your mistakes, which will be legion at this stage of your training. You will find me to be somewhat slack and subjective in this department. Newly minted OJTIs tend to write everything down. I tend to concentrate on the big stuff like separation rather than nickel and dime you on technicalities, unless you do not improve the small stuff as time passes.

In the event we do not connect, you can modify your training plan to some extent. Let's say we have a personality conflict, then it might be in your best interests to change OJTIs. The person to talk to about this is your supervisor of record. If necessary, I can be replaced by another primary OJTI, although you might have to change RDOs (and thus controller teams) to make a start with another OJTI.

As I said earlier, every day you train, you log and track your OJT hours and keep a running balance. Every day you train, your OJTI fills out a training form, which goes in your folder. Your primary OJTI will be talking to your secondary OJTI and any other OJTIs that might have a session with you. He will then use this information plus his own experience with you to keep your supervisor informed of your progress. The supervisor will also review all of your OJTI training forms every week so he can keep up with how you are doing.

At least once every 30 days, the supervisor will plug in on position with you to conduct a Skills Check. This is like a progress report and is used to officially document your strengths and weaknesses. At ZTL, the supervisor is looking to see you work moderate or busier traffic when he does a routine skills check. Your time during a skills check does not count against your target hours. At the end, the supervisor will write a fairly detailed summary of your performance and will identify specific areas where you may need improvement. He or she must also recommend one of the following options:

- Continuation of OJT. This is by far the most common recommendation for routine skills checks at ZTL.

- Skill enhancement training (SET). This is special training where the supervisor, your OJTI and ZTL-520 set up some tailor-made problems for you to run in the DYSIM lab, targeting specific weaknesses you may have. Skill enhancement training can also be a CBI course in the CBI lab, or rarely, extra classroom time. It is very rare to have SET assigned during D-side OJTI at ZTL.

- Suspension of OJT. This only happens when you have burned up all of your target hours and screw up the skills check so badly that the supervisor cannot recommend certification, SET, or continued OJTI.

- Certification skills check. Provided you have surpassed at least 20 percent of your target hours (the minimum level of OJTI for certification at ZTL), a routine skills check can morph into a certification checkride with the wave of a pen. Some supervisors conduct a routine skills check, recommend certification, and then hold a certification checkride to sign you off. Others, if they are convinced you are ready to certify, plug in to observe you and eventually just get up and walk away, leaving you to work the position all by yourself. Note that only your supervisor of record can sign you off at a position, so if you are getting a skills check from a different supervisor than your own, this latter method will not happen. Obviously, there is a lot of supervisor discretion built in to the certification process.

Let's take a closer look at the certification process. You've been training for almost three months now at North and Hinch. Your training log shows that you have a total of 100 hours at North and 86 hours at Hinch. For the last two weeks or so, I have not had a whole lot left to teach you. You are doing alright at moderate to heavy traffic volume, and you keep up with the R-side to my satisfaction. Debbie and I think you are ready for certification. We communicate our opinion to Jane the Supervisor. Jane has already given you a couple of monthly skills checks, and agrees to give you a checkride. You will undergo a skills check at Sector 38, then one at Sector 41, get recommended for certification on paper, and then have a certification checkride at both North and Hinch. After the skills checks, she recommends certification. Officially, she also considers your performance during OJTI over the last three months and during the skills checks, and the recommendations of the primary and secondary OJTI. Many supervisors also have a secret, arbitrary line you have to cross to get certified. Nobody knows what the line is except the individual supervisor, but usually it relates to how many hours of OJTI you have acquired when the question of certification comes up. I have seen supervisors refuse to certify developmentals after flawless checkrides, simply because the supervisor wanted the developmental to have more hours under his belt before being turned loose.

All you have to do to pass the certification checkride is to perform all job tasks at a satisfactory level or above. The supervisor checks a few boxes and you are now a certified radar associate controller in Area 7. There will be a lot of paperwork involved, more than when you got signed off on the A-side. You can now work D38, D41 and any A-side in Area 7. To your peers, you are a "one-armer." To area management, you are a "Limited D-side." You are eligible to work credit hours and overtime. You will season at either D-38 or D-41 (or any A-side) for a period of 45 days before you can start training on the next pair of D-sides.

This process will be repeated for all six D positions in Area 7 until you are certified on all of them. It will probably take you anywhere from eight months if you are really sharp (and lucky enough to train every day) to 14 months to certify on all of your D-sides. After that, you will work as a radar associate controller under general supervision in Area 7 until the facility can slide you in to a Stage IV slot.

If you should fail to certify within your target hours, your supervisor can extend to you an additional 20 percent of the original target hours. Traditionally on your first two D-sides, this is almost a guarantee. The supervisor can terminate your training, but most will not, even if you suck mightily. If you should blow through this extra 20 percent without certifying, the supervisor has no other option but to suspend your OJTI. You will then be referred back to ZTL-520 for a training review process. At ZTL, these are called Training Review Boards. Your career is on the line at this point.

The purpose of the training review process is to ensure all opportunities for training success were employed while maintaining the integrity of the training program. Reviews are conducted when requested by an ATM/hub manager or when training has been suspended due to the developmental's training performance. The training review will consist of the following group of people:

1. At least two of the following individuals selected by the ATM/hub manager: An operational supervisor other than the developmental's supervisor. (If not available onsite, the hub manager may assign this duty to any operational supervisor within the hub.) A support manager at facilities where this position is staffed. (If not available onsite, the hub manager may assign this duty to any support manager in the hub.) A TA/support specialist. (If not available onsite, the hub manager may designate any of these individuals from within the hub.)

2. A representative designated by the union.

The ATM and/or training team members may be asked to provide information during the training review, but they will not be part of the training review group. This training review will include an assessment of the training history on the position. Interviews of the training team members and/or other persons may be conducted. At the completion of the review, recommendation(s) are forwarded to the ATM/hub manager. Recommendations will include one or both of the following:

1. Continuation of training, which may include reassignment to a new training team; assignment of skill enhancement training; assignment of a new amount of OJT hours, and/or other actions that would help the individual to certify.

2. Discontinuation of training.

The ATM/hub manager considers the recommendation(s) resulting from the training review in making a final determination for continuation or discontinuation of training for the developmental. The results of this training review process are communicated to the developmental as soon as possible; the training review process cannot exceed 30 days from the date of the OJT suspension. The regional Air Traffic division manager has the authority to approve any exceptions to this process.

If at the end of the training review, you will either have a do-or-die reprieve, or your developmental training at ZTL will be terminated. If the latter happens, you will be processed in accordance with appropriate agency directives.

How To Survive D-side Training

Every sector will have slightly different D-side requirements. However, there are eight universal rules on how to be a successful D-side trainee at ZTL. They involve both your actual performance on the boards, and almost as important, your reputation as a developmental. Your reputation as a developmental can go a long way toward making or breaking you as an ATC trainee. Be concerned with it.

Never, ever, ever lie about anything that happens on the sector. EVER. Your OJTI is supposed to be watching you like a hawk. He listens to everything you do and watches your every move. He sits behind you, engaged with his own tasks while watching what you are doing. It is possible for him to miss something you have done because he is focused on another task, but if he asks you a simple question, like "Did we point that Delta out to Sector 5?" be honest when you answer. We once had a developmental who answered such questions based on what she thought the OJTI wanted to hear. Consequently, a deviation occurred, which went on her trainer's record. The trainer resigned from her training team. She eventually washed out.

Rule #1:

In ATC is never lie about what happens on a sector. This applies equally to air safety stuff once you make CPC. You cannot get fired for making a mistake, but they can fire you in a heartbeat for lying about it. Controllers do not lie about air traffic control safety.

Rule #2:

Save your excuses. If you did not do something that needs to be done, just do it when prompted. Do not verbalize why it is not done. The best thing for your personal reputation is to be a no-nonsense, no-excuses kind of person. When you screw up, take it in stride and move on. That is what training is all about. Do not garner the reputation of excusing your failures.

Rule #3:

Keep it simple. ATC is a complicated quilt made up of hundreds of simple pieces. Focus on the simple and stay there. I tell my trainees to do things the same way every time, as much as possible. The goal is to eliminate as many variables as possible, which makes the job simpler. One example is phraseology. Up in the classroom and in the DYSIM lab, you will learn the formula for making a point-out to another controller via the landline. Use the correct phraseology every time, regardless of what you hear and see CPCs using on the floor. If you always use the same formula for making a point-out, then you will not have to think about the "how," and you can concentrate on the "why, when, and what" instead.

Rule #4:

The sin of commission is better than the sin of omission. Be aggressive. Be very aggressive. If you think that something might need to be done, go ahead and do it. Your OJTI will gently correct you if you are jumping the gun. On the other hand, if it needed to be done and you failed to do it, your OJTI might not be so gentle when they get on you for not doing it.

Here is an example. We are training at North Departure. We are in the throws of a mad departure push out of Atlanta. It is July and 98 degrees F outside, with 80 percent humidity. Air carrier departures are climbing like rocks. The guys climbing out to the northwest are having trouble topping our boundary with the DALAS sector. You notice a Regional Jet out of FL190, climbing at 500 FPM, 30 miles from the DALAS boundary. Too early to tell if this airplane needs a point-out to DALAS. You are busy trying to keep up with the R-side. Do you point this guy out now or wait until later? The answer is that an experienced CPC would wait until the last minute, but that is because they have the experience. If you wait until later, you might forget to do it at all, because you are one busy dude right now. So you call with an early point-out and the RJ actually tops DALAS with a few hundred feet to spare, making your point-out unnecessary. This is a sin of commission, because you made a point-out where one was not needed, but so what? As your OJTI, I have no problem with this.

On the other hand, let's say you decided to wait and see and then forgot to make a point-out when required. As your OJTI, I have a problem with this. See how rule #4 works?

Rule #5:

Come to work on time, every day, ready to train. Do yourself a favor and consistently show up for training. You want to concentrate on learning how to be a D-side. This will require intense application on your part. Every day you do not train is a day longer toward certification. A week of annual leave in the middle of training can set you back a month, mentally. Avoid it. Also try to avoid as much outside stress as you can while you are training. Things like getting married, buying a house, or moving can really affect your performance as a developmental. If you can, plant yourself in a simple, stable outside situation and concentrate on work. Once you check out, there will be plenty of time for external stresses.

Rule #6:

Be a team player. Remember that your training is not just about you. Your area is going to be running an intense ATC operation with or without you. There will be times when you will have to fall out of training and rip strips or something else because staffing is low that day. Be cheerful and take one for the team when you are asked to do so. People notice this right away.

Rule #7:

Be hungry, interested and eager to learn. One of the biggest complaints out there about today's trainees (which would include CTIs and MARCs) is that some of them seem to have a sense of entitlement. That is, some of them seem to think that no matter what, they are going to make CPC just because they are in the training program. Avoid this reputation like the plague. Never come across as unconcerned or lazy about making CPC. The other CPCs will crucify your reputation and you will have to move heaven and earth to shed your bad rap.

Rule #8:

Know your airspace. Occasionally a developmental actually makes it all the way to the OJT portion of Stage III without having a rock solid grip on his or her airspace. You will not check out on any D-side in ZTL if you do not know your airspace and procedures. There is no excuse not to know them by this point, but still expect to be asked obscure questions from the supervisor giving you a checkride. And if you do not know the answer, your answer should always be "I don't know, but I'll find out."

Stage III, Part 3

In Part 3, we will first take a look at what factors effect your selection for Stage III training, and then we'll look at salary and the promotion schedule associated with controller training.

As we already established, the main bottleneck for developmental training at ZTL is the DYSIM lab. Both Stage III and Stage IV classes compete for DYSIM time. In addition, all of the various sorts of CPC DYSIM training needs also compete for the lab. Usually, CPC needs outweigh developmental needs. It is possible for up to two developmental classes (either Stage III or IV, or one of each, 16 developmentals total) to run concurrently, one doing days shifts and one doing evening shifts. It is also possible for ZTL to be training in other areas, so the whole facility is trying to squeeze through the DYSIM lab at the same time.

Because of this, it is possible that there could be more ZTL developmental controllers waiting on a Stage III or Stage IV slot than there are slots available. Say there are 10 new people in the various areas. All of these people have completed Stage II and are pulling strips as certified A-sides. All of these people are chomping at the bit to get into Stage III. Yet there are only 8 slots in the next Stage III class. How does ZTL-520 pick who gets in, and who has to wait for the next class (weeks away)?

At ZTL, Stage III assignment criteria is as follows. To be eligible, you must have satisfactorily completed Stage II training, which means you are a certified assistant controller. You will be assigned to Stage III training based on your eligibility, which is based on seniority and then a series of tie breakers. The criteria that ZTL-520 considers are first, your appointment date as an AT-2152 (i.e., air traffic controller); then your entry-on-duty (EOD) FAA; next is your EOD ZTL, then your SCD; finally, your FAA Academy composite score. It is not arbitrary, and it is not always exactly first come, first served.

Stage IV, Part 1

For the past few months, you have been working as a radar associate controller (D-side controller) in Area 7. You are getting a bit tired of being the Area 7 D-side fireman. Fireman? Yep! You find yourself constantly on the move between busy sectors as the area supervisor feeds help to his overwhelmed R-side controllers when the heat is on. You are the go-to guy. The supervisor would much rather move you around the area as the traffic moves than to move a CPC on a D-side. Your day consists of a constant rotation between busy sectors or working the A-side. Due to FAA policy, Area 7 has to plug in minimum one D-side at 0800 and keep that D-side position staffed until at least 2200 at night, regardless of traffic or area staffing. As a fireman moving from sector to sector as the traffic ebbs and flows through the area, you will be referred to as a floater.

The advantage to being a floater is that you will see plenty of action while you await a Stage IV slot. Before long, you should be feeling like an actual air traffic controller. You work the traffic, you work the break rotation, you have weekdays off, and you endure the long hours on positions with the rest of the troops. You're bonding with your area. Likely, you break with your peers, eat with your peers, drink and party with your peers. The point is, you are getting comfortable with the environment and starting to fit in. You have gone out of your way to establish your reputation on a good footing, and the daily work routine is something you are growing comfortable with. Also, if you are good, you are positively chomping at the bit to start working the radios and radar. Be patient, the time will come.

Things that affect the timing of your Stage IV classroom and DYSIM training are identical to the ones that impact Stage III. The bottleneck will always be the DYSIM lab and what ZTL is doing overall. Stage IV classes, like Stage III, consist of eight radar developmentals. Normally, the timing between completing Stage III and beginning Stage IV depends on your own performance and the performance of seven other D-side developmentals. ZTL-520 traditionally waits for 8 people to qualify for a Stage IV class before starting one. If ZTL is running all the CPCs through annual refresher training, URET training, or any other training, your Stage IV class will take a back seat until the facility is finished.

One thing that is slightly different between Stage III and Stage IV is the assignment criteria. Let's say 10 people have been certified on all of their D-sides before the next Stage IV class is scheduled to begin. Because of space limitations, only 8 can make the class. The other two will have to wait for the next one. The official tie-breakers for Stage IV assignment are as follows, in order of importance:

Controller date	EOD ZTL
Appointment to 2152 series	SCD
EOD FAA	FAA Academy Composite Score

Your controller date is the date that you get fully certified as a radar associate controller at ZTL, that is you get all of your D-sides and end Stage III. Everything else plays second fiddle to this date. Basically, you are in an unheralded race during your Stage III training to secure priority in Stage IV. Regardless of your seniority, your priority for a Stage IV slot depends on when you get checked out as a D-side. Since your raises depend on your progress through the various stages of training, the faster you progress, the quicker you make bank.

Unfortunately, once you make CPC, bargaining unit seniority returns to primacy. For example, I made CPC eight years before the guy one slot below me on the Area 7 seniority list, yet he is only one month my junior. I made CPC two to four years before several of my immediate peers who occupy slots right above me on the area seniority list. They started Stage III training before I did, I caught them during D training and went to Stage IV R-school before them. Thus, I made CPC well before them. Yet once they made CPC, they reclaimed their linear seniority ahead of me by virtue of their bargaining unit date. This means they pick their RDOs and annual leave before me. However, because I made CPC before they did, I make more money than they do.

Here is a cut and dried look at your upstairs R-side training. A lot of Stage IV training is similar in structure to Stage III. The main difference is the curriculum. The objective of your Stage IV at ZTL is to qualify you to perform the full range of ATC duties in Area 7 and for you to attain certification on all radar positions in the area. Stage IV, like Stages II and III, are conducted on site under the tutelage of ZTL-520. The course is a combination of classroom material from the FAA Academy and locally developed material like simulation scenarios in the DYSIM lab. The upstairs portion of Stage IV is almost identical in elapsed time to Stage III, except there is no non-radar work, so you finish sooner.

Stage IV training consists of classroom instruction and radar simulation scenarios in the DYSIM lab on two sectors from your Area of Specialization. It is comprehensive, job-related and designed to minimize the amount of live OJTI training as much as possible. The idea is that the DYSIM lab will expose you to routine traffic situations on the floor, teach you how to handle them, and throw unusual situations at you. Because the instructor can stop the clock to teach, the lab is a great R-side training tool.

ZTL radar controller training consists of about 60 hours of classroom instruction. You learn how the ARTCC radar operates, what DARC is, how HOST works, how flight data and radar feeds are meshed, what radar symbology signifies, etc. You also go over strip marking and phraseology. You draw your Area of Specialization map again from memory. Officially, this part of the training eats up about two weeks. Like Stage III, you will probably be working 0800-1630 with weekends off.

Before you enter the DYSIM lab, you must pass the national radar qualification examination at the FAA Academy. The local classroom portion of Stage IV will teach you everything you need to know to pass the national radar exam. It is not a tough test, in my opinion. It deals with radar basics like symbology (i.e., the difference between flat track targets, free track targets, primary targets and coast track targets, or the difference between correlated versus uncorrelated targets, etc.), and the ARSR radar mosaic. It is not hard to study for and everyone passes. If you have made it this far, you will find these standard national tests easy.

The reason you have to pass this test is because the FAA used to require ZTL people to head out to the Academy at OKC for a national standardized radar school called RTF, but now the testing is done in-house. The national test is to ensure our local training meets basic national guidelines.

In the lab, as an Area 7 developmental, you will be training at Sector 38 (North Departure) and Sector 41 (Hinch Mountain). These sectors own from the ground to FL230, so you get to see the full gamut of enroute ATC in this airspace. Your DYSIM lab training consists of adequate time in the lab to run two familiarization problems and 18 instructional simulated scenarios on each of the two sectors. Problems 1 and 2 are the FAM problems, where you get your feet wet. Problems 3 through 10 are instructional. Problem 11 is a preparatory evaluation. Problems 12 and 13 are instructional. Problem 14 is a pass/fail eval. Problems 15 and 16 are instructional. Problem 17 is a pass/fail eval. Problems 18 and 19 are instructional. Problem 20 is a pass/fail eval.

Like Stage III, the radar problems start out at less than 100 percent in complexity and volume and slowly ratchet up to 100 percent. They start out at 70 percent with problem 1. The first eval (problem 14) is at 90 percent. The last eval (problem 20) is at 100 percent. The instructors (the same WCG contract guys from Stage III) will throw everything they can at you during the instructional problems. During the evals, everyone is serious business, and they will unofficially back off with some of the non-routine stuff like emergencies.

Having survived DYSIM training in Stage III, this lab training should all be old hat to you. However, you will find that as the R-side, you have to do your job and much of the D-side's job as well. You will have one of your WCG instructors (minimum four per class) working the D-side as you do the lab, while the other will be either teaching the problem or evaluating it, in the case of pass/fail. You tell the D-side what to do, things like "Get me control to turn that guy" or "Call in this military change of destination," etc. The idea is to teach you that the R-side is the captain of the sector. Except for a few specific duties, the R-side is ultimately responsible for everything that happens on a sector. If the D-side fails to do something (say like pass a speed, or APREQ a wrong-for-direction), the R-side is responsible for ensuring it gets done. We really get into the meat of this in Part 2 when we head down to the floor to begin R-side OJTI in our area.

Back to the DYSIM

The training order specifies that the developmental shall satisfactorily complete all pass/fail simulation problems. The simulation pass/fail criteria must be in accordance with FAA Order 3120.4 Appendix 2, which means there are specific national standards to follow. A determination for additional training will be made by ZTL-520 after each bust of an eval problem. Additional training, if warranted, will include up to two instructional scenarios and one reevaluation at the volume/complexity level where the bust occurred. (Additional training is usually not warranted in the lab phase of Stage IV, so do not count on getting it.) If requirements are not met for certification or additional training is not warranted, ZTL-520 will inform you, in writing, stating why. You will then be withdrawn from training and processed in accordance with agency directives. At this phase, this usually means your employment is terminated. Washouts from Stage IV used to have a shot at an FSS job, or a Level One VFR tower, but FSS is gone, Level One has been privatized, and there are few other FAA jobs available to Stage IV training failures. The retention picture will change as you progress through R-side OJTI on the floor. Get two R-sides and you get a promotion to developmental 3 and a fighting chance to go elsewhere if you cannot make CPC. (More on this later.)

Expect to be upstairs in Stage IV training for 11 to 12 weeks at least. Once you pass this portion, you will return to the control room floor as a radar developmental. You will be assigned to a training team, have a training team meeting, and begin your final OJTI on the road to CPC.

Stage IV Part 2

The OJT structure of enroute radar training is virtually identical to that of Stage III D-side training. That is, you will do almost all of the same things structurally as you did a year or two ago in Stage III. You will be assigned a training team consisting of a primary OJTI, a secondary OJTI, a supervisor, and you. However, when you get to the meeting, you notice there is only me and a supervisor you do not recognize. You were expecting Jane and Debbie to attend. I will explain where they are in just a minute.

Just like when you graduated from D-school, your upstairs instructors will set up a meeting with your downstairs OJTI team. This will be your first R-side training team meeting. In this meeting, the instructors will have a frank discussion with the OJTI team and you. They will highlight your strengths and catalogue your weaknesses. The WCG instructors will then turn you over to the area via your training team, and your work upstairs with ZTL-520 will be over for good. Gone are the admin hours, the eight and a half hour days, and the weekends and holidays off. From here on out, you will be training downstairs on the floor with live traffic. Within the next year or 18 months, you will either make CPC or hang up your headset forever.

A Few Stage IV points

Your radar OJTI will mimic D-side OJTI in most ways. For example, in Area 7 you will get 130 hours per sector on your first two R-side sectors. You will get 110 on your second two, and 90 on your last two. Also, when you train on Burne Sector, you will get 130 hours regardless of its position in your training lineup. Because Burne is the Area 7 bugbear, you will train on R-39 last. R-side OJTI consists of you and me getting assigned to two sectors in the area, probably two sectors that routinely combine. Likely candidates for your first two in Area 7 will be North Departure and Hinch Mountain. We will exclusively train on these two until you know them like the back of your hand.

You have to know everything about these two sectors—all the LOAs, all the mileages, every approach by heart, all the frequencies for adjacent airspace, etc. As the R-side, you are the captain of the sector. Remember D-side OJTI, where you found yourself doing a lot of R-side tasks like point-outs, handoffs, and radar data entry? As an R-side trainee, you will discover that you are responsible for the D-side tasks also, like strip marking, dupe strips, and WAFDOF. You will get a promotion from developmental 2 to developmental 3 once you certify on your first two

R-sides. Currently, this is good for about $95,000 a year. Once you certify on your first two R-sides, ZTL has a mandatory "seasoning" phase of 45 calendar days before you can begin on your second two. The more R-sides you certify on, the more useful you become to Area 7. The more useful you become, the more likely you are to be pulled out of training and used for coverage, which will delay your trek to CPC.

Remember, just like on the D-side, you can get into trouble with your training. R-side training is harder than D-side training in many ways for most people, but radar controllers have some kind of indescribable ability to see in four dimensions simultaneously. This does not seem to be a common human trait. If you do not come genetically equipped with what we call the "sight," all the training in the world will not help you succeed, and eventually you will discover that the radar ATC world is not your calling.

You must also be able to multitask and get things done by constantly changing priorities. Good instructors will teach you how to prioritize duty. They will impart survival skills on scan, clearances, and phraseology. I really think a good OJTI can teach a person everything except how to see traffic. Even so, some people just cannot make the leap to radio, even though they were stellar D-sides. And I have seen slow D-side developmentals take to the radio with a gusto and turn into excellent radar controllers. Overall though, my experience has shown me that people are generally consistent, with good D-side trainees being good R-side trainees, and poor D-side trainees washing out on the radar.

The washout procedures are identical with Stage III. The supervisor can grant you an extra 20 percent of target hours, after which you go to a review board. Usually, the review board grants you more hours, at least once. Your training will also progress from easier sectors through the harder ones, with Burne waiting your last effort in Area 7. There are few people in the system who can work a sector like Burne, but any decent enroute CPC can, given enough training and motivation. So if you can certify on at least two radar positions, you gain an intangible benefit as far as job termination goes.

If you get the chance to train with another OJTI, take it. The best way to learn the R-side is to work with as many OJTIs as possible. In real life at ZTL, you probably will not have the opportunity, but ideally you should try to change OJTIs between each pair of R-sides that you qualify on. In the enroute environment, there are usually two or more ways to resolve a given tactical conundrum. Your goal as a radar developmental is to soak up as many different control techniques as you can, and then put together your own bag of tricks. Even when you are not actively training on the radar, observe how other controllers handle situations. You'll learn some new things.

Eventually, you will certify on every radar position in Area 7. Along the way, we will toss in a bit of tracker training so you know what do when the a sector calls for a third set of eyes (you). Tracker training is not formalized. You are required to have it, but the when and where is usually an afterthought. You will also have some DARC training. At ZTL, the requirement is one hour during live Stage IV training. DARC is our backup radar system, a primitive version of the NAS-Host we use daily. You can get active DARC training by working a mid shift. Often, the main system is taken off line for maintenance in the wee hours, and those of us who work the graveyard get plenty of hands-on time with DARC. So you will want to work a mid or two so that you can see what happens on that shift. Once you make CPC, you can expect to be scheduled the occasional mid every month—and they are easy to swap out of or into.

Hope this helps those of you ZTL bound. Hurry up and get here. We need you!

Chapter Three
The AT-SAT Test

Introduction

The Air Traffic Selection and Training (AT-SAT) Examination is divided into eight separate parts—seven cognitive tests and one non-cognitive. The cognitive tests are Applied Math, Air Traffic Scenarios, Scan, Letter Factory, Analogies, Angles, and Dial Reading. The non-cognitive test is the Experience Questionnaire, which is part of the test but not counted into your score. "The non-cognitive measure was included in the AT-SAT composite score, but was not used independently in the current study, as the focus of the study was on cognitive ability tests. In addition to the AT-SAT composite score based on total test performance, scores were also calculated for each cognitive test included in the battery." (Heil and Agnew, 2000, p.3; see note below.*)

Those who have taken this test reported the most difficult parts to be the Air Traffic Scenarios and the Applied Math. They also reported that one needs basic computer skills and familiarity with using a computer keyboard and mouse to take the test.

If your AT-SAT exam score is between 70 and 84.9, you will be in the qualified group; over 85 is well qualified. Anecdotal data indicate that students enrolled or graduated from the CTI schools had an average AT-SAT score of 85 to 90 and a few 90 plus, but no data exist for non-CTI students/graduates.

The sample tests in this book illustrate the types of questions you will encounter on the exam, and are meant for practicing. The material is not intended to represent an actual AT-SAT exam; the actual exam may appear more difficult than this practice material. Each test in the actual AT-SAT exam is conducted via computer terminal and no paper and pencils will be allowed into the test area.

The practice tests on the enclosed CD-ROM are meant to simulate the FAA AT-SAT test. Our programming team worked with documents related to the AT-SAT that were in public domain and we gathered anecdotal data to verify the format of the tests. All of your actual exams will be on computer—so it will be helpful to prepare by first getting a preview from reading these descriptions and sample tests here in the book, and then by using the CD-ROM to practice test-taking.

---

* The explanations for each test description are taken from Heil, M. and Agnew, B., *The effects of previous computer experience on air traffic-selection and training (AT-SAT) test performance*, DOT/FAA/AM-00/12 (FAA Civil Aeromedical Institute, Oklahoma City, April 2000).

Even though this information was written for a research report in 2000, it remains a fairly accurate reflection of the exam. The other source for information is an undated FAA pamphlet that was published a few years ago and distributed to CTI schools.

The Air Traffic (ATST) and Letter Factory (LF) tests are dynamic scenario-based tests that require the use of the mouse. The scan test is also a dynamic test but requires use of the keyboard number pad. The analogies test is a static test that requires use of the mouse to view different parts of the screen and to select the correct response. The applied math, angles, and dial reading tests are static, page-turner tests that require only the use of the keyboard to select the correct response for multiple-choice questions. (Information taken from Heil and Agnew, 2000, p. 4)

Test-Taking Strategies

You will probably find a mix of very easy and extremely hard questions on the tests. Prioritize your work to achieve the highest possible score by skipping the hard ones and going back to them after you have answered all the easy ones. Determine what the question is asking; often the answer can be narrowed down quickly. If a particular question seems too difficult, make a mark by it and return to it later. Learn to use the process of elimination. This is especially helpful on questions that seem to demand a difficult solution. Some answers are obviously incorrect and can be eliminated immediately. For example, on the radar questions, first check the altitudes; this may eliminate the need to trace the route information to find the answer.

When you take the actual test, read the instructions for each part very carefully as the test monitor reads them aloud. Listen to everything that he or she says. If you do not understand something, ask questions. There is no such thing as a dumb question!

Use your time wisely as this is a timed test. Bring a watch with a second hand on it; place it in front of you on your table so you can keep accurate track of the time left for each section.

Stay calm and work rapidly. All the study material you acquired will serve you well; you should feel confident, but not overconfident. Do not worry that the person next to you has finished in supersonic time. When the exam is over you could have more correct answers and a higher score without finishing all of the questions.

Once you select or mark an answer, do not change it unless you are positive of your new answer. Studies have shown that 70 percent of the time in multiple-choice tests, people will change an answer to the wrong choice.

Get a good night's sleep before exam day and eat a light breakfast. If you are tired, hungover, or eat too much, you will not be at your best. Arrive early to secure the seat you want, be mindful of where you park (not the short-term lot), and use the bathroom before the test starts. You will work mostly on the computer, but it is not a bad idea to bring pens or pencils in case you have to fill out any forms. Also bring two forms of identification, one with a photo.

Cheating on the exam is a serious offense and can disqualify a candidate. If you studied and are feeling confident, you should do well on the test. Take the time to read this book in its entirety and work through all of the practice tests. This book has valuable information about the FAA, how to fill out the application forms, and related applicant information.

The Practice Tests

The practice tests in this book—even though they are presented on paper, as opposed to the actual exam on computer—are similar to the actual exam's tests for which you are given 8 hours to work at your own pace. Indivdual test times will vary, but we believe these reflect and simulate true exam conditions. Complete each test, correct for accuracy, then review your incorrect answers to determine how the mistakes were made. Concentrate on accuracy first, then speed. See the sample tests following each individual test's description to get an idea of test content; then use the CD to practice taking a simulated AT-SAT exam.

Air Traffic Scenarios

"This test simulates air traffic situations and measures the ability to safely and efficiently guide airplanes. The test uses simple rules and does not require that candidates have knowledge of air traffic control. Candidates are presented with simulated air traffic situations as aircraft appear on the screen and must be routed to an appropriate exit or airport. All situations involve the movement of aircraft and scoring of the test is based on how quickly and accurately the aircraft are directed to their destinations. There are practice and graded scenarios of different lengths and numbers of aircraft. All inputs to the computer are by mouse button." (FAA pamphlet, p. 11)

The Air Traffic Scenarios Test (ATST) is a low-fidelity simulation of an ATC radar screen that is updated every seven seconds. The goal is to maintain, as efficiently as possible, separation and control of a varying number of simulated aircraft—represented as data blocks—within the designated airspace. Aircraft in flight can pass through the airspace or land at one of two airports within the airspace. Each aircraft's data block indicates its present heading, speed, and altitude. There are eight different headings representing 45 degree increments, three different speeds (slow, moderate, fast), and four different altitude levels (1=lowest and 4=highest). You will use your computer mouse to communicate and coordinate with each aircraft by clicking on the data block representing the aircraft and providing instructions such as changes to the current heading, speed, or altitude. This is how you will achieve separation and control. The ATST produces three scores for air traffic (AT): AT Efficiency, AT Safety, and AT Procedural Accuracy. (This information is from Heil and Agnew, 2000, p. 3.)

The basic rule for the ATC scenarios is aircraft must have five miles of radar or 1,000 feet vertical separation when flying over the same point or intersection. If these criteria are not met then they are said to be in conflict or on a collision course.

An airplane is shown with an arrow pointing in the direction of flight along with a data block. The data block shows speed (S)slow, (M)medium, or (F)fast, and altitude is indicated by 1, 2, 3, or 4 (1 is the lowest, 4 is the highest). Destination is represented by A, B, C, D being external gates, and e & f are airports. An example data block might look like "M4D fl". This plane is flying west at medium speed at the highest altitude, and will exit gate D. Planes going through an exit must leave fast and at the highest altitude, and those going to an airport need to be slow and at the lowest altitude. All planes must also be kept at least 5 miles apart from other planes or the boundary, except for airports. The plane must not touch the airport boundary.

Select a plane by clicking on the arrow. Then select the item you want to change from the list on the side of the screen. For example, click the compass to change the heading. The landing direction required for the planes to land at the airports may change randomly from the left or the right. The pilot response will be through your headset, but sometimes they ignore commands or say the wrong response. Aircraft targets will appear at random on your screen and sometimes pilots will not follow your commands. Pay attention to everything that is happening on the screen in case a pilot responds or acts incorrectly to the commands and you have to take corrective action. Separation errors, aircraft wrong exits, altitudes, or speeds are considered operational or procedural errors and points are deducted from your score. Perseverance in spite of mistakes seems to matter in the test scoring.

Some test takers have said experience with PC gaming can help with this type of test (multitasking after gathering a lot of information). A screen similar to that shown in Figure 3-1 will be presented and your task is to answer 30 questions in about 30 minutes. It is possible that an electronic version of the AT scenarios practice test may be developed in the future, so you might want to use some of these programs to help you practice. These websites also may help:

ATCSimulator2 http://www.atcsimulator.com/

Air Traffic Simulation Project at http://www.cs.bham.ac.uk/~mzk/projects/webATC/

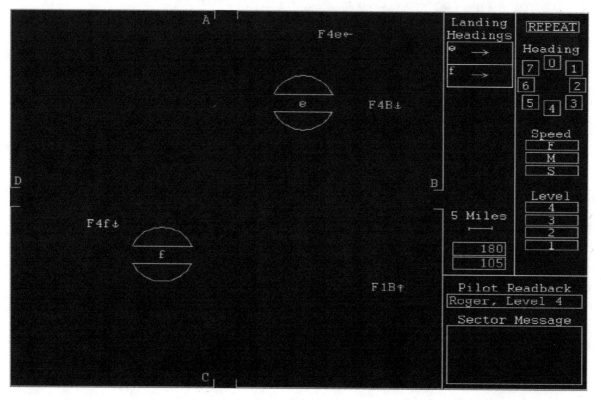

Figure 3-1. ATC Scenarios test screen

Analogies

"Air traffic controllers must solve reasoning problems by knowing which rules apply to a situation and then applying those rules. The analogies test measures reasoning ability in applying the correct rules to solve the problem." (FAA pamphlet, p. 9)

Note in the word and symbol examples (Figures 3-2 and 3-3) that some boxes are covered. You will be able to view only one at a time. As you move the mouse over a box, it will reveal the information; when you move it off, the box is covered again (follow the steps 1-4 in the figures below). The top left box contains the first word or object pair, and the top right box contains only the first word or object of the second pair. The bottom box contains the choices of the second word or object of the second pair. You can continuously go back and forth between boxes. At the time this book went to press, an electronic version of the analogy practice test was in development. Samples of analogies are provided for you to practice. The test has 57 items: 30 word analogies and 27 visual analogies. You will have 45 minutes to complete the test.

The analogies test measures a person's ability to apply correct rules and their efficient use of the rules to solve a given problem. Analogies are based on words, pictures, or figures and appear in three windows on the same screen for a given item. Test takers use a mouse to move freely between the three windows, view the different parts of the analogy, and select their answer. However, they can view only one window at a time. Window A presents the first part of the analogy, which requires subjects to infer the underlying rule. Window B contains the second part of the analogy, which requires subjects to apply the inferred rule. Window C provides subjects the opportunity to confirm their choice by selecting their answer from the available response options. (This information is from Heil and Agnew, 2000, p. 3.)

An electronic version of this test may also be developed in the future. You might want to check with your local college or technical school career assessment office to see if they offer help in practicing with these types of tests. Additionally, these websites might help you practice:

GRE Test Preparation Practice Exercises: http://www.syvum.com/gre/

Miller Analogy Test Online Course: http://www.testpreview.com/mat_practice.htm

Abstract Reasoning Symbols: http://www.kent.ac.uk/careers/tests/spatialtest.htm

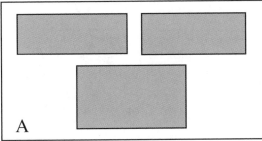

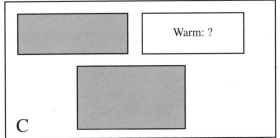

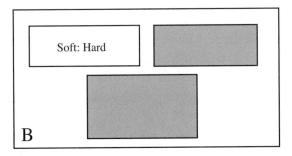

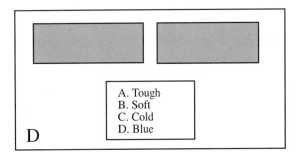

Figure 3-2. Word example

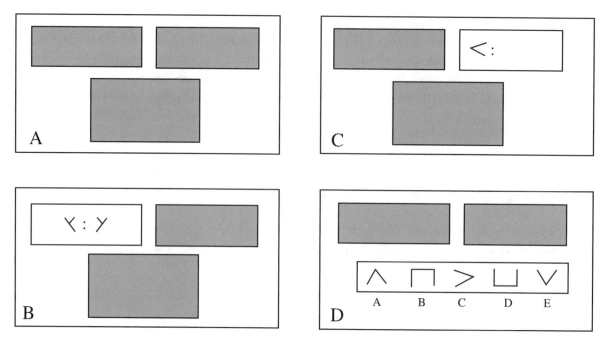

Figure 3-3. Symbols example

Letter Factory

"This test measures three abilities required to perform the air traffic controller job (1) pre-planning and decision making; (2) thinking ahead, and (3) maintaining situational awareness. In the first of several scenarios, letters move down each conveyer belt as shown in [Figure 3-4]. Candidates must place the correctly colored letter in the correct color box at the bottom of the diagram using the computer mouse. Candidates are asked to move empty boxes from the storage area to the loading area, order new boxes when supplies become low, and call Quality Control when "defective" letters appear. Using the mouse, the student clicks on a colored box to fill with the same color letters." (FAA pamphlet, p. 10)

The Letter Factory test (LF) simulates four factory assembly lines, each of which manufactures one of four letters of the alphabet (A, B, C, or D) in one of three colors. The test requires that subjects use a mouse to perform multiple and concurrent tasks. Each test section begins with letters that appear at the top of the conveyor belts and move down toward the loading area, as shown in Figure 3-4. The object of the test is to load each of the colored letters into boxes that correspond to the letter's color (e.g., an orange letter must go into an orange box). Based on the letters on the conveyor belts, subjects immediately begin selecting and moving boxes to the loading area to provide just the right number and color of boxes to correctly place all letters. Other tasks performed during the simulated factory settings include ordering new boxes when supplies become low and calling Quality Control when defective letters appear (letters that are not As, Bs, Cs, or Ds). The LF test produces two scores: LF situational awareness and LF planning and thinking ahead. (Information taken from Heil and Agnew, 2000, p. 3)

Every now and then the system will pause and ask a series of four questions pertaining to the previous situation. Candidates are asked to answer multiple situational awareness questions based on the rules provided for this test and previous test scenarios. A sample question would be "Which letter caused you to move the green box over?" or, "If all the letters remaining on the belt were put in their respective boxes, which letter would you need to complete the orange box?" Figure 3-5 shows the second type of question used in this test. Figure 3-4 cannot be used to answer Figure 3-5. (The figures on the actual test may be different than those depicted here.)

If an electronic version of the Letter Factory is developed in the future, you may want to practice using a computer game that requires you to focus on the screen action along with keyboard input (such as "Pong" or "Tetris").

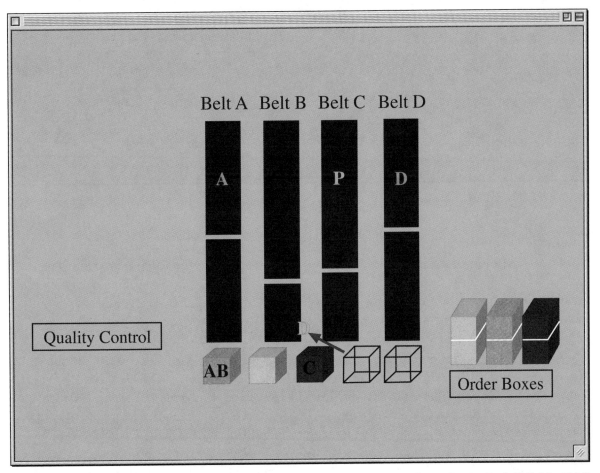

Figure 3-4. Letter factory #1–Control room (Source: Morath, R., Cronin, B. & Heil, M., 2004)

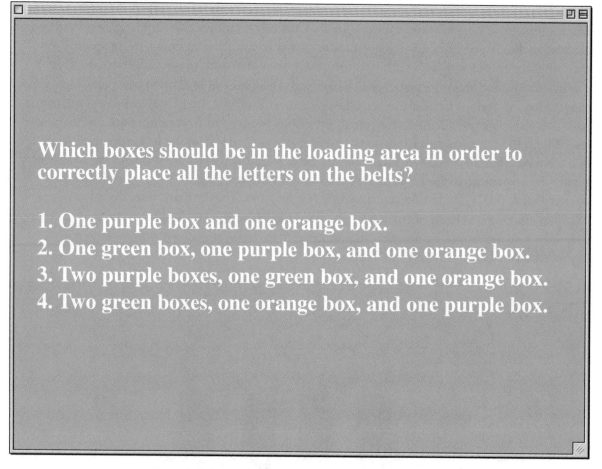

Which boxes should be in the loading area in order to correctly place all the letters on the belts?

1. One purple box and one orange box.
2. One green box, one purple box, and one orange box.
3. Two purple boxes, one green box, and one orange box.
4. Two green boxes, one orange box, and one purple box.

Figure 3-5. Letter factory #2–Questions (Source: Morath, R., Cronin, B. & Heil, M., 2004)

Scan

"In this test, multiple moving blocks of data appear at random on the computer screen. The numbers that appear in the data blocks will be either inside or outside a specific range displayed on the bottom of the computer screen. Scoring is based on how quickly and accurately candidates can identify data blocks with numbers outside the specified range. You will have 18 minutes to answer as many questions as you can correctly." (FAA pamphlet, p. 4)

After the test proctor explains this test, you will be given time to practice. In the Scan test, subjects monitor a field on the screen that contains discrete objects (data blocks) that are ½-inch tall and are moving in different directions. Data blocks appear in the field, travel in a straight line for a short period of time, and then disappear. During the test, the subject sees a blue field that fills the screen, except for a two-inch white bar at the bottom. In this field, up to 12 green data blocks may be present. Each data block contains two lines of letters and numbers separated by a horizontal line. The upper line is the identifier and begins with a letter followed by a two-digit number. The lower line contains a three-digit number. Throughout the test, a range of numbers (for example 360-710) is displayed at the bottom of the screen. Subjects are scored on the time it takes them to notice and respond to lower line numbers that fall outside the specified range. To respond, the subject types the two-digit number from the upper line of the block and presses enter. (Information taken from Heil and Agnew, 2000, p. 3)

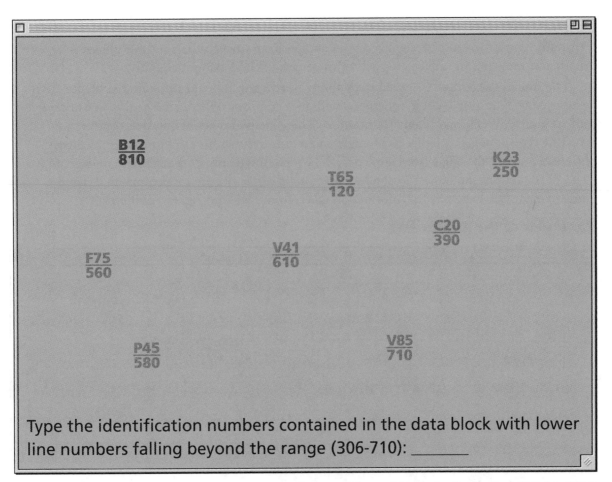

Type the identification numbers contained in the data block with lower line numbers falling beyond the range (306-710): _____

Figure 3-6. Scan Test screen (Source: Morath, R., Cronin, B. & Heil, M., 2004)

Planes appear and disappear on the computer screen seemingly from out of nowhere, and the targets move in all different directions at dissimilar speeds. Each target will be tagged with data consisting of a name (call sign is letter and two numbers) and its speed. A speed range will be printed at the bottom of the screen, which may change at any given time during the test. You have to eliminate all planes outside of this range and ignore all those within it. To eliminate a plane, you type in the two-number designation from the call sign and press enter; the plane will change color and disappear. Your score is based on accuracy and speed.

Say your screen shows these planes: F75/560, V41/610, T65/120, and the range given is 470-630. You will type 75, hit enter; 65, hit enter, etc., until the clock stops or you have no more planes to enter. Knowledge and proficiency with the computer numeric keypad on right side of a keyboard may give you an advantage.

You can practice for this test with a computer game, like Pong or Tetris, which requires you to focus on the screen action along with keyboard input.

Angles

"Air traffic controllers must recognize angles and perform calculations on those angles. The Angles test measures the ability to perform these tasks." (FAA pamphlet, p. 6)

The Angles test measures the subject's ability to recognize the measurement of angles. This test contains 30 multiple-choice questions with four response options; the goal is to work quickly and accurately (you'll have about 10 minutes). There are two types of questions on the test. The first type presents a picture of an angle and requires the subject to estimate (in degrees) the correct size of the angle (see Figure 3-7). The second type presents a measure in degrees (e.g., 35°) and asks the subject to choose the depicted angle that best represents that degree measurement (see Figure 3-8). (Information taken from Heil and Agnew, 2000, p. 4)

Examples of the Angles Test

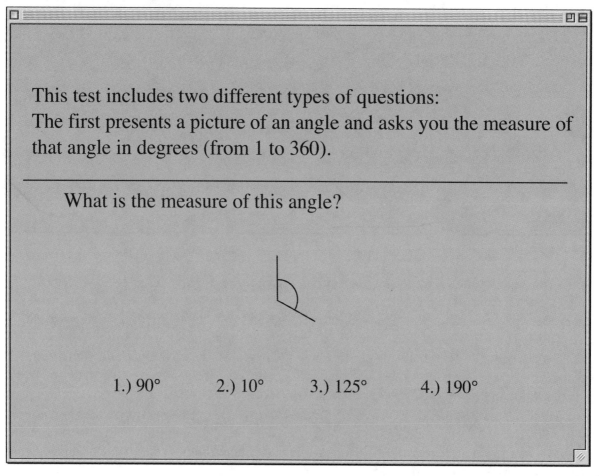

Figure 3-7. Angles test screen example (Source: FAA Pamphlet)

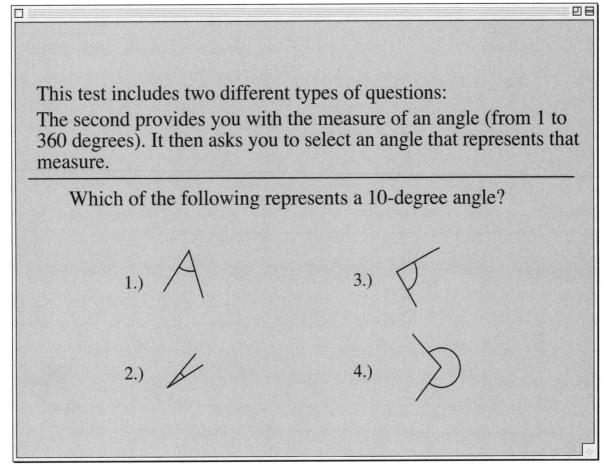

This test includes two different types of questions:

The second provides you with the measure of an angle (from 1 to 360 degrees). It then asks you to select an angle that represents that measure.

Which of the following represents a 10-degree angle?

1.)

2.)

3.)

4.)

Figure 3-8. Angles test screen example (Source: FAA Pamphlet)

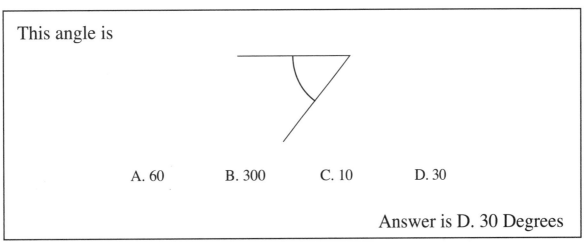

This angle is

A. 60   B. 300   C. 10   D. 30

Answer is D. 30 Degrees

Figure 3-9. Angles test

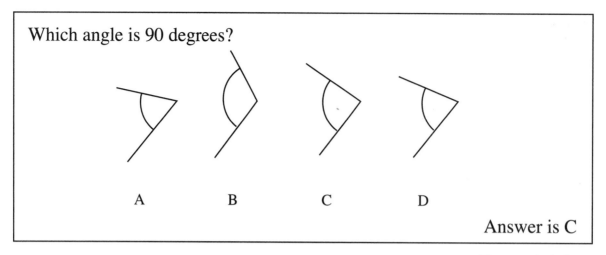

Which angle is 90 degrees?

A   B   C   D

Answer is C

Figure 3-10. Angles test

Angles Sample Test

1. Which angle is 45 degrees?

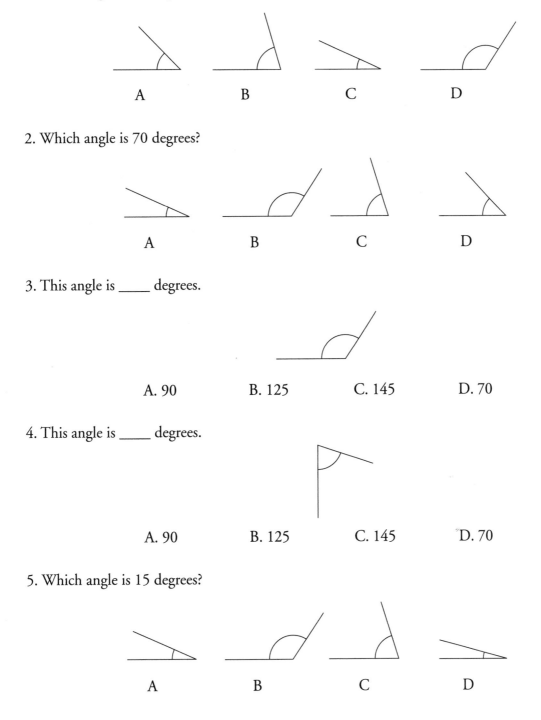

A   B   C   D

2. Which angle is 70 degrees?

A   B   C   D

3. This angle is _____ degrees.

A. 90   B. 125   C. 145   D. 70

4. This angle is _____ degrees.

A. 90   B. 125   C. 145   D. 70

5. Which angle is 15 degrees?

A   B   C   D

6. Which angle is 40 degrees?

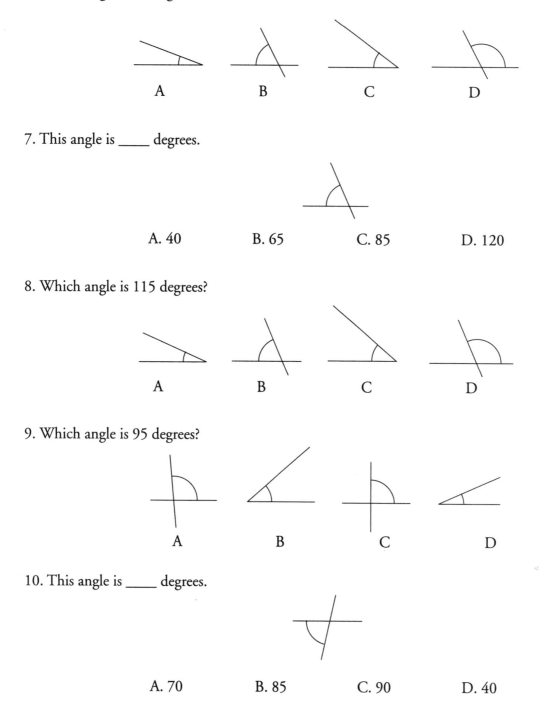

     A   B   C   D

7. This angle is _____ degrees.

     A. 40   B. 65   C. 85   D. 120

8. Which angle is 115 degrees?

     A   B   C   D

9. Which angle is 95 degrees?

     A   B   C   D

10. This angle is _____ degrees.

     A. 70   B. 85   C. 90   D. 40

11. Which angle is 125 degrees?

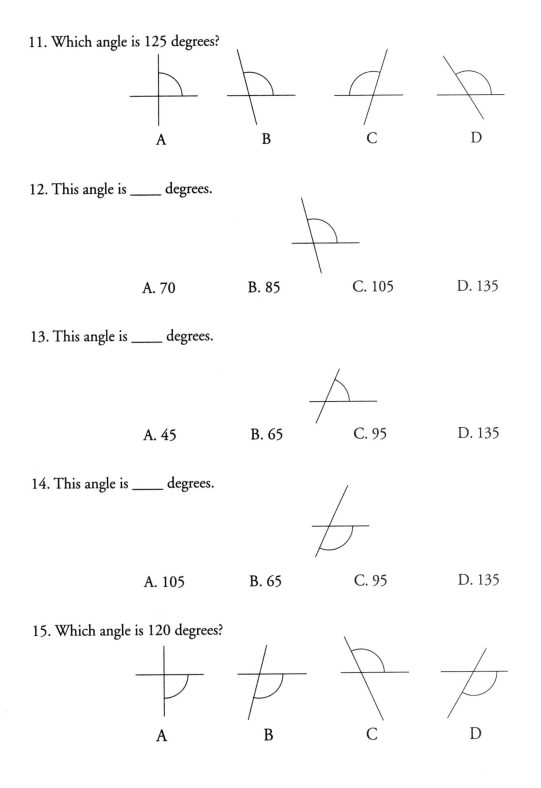

A   B   C   D

12. This angle is ____ degrees.

A. 70   B. 85   C. 105   D. 135

13. This angle is ____ degrees.

A. 45   B. 65   C. 95   D. 135

14. This angle is ____ degrees.

A. 105   B. 65   C. 95   D. 135

15. Which angle is 120 degrees?

A   B   C   D

16. Which angle is 80 degrees?

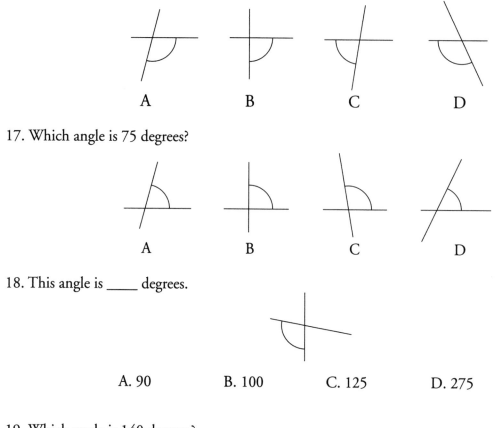

A   B   C   D

17. Which angle is 75 degrees?

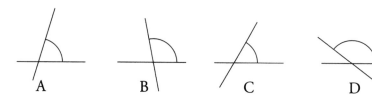

A   B   C   D

18. This angle is _____ degrees.

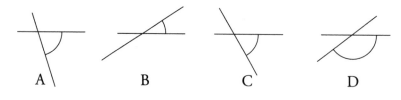

A. 90   B. 100   C. 125   D. 275

19. Which angle is 140 degrees?

A   B   C   D

20. Which angle is 35 degrees?

A   B   C   D

21. This angle is _____ degrees.

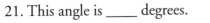

      A. 75   B. 100   C. 90   D. 10

22. This angle is _____ degrees.

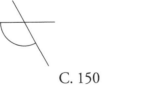

      A. 125   B. 100   C. 150   D. 45

23. Which angle is 55 degrees?

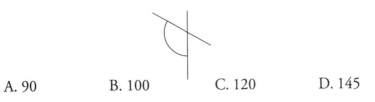

     A   B   C   D

24. This angle is _____ degrees.

      A. 10   B. 120   C. 150   D. 145

25. This angle is _____ degrees.

      A. 90   B. 100   C. 120   D. 145

26. Which angle is 35 degrees?

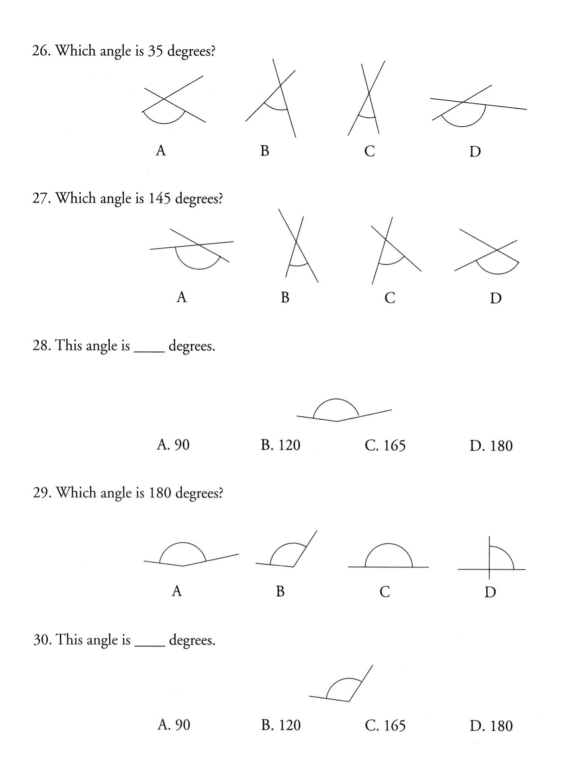

        A   B   C   D

27. Which angle is 145 degrees?

        A   B   C   D

28. This angle is _____ degrees.

      A. 90   B. 120   C. 165   D. 180

29. Which angle is 180 degrees?

        A   B   C   D

30. This angle is _____ degrees.

      A. 90   B. 120   C. 165   D. 180

Applied Math

"This test consists of word math problems with four possible answers for each problem. All of the questions involve calculating time, distance, or speed based on information given in the problem. All problems involve the movement of aircraft. Knowledge of knots or nautical mile terminology is not required to determine the answer. Scoring of the test is based on the number of problems answered correctly." (FAA pamphlet, p. 7)

Use the following formula (Figure 3-11) to calculate the time for the applied math part of the exam: Where T is time in minutes (60 minutes is one hour), speed is in knots or miles per hour; most questions will need this translated into miles per minute. (360 KPH or MPH / 60 minutes = 6 miles per minute.)

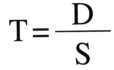

$$T = \frac{D}{S}$$

Figure 3-11. Calculating time

The Applied Math test contains 30 multiple-choice questions. The first five items are practice questions followed by 25 scored questions. An example of an Applied Math question is: "A plane has flown for three hours with a ground speed of 210 knots. How far did the plane travel?" Each of these questions requires the subject to make calculations based on time, speed, and distance to identify the correct answer from among four choices. (This information is from Heil and Agnew, 2000, p. 3.)

An aircraft has flown 375 miles in 90 minutes. What is the aircraft's ground speed?

A. 150 kts
B. 200 kts
C. 250 kts
D. 300 kts

Answer is C. 250 knots (375=D/1.5). 1.5 is 90 minutes in hourly format.

Figure 3-12. Math problem example (Source: FAA Pamphlet)

These basic math problems deal with time, speed, and distance (D = S x T). Practicing with standard math word problems might help you prepare for this test. No calculator or scratch paper is provided, and you must figure everything out in your head, similar to what a controller has to do on the job. Examples:

---

1. A jet at 2,000 feet is climbing at 500 feet per minute after 12 minute; what is the altitude?

     A. 10,000   B. 5,000   C. 8,000   D. 6,000

Answer: C (D = 500 x 12)

2. How far will a plane travel in 75 minutes if its speed is 300 KPH?

     A. 250   B. 375   C. 300   D. 150

Answer: B (D = S x 1.25) 1.25 is 75 minutes in hour format.

Figure 3-13. More math problem examples

Applied Math Sample Test

All distances are in miles; the speed is given or calculated in miles per hour (MPH).

1. How many miles has the aircraft traveled if it flies at 450 MPH for 2½ hours?

   A. 1050
   B. 1075
   C. 1100
   D. 1125

2. If a plane was traveling 200 MPH with a 15 MPH tailwind, how many miles would the plane fly in 1 hour and 45 minutes?

   A. 315
   B. 376
   C. 350
   D. 370

3. How many miles will an aircraft cover if it flies for 4 hours at 220 MPH?

   A. 820
   B. 880
   C. 900
   D. 980

4. The distance from Minneapolis to Milwaukee is 350 miles. What speed will N2540G have to maintain in order to fly this route under three hours?

   A. 100
   B. 110
   C. 117
   D. 105

5. An aircraft takes 9 hours to fly 1800 miles; what is the average speed in MPH?

   A. 250
   B. 150
   C. 180
   D. 200

6. An aircraft (150 MPH) flew over ABC airport at 1000Z and touched down at XYZ airport at 1230Z. How many miles apart are the two airports?

    A. 375
    B. 500
    C. 300
    D. 200

7. What time will N4105C (180 MPH) arrive at ABC airport if they departed XYZ airport (360 miles apart) at 0615Z?

    A. 0800Z
    B. 0915Z
    C. 0815Z
    D. 2015

8. How many miles did N74810 fly if it flew for 3½ hours at a speed of 155 MPH?

    A. 425
    B. 543
    C. 625
    D. 245

9. An aircraft flies from ABC to CDE to EFG and back to ABC airports every day. The distance between ABC and CDE is 90 miles; CDE to EFG 120 miles and ABC and EFG is 90. What is the average speed of the aircraft if the total flight time takes 2 hours?

    A. 200
    B. 180
    C. 150
    D. 250

10. N74JPC (180 MPH) is 20 minutes from flying over ABC airport. How many miles is the aircraft from this airport?

    A. 60
    B. 90
    C. 20
    D. 45

11. About how long would it take an aircraft (180 MPH) to make a round trip of 345 miles?

    A. 1 hour, 30 minutes
    B. 1 hour, 50 minutes
    C. 2 hours, 30 minutes
    D. 2 hours, 10 minutes

12. The distance between Akron, OH and Pittsburgh is 120 miles. If an aircraft can make the trip in 1 hour, 30 minutes what is the average speed in MPH?

    A. 120
    B. 180
    C. 60
    D. 80

13. If a plane was descending at 500 feet per second from an altitude of 18,000 feet traveling at 165 MPH, how many miles would the plane have traveled as it descended to 14,500 feet?

    A. 25
    B. 19
    C. 12
    D. 30

14. What altitude will N74985 be at after 3½ minutes if they are passing 10,000 feet and climbing at 500 feet per minute?

    A. 12500
    B. 11500
    C. 11750
    D. 12000

15. N34285 just left 8,000 feet descending and will reach 6,000 feet in 4 minutes; what is the descent rate per minute?

    A. 750
    B. 250
    C. 500
    D. 150

16. If N44285 (120 MPH) left ABC airport at the same time as N72085 (180 MPH) going in opposite directions, how many miles apart would they be in 9 minutes?

    A. 45
    B. 27
    C. 18
    D. 30

17. After passing each other how many miles apart will N74JPC (150 MPH) and N9502A (90 MPH) be in 3 minutes?

    A. 20
    B. 15
    C. 24
    D. 12

18. How many miles has N74GJM flown after 18 minutes at a speed of 360 MPH?

    A. 208
    B. 108
    C. 125
    D. 648

19. The distance from Omaha to Des Moines is 135 miles. What is N700SC's speed if it takes 75 minutes to fly this route?

    A. 108
    B. 170
    C. 135
    D. 216

20. How many miles has the aircraft traveled if it flies at 250 MPH for 2 hours 45 minutes?

    A. 500
    B. 857.5
    C. 1100
    D. 687.5

21. N74985 (240 MPH) is climbing at 1,500 feet per minute and has just left ABC airport. How far from the airport and at what altitude will the aircraft be at after 5 minutes of flight?

    A. 10 miles, 5500 feet
    B. 40 miles, 7500 feet
    C. 20 miles, 7500 feet
    D. 75 miles, 500 feet

22. How many miles apart are New York City and Cleveland if N74985 (280 MPH) takes 1 hour, 30 minutes to fly between these cities?

    A. 500
    B. 420
    C. 280
    D. 685

23. What is N700SC's speed (in MPH) if it can fly 75 miles every 15 minutes?

    A. 450
    B. 150
    C. 275
    D. 300

24. How many minutes will it take N74GJM (360 MPH) to fly from Des Moines to Omaha (135 miles).

    A. 23
    B. 36
    C. 15
    D. 30

25. Phoenix to Tucson roundtrip is 200 miles. How many minutes will it take N74985 to fly from Tucson to Phoenix at a speed of 240 MPH?

    A. 15
    B. 35
    C. 50
    D. 30

26. How many miles will an aircraft cover if it flies for 1 hour, 15 minutes at 180 MPH?

    A. 175
    B. 225
    C. 180
    D. 360

27. After passing each other how many miles apart will N74985 (180 MPH) and N1502E (180 MPH) be in 5 minutes?

    A. 16
    B. 12
    C. 24
    D. 30

28. If a plane was taking off and climbing at 380 feet per minute at 205 MPH, what is the altitude of the plane after it traveled 115 miles?

    A. 12,750
    B. 10,500
    C. 18,000
    D. 15,000

29. N749PA (150 MPH) is climbing at 600 feet per minute and has just left CDE airport. What altitude and how far from the airport will the aircraft be after 10 minutes of flight?

    A. 5500 feet, 20 miles
    B. 7500 feet, 40 miles
    C. 6000 feet, 25 miles
    D. 60000 feet, 25 miles

30. How many miles did N48101 (270 MPH) fly if it if it took 1hour, 30 minutes to get to the destination airport?

    A. 270
    B. 405
    C. 135
    D. 540

Dial Reading

"Air traffic controllers must be able to perceive visual information quickly and accurately and perform simple processing tasks like comparisons. The Dial Reading test assesses ability to read dials quickly and accurately." (FAA pamphlet, p. 5).

The Dial Reading test measures the subject's ability to quickly identify and accurately read certain dials on an instrument panel. Subjects are asked to choose from one of five answers for each question about a given display. The test consists of 20 questions. Individuals pace themselves against the display of time remaining in the subtest. They are advised to skip difficult items and return to them at the end of the test. Each panel consists of seven dials in two rows. Each of the seven dials contains unique flight information (e.g., air speed, fuel, temperature). (This information is from Heil and Agnew, 2000, p. 4.)

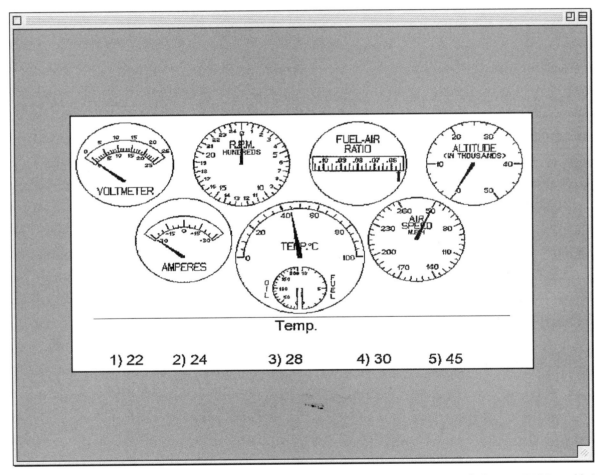

Figure 3-14. Dials test screen example (Source: FAA Pamphlet)

This test requires the applicant to answer multiple-choice questions based on information presented in multiple airplane instruments (explanation on how to read each instrument is given). Examples of the questions:

What is the altimeter reading?
 A. 10,500 ft.   B. 13,000 ft.   C. 10,000 ft.   D. 1,050 ft.

Answer: D

What is the voltmeter reading?
 A. 8 Volts   B. -8 Volts   C. 10.5 Volts   D. 9 Volts

Answer: B

Figure 3-15. Dials test questions example

Dials Sample Test

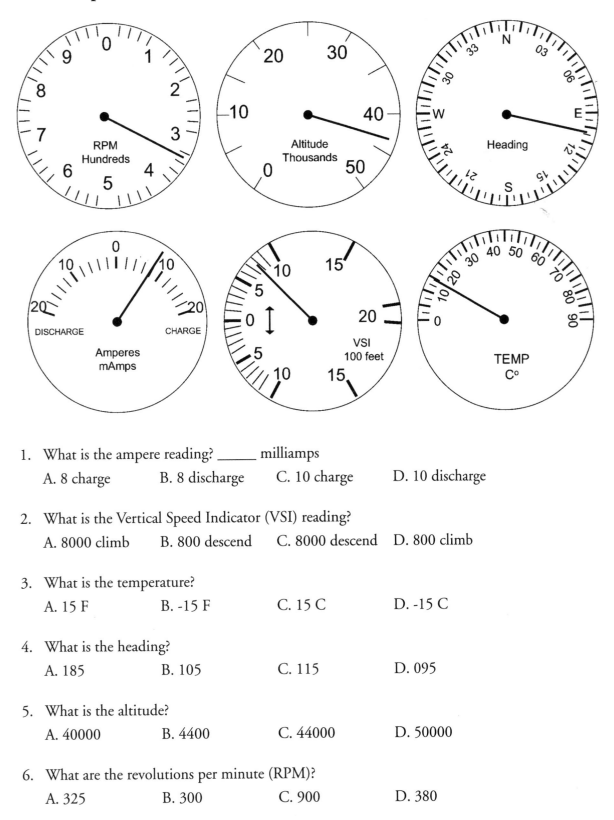

1. What is the ampere reading? _____ milliamps

   A. 8 charge   B. 8 discharge   C. 10 charge   D. 10 discharge

2. What is the Vertical Speed Indicator (VSI) reading?

   A. 8000 climb   B. 800 descend   C. 8000 descend   D. 800 climb

3. What is the temperature?

   A. 15 F   B. -15 F   C. 15 C   D. -15 C

4. What is the heading?

   A. 185   B. 105   C. 115   D. 095

5. What is the altitude?

   A. 40000   B. 4400   C. 44000   D. 50000

6. What are the revolutions per minute (RPM)?

   A. 325   B. 300   C. 900   D. 380

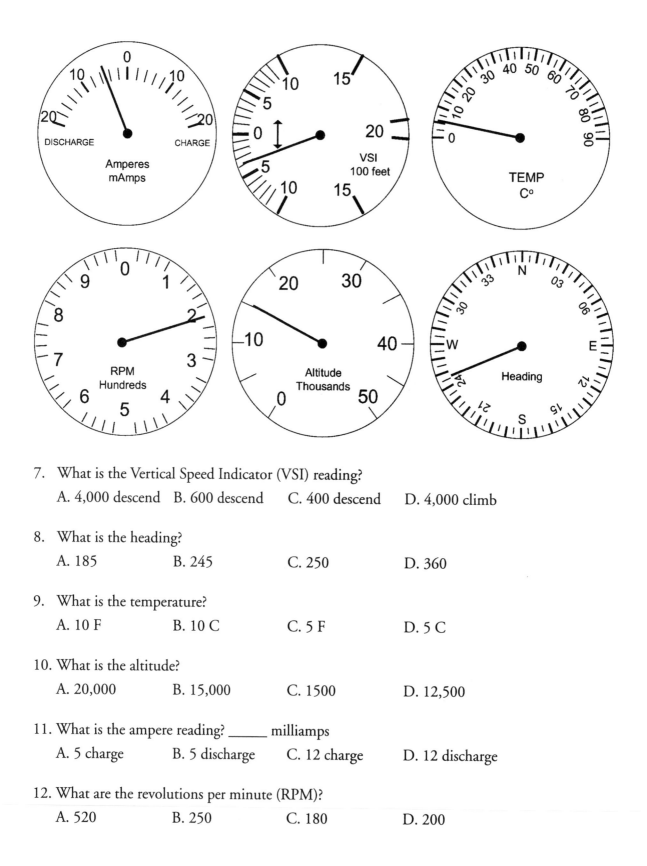

7. What is the Vertical Speed Indicator (VSI) reading?

    A. 4,000 descend   B. 600 descend   C. 400 descend   D. 4,000 climb

8. What is the heading?

    A. 185   B. 245   C. 250   D. 360

9. What is the temperature?

    A. 10 F   B. 10 C   C. 5 F   D. 5 C

10. What is the altitude?

    A. 20,000   B. 15,000   C. 1500   D. 12,500

11. What is the ampere reading? _____ milliamps

    A. 5 charge   B. 5 discharge   C. 12 charge   D. 12 discharge

12. What are the revolutions per minute (RPM)?

    A. 520   B. 250   C. 180   D. 200

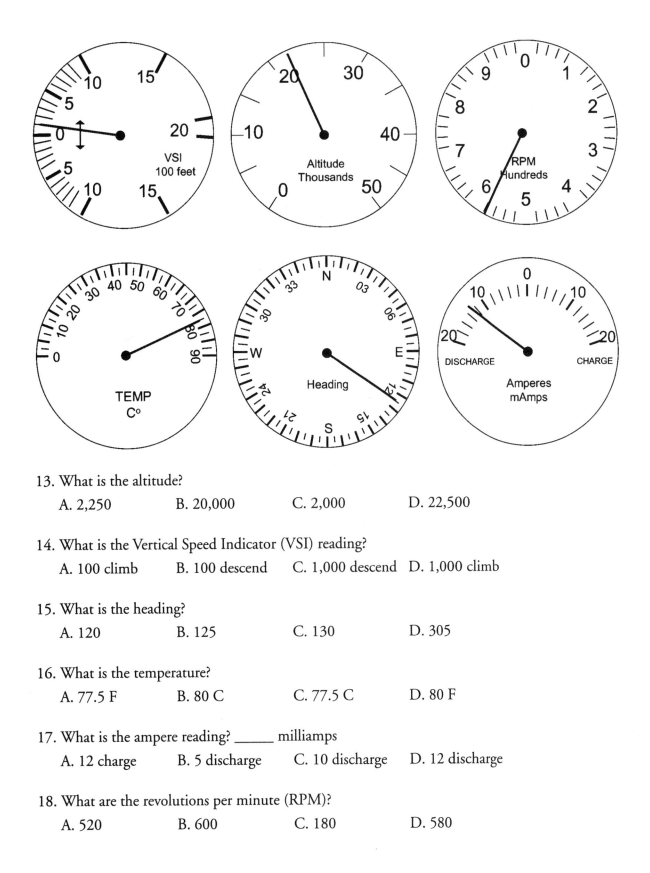

13. What is the altitude?

    A. 2,250   B. 20,000   C. 2,000   D. 22,500

14. What is the Vertical Speed Indicator (VSI) reading?

    A. 100 climb   B. 100 descend   C. 1,000 descend D. 1,000 climb

15. What is the heading?

    A. 120   B. 125   C. 130   D. 305

16. What is the temperature?

    A. 77.5 F   B. 80 C   C. 77.5 C   D. 80 F

17. What is the ampere reading? _____ milliamps

    A. 12 charge   B. 5 discharge   C. 10 discharge   D. 12 discharge

18. What are the revolutions per minute (RPM)?

    A. 520   B. 600   C. 180   D. 580

19. What is the heading?
    A. 170   B. 165   C. 160   D. 345

20. What is the temperature?
    A. 65 C   B. 75 C   C. 65 F   D. 75 F

21. What are the revolutions per minute (RPM)?
    A. 700   B. 670   C. 660   D. 6600

22. What is the altitude?
    A. 30,000   B. 35,000   C. 3,500   D. 40,000

23. What is the Vertical Speed Indicator (VSI) reading?
    A. 500 descend   B. 5,000 descend   C. 5,000 climb   D. 500 climb

24. What is the ampere reading? _____ milliamps
    A. 10 charge   B. 7 discharge   C. 7 charge   D. 10 discharge

Experience Questionnaire

"Air traffic controllers must possess certain work-related attributes to perform their job well. This test determines whether candidates have these attributes by asking about past experience. There are no correct or incorrect answers. People respond differently based on what is true for themselves." (FAA pamphlet, p. 8)

This questionnaire does not count towards your test score. It is similar to the psychological PF-16 exam, and responses are kept confidential. On the following example pages, there are phrases describing people's behaviors. The test will have one of the rating scales below for you to describe how accurately each statement describes you. Describe yourself as you generally are now, not as you wish to be in the future. Describe yourself as you honestly see yourself in relation to other people of the same sex and similar age. Read each statement carefully and then answer with the response that corresponds to the number on the scale. Scale values could be something similar to the list below. There are no correct answers—respond to each statement as if you are saying. "I [statement]."

A. Definitely True
B. Somewhat True
C. Neither True nor False

D. Somewhat False
E. Definitely False

Experience Questionnaire Sample

1. Am a very private person.
2. Am hard to get to know.
3. Am not interested in other people's problems.
4. Am skilled in handling social situations.
5. Can handle a lot of information.
6. Do things according to a plan.
7. Enjoy being reckless.
8. Feel others' emotions.
9. Get caught up in my problems.
10. Get upset easily.
11. Have a strong need for power.
12. Have persuaded others to do something really adventurous or crazy.
13. Leave a mess in my room.
14. Love order and regularity.
15. Make plans and stick to them.
16. Pay attention to details.
17. Rarely get irritated.
18. Start conversations.
19. Talk to a lot of different people at parties.
20. Waste my time.
21. Am always prepared.
22. Am indifferent to the feelings of others.

23. Am on good terms with nearly everyone.
24. Am the life of the party.
25. Carry the conversation to a higher level.
26. Don't get excited about things.
27. Feel at ease with people.
28. Feel threatened easily.
29. Get caught up in the excitement when others are celebrating.
30. Grumble about things.
31. Have a vivid imagination.
32. Inquire about others' well-being.
33. Leave my belongings around.
34. Love to help others.
35. Neglect my duties.
36. Prefer friends who are excitingly unpredictable.
37. Rarely worry.
38. Sympathize with others' feelings.
39. Think of others first.
40. Will not probe deeply into a subject.
41. Am exacting in my work.
42. Am interested in people.
43. Am quick to understand things.
44. Avoid dangerous situations.
45. Catch on to things quickly.
46. Don't like to draw attention to myself.
47. Feel comfortable around people.
48. Find it difficult to approach others.
49. Get chores done right away.
50. Have a good word for everyone.
51. Have difficulty imagining things.
52. Know how to captivate people.
53. Like order.
54. Love to think up new ways of doing things.
55. Often feel uncomfortable around others.
56. Push myself very hard to succeed.
57. Shirk my duties.
58. Take charge.
59. Try to surpass others' accomplishments.
60. Worry about things.
61. Am full of ideas.
62. Am not highly motivated to succeed.

63. Am quiet around strangers.
64. Become overwhelmed by events.
65. Continue until everything is perfect.
66. Don't mind being the center of attention.
67. Feel excited or happy for no apparent reason.
68. Follow a schedule.
69. Get irritated easily.
70. Have a rich vocabulary.
71. Have excellent ideas.
72. Know how to comfort others.
73. Like to act spontaneously.
74. Make friends easily.
75. Often forget to put things back in their proper place.
76. Rarely enjoy behaving in a silly manner.
77. Show my gratitude.
78. Take offense easily.
79. Wait for others to lead the way.
80. Worry about what people think of me.
81. Am good at many things.
82. Am not interested in abstract ideas.
83. Am relaxed most of the time.
84. Begin to panic when there is danger.
85. Do not have a good imagination.
86. Don't talk a lot.
87. Feel little concern for others.
88. Get angry easily.
89. Get so happy or energetic that I am almost giddy.
90. Have a soft heart.
91. Have little to say.
92. Know how to get around the rules.
93. Like to tidy up.
94. Make people feel at ease.
95. Often worry about things that turn out to be unimportant.
96. Rarely get caught up in the excitement.
97. Spend time reflecting on things.
98. Take time out for others.
99. Want to be in charge.
100. Would never go hang gliding or bungee jumping.

From "International personal Item Pool: (http://ipip.ori.org), 2001.

Chapter Four
ATC Knowledge Questions

These questions are not on the AT-SAT test, but you should start acquiring this knowledge if you plan to pursue an ATC career. This knowledge comes from study of the FAA's *Air Traffic Control Handbook*, or "Order FAAH 7110.65," and the *Aeronautical Information Manual* (AIM)'s sections on air traffic control and procedures. Answers with explanations and references for these questions begin on page 120.

1. Course alignment accuracy of the VOR is plus/minus _____ degrees.

    A. 1
    B. 3
    C. 2
    D. 4

2. It is the responsibility of the _____ to determine the final (within 2 miles of the airport) landing sequence between aircraft under its control.

    A. approach controller
    B. center controller
    C. flight service station
    D. control tower

3. When the wind is less than 5 knots, which of the following runways should be used?

    A. Pilot's choice
    B. Any runway
    C. Controller's choice
    D. Calm wind

4. The _____ controller manages aircraft operations on the airport movement area except the active runway(s).

   A. ground
   B. local
   C. radar
   D. non-radar

5. Airport Traffic Control Towers (ATCT) provide for both preventive and positive control of VFR and IFR aircraft around airports where they are located.

   A. True
   B. False

6. What is the minimum vertical separation (in feet) required between IFR aircraft below FL 290?

   A. 1,000
   B. 2,000
   C. 3,000
   D. 4,000

7. A controller provides _____ separation until some other type of separation can be established for IFR aircraft on the same route in the same direction.

   A. visual
   B. lateral
   C. vertical
   D. longitudinal

8. In radio communications, the phrase *"have numbers"* is not the same as the pilot having the information contained in the current ATIS broadcast.

   A. True
   B. False

9. Glidepath information for the ILS is useable when flying

   A. outbound-back course.
   B. inbound-front course.
   C. inbound-back course.
   D. outbound-front course.

10. In handling a normal IFR aircraft on a flight from Chicago to Las Vegas, the facilities involved could include _____.

    A. center
    B. tower
    C. approach control
    D. all of the above

11. Letters of Agreement (LOA) are used between centers and towers to ensure correct procedures or delegate airspace control.

    A. True
    B. False

12. What is the first duty priority of controllers?

    A. providing advisories within 10 miles of the airport
    B. issuing weather advisories
    C. vectoring aircraft to the airport
    D. none of the above are correct

13. Tower Local Control provides both positive and preventive control instructions.

    A. True
    B. False

14. Spaces 10-18 on the approach/departure control flight progress strip are used for

    A. altitude data.
    B. route information.
    C. facility specific data.
    D. aircraft identification data.

15. A degree divergence chart is primarily used to apply _____ non-radar separation.

    A. vertical
    B. lateral
    C. longitudinal
    D. visual

16. Which aircraft equipment suffix (transponder) indicates the aircraft is equipped with DME and altitude data capabilities displayed on ATC radar scopes?

    A. X

    B. C

    C. A

    D. T

17. Flight progress strips are pieces of paper used to record aircraft movement.

    A. True

    B. False

18. Corrections for altitude data on a flight progress strip are made by using a single line to delete the wrong information.

    A. True

    B. False

19. _____ is usually the lowest altitude that can be assigned by ATC on a Victor airway.

    A. MXA

    B. MSA

    C. MVA

    D. MEA

20. The transfer of _____ point is _____.

    A. communications; after the aircraft crosses the receiving controller's airspace.

    B. control; after the aircraft crosses the receiving controller's airspace.

    C. communications; before the aircraft crosses the receiving controller's airspace.

    D. control; before the aircraft crosses the receiving controller's airspace.

21. When using vertical separation, the lead aircraft must always be same speed or faster.

    A. True

    B. False

22. When using lateral separation, the lead aircraft must always be same speed or faster.

    A. True

    B. False

23. When using longitudinal separation, the lead aircraft must always be same speed or faster.

    A. True

    B. False

24. Holding pattern airspace to be protected is a form of lateral separation.

    A. True

    B. False

25. Radar separation is ___ miles when both aircraft are less than 40 miles from the antenna.

    A. 3

    B. 5

    C. 10

    D. none of the above

26. Two or more aircraft estimated to occupy the same airspace in less than ten minutes are considered to be

    A. separated.

    B. in conflict.

    C. separated if they are talking to different ATC facilities.

    D. no problem, if one of the aircraft are in the clouds (the no-see'em factor).

27. Two of more air traffic control facilities can control an aircraft at the same time.

    A. True

    B. False

28. _____ are used between two facilities (external coordination) and _____ are used for facilities (external coordination).

    A. Letters of Agreement; Ops letters

    B. Ops letters; Letters of Agreement

    C. AIM; Ops letters

    D. Letters of Agreement; 7110.65

29. When using _____ separation minima the transfer of communication shall be made ____ minutes before the aircraft is estimated to reach the boundary unless otherwise agreed to by the control and/or communication facilities concerned.

    A. nonradar; 3

    B. nonradar; 5

    C. radar; 3

    D. radar; 5

30. Air traffic control is defined as the orderly, safe and careful flow of airplanes through designated airspace.

    A. True

    B. False

31. Letters of Agreement (LOA) are used between centers and pilots to ensure correct phraseology.

    A. True

    B. False

32. The transfer of control point is _____ the aircraft crosses the receiving controller's airspace.

    A. any time after

    B. five minutes after

    C. five minutes before

    D. when

33. ATC is described as being "situational" with weather conditions being the primary factor in delays.

    A. True

    B. False

34. A Certified Professional Controller (CPC) has all the appropriate ratings for his or her area of assignment.

    A. True

    B. False

35. The first three items in an ATC departure clearance are aircraft identification,

    A. clearance limit, and route of flight.

    B. clearance limit, and altitude.

    C. altitude, and route of flight.

    D. clearance limit, and holding instructions.

36. The pilot-in-command of an aircraft shall comply with all provisions of an ATC clearance unless an amended clearance has been obtained or

    A. conducting formation flight operations.

    B. participating in a speed run.

    C. operating aircraft in IFR conditions.

    D. in an emergency situation.

37. The purpose of an ATC clearance is to

   A. relieve controller stress.
   B. provide classified instructions to pilots.
   C. prevent collision between known aircraft.
   D. provide for emergency situations.

38. VFR aircraft operating in uncontrolled airspace

   A. should set their transponder to 1200.
   B. must always use air traffic control services.
   C. can contact ATC by radio.
   D. are prohibited from contacting ATC.
   E. A and C are correct.

39. Flight progress strips are unofficial government documents used to record aircraft movements.

   A. True
   B. False

40. Which is NOT a part of the clearance items spoken by a controller?

   A. aircraft ID
   B. departure speed
   C. clearance limit
   D. route of flight

41. ATIS is the continuous broadcast of recorded

   A. information alerting pilots of radar-identified aircraft when their aircraft is in dangerous proximity to terrain or an obstruction.
   B. nonessential information to reduce radio congestion.
   C. non-control information in selected high activity terminal areas.
   D. sky conditions report limited to ceilings below 1,000 feet and visibility less than 3 miles.

42. A conflict is defined as two or more aircraft

   A. (IFR) estimating the same fix at the same altitude within 10 minutes of each other.
   B. (IFR) holding at the same fix at the same altitude at the same time.
   C. IFR and VFR departures within one minute of each other.
   D. all of the above are correct.
   E. A and B are correct.

43. A departure leaves the airport climbing through an arrival, which is over a point 45 miles northwest; both are converging toward the same VORTAC (ETA within 10 minutes).

    A. Separation is required as the protected airspace for each does NOT overlap.

    B. The controller must provide some type of separation.

    C. The transferring controller must make sure there are at least 1,000 feet between the two aircraft.

    D. No separation is required as there is no conflict.

44. Two aircraft are arriving at the same airport and one is estimating to be over IAF for the ILS twenty (20) minutes before the second aircraft.

    A. Separation is required as the protected airspace for each does NOT overlap.

    B. The controller must provide some type of separation.

    C. The transferring controller must make sure there are at least 1,000 feet between the two aircraft.

    D. No separation is required as there is no conflict.

45. An aircraft, arriving at the airport, has reported leaving 8,000 for 4,000 and another aircraft is overflying the airport VORTAC at 6,000 (both estimating a common fix at 9 minutes apart).

    A. Separation is required as the protected airspace for each does NOT overlap.

    B. The controller must provide some type of separation.

    C. The transferring controller must make sure there are at least 1,000 feet between the two aircraft.

    D. No separation is required as there is no conflict.

46. Two aircraft are in the approach controller's airspace and are arriving at the same airport, assigned to hold over the IAF fix for the ILS at least 1,000 feet apart.

    A. Separation is required as the protected airspace for each does NOT overlap.

    B. The controller must provide some type of separation.

    C. The transferring controller must make sure there are at least 1,000 feet between the two aircraft.

    D. No separation is required as there is no conflict.

47. Two aircraft are requesting to depart the same airport at the same time and are assigned courses which will take one northeast and the other to the west (courses diverge by 135 degrees).

    A. Separation is required as the protected airspace for each does NOT overlap.

    B. The controller must provide some type of separation.

    C. The transferring controller must make sure there are at least 1,000 feet between the two aircraft.

    D. No separation is required as there is no conflict.

48. VORs are identified by _____ letters in Morse Code.

    A. 1
    B. 2
    C. 3
    D. 4

49. The navigational aid designed specifically for military needs is

    A. VORTAC.
    B. VOT.
    C. TACAN.
    D. VOR.

50. What is the correct phraseology for issuing the runway?

    A. Runway Thirty
    B. Runway One Zero
    C. Nine is the Runway
    D. Runway Forty

51. The President of the United States uses what call sign when flying aboard a civil aircraft?

    A. Air Force One
    B. Marine One
    C. Executive One
    D. President One

52. Pilots can be cleared for the contact approach

    A. only between sunset and sunrise.
    B when issued by the controller.
    C. anytime a controller feels they will have an operationally advantage.
    D. if pilot requests and ground visibility is at least 1 SM.

53. What are the emergency radio frequencies for aviation use?

    A. 122.5 and 243.0
    B. 121.5 and 240.1
    C. 121.5 and 243.0
    D. 122.0 and 235.0

54. Which of the following can be found on a Sectional Chart?

    A. Airports
    B. Airspace
    C. NAVAIDs
    D. All of the above

55. What does the abbreviation ATIS mean?

    A. Aviation Training in Service
    B. Automatic Traffic Information Service
    C. Automatic Terminal Information Service
    D. Applied Traffic Intrail Separation

56. _____ need not be given when radar identification is made by position correlation.

    A. Location
    B. Turns
    C. Time check
    D. Position information

57. The number 9 is spoken

    A. nine.
    B. niner.
    C. neine.
    D. none of the above.

58. Aircraft may discontinue reporting over compulsory reporting points

    A. after the first fix.
    B. never.
    C. any time they feel like it.
    D. after radar contact by ATC.

59. The first duty priority of an air traffic controller is

    A. providing radar advisories.
    B. separation of IFR traffic.
    C. coordinating search and rescue.
    D. relaying traffic advisories to VFR aircraft.

60. The emergency transponder code is
    A. 7700.
    B. 7100.
    C. 7600.
    D. 1200.

61. Clear aircraft to hold over different fixes at the same altitude whose holding pattern airspace areas
    A. do not touch.
    B. are at least 7 miles apart.
    C. do not overlap.
    D. are at least 10 miles apart.

62. Standard Instrument Departure (SID) procedure is
    A. used to simplify clearance delivery.
    B. used to assist IFR pilots to avoid obstacles during departure.
    C. an ATC coded departure procedure.
    D. all of the above are correct.

63. How does a controller make corrections on a flight progress strip?
    A. Draw a single line through the error (except altitude data; "X" that out).
    B. Erase the mistake completely.
    C. Scratch out the error.
    D. Inform his/her supervisor.

64. A Category III aircraft landing behind a Category I aircraft requires _____ feet of runway separation.
    A. 1,500
    B. 6,000
    C. 4,500
    D. 3,000

65. A red "E" marked on a flight progress strip is used to show
    A. an aircraft in excellent condition.
    B. clearance has been issued to land.
    C. the type of fuel on board a VFR aircraft.
    D. an aircraft in an emergency condition.

66. The correct phraseology to determine the altitude of an aircraft is "_____ altitude."

    A. Report
    B. Say
    C. Verify
    D. What is your

67. The standard longitudinal separation minima required between two IFR aircraft is _____ DME or _____ minutes.

    A. 10, 20
    B. 20, 10
    C. 5, 10
    D. 15, 5

68. If the runway is not reported in sight by a pilot making a radar approach prior to a prescribed point, tell the pilot to

    A. execute a missed approach.
    B. continue approach to mid-runway area.
    C. contact the weather station.
    D. contact the tower immediately.

69. How can a military airport be identified at night?

    A. Alternate white and green beacon light flashes.
    B. Dual peaked (two quick) white flashes between green flashes.
    C. White flashing beacon lights with steady green at the same site.
    D. Alternate white and red beacon light flashes.

70. Airport taxiway edge lights are identified at night by

    A. white directional lights.
    B. blue omnidirectional lights.
    C. white and red lights.
    D. a green, yellow, and white rotating beacon.

71. An airport's rotating beacon operated during the daylight hours shows

    A. there are obstructions on the airport.
    B. the airport is temporarily closed.
    C. the Airport Traffic Area is not in operation.
    D. that weather at the airport is below basic VFR weather.

72. Prior to entering Class D airspace, a pilot

    A. must contact the tower for clearance to enter.

    B. should monitor ATIS for weather and traffic advisories.

    C. should contact approach control for vectors to the traffic pattern.

    D. should contact the AFSS for airport and traffic advisories.

73. Basic radar service in the terminal area is described as

    A. traffic advisories and limited vectoring to VFR aircraft.

    B. mandatory radar service provided by the ARTS program.

    C. windshear warning at participating airports.

    D. sequencing an d separation service to IFR aircraft only.

74. An ATC radar facility issues the following advisory to a pilot flying on a heading of 090: "TRAFFIC 3 O'CLOCK, 2 MILES, SOUTHBOUND..." Where should the pilot look for this traffic?

    A. East

    B. South

    C. West

    D. North

75. An ATC radar facility issues the following advisory to a pilot flying on a heading of 360: "TRAFFIC 10 O'CLOCK, 2 MILES, SOUTHBOUND..." Where should the pilot look for this traffic?

    A. Northwest

    B. Northeast

    C. Southwest

    D. Southeast

76. An ATC radar facility issues the following advisory to a pilot during a local flight: "TRAFFIC 2 O'CLOCK, 5 MILES, NORTHBOUND..." Where should the pilot look for this traffic?

    A. Directly ahead.

    B. Between directly ahead and 90 to the left.

    C. Between directly behind and 90 to the right.

    D. Between directly ahead and 90 to the right.

77. An ATC radar facility issues the following advisory to a pilot flying north in a calm wind: "TRAFFIC 9 O'CLOCK, 2 MILES, SOUTHBOUND..." Where should the pilot look for this traffic?

    A. East

    B. South

    C. West

    D. North

78. After landing at a tower controlled airport, where should the pilot contact ground control?

    A. Prior to turning off the runway.

    B. After reaching a taxiway that leads directly to the parking area.

    C. After leaving the runway and crossing the runway holding lines.

    D. When advised by the tower to change frequencies.

79. NonRadar separation includes

    A. vertical.

    B. lateral.

    C. longitudinal.

    D. all of the above.

80. The ATC facility that provides air traffic control services to aircraft on IFR flight plans during the enroute phase of flight is

    A. ATCT.

    B. ARTCC.

    C. TRACON.

    D. AFSS.

81. If instructed by ground control "Taxi to Runway 9," a pilot may proceed

    A. via taxiways and across runways to, but not onto, Runway 9.

    B. to the next intersecting runway where clearance is required.

    C. via taxiways and across runways to Runway 9, and make an immediate takeoff.

    D. via any route at the pilot's discretion onto Runway 9 and hold until cleared for takeoff.

82. The definition of nighttime is

    A. sunset to sunrise.

    B. 30 minutes after sunset to 30 minutes before sunrise.

    C. 1 hour after sunset to 1 hour before sunrise.

    D. from the end of evening twilight to the beginning of morning twilight.

83. Unless otherwise authorized or required by Air Traffic Control, what is the maximum indicated airspeed (knots) at which a pilot may operate an aircraft below 10,000 ft. MSL?

A. 156

B. 180

C. 200

D. 250

84. When may Air Traffic Control request a detailed report of an emergency even though a rule has not been violated?

A. After priority has been given.

B. Anytime an emergency is declared.

C. When the emergency occurs in controlled airspace.

D. None of the above.

85. An Air Traffic Control clearance provides

A. authorization for flight in uncontrolled airspace.

B. priority over all other traffic.

C. separation from all traffic.

D. authority to go under specified conditions in controlled airspace.

86. A steady green ATC light signal directed to an aircraft in flight is a signal that the pilot

A. is cleared to land.

B. should give way to other aircraft and continue circling.

C. should return for landing.

D. should exercise extreme caution.

87. A flashing white light signal from the control tower to an aircraft taxiing is an indication

A. to taxi at a faster speed.

B. to taxi only on taxiways and not cross runways.

C. to return to the starting point on the airport.

D. that instrument conditions exist.

88. If the control tower uses a light signal to direct a pilot in flight to give way to other aircraft and continue circling, the light will be

A. flashing red.

B. steady red.

C. alternating red and green.

D. flashing green

89. Which light signal from a control tower clears a pilot to taxi?

   A. Flashing green
   B. Flashing white
   C. Steady green
   D. Steady red

90. Unless otherwise authorized, two-way radio communications with ATC are required for landing and takeoffs

   A. within control zones regardless of the weather conditions.
   B. at all tower controlled airports regardless of the weather.
   C. at all tower controlled airports only when weather conditions are less than VFR.
   D. at tower controlled airports within control zones only when weather conditions are less than VFR.

91. Ceiling, as used in weather reports, is the height above the Earth's surface of the

   A. lowest reported obscuration and the highest layer of clouds reported as overcast.
   B. lowest layer of clouds reported as broken or overcast and not classified as thin.
   C. lowest layer of clouds reported as scattered, broken, or thin.
   D. highest layer of clouds reported as broken or thin.

92. What leg(s) of a standard traffic pattern is (are) flown perpendicular to the downwind leg?

   A. Base, crosswind
   B. Base, final
   C. Crosswind, final
   D. Final only

93. A VOR federal airway is considered

   A. controlled airspace.
   B. a control zone.
   C. a positive control area
   D. a transition area.

94. What is the correct way to state radio frequency of 122.95?

   A. One two two niner five
   B. One two two point niner five
   C. One hundred two two point niner five
   D. Twenty-two niner five

95. What is the correct way to identify Piper N431AQ on initial radio contact?

    A. Piper Alpha Quebec
    B. Piper four three one A Q
    C. Piper four three one Alpha Quebec
    D. Piper four thirty one A Q

96. Which of the following terms means that a transmission has been received and understood?

    A. Affirmative
    B. Over
    C. Roger
    D. Verify

97. The primary training facility for new FAA ATC candidates is in

    A. Atlantic City, NJ.
    B. Washington, DC.
    C. Oklahoma City, OK.
    D. Minneapolis, MN.

98. The National Airspace System includes

    A. ATC.
    B. airmen and aircraft.
    C. airports.
    D. all of the above.

99. The FAA has operated under the DOT since 1967 and has a dual role in aviation—the promotion and regulation of air transportation.

    A. True
    B. False

100. The first enroute ARTCC was established by the airlines about 1940.

    A. True
    B. False

Appendices

Appendix 1: Answers to Practice Exams

All answers are listed so you can check your work on each sample test.

Angles	Math	Dials
1. A	1. D	1. A
2. C	2. B	2. D
3. B	3. B	3. C
4. D	4. C	4. B
5. D	5. D	5. C
6. C	6. A	6. A
7. B	7. C	7. C
8. D	8. B	8. B
9. A	9. C	9. D
10. A	10. A	10. B
11. D	11. B	11. B
12. C	12. D	12. D
13. B	13. B	13. D
14. A	14. C	14. A
15. D	15. C	15. B
16. C	16. A	16. C
17. A	17. D	17. D
18. B	18. B	18. D
19. D	19. A	19. B
20. B	20. D	20. A
21. C	21. C	21. C
22. A	22. B	22. B
23. B	23. D	23. D
24. B	24. A	24. B
25. C	25. C	
26. C	26. B	
27. A	27. D	
28. C	28. A	
29. C	29. C	
30. B	30. B	

Answers and Explanations — Chapter 4 ATC Knowledge Test

Below are the answers (correct letter choice) for the test given in Chapter 4 on air traffic control knowledge, along with a reference and explanation for the correct answer. The references give the source from which the answers and explanations were derived, so you can go back to those sources for further reading. The principle source is the FAA Order (FAAO) 7110.65 *Air Traffic Control Handbook,* along with the *Aeronautical Information Manual* (AIM) and other FAA handbooks.

1. A. 1
   The Aeronautical Information Manual (AIM), in paragraph 1-1-3 states that the accuracy of course alignment of the VOR is excellent, being generally plus or minus 1 degree.

2. D. control tower
   At a towered airport, the local controller has Class D airspace and will set the spacing and landing sequence instructions.

3. D. calm wind
   In FAA Order 7110.65 Section 3-5-1 it says the calm wind runway is used when the wind is less than 5 knots.

4. A. ground controller
   See FAAO 7110.65 Section 3-1-4: The ground controller is responsible for the safe and efficient use of airport movement areas.

5. A. True
   Towers use a mix of instructions to provide positive control (landing and takeoff clearances) of aircraft and they issue safety alerts when they know where other aircraft are. VFR aircraft are responsible to see and avoid each other.

6. A. 1,000 feet
   See FAAO 7110.65 Section 4-5-1: "Vertical Separation Minima."

7. C. vertical
   Vertical separation is applied first, as this is sometimes the easiest, first-used separating method until a better one is found and applied.

8. A. True
   See AIM paragraph 4-1-8: Note that pilot use of "have numbers" does not indicate receipt of the ATIS broadcast.

9. B. inbound—front course.

AIM 1-1-9: glide slope radiates its signal in the direction of the localizer front course.

10. D. all of the above.

Chicago tower to depart, center once en route, and Las Vegas approach once you're in the Las Vegas area (see FAA-H-8083-15, Instrument Flying Handbook for reference).

11. A. True

In FAAO 7110.65 Section 1-1-8, the letters of agreement spell out the procedures that are applied jointly or require the cooperation of more than one facility.

12. D. none of the above are correct

Instead, read FAAO 7110.65 Section 2-1-2: "Duty Priority. Give first priority to separating aircraft and issuing safety alerts as required in this order. Good judgment shall be used in prioritizing all other provisions of this order based on the requirements of the situation at hand."

13. A. True

See FAAO 7110.65 Section 3-1-2 and 3-1-3: "Preventive Control. Provide preventive control service only to aircraft operating in accordance with a letter of agreement. When providing this service, issue advice or instructions only if a situation develops which requires corrective action. …The local controller has primary responsibility for operations conducted on the active runway and must control the use of those runways."

14. C. facility specific data.

See FAAO 7110.65 Section 2-3-3: "Terminal Data Entries. Facility managers can authorize omissions and/or optional use of spaces 2A, 8A, 8B, 9A, 9B, 9C, and 10–18, if no misunderstanding will result. These omissions and/or optional uses shall be specified in a facility directive."

15. B. lateral

See FAAO 7110.65 Section 6-5, Lateral Separation: (6-5-2-b.) "…to determine the distance required for various divergence angles to clear the airspace to be protected. For divergence that falls between two values, use the lesser divergence value to obtain the distance."

16. A. X

See FAAO 7110.65 Table 2-3-7, Aircraft Equipment Suffixes.

17. A. True

See FAAO 7110.65 Section 2-3-1: "Flight Progress Strips. General—Unless otherwise authorized in a facility directive, use flight progress strips to post current data on air traffic and clearances required for control and other air traffic control services."

18. B. False

FAAO 7110.65 Section 2-3-1 (a)(1) reads as follows: 1. Do not erase or overwrite any item. Use an "X" to delete a climb/descend and maintain arrow, an at or above/below symbol, a cruise symbol, and unwanted altitude information. Write the new altitude information immediately adjacent to it and within the same space. (See also 2-3-1 (a)(2).)

19. D. MEA

FAAO 7110.65 Section 4-5-6 says "Except as provided in subparagraphs (a) and (b) below, assign altitudes at or above the MEA for the route segment being flown."

20. C. communications; before the aircraft crosses the receiving controller's airspace.

See FAAO 7110.65 Section 8-2-2: "Transfer of Control and Communications. The control of an aircraft shall be transferred from one control unit to another at the time the aircraft is estimated to cross the control boundary or at such other point or time agreed upon by the two units. Where nonradar separation minima are being applied, the transfer of air-ground communications with an aircraft shall be made 5 minutes before the time at which the aircraft is estimated to reach the boundary unless otherwise agreed to by the control and/or communication units concerned."

21. B. False

In FAAO 7110.65 Section 4-5-1, "Altitude Assignment and Verification," under "Vertical Separation Minima," there is no mention of speed in this section with regard to separation purposes.

22. B. False

See FAAO 7110.65 Section 6-5-1, Lateral Separation, Separation Methods: the application of lateral separation is not based on aircraft speed.

23. A. True

FAAO 7110.65 Section 6-4, Longitudinal Separation: The lead aircraft and trailing aircraft must be 10 minutes or 20 NM apart with DME.

24. A. True

Controllers must provide vertical and, in the case of adjacent airspace, lateral separation when placing aircraft into a holding pattern.

25. A. 3

See FAAO 7110.65 Section 5-5-1, Radar Separation Application.

26. B. in conflict.

IFR aircraft must be at least 10 minutes apart in a nonradar situation.

27. B. False

See FAAO 7110.65 Section 8-2-2(a). Only one facility can control aircraft until transfer of control has been issued.

28. A. Letters of Agreement; Ops letters

See FAAO 7110.65 Section 5-4-5.

29. B. nonradar; 5

See FAAO 7110.65 Section 8-2-2.

30. B. False

"The safe, orderly, and expeditious flow of air traffic" is the commonly accepted definition of ATC; note that the order of words is important.

31. B. False

These are only used to coordinate between facilities (FAAO 7110.65 Section 1-1-9).

32. D. when

See FAAO 7110.65 Section 8-2-2(b). This transfer occurs when the aircraft reaches or crosses this point, because only one air traffic control unit shall control an aircraft at any given time.

33. A. True

ATC is based on situations arising out of a controller actions when he/she reacts to pilots flying through assigned airspace (in the controller's area of responsibility). ATC often gets the blame for delays, however it is the weather that causes most delays in the aviation system.

34. A. True

According to the U.S. Department of Labor, CPCs are to be certified for all of the ATC positions within a defined area of a given facility.

35. A. clearance limit, and route of flight.

See FAAO 7110.65 Section 4-3-2, Departure Clearances.

36. D. in an emergency situation.
   See FAAO 7110.65 Section 4-4-1, "Clearance: Pilots are required to obey clearances unless they are at risk of an incident or accident."

37. C. prevent collision between known aircraft.
   See FAAO 7110.65 Glossary definition for air traffic clearance.

38. E. A and C are correct
   Aircraft flying VFR, if transponder equipped, should set their transponder to 1200. Aircraft flying in uncontrolled airspace can contact ATC, if desired, by radio.

39. B. False
   See FAAO 7110.65 Section 2-3: "Flight Progress Strips. Flight progress strips are official government documents kept on file for future reference."

40. B. departure speed
   See FAAO 7110.65 Section 4-4-1, "Clearance." Departure speed is not one of the required listed parts of a clearance.

41. C. non-control information in selected high activity terminal areas.
   See FAAO 7110.65 or AIM Glossary definition of ATIS.

42. E. A and B are correct
   A conflict is defined as two IFR aircraft occupying the same airspace while violating ATC safe airspace rules and regulations.

43. B. The controller must provide some type of separation.
   A conflict is defined as two IFR aircraft occupying the same airspace while violating ATC safe airspace rules and regulations. If there is a conflict, a controller is responsible to separate the aircraft.

44. D. No separation is required as there is no conflict.
   No separation is required because there has not and will not be a violation of ATC rules and regulations.

45. B. The controller must provide some type of separation.
   FAAO 7110.65 Section 6-4-2 explains that some type of separation is required since both airplanes are estimated to be over the same fix within 10 minutes of each other.

46. D. No separation is required as there is no conflict.
    FAAO 7110.65 Section 6 (nonradar) states that 1,000 feet of vertical separation is required.

47. B. The controller must provide some type of separation.
    See FAAO 7110.65 Section 6-3, "Initial Separation of Departing and Arriving Aircraft": clear departing aircraft to fly specified headings which diverge by at least 45 degrees.

48. C. 3
    This is the signal put out electronically in international Morse Code.

49. C. TACAN.
    See FAAO 7110.65 or AIM Glossary for tactical air navigation (TACAN) definition.

50. B. Runway One Zero
    FAAO 7110.65 Section 2-4-17 explains number usage for ATC and pilots—the correct way to say the runway would be One Zero.

51. C. Executive One
    FAAO 7110.65 Section 2-4-20, Example 7(b) states that when the president is aboard a civil aircraft, it is called Executive One.

52. D. if pilot requests and ground visibility is at least 1 SM.
    FAAO 7110.65 Section 7-4-6 states that the pilot must request it, and you need one statue mile of ground visibility.

53. C. 121.5 and 243.0
    See FAAO 7110.65 10-2-2: emergency frequencies are 121.5 and 243.0.

54. D. All of the above
    See the FAA's Aeronautical Chart User's Guide for legends and examples of all the items found on a sectional chart.

55. C. Automatic Terminal Information Service
    See FAAO 7110.65 Section 1-2-6, Abbreviations.

56. D. Position information
    In FAAO 7110.65 Section 5-3-6, it states, "Inform an aircraft of its position whenever radar identification is established by means of identifying turns or by any of the beacon identification method."

57. The number 9 is spoken
    B. niner.
    See FAAO 7110.65 Section 2-4-17, number clarification.

58. D. after radar contact by ATC.
    FAAO 7110.65 Section 5-1-12: After an aircraft receives the statement "radar contact" from ATC, it discontinues reporting over compulsory reporting points. It resumes normal position reporting when ATC informs it "radar contact lost" or "radar service terminated."

59. B. separation of IFR traffic.
    In FAAO 7110.65 Section 2-1-2, it states the first duty is to separate aircraft.

60. A. 7700
    See FAAO 7110.65 Glossary, "discreet codes."

61. C. do not overlap.
    FAAO 7110.65 Section 4-6-1 says holding pattern airspace may touch, but cannot overlap.

62. D. all of the above are correct.
    FAAO 7110.65 Section 3-9-1, and Section 4-3-1: The SID is only valid if you are following all of the directions on the chart. If anything changes, altitude, heading etc., then the SID is no longer in effect. SIDs are an effective way to send aircraft out on their various routes in a planned and organized fashion.

63. A. Draw a single line through the error (except altitude data; "X" that out).
    See FAAO 7110.65 Section 2-3-1.

64. B. 6,000
    FAAO 7110.65 Section 3-10-3 states, when a category III is involved, there is an automatic 6,000 feet runway of separation needed.

65. D. an aircraft in an emergency condition.
    In FAAO 7110.65 Fig. 2-3-7, the red E means emergency.

66. B. Say
    FAAO 7110.65 Section 4-5-7: to get altitude information, you must state "Say altitude" to the aircraft.

67. A. 10, 20

In FAAO 7110.65 Section 6-4-2, there must be 10 miles of separation when two aircraft are on the same path.

68. A. execute a missed approach.

FAAO 7110.65 Section 5-10-14, Final Approach Abnormalities: "Instruct the aircraft if runway environment not in sight, execute a missed approach if previously given; or climb to or maintain a specified altitude and fly a specified course whenever the completion of a safe approach is questionable because one or more of the following conditions exists. The conditions in subparas a, b, and c do not apply after the aircraft passes decision height on a PAR approach."

69. B. Dual peaked (two quick) white flashes between green flashes.

See FAAO 7110.65 Glossary, airport rotating beacon.

70. B. blue omni-directional lights.

See FAA-H-8083-15 Instrument Flying Handbook.

71. D. that weather at the airport is below basic VFR weather.

Operation of an airport beacon during daylight hours at a controlled airport may indicate that the visibility at the surface may be less that 3 statute miles and/or a ceiling of less than 1,000 feet.

72. A. must contact the tower for clearance to enter.

FAAO 7110.65 Section 3-1-13: Pilots are required to establish two-way radio communications before entering the Class D airspace. If the controller responds to a radio call with, "(a/c call sign) standby," radio communications have been established and the pilot can enter the Class D airspace. If workload or traffic conditions prevent immediate provision of Class D services, inform the pilot to remain outside the Class D airspace until conditions permit the services to be provided.

73. A. traffic advisories and limited vectoring to VFR aircraft.

Read FAAO 7110.65 Section 7-6-1, "Application."

74. B. South

Pilots are given traffic information relative to their own position, and are provided distance in nautical miles, direction of flight, altitude, and type of aircraft. When calling out traffic, controllers use the 12-hour clock. Visualize a clock face and the numbers 12 (top-north), 3 (right-east), 6 (bottom-south), and 9 (left-west). Example: traffic 3-o'clock means the traffic is off the right wing.

75. A. Northwest
Pilots are given traffic information relative to their own position, and are provided distance in nautical miles, direction of flight, altitude, and type of aircraft. When calling out traffic, controllers use the 12-hour clock. Visualize a clock face and the numbers 12 (top-north), 3 (right-east), 6 (bottom-south), and 9 (left-west). Example: traffic 3-o'clock means the traffic is off the right wing.

76. D. Between directly ahead and 90 to the right
Pilots are given traffic information relative to their own position, and are provided distance in nautical miles, direction of flight, altitude, and type of aircraft. When calling out traffic, controllers use the 12-hour clock. Visualize a clock face and the numbers 12 (top-north), 3 (right-east), 6 (bottom-south), and 9 (left-west). Example: traffic 3-o'clock means the traffic is off the right wing.

77. C. West
Pilots are given traffic information relative to their own position, and are provided distance in nautical miles, direction of flight, altitude, and type of aircraft. When calling out traffic, controllers use the 12-hour clock. Visualize a clock face and the numbers 12 (top-north), 3 (right-east), 6 (bottom-south), and 9 (left-west). Example: traffic 3-o'clock means the traffic is off the right wing.

78. C. After leaving the runway and crossing the runway holding lines.
Hold lines are used to keep aircraft clear of runways and at controlled airports are used as that separates the responsibilities of ground control and tower. (See FAA-H-8083-15, Instrument Flying Handbook.)

79. D. all of the above.
In FAAO 7110.65 Section 6-2, the diagrams indicate all 3 methods are used in the separation of aircraft.

80. B. ARTCC
AIM paragraph 4-1-1: "Centers are established primarily to provide air traffic service to aircraft operating on IFR flight plans within controlled airspace, and principally during the en route phase of flight."

81. D. via any route at the pilot's discretion onto Runway 9 and hold until cleared for takeoff.
AIM paragraph 4-3-18 (a)(5): "When ATC clears an aircraft to 'taxi to' an assigned takeoff runway, the absence of holding instructions authorizes the aircraft to 'cross' all runways which the taxi route intersects except the assigned takeoff runway. It does not include authorization to 'taxi onto' or 'cross' the assigned takeoff runway at any point."

82. D. from the end of evening twilight to the beginning of morning twilight.

14 CFR Section 1.1 (definitions): Night means the time between the end of evening civil twilight and the beginning of morning civil twilight, as published in the American Air Almanac, converted to local time.

83. D. 250

14 CFR Section 91.117(a): Unless otherwise authorized by the Administrator, no person may operate an aircraft below 10,000 feet MSL at an indicated airspeed of more than 250 knots (288 m.p.h.).

84. B. Anytime an emergency is declared.

This is the voluntary NASA safety reporting system.

85. D.

AIM paragraph 4-4-1(a): A clearance issued by ATC is predicated on known traffic and known physical airport conditions. An ATC clearance means an authorization by ATC, for the purpose of preventing collision between known aircraft, for an aircraft to proceed under specified conditions within controlled airspace.

86. A. is cleared to land.

FAAO 7110.65 Section 3-2-1: The table indicates aircraft in flight are cleared to land when a steady green light is indicated.

87. C. to return to the starting point on the airport.

FAAO 7110.65 Section 3-2-1: The table indicates aircraft on the ground are cleared to land when a flashing white light is indicated.

88. B. steady red.

FAAO 7110.65 Section 3-2-1: The table indicates aircraft in flight are cleared to land when a steady red light is indicated.

89. A. Flashing green

FAAO 7110.65 Section 3-2-1: The table indicates aircraft on the ground are cleared to land when a flashing green light is indicated.

90. B. at all tower controlled airports regardless of the weather.

FAAO 7110.65 Section 3-1-13: Pilots are required to establish two-way radio communications before entering the Class D airspace.

91. B. lowest layer of clouds reported as broken or overcast and not classified as thin.
   A ceilometer is a device that uses a laser or other light source to determine the height of a cloud base. Meteorologists also make visual and balloon observations to determine ceiling height. Ceilings are either broken (5/8 to 7/8 sky cover) or overcast (sky is completely covered) and can be estimated, measured, or indefinite.

92. A. Base, crosswind
   See AIM Figure 4-3-2: "Traffic Pattern Operations."

93. A. controlled airspace
   See AIM Paragraph 3-2-6, Class E Airspace.

94. B. One two two point niner five
   FAAO 7110.65 Section 2-4-17, Numbers Usage… "j. Frequencies. 1. The separate digits of the frequency, inserting the word "point" where the decimal point occurs."

95. C. Piper four three one Alpha Quebec

96. C. Roger
   See FAAO 7110.65 Glossary.

97. C. Oklahoma City, OK.
   See FAA Air Traffic Control internet home page.

98. D. all of the above.
   It is a common misconception in the aviation industry that the NAS consists of only air traffic control. All parts (ATC, airmen and aircraft, and airports) must be considered in order to reflect a true systems approach to aviation.

99. A. True
   Although their role in the promotion of aviation has diminished over the past decade and the FAA seems more involved in regulation today, this is their history.

100. A. True
   FAA and Air Traffic Control Association (ATCA) history says that the airlines were concerned about safety during the early years of commercial flight and the eastern routes were becoming congested.

Appendix 2: Instruction/Evaluation Report, FAA Form 3120-25

This is the form the FAA uses during On-the-Job (OTJ) training/instruction to allow the trainer to document progress and deficiencies of the developmental or controller in training.

3120.4L
Appendix 2

6/22/05

FIGURE 2. FAA FORM 3120-25

ATCT/ARTCC OJT
INSTRUCTION/EVALUATION REPORT

1. Name		2. Date	3. Scenario/Position(s)

4. Weather	5. Workload	6. Complexity	7. Hours
☐ VFR ☐ MVFR ☐ IFR ☐ Other_____	☐ Light ☐ Moderate ☐ Heavy	☐ Not Difficult ☐ Occasionally Difficult ☐ Mostly Difficult ☐ Very Difficult	8. Total Hours This Position

9. Purpose ☐ OJT ☐ OJF ☐ Familiarization Scenario ☐ Instructional Scenario ☐ Evaluation Scenario **10. Routing**

☐ Skill Check ☐ Certification ☐ Recertification ☐ Skill Enhancement ☐ Other

11.	Job Task	Job Subtask	Observed	Comment	Satisfactory	Needs Improvement	Unsatisfactory	Simulation Training
Performance	A. Separation	1. Separation is ensured.						
		2. Safety alerts are provided.						
	B. Coordination	3. Performs handoffs/pointouts.						
		4. Required coordinations are performed.						
	C. Control Judgment	5. Good control judgment is applied.						
		6. Priority of duties is understood.						
		7. Positive control is provided.						
		8. Effective traffic flow is maintained.						
	D. Methods and Procedures	9. Aircraft identity is maintained.						
		10. Strip posting is complete/correct.						
		11. Clearance delivery is complete/correct and timely.						
		12. LOAs/directives are adhered to.						
		13. Additional services are provided.						
		14. Rapidly recovers from equipment failures and emergencies.						
		15. Scans entire control environment.						
		16. Effective working speed is maintained.						
	E. Equipment	17. Equipment status information is maintained.						
		18. Equipment capabilities are utilized/understood.						
	F. Communication	19. Functions effectively as a radar/tower team member.						
		20. Communication is clear and concise.						
		21. Uses prescribed phraseology.						
		22. Makes only necessary transmissions.						
		23. Uses appropriate communications method.						
		24. Relief briefings are complete and accurate.						
	G. Other							

FAA Form 3120-25 (5-98) Supersedes Previous Edition

NSN: 0052-00-900-2002

FIGURE 2. FAA FORM 3120-25
(Continued)

12. Comments	12A. References

Signature: _____ Date: _____

13. Recommendation
☐ Certification Skill Check ☐ Certification
☐ Continuation of OJT ☐ Skill Enhancement Training ☐ Suspension of OJT

14. Employee's Comments:

This report has been discussed
with me (Signature) _____ Date: _____

15. Certification/Recertification
I certify that this employee meets qualification requirements and is capable of working under general supervision.

Signature of Certifier: _____ Date: _____

FAA Form 3120-25 (5-98) Supersedes Previous Edition   NSN: 0052-00-900-2002

Appendix 3: FAA FG-2152-1 Documents

These three documents show the FAA ATC new-hire qualifications for initial employment and pay they will receive while attending the Oklahoma City Academy. These documents replaced the long-standing practice of paying new ATC hires their initial facility level salary and per diem rates while undergoing initial screening and training. Appendix 6 lists the URLs for these documents.

1. Position Description Academy ATC Specialist Trainee:

POLICY BULLETIN #33: QUALIFICATION STANDARD FOR AIR TRAFFIC CONTROL SPECIALIST TRAINEE – FAA ACADEMY (FG-2152-1)

Standard Position Description (SPD)
Air Traffic Control Specialist TRAINEE
Federal Aviation Administration (FAA) Academy
FG-2152-1

I. Introduction

This position serves as a trainee in the air traffic control occupation. Upon initial hire the employee has met either basic or specialized air traffic control qualifications, and serves in a temporary appointment while in training status at the FAA Academy.

These are not permanent positions. The trainees who successfully complete training and pass all required evaluations established by the Air Traffic Organization may be given permanent appointments in terminal or en route air traffic facilities at the appropriate pay level at their assigned facilities.

II. Major Duties and Responsibilities

Academy students receive basic air traffic control training at the FAA Academy, which includes:

   a. A complete occupational indoctrination including highlights of Federal employment, familiarization with organizational structure and functions, aircraft, the air traffic control system, and the aviation industry.

   b. Classroom instruction and workshop exercises relating to the air traffic control system.

   c. Skills training related to the work of air traffic control specialists in the target option, i.e., at air traffic control terminal facilities and air route traffic control centers.

III. Supervision Received

While at the FAA Academy, the trainees are under the direct supervision of instructors and FAA Mike Monroney Aeronautical Center staff who observe the work on a continuing basis to insure the proper performance of tasks and to provide training in basic controller skills.

2. Qualification Standard Academy ATC Specialist Trainee:

QUALIFICATION STANDARD
AIR TRAFFIC CONTROL SPECIALIST TRAINEE
FEDERAL AVIATION ADMINISTRATION (FAA) ACADEMY (FG-2152-1)

This is a single agency qualification standard for terminal and en route air traffic control specialists participating in initial air traffic control training at the FAA Academy.

The provisions of EMP. 1.13 Citizenship Requirements, EMP 1.20 Maximum Entry and Retention Age for Air Traffic Control Specialists, and EMP. 1.24 Suitability apply to these positions. Security clearances may be required in accordance with applicable rules, policies, and regulations.

The following qualification requirements apply to these positions:

EXPERIENCE AND EDUCATION REQUIREMENTS

Applicants may meet minimum qualification requirements on the basis of experience, education, or one of the alternate provisions as described below.

EXPERIENCE

General Experience Three years of progressively responsible experience that demonstrated the potential for learning and performing air traffic control work.

OR

Specialized Experience: Experience in a military or civilian air traffic facility that demonstrated possession of the knowledge, skills, and abilities required to perform the level of work of the specialization for which application is made. This experience must have provided a comprehensive knowledge of appropriate air traffic control laws, rules, and regulations.

- Examples of specialized experience include:

For Terminal Positions: Issuing control instructions and advice to pilots in the vicinity of airports to assure proper separation of aircraft and to expedite their safe and efficient movement. This specialization also requires:

- Ability to act decisively under stressful situations and to maintain alertness over sustained periods of pressure;

- kill to coordinate plans and actions with pilots and other controllers; and

- Judgment to select and take the safest and most effective course of action from among several available choices.

For Center Positions: Controlling aircraft operating enroute along the airways to assure proper separation and safe and expeditious movement of such aircraft. This specialization also requires:

- Skill to control aircraft operating at very high speeds over great distances;

- Skill to arrange air traffic in patterns that assure maximum safety and minimum delay at points where such aircraft are "handed off" or transferred to other facilities or other sectors within the center; and

- Judgment to estimate when and where traffic congestion will build to a point that necessitates changing patterns, and to plan accordingly.

For all specializations, qualifying specialized experience must have provided the ability to:

- Arrive quickly at well-reasoned solutions to complex problems;

- Adjust quickly to different assignments, changing conditions, and workload fluctuations;

- Remain calm and controlled during and after long periods of tension and fatigue; and

- Speak rapidly, clearly, and distinctly.

Level of Experience: Creditable experience must have equipped applicants with the knowledge, skills, and abilities to perform the full range of duties of the position for which application is being made.

OR

EDUCATION
Superior academic achievement at the baccalaureate level or 1 full year of graduate study.

OR

ALTERNATE REQUIREMENTS
Applicants who pass the written test qualify if they:

- Hold or have held an appropriate facility rating and have actively controlled air traffic in civilian or military air traffic control terminals or centers;

- Hold or have held an FAA certificate as a dispatcher for an air carrier;

- Hold or have held an instrument flight rating;

- Hold or have held an FAA certificate as a navigator or have been fully qualified as a Navigator/Bombardier in the Armed Forces;

- Have 350 hours of flight time as a copilot or higher and hold or have held a private certificate or equivalent Armed Forces rating;

- Have served as a rated Aerospace Defense Command Intercept Director; or

- Have three years of progressively responsible experience that demonstrated the potential for learning and performing air traffic control work and pass the written test with an appropriately higher score.

MAXIMUM ENTRY AGE
Under the provisions of 5 U.S.C. 3307, a maximum entry age has been established for Terminal and Center positions.

TEST REQUIREMENTS
Applicants for appointment and inservice placement to all positions covered by this standard must pass a written test unless the individuals have previously been certified as control tower operators according to FAA standards or received air traffic control specialist certification according to FAA standards.

PERSONAL QUALITIES
In addition to meeting all other requirements, applicants must demonstrate possession of the traits and characteristics important in air traffic control work. Applicants who qualify in the written test and/or meet the experience and training requirements will be required to appear for a pre-employment interview to determine whether they possess the personal characteristics necessary for performance of air traffic control work.

ADDITIONAL SCREENING REQUIREMENTS
Applicants who have passed the written test (and the interview, if required) may be required to pass additional air traffic control aptitude screening for positions in the Department of Transportation, Federal Aviation Administration. Persons who do not pass the aptitude evaluation testing requirements will not be appointed to these positions.

TRAINING REQUIREMENTS
At all trainee and developmental levels, employees must learn the skills needed for operation at

higher levels of responsibility. Failure of employees to meet training requirements for or accept promotion to higher grade air traffic control specialist positions may constitute grounds for reassignment, demotion, or separation from employment.

CERTIFICATE AND RATING REQUIREMENTS

Air traffic control specialists in all specializations must possess or obtain, within uniformly applicable time limits, the facility ratings required for full performance at the facility where the position is located.

Applicants must possess or obtain a valid Air Traffic Control Specialist Certificate and/or Control Tower Operator Certificate, if appropriate. These certificates require demonstrating knowledge of basic meteorology, basic air navigation, standard air traffic control and communications procedures, the types and uses of air navigation aids, and regulations governing air traffic.

Facility ratings require demonstration of a knowledge of the kind and location of radio aids to air navigation, the terrain, the landmarks, the communications systems and circuits, and the procedures peculiar to the area covered by the facility.

MEDICAL REQUIREMENTS

In general, air traffic control specialist applicants and employees must have the capacity to perform the essential functions of these positions without risk to themselves or others. The provision of sufficient information about physical capacity for employment requires that before appointment applicants undergo appropriate pre-employment physical/medical evaluations. The medical standards for initial entry into terminal and en route air traffic control specialist positions apply to positions covered by this standard and are published in FAA Directive 3933A ATCS Health Program (or successor document).

3. Entry-Level Pay Grade for ATC Academy Trainee:
ENTRY-LEVEL PAY AND GRADE FOR AIR TRAFFIC ACADEMY TRAINEES
POLICY BULLETIN #33

This policy bulletin applies to: All air traffic control specialist new hires serving on temporary excepted appointments who receive air traffic control specialist training at the FAA Academy.

Policy bulletin effective date: March 25, 2005. This policy bulletin remains in effect until cancelled by AHR-1. **Use this policy bulletin in conjunction with:** EMP-1.11 Temporary External Hiring and Policy Bulletin #31 Eligibility Period for Air Traffic Control Collegiate Training Initiative Graduates.

1. **PURPOSE:** This policy bulletin establishes that new air traffic control hires who must attend initial (entry-level) air traffic control training at the FAA Academy are to be hired at grade FG-1 on temporary excepted appointments. Individuals in these positions who successfully complete the entry-level training at the FAA Academy and successfully complete all other requirements for continuing employment, including all evaluations required by the Air Traffic Organization (ATO), may be given permanent appointments in air traffic terminal and en route facilities at the appropriate pay levels for Academy graduates at the facilities.

2. **POLICY:**

(a) Temporary Excepted Appointments: New hires into air traffic control positions who must attend initial (entry-level) training at the FAA Academy will be placed on temporary excepted appointments not to exceed six months while they are attending initial training.

(b) Position Description: The Air Traffic Control Specialist Trainee – FAA Academy standard position description (SPD) shall be used as the position description for these positions. This SPD will be entered into PDLibrary. However, it is to be used effective immediately.

(c) Grade: These trainees will be assigned grade FG-1 and paid according to the pay for that grade, including any appropriate locality pay that applies to employees with a duty station at the Mike Monroney Aeronautical Center.

(d) Qualification Standard: The single agency qualification standard for air traffic control specialist trainee – FAA Academy shall be used for making qualifications and eligibility determinations, as appropriate.

(e) Permanent Appointments: Individuals in these positions who successfully complete the initial training at the FAA Academy and all other requirements for continuing employment, including all evaluations required by the ATO, may be given permanent appointments as developmental air traffic control specialists in air traffic terminal and en route facilities and be paid at the appropriate pay levels for Academy graduates at the facilities.

3. EFFECT ON OTHER POLICIES:

(a) This policy bulletin does not change any training requirements for the subject positions.

(b) This policy bulletin applies to candidates and selectees from the following sources: former Office of Personnel Management inventory/register, Air Traffic Collegiate Training Initiative (AT-CTI) inventory, and applicants/selectees from the general public if they must attend initial (entry-level) air traffic control training at the FAA Academy. This policy bulletin does not apply to candidates or selectees from the following recruitment sources: former PATCO inventory, former military controllers hired under Veterans Readjustment Appointments, and Employment of Retired Military Air Traffic Controllers (RMC) Program.

(c) Candidates from the covered inventories who are not currently officially referred for employment consideration to FAA regions or service areas: Individuals who are officially notified of the new policy established by this policy bulletin and who choose to continue to be considered for positions under the new policy shall have their eligibility on the inventory extended as if they first entered into the inventory on the date their acceptance is received by AMH-300. This does not apply to AT-CTI candidates.

(d) Individuals from the covered sources who are currently referred on certificates of eligibles/referral lists for the subject positions or who have been selected for the subject positions:

   (1) If the candidates are officially notified of the new policy established by this policy bulletin and choose to continue to be considered for positions under the new policy, the change in policy shall not remove them from consideration for employment by the region or service area.

   (2) If the candidates who choose to continue to be considered for positions under the new policy were considered to be in-process under Policy Bulletin #12, In-Process Rule for Air Traffic Control Specialist Positions, the change in policy shall not remove them from being in-process under Policy Bulletin #12.

4. POINTS OF CONTACT: Questions about this guidance should be directed to Jay Aul, Manager, ATO Support Team, AHR-4, on (202) 267-9862.

Appendix 4: Study Maps and Symbology

These maps are used for the nonradar and radar training at the Academy. A supplemental document is included to assist the reader in understanding the AeroCenter map symbols. The material from the FAA-H-7110.65 starting on page 143 is a list of sections from the air traffic manual that a new-hire would need to know for initial Academy nonradar and radar training.

AeroCenter map (ZME 66 sector) [Appdx 4-A]

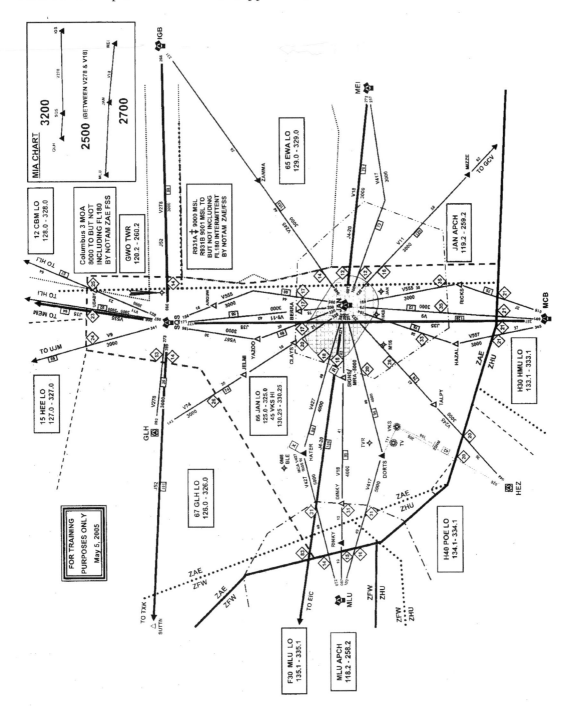

AeroCenter blank map (ZME 66 sector) [Appdx 4-B]

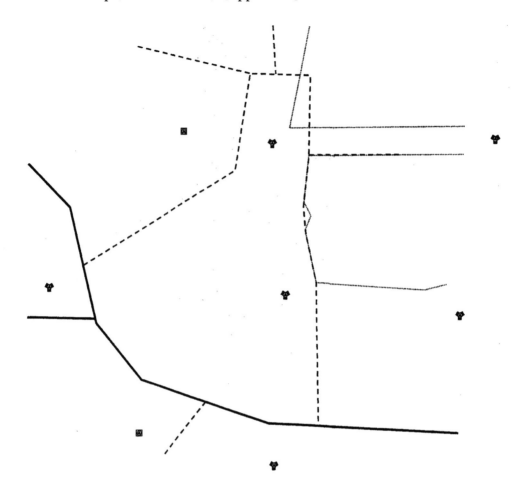

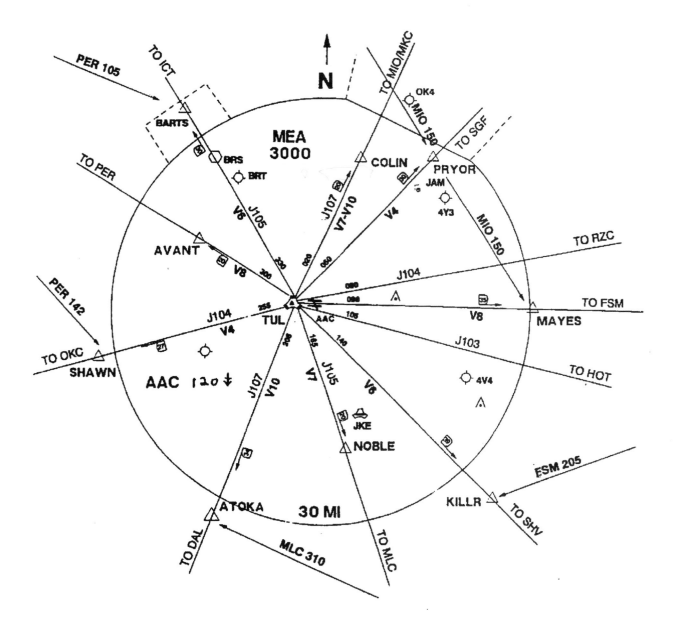

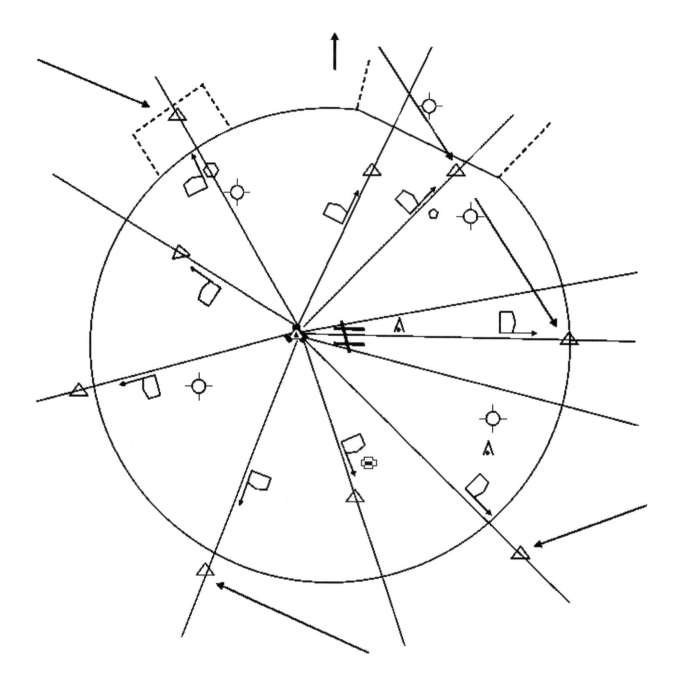

7110.65 Sections NonRadar

Flight Strip Marking: Chapter 2-3-2. Enroute Data Entries 2-3-3 and 2-3-4; 2-3-10 to 2-3-13
NonRadar Procedures Chapter 6.

Appendix D. Standard Operating Practice (SOP) for the Transfer of Position Responsibility

7110.65 Sections Radar

Full Data Blocks: 5-4-11;

Beacon Code Assignment: 5-2-1 thru 5-2-10, 5-2-13, 5-2-14, 5-2-16, 5-2-21, 5-2-22, 10-2-6

Radar Identification: 5-1-12, 5-1-13, 5-3-1 thru 5-3-8

Radar Handoff & Point-out: 2-1-17, 2-3-1, 2-3-9, 5-4-2 thru 5-4-11,

Radar Separation & Safety Alerts: 2-1-2, 2-1-6, 2-1-21, 5-1-8, 5-2-9, 5-2-17 thru 5-2-20, 5-5-1 thru 5-5-11, 5-14-1, 5-14-2, 5-14-7, 7-2-1, 9-4-2

Radar Vectoring: 5-6-1 thru 5-6-3

Radar Departures & Arrivals: 4-2-8, 5-8-1, 5-9-1 thru 5-9-4, 7-4-1 thru 7-4-6

Speed Adjustment: 3-1-11, 5-7-1 thru 5-7-4

Emergencies: 5-1-3, 5-1-6, 5-2-15, 5-3-3, 10-1-1 thru 10-1-5, 10-2-1 thru 10-2-17, 10-3-1, 10-3-4 thru 10-3-7, 10-4-3, 10-4-4, 10-5-1, 10-7-1 thru 10-7-5

Additional Services: 2-1-2, 2-1-21, 2-1-22, 2-6-2 thru 2-6-4, 5-1-8 thru 5-1-10

Military Operations: 2-1-4, 2-1-12, 2-1-13, 4-5-7, 5-3-1, 5-1-13, 5-5-5, 5-5-8, 9-3-6 thru 9-3-8, 9-3-12, 9-3-16, 9-4-1 thru 9-4-3, 9-5-1 thru 9-5-5

Position Relief Briefing: Reference Appendix D

Map Symbology Review

Extending from NAVAIDs (such as JAN, SQS, MLU, MCB, MEI, etc.) are the Victor airways and Jet Routes. Victor airways are routes which typically extend from 1,200 AGL up to but NOT including FL180, and the protected airspace is 4 miles either side. Jet routes are from FL180 up to FL450. Each airway is labeled. A Victor airway is named with a V and a number (ex.: V245), pronounced "Victor Two Forty-Five"; a jet route is J52, "J Fifty-Two." Along each airway are boxes with numbers in them indicating the distances between NAVAIDs and the intersections (triangles).

NAVAIDS

TXK   Texarkana VORTAC, AR
GLH   Greenville VOR/DME, MS
HEE   Thompson-Robbins NDB (Helena-West, AR)
UJM   Marvell VOR/DME (Helena-West, AR)
MEM   Memphis VORTAC, TN
HLI   Holly Springs VORTAC, MS
SQS   Sidon VORTAC, MS
CBM   Caledonia VORTAC (Columbus, MS)
IGB   Bigbee VORTAC (Columbus, MS)
EWA   Kewanee VORTAC, MS
MEI   Meridian VORTAC, MS
JAN   Jackson VORTAC, MS
GCV   Greene County VORTAC (Leakesville, MS)
MCB   Mc Comb VORTAC, MS
VKS   Vicksburg NDB, MS

POE South Fan MARKER (Fort Polk, LA)
HMU Hammond VOR, LA
MLU Monroe VORTAC, LA
BLE Lake Providence NDB, LA
EIC Belcher VORTAC (Shreveport, LA)
HEZ Natchez VORTAC
BLE Byerly NDB
TV Outer Marker/NDB for TVR

Airports
JAN Jackson
GWO Greenwood
VKS Vicksburg
0M8 Byerley Lake Providence, Louisiana
M16 John Bell Williams Raymond, MS
TVR Vicksburg Tallulah, MS
HKS Hawkins Field Airport (Jackson, MS)
MLU Monroe
TVR Tallualah

Centers
ZAE Aero Center
ZHU Houston
ZFW Fort Worth

Appendix 5: FAA Flight Progress Strips

These are examples and explanations for the paper flight progress strips that controllers use in their jobs every day. If you are assigned to an ARTCC (the Zs) you should search the internet for User Request and Evaluation Tool (URET) information, as this system is slowly being introduced into all ARTCCs and will replace paper strips. This material is taken directly from the FAA-H-7110.65 document.

2-3-2. EN ROUTE DATA ENTRIES (ARTCC)

FIG 2-3-2
Flight Progress Strip
(7230-19)

3 4 5 6 7 1 2 8 9 10	11 12 13 14 14a	15 16 17 18 19	20 20a	21 22 23 24	25 26	27 28 29 30

DAL542 1 H/B753/A T468 G555 16 16 486 09	7HQ 1827	18 30 PXT	330 RA↑1828		FLLJ14 ENO 000212 COD PHL	2675 *ZCN

a. Information recorded on the flight progress strips (FAA Forms 7230-19) shall be entered in the correspondingly numbered spaces:

TBL 2-3-1

Block	Information Recorded
1.	Verification symbol if required.
2.	Revision number. DSR–Not used.
3.	Aircraft identification.
4.	Number of aircraft if more than one, heavy aircraft indicator "H/" if appropriate, type of aircraft, and aircraft equipment suffix.
5.	Filed true airspeed.
6.	Sector number.
7.	Computer identification number if required.
8.	Estimated ground speed.
9.	Revised ground speed or strip request (SR) originator.
10.	Strip number. DSR– Strip number/Revision number.
11.	Previous fix.
12.	Estimated time over previous fix.
13.	Revised estimated time over previous fix.

Block	Information Recorded
14.	Actual time over previous fix, or actual departure time entered on first fix posting after departure.
14a.	Plus time expressed in minutes from the previous fix to the posted fix.
15.	Center–estimated time over fix (in hours and minutes), or clearance information for departing aircraft.
16.	Arrows to indicate if aircraft is departing (↑) or arriving (↓).
17.	Pilot–estimated time over fix.
18.	Actual time over fix, time leaving holding fix, arrival time at nonapproach control airport, or symbol indicating cancellation of IFR flight plan for arriving aircraft, or departure time (actual or assumed).
19.	Fix. For departing aircraft, add proposed departure time.
20.	Altitude information (in hundreds of feet) or as noted below.

NOTE– *Altitude information may be written in thousands of feet provided the procedure is authorized by the facility manager, and is defined in a facility directive, i.e. FL 330 as 33, 5,000 feet as 5, and 2,800 as 2.8.*

Block	Information Recorded
20a.	**OPTIONAL USE,** when voice recorders are operational; **REQUIRED USE,** when the voice recorders are not operating and strips are being use at the facility. This space is used to record reported RA events. The letters RA followed by a climb or descent arrow (if the climb or descent action is reported) and the time (hhmm) the event is reported.
21.	Next posted fix or coordination fix.
22.	Pilot's estimated time over next fix.
23.	Arrows to indicate north (↑), south (↓), east (→), or west (←) direction of flight if required.
24.	Requested altitude.
NOTE–	*Altitude information may be written in thousands of feet provided the procedure is authorized by the facility manager, and is defined in a facility directive, i.e., FL 330 as 33, 5,000 feet as 5, and 2,800 as 2.8.*
25.	Point of origin, route as required for control and data relay, and destination.

Block	Information Recorded
26.	Pertinent remarks, minimum fuel, point out/radar vector/speed adjustment information or sector/position number (when applicable in accordance with para 2–2–1, Recording Information), or NRP. High Altitude Redesign (HAR) or Point–to–point (PTP) may be used at facilities actively using these programs.
27.	Mode 3/A beacon code if applicable.
28.	Miscellaneous control data (expected further clearance time, time cleared for approach, etc.).
29–30.	Transfer of control data and coordination indicators.

b. Latitude/longitude coordinates may be used to define waypoints and may be substituted for nonadapted NAVAIDs in space 25 of domestic en route flight progress strips provided it is necessary to accommodate a random RNAV or GNSS route request.

c. Facility Air Traffic managers may authorize the optional use of spaces 13, 14, 14a, 22, 23, 24, and 28 for point out information, radar vector information, speed adjustment information, or transfer of control data.

2-3-3. TERMINAL DATA ENTRIES (ATCT)

a. Arrivals:

Information recorded on the flight progress strips (FAA Forms 7230–7.1, 7230–7.2, and 7230–8) shall be entered in the correspondingly numbered spaces. Facility managers can authorize omissions and/or optional use of spaces 2A, 8A, 8B, 9A, 9B, 9C, and 10–18, if no misunderstanding will result. These omissions and/or optional uses shall be specified in a facility directive.

FIG 2–3–3

1 2 3 4	2A	5 6 7	8 8A 8B	9 9A	9B 9C	10 13 16	11 14 17	12 15 18

TBL 2–3–2

Block	Information Recorded
1.	Aircraft identification.
2.	Revision number (FDIO locations only).
2A.	Strip request originator. (At FDIO locations this indicates the sector or position that requested a strip be printed.)
3.	Number of aircraft if more than one, heavy aircraft indicator "H/" if appropriate, type of aircraft, and aircraft equipment suffix.
4.	Computer identification number if required.
5.	Secondary radar (beacon) code assigned.
6.	(FDIO Locations.) The previous fix will be printed. (Non–FDIO Locations.) Use of the inbound airway. This function is restricted to facilities where flight data is received via interphone when agreed upon by the center and terminal facilities.
7.	Coordination fix.
8.	Estimated time of arrival at the coordination fix or destination airport.
8A.	**OPTIONAL USE.**

Block	Information Recorded
8B.	**OPTIONAL USE,** when voice recorders are operational; **REQUIRED USE,** when the voice recorders are not operating and strips are being used at the facility. This space is used to record reported RA events when the voice recorders are not operational and strips are being used at the facility. The letters RA followed by a climb or descent arrow (if the climb or descent action is reported) and the time (hhmm) the event is reported.
9.	Altitude (in hundreds of feet) and remarks.
NOTE–	*Altitude information may be written in thousands of feet provided the procedure is authorized by the facility manager, and is defined in a facility directive, i. e., FL 230 as 23, 5,000 feet as 5, and 2,800 as 2.8.*
9A.	Minimum fuel, destination airport/point out/radar vector/speed adjustment information. Air Traffic managers may authorize in a facility directive the omission of any of these items, **except minimum fuel,** if no misunderstanding will result.
NOTE–	*Authorized omissions and optional use of spaces shall be specified in the facility directive concerning strip marking procedures.*
9B.	**OPTIONAL USE.**
9C.	**OPTIONAL USE.**
10–18.	Enter data as specified by a facility directive. Radar facility personnel need not enter data in these spaces except when nonradar procedures are used or when radio recording equipment is inoperative.

b. Departures:

Information recorded on the flight progress strips (FAA Forms 7230–7.1, 7230–7.2, and 7230–8) shall be entered in the correspondingly numbered spaces. Facility managers can authorize omissions and/or optional use of spaces 2A, 8A, 8B, 9A, 9B, 9C, and 10–18, if no misunderstanding will result. These omissions and/or optional uses shall be specified in a facility directive.

FIG 2–3–4

1 2 3 4	2A	5 6 7	8 8A 8B	9 9A	9B 9C	10 13 16	11 14 17	12 15 18

TBL 2–3–3

Block	Information Recorded
1.	Aircraft identification.
2.	Revision number (FDIO locations only).
2A.	Strip request originator. (At FDIO locations this indicates the sector or position that requested a strip be printed.)
3.	Number of aircraft if more than one, heavy aircraft indicator "H/" if appropriate, type of aircraft, and aircraft equipment suffix.
4.	Computer identification number if required.
5.	Secondary radar (beacon) code assigned.
6.	Proposed departure time.
7.	Requested altitude.
NOTE–	*Altitude information may be written in thousands of feet provided the procedure is authorized by the facility manager, and is defined in a facility directive, i. e., FL 230 as 23, 5,000 feet as 5, and 2,800 as 2.8.*
8.	Departure airport.
8A.	**OPTIONAL USE.**

Block	Information Recorded
8B.	**OPTIONAL USE,** when voice recorders are operational; **REQUIRED USE,** when the voice recorders are not operating and strips are being used at the facility. This space is used to record reported RA events when the voice recorders are not operational and strips are being used at the facility. The letters RA followed by a climb or descent arrow (if the climb or descent action is reported) and the time (hhmm) the event is reported.
9.	**Computer–generated:** Route, destination, and remarks. Manually enter altitude/altitude restrictions in the order flown, if appropriate, and remarks.
9.	**Hand–prepared:** Clearance limit, route, altitude/altitude restrictions in the order flown, if appropriate, and remarks.
NOTE–	*Altitude information may be written in thousands of feet provided the procedure is authorized by the facility manager, and is defined in a facility directive, i.e., FL 230 as 23, 5,000 feet as 5, and 2,800 as 2.8.*
9A.	**OPTIONAL USE.**
9B.	**OPTIONAL USE.**
9C.	**OPTIONAL USE.**
10–18.	Enter data as specified by a facility directive. Items, such as departure time, runway used for takeoff, check marks to indicate information forwarded or relayed, may be entered in these spaces.

c. Overflights:

Information recorded on the flight progress strips (FAA Forms 7230–7.1, 7230–7.2, and 7230–8) shall be entered in the correspondingly numbered spaces. Facility managers can authorize omissions and/or optional use of spaces 2A, 8A, 8B, 9A, 9B, 9C, and 10–18, if no misunderstanding will result. These omissions and/or optional uses shall be specified in a facility directive.

FIG 2–3–5

1		5	8	9		9B	10	11	12
2	2A		8A				13	14	15
3		6							
4		7	8B	9A		9C	16	17	18

TBL 2–3–4

Block	Information Recorded
1.	Aircraft identification.
2.	Revision number (FDIO locations only).
2A.	Strip request originator. (At FDIO locations this indicates the sector or position that requested a strip be printed.)
3.	Number of aircraft if more than one, heavy aircraft indicator "H/" if appropriate, type of aircraft, and aircraft equipment suffix.
4.	Computer identification number if required.
5.	Secondary radar (beacon) code assigned.
6.	Coordination fix.
7.	Overflight coordination indicator (FDIO locations only).
NOTE–	*The overflight coordination indicator identifies the facility to which flight data has been forwarded.*
8.	Estimated time of arrival at the coordination fix.
8A.	**OPTIONAL USE.**

Block	Information Recorded
8B.	**OPTIONAL USE,** when voice recorders are operational; **REQUIRED USE,** when the voice recorders are not operating and strips are being used at the facility. This space is used to record reported RA events when the voice recorders are not operational and strips are being used at the facility. The letters RA followed by a climb or descent arrow (if the climb or descent action is reported) and the time (hhmm) the event is reported.
9.	Altitude and route of flight through the terminal area.
NOTE–	*Altitude information may be written in thousands of feet provided the procedure is authorized by the facility manager, and is defined in a facility directive, i.e., FL 230 as 23, 5,000 feet as 5, and 2,800 as 2.8.*
9A.	**OPTIONAL USE.**
9B.	**OPTIONAL USE.**
9C.	**OPTIONAL USE.**
10–18.	Enter data as specified by a facility directive.

NOTE–
National standardization of items (10 through 18) is not practical because of regional and local variations in operating methods; e.g., single fix, multiple fix, radar, tower en route control, etc.

Appendix 6: Internet Resources

The following are the specific URLs for the websites referenced within the chapters. You'll find these sites very useful in researching your ATC options.

Chapter 1 Internet links

Wikipedia.com—Air Traffic Controller
    http://en.wikipedia.org/wiki/Air_traffic_controller

How Stuff Works—Air Traffic Control
    http://travel.howstuffworks.com/air-traffic-control.htm

Work Roles
    http://www.faa.gov/careers/employment/atc.htm

Occupational Outlook Handbook, 2004-05
    http://stats.bls.gov/oco/pdf/ocos108.pdf

Pay and benefits
    http://www.nw.faa.gov/ats/zdvartcc/careers.htm
    http://atpayplan.natca.net/

FAA
    http://www.faa.gov

FAA ATC staffing
    http://www.faa.gov/airports_airtraffic/air_traffic/controller_staffing/

Denver Center
        http://www.nw.faa.gov/ats/zdartcc/careers.htm

Chapter 2 Internet Links and Sources

"ATCCTI.com:– CTI information website
    http://www.atccti.com/index.html

FAA Staffing Plan
    http://www.faa.gov/airports_airtraffic/air_traffic/controller_staffing/

FAA ATC qualifications
    http://www.faa.gov/careers/employment/atc-quals.htm

Williams. T. P. (2005, May). 2005-2014 Air Traffic Controller Workforce Plan En Route.
    Briefing to the National Hispanic Coalition of Federal Aviation Employees (NHCFAE).

FAA HR Policies
    http://faa.gov/ahr/policy/

FAA Careers CTI
    http://www.faa.gov/careers/employment/at-cti.htm
    http://faa.gov/ahr/policy/hrpm/emp/emp-1-20.cfm
    http://faa.gov/ahr/policy/hrpm/emp/emp-1-13.cfm

FAAH 3120.4
    http://www.faa.gov/atpubs/TRN/TRN.pdf

AvWeb
    http://www.avweb.com/news/columns/182651-1.html

FAAH 7110.65
   http://www.faa.gov/ATpubs/ATC/

NASA ATC Tutorial
   http://virtualskies.arc.nasa.gov/

ZTL Live audio
   http://atcmonitor.com/

Collegiate Training Iniative Schools (state where school is located)
http://www.uaa.alaska.edu/ (Alaska)
http://www.mtsac.edu/ (California)
http://www.db.erau.edu/ (Florida)
http://www.mdcc.edu/ (Florida)
http://www.purdue.edu/ (Indiana)
http://minneapolis.edu/airTraffic/ (Minnesota)
http://www.dwc.edu/ (New Hampshire)
http://www.vaughn.edu/ (New York)
http://www.dowling.edu/ (New York)
http://www.und.nodak.edu/ (North Dakota)
http://www.ccbc.edu/ (Pennsylvania, also has CTO training)
http://bc.inter.edu/ (Puerto Rico)
http://www.mtsu.edu/ (Tennessee)
http://www.hamptonu.edu (Virginia)

FORM NUMBER	FORM NAME
OF-612	Application for Employment
OF-306	Declaration for Federal Employment
SF-15	Application for 10-Point Veteran Preference
SF-181	Race and National Origin Identification
FAA-3330-473	2181/1825 Supplemental Qualifications Statement
FAA-52569	Retired Military Air Traffic Control Specialist
ACForm3300-70	VRA-GFP
Standard Form 86	Questionnaire for National Security Positions

Chapter 3 Internet links and sources

Heil, M. and Agnew, B. (2000, April) as noted. The Effects of previous computer experience on air traffic-selection and training (AT-SAT) test performance DOT/FAA/AM-00/12. Civil Aeromedical Federal Aviation Oklahoma City, OK. (http://www.hf.faa.gov/docs/508/docs/cami/00_12.pdf)

Morath, R., Cronin, B. & Heil, M. (2004). Dynamic and interactive computerized tests of cognitive, perceptual, and psychomotor abilities: A comparison of a computerized test battery with the ASVAB in predicting training and job performance among airmen and sailors. IPMAAC Conference presentation. (http://www.ipmaac.org/conf/04/morath.pdf

Federal Aviation Administration (FAA). (no date). Pamphlet: Air traffic-selection and training (AT-SAT) for the next generation of air traffic control.

GAO FAA Needs to Better Prepare for Impending Wave of Controller Attrition http://www.gao.gov/new.items/d02591.pdf

FAA Staffing http://www.faa.gov/airports_airtraffic/air_traffic/controller_staffing/

FAA testing policy http://www.faa.gov/ahr/policy/hrpm/bulletin/bullet8.cfm

Professional Women Controller News http://www.pwcinc.org/docs/news/FAArecruitmentFAQ_0805.pdf

FAA ATO presentation May 7, 2005. 2005-2014 Air Traffic Controller Workforce Plan En Route.

ATCSimulator2 http://www.atcsimulator.com/

Air Traffic Simulation Project at http://www.cs.bham.ac.uk/~mzk/projects/webATC/

GRE Test Preparation Practice Exercises: http://www.syvum.com/gre/

Miller Analogy Test Online Course: http://www.testpreview.com/mat_practice.htm

Abstract Reasoning Symbols: http://www.kent.ac.uk/careers/tests/spatialtest.htm

Web addresses for the document in Appendix 3, FAA FG-2152-1:
http://www.faa.gov/AHR/POLICY/hrpm/bulletin/pb33pd.doc
http://www.faa.gov/ahr/policy/hrpm/bulletin/pb33stan.doc
http://www.faa.gov/AHR/policy/hrpm/bulletin/bullet33.cfm

Glossary

Pilot/Controller Glossary

This glossary was compiled to promote a common understanding of the terms used in the Air Traffic Control system. It includes those terms which are intended for pilot/controller communications. The definitions are primarily defined in an operational sense applicable to both users and operators of the National Airspace System. Use of the Glossary will preclude any misunderstandings concerning the system's design, function, and purpose.

A

AAI. (See ARRIVAL AIRCRAFT INTERVAL.)

AAR. (See AIRPORT ARRIVAL RATE.)

ABBREVIATED IFR FLIGHT PLANS. An authorization by ATC requiring pilots to submit only that information needed for the purpose of ATC. It includes only a small portion of the usual IFR flight plan information. In certain instances, this may be only aircraft identification, location, and pilot request. Other information may be requested if needed by ATC for separation/control purposes. It is frequently used by aircraft which are airborne and desire an instrument approach or by aircraft which are on the ground and desire a climb to VFR-on-top. (See VFR-ON-TOP.) (Refer to AIM.)

ABEAM. An aircraft is "abeam" a fix, point, or object when that fix, point, or object is approximately 90 degrees to the right or left of the aircraft track. Abeam indicates a general position rather than a precise point.

ABORT. To terminate a preplanned aircraft maneuver; e.g., an aborted takeoff.

ACC [ICAO]. (See ICAO term AREA CONTROL CENTER.)

ACCELERATE-STOP DISTANCE AVAILABLE. The runway plus stopway length declared available and suitable for the acceleration and deceleration of an airplane aborting a takeoff.

ACCELERATE-STOP DISTANCE AVAILABLE [ICAO]. The length of the take-off run available plus the length of the stopway if provided.

ACDO. (See AIR CARRIER DISTRICT OFFICE.)

ACKNOWLEDGE. Let me know that you have received my message. (See ICAO term ACKNOWLEDGE.)

ACKNOWLEDGE [ICAO]. Let me know that you have received and understood this message.

ACL. (See AIRCRAFT LIST.)

ACLS. (See AUTOMATIC CARRIER LANDING SYSTEM.)

ACLT. (See ACTUAL CALCULATED LANDING TIME.)

ACROBATIC FLIGHT. An intentional maneuver involving an abrupt change in an aircraft's attitude, an abnormal attitude, or abnormal acceleration not necessary for normal flight. (See ICAO term ACROBATIC FLIGHT.) (Refer to 14 CFR Part 91.)

ACROBATIC FLIGHT [ICAO]. Maneuvers intentionally performed by an aircraft involving an abrupt change in its attitude, an abnormal attitude, or an abnormal variation in speed.

ACTIVE RUNWAY. (See RUNWAY IN USE/ACTIVE RUNWAY/DUTY RUNWAY.)

ACTUAL CALCULATED LANDING TIME. ACLT is a flight's frozen calculated landing time. An actual time determined at freeze calculated landing time (FCLT) or meter list display interval (MLDI) for the adapted vertex for each arrival aircraft based upon runway configuration, airport acceptance rate, airport arrival delay period, and other metered arrival aircraft. This time is either the vertex time of arrival (VTA) of the aircraft or the tentative calculated landing time (TCLT)/ACLT of the previous aircraft plus the arrival aircraft interval (AAI), whichever is later. This time will not be updated in response to the aircraft's progress.

ACTUAL NAVIGATION PERFORMANCE (ANP). (See REQUIRED NAVIGATION PERFORMANCE.)

ADDITIONAL SERVICES. Advisory information provided by ATC which includes but is not limited to the following:
a. Traffic advisories.
b. Vectors, when requested by the pilot, to assist aircraft receiving traffic advisories to avoid observed traffic.
c. Altitude deviation information of 300 feet or more from an assigned altitude as observed on a verified (reading correctly) automatic altitude readout (Mode C).
d. Advisories that traffic is no longer a factor.
e. Weather and chaff information.
f. Weather assistance.
g. Bird activity information.
h. Holding pattern surveillance. Additional services are provided to the extent possible contingent only upon the controller's capability to fit them into the performance of higher priority duties and on the basis of limitations of the radar, volume of traffic, frequency congestion, and controller workload. The controller has complete discretion for determining if he/she is able to provide or continue to provide a service in a particular case. The controller's reason not to provide or continue to provide a service in a particular case is not subject to question by the pilot and need not be made known to him/her.

(See TRAFFIC ADVISORIES.) (Refer to AIM.)

ADF. (See AUTOMATIC DIRECTION FINDER.)

ADIZ. (See AIR DEFENSE IDENTIFICATION ZONE.)

ADLY. (See ARRIVAL DELAY.)

ADMINISTRATOR. The Federal Aviation Administrator or any person to whom he/she has delegated his/her authority in the matter concerned.

ADR. (See AIRPORT DEPARTURE RATE.)

ADS [ICAO]. (See ICAO term AUTOMATIC DEPENDENT SURVEILLANCE.)

ADS-B. (See AUTOMATIC DEPENDENT SURVEILLANCE–BROADCAST.)

ADS-C. (See AUTOMATIC DEPENDENT SURVEILLANCE–CONTRACT.)

ADVISE INTENTIONS. Tell me what you plan to do.

ADVISORY. Advice and information provided to assist pilots in the safe conduct of flight and aircraft movement. (See ADVISORY SERVICE.)

ADVISORY FREQUENCY. The appropriate frequency to be used for Airport Advisory Service. (See LOCAL AIRPORT ADVISORY.) (See UNICOM.) (Refer to ADVISORY CIRCULAR NO. 90-42.) (Refer to AIM.)

ADVISORY SERVICE. Advice and information provided by a facility to assist pilots in the safe conduct of flight and aircraft movement. (See ADDITIONAL SERVICES.) (See EN ROUTE FLIGHT ADVISORY SERVICE.) (See LOCAL AIRPORT ADVISORY.) (See RADAR ADVISORY.) (See SAFETY ALERT.) (See TRAFFIC ADVISORIES.) (Refer to AIM.)

AERIAL REFUELING. A procedure used by the military to transfer fuel from one aircraft to another during flight. (Refer to VFR/IFR Wall Planning Charts.)

AERODROME. A defined area on land or water (including any buildings, installations and equipment) intended to be used either wholly or in part for the arrival, departure, and movement of aircraft.

AERODROME BEACON [ICAO]. Aeronautical beacon used to indicate the location of an aerodrome from the air.

AERODROME CONTROL SERVICE [ICAO]. Air traffic control service for aerodrome traffic.

AERODROME CONTROL TOWER [ICAO]. A unit established to provide air traffic control service to aerodrome traffic.

AERODROME ELEVATION [ICAO]. The elevation of the highest point of the landing area.

AERODROME TRAFFIC CIRCUIT [ICAO]. The specified path to be flown by aircraft operating in the vicinity of an aerodrome.

AERONAUTICAL BEACON. A visual NAVAID displaying flashes of white and/or colored light to indicate the location of an airport, a heliport, a landmark, a certain point of a Federal airway in mountainous terrain, or an obstruction. (See AIRPORT ROTATING BEACON.) (Refer to AIM.)

AERONAUTICAL CHART. A map used in air navigation containing all or part of the following: topographic features, hazards and obstructions, navigation aids, navigation routes, designated airspace, and airports. Commonly used aeronautical charts are:

a. Sectional Aeronautical Charts (1:500,000). Designed for visual navigation of slow or medium speed aircraft. Topographic information on these charts features the portrayal of relief and a judicious selection of visual check points for VFR flight. Aeronautical information includes visual and radio aids to navigation, airports, controlled airspace, restricted areas, obstructions, and related data.

b. VFR Terminal Area Charts (1:250,000). Depict Class B airspace which provides for the control or segregation of all the aircraft within Class B airspace. The chart depicts topographic information and aeronautical information which includes visual and radio aids to navigation, airports, controlled airspace, restricted areas, obstructions, and related data.

c. World Aeronautical Charts (WAC) (1:1,000,000). Provide a standard series of aeronautical charts covering land areas of the world at a size and scale convenient for navigation by moderate speed aircraft. Topographic information includes cities and towns, principal roads, railroads, distinctive landmarks, drainage, and relief. Aeronautical information includes visual and radio aids to navigation, airports, airways, restricted areas, obstructions, and other pertinent data.

d. En Route Low Altitude Charts. Provide aeronautical information for en route instrument navigation (IFR) in the low altitude stratum. Information includes the portrayal of airways, limits of controlled airspace, position identification and frequencies of radio aids, selected airports, minimum en route and minimum obstruction clearance altitudes, airway distances, reporting points, restricted areas, and related data. Area charts, which are a part of this series, furnish terminal data at a larger scale in congested areas.

e. En Route High Altitude Charts. Provide aeronautical information for en route instrument navigation (IFR) in the high altitude stratum. Information includes the portrayal of jet routes, identification and frequencies of radio aids, selected airports, distances, time zones, special use airspace, and related information.

f. Instrument Approach Procedures (IAP) Charts. Portray the aeronautical data which is required to execute an instrument approach to an airport. These charts depict the procedures, including all related data, and the airport diagram. Each procedure is designated for use with a specific type of electronic navigation system including NDB, TACAN, VOR, ILS/MLS, and RNAV. These charts are identified by the type of navigational aid(s) which provide final approach guidance.

g. Instrument Departure Procedure (DP) Charts. Designed to expedite clearance delivery and to facilitate transition between takeoff and en route operations. Each DP is presented as a separate chart and may serve a single airport or more than one airport in a given geographical location.

h. Standard Terminal Arrival (STAR) Charts. Designed to expedite air traffic control arrival procedures and to facilitate transition between en route and instrument approach operations. Each STAR procedure is presented as a separate chart and may serve a single airport or more than one airport in a given geographical location.

i. Airport Taxi Charts. Designed to expedite the efficient and safe flow of ground traffic at an airport. These charts are identified by the official airport name; e.g., Ronald Reagan Washington National Airport.

(See ICAO term AERONAUTICAL CHART.)

AERONAUTICAL CHART [ICAO]. A representation of a portion of the earth, its culture and relief, specifically designated to meet the requirements of air navigation.

AERONAUTICAL INFORMATION MANUAL (AIM). A primary FAA publication whose purpose is to instruct airmen about operating in the National Airspace System of the U.S. It provides basic flight information, ATC Procedures and general instructional information concerning health, medical facts, factors affecting flight safety, accident and hazard reporting, and types of aeronautical charts and their use.

AERONAUTICAL INFORMATION PUBLICATION (AIP) [ICAO]. A publication issued by or with the authority of a State and containing aeronautical information of a lasting character essential to air navigation.

A/FD. (See AIRPORT/FACILITY DIRECTORY.)

AFFIRMATIVE. Yes.

AIM. (See AERONAUTICAL INFORMATION MANUAL.)

AIP [ICAO]. (See ICAO term AERONAUTICAL INFORMATION PUBLICATION.)

AIR CARRIER DISTRICT OFFICE. An FAA field office serving an assigned geographical area, staffed with Flight Standards personnel serving the aviation industry and the general public on matters related to the certification and operation of scheduled air carriers and other large aircraft operations.

AIR DEFENSE EMERGENCY. A military emergency condition declared by a designated authority. This condition exists when an attack upon the continental U.S., Alaska, Canada, or U.S. installations in Greenland by hostile aircraft or missiles is considered probable, is imminent, or is taking place. (Refer to AIM.)

AIR DEFENSE IDENTIFICATION ZONE (ADIZ). The area of airspace over land or water, extending upward from the surface, within which the ready identification, the location, and the control of aircraft are required in the interest of national security.
  a. Domestic Air Defense Identification Zone. An ADIZ within the United States along an international boundary of the United States.
  b. Coastal Air Defense Identification Zone. An ADIZ over the coastal waters of the United States.
  c. Distant Early Warning Identification Zone (DEWIZ). An ADIZ over the coastal waters of the State of Alaska.
  d. Land-Based Air Defense Identification Zone. An ADIZ over U.S. metropolitan areas, which is activated and deactivated as needed, with dimensions, activation dates and other relevant information disseminated via NOTAM.

Note: ADIZ locations and operating and flight plan requirements for civil aircraft operations are specified in 14 CFR Part 99.
(Refer to AIM.)

AIR NAVIGATION FACILITY. Any facility used in, available for use in, or designed for use in, aid of air navigation, including landing areas, lights, any apparatus or equipment for disseminating weather information, for signaling, for radio-directional finding, or for radio or other electrical communication, and any other structure or mechanism having a similar purpose for guiding or controlling flight in the air or the landing and takeoff of aircraft. (See NAVIGATIONAL AID.)

AIR ROUTE SURVEILLANCE RADAR. Air route traffic control center (ARTCC) radar used primarily to detect and display an aircraft's position while en route between terminal areas. The ARSR enables controllers to provide radar air traffic control service when aircraft are within the ARSR coverage. In some instances, ARSR may enable an ARTCC to provide terminal radar services similar to but usually more limited than those provided by a radar approach control.

AIR ROUTE TRAFFIC CONTROL CENTER. A facility established to provide air traffic control service to aircraft operating on IFR flight plans within controlled airspace and principally during the en route phase of flight. When equipment capabilities and controller workload permit, certain advisory/assistance services may be provided to VFR aircraft. (See EN ROUTE AIR TRAFFIC CONTROL SERVICES.) (See NAS STAGE A.) (Refer to AIM.)

AIR TAXI. Used to describe a helicopter/VTOL aircraft movement conducted above the surface but normally not above 100 feet AGL. The aircraft may proceed either via hover taxi or flight at speeds more than 20 knots. The pilot is solely responsible for selecting a safe airspeed/altitude for the operation being conducted. (See HOVER TAXI.) (Refer to AIM.)

AIR TRAFFIC. Aircraft operating in the air or on an airport surface, exclusive of loading ramps and parking areas. (See ICAO term AIR TRAFFIC.)

AIR TRAFFIC [ICAO]. All aircraft in flight or operating on the maneuvering area of an aerodrome.

AIR TRAFFIC CLEARANCE. An authorization by air traffic control for the purpose of preventing collision between known aircraft, for an aircraft to proceed under specified traffic conditions within controlled airspace. The pilot-in-command of an aircraft may not deviate from the provisions of a visual flight rules (VFR) or instrument flight rules (IFR) air traffic clearance except in an emergency or unless an amended clearance has been obtained. Additionally, the pilot may request a different clearance from that which has been issued by air traffic control (ATC) if information available to the pilot makes another course of action more practicable or if aircraft equipment limitations or company procedures forbid compliance with the clearance issued. Pilots may also request clarification or amendment, as appropriate, any time a clearance is not fully understood, or considered unacceptable because of safety of flight. Controllers should, in such instances and to the extent of operational practicality and safety, honor the pilot's request. 14 CFR Part 91.3(a) states: "The pilot in command of an aircraft is directly responsible for, and is the final authority as to, the operation of that aircraft." THE PILOT IS RESPONSIBLE TO REQUEST AN AMENDED CLEARANCE if ATC issues a clearance that would cause a pilot to deviate from a rule or regulation, or in the pilot's opinion, would place the aircraft in jeopardy. (See ATC INSTRUCTIONS.) (See ICAO term AIR TRAFFIC CONTROL CLEARANCE.)

AIR TRAFFIC CONTROL. A service operated by appropriate authority to promote the safe, orderly and expeditious flow of air traffic. (See ICAO term AIR TRAFFIC CONTROL SERVICE.)

AIR TRAFFIC CONTROL CLEARANCE [ICAO]. Authorization for an aircraft to proceed under conditions specified by an air traffic control unit.

Note 1: For convenience, the term air traffic control clearance is frequently abbreviated to clearance when used in appropriate contexts.

Note 2: The abbreviated term clearance may be prefixed by the words taxi, takeoff, departure, en route, approach or landing to indicate the particular portion of flight to which the air traffic control clearance relates.

AIR TRAFFIC CONTROL SERVICE. (See AIR TRAFFIC CONTROL.)

AIR TRAFFIC CONTROL SERVICE [ICAO]. A service provided for the purpose of:
a. Preventing collisions:
  1. Between aircraft; and
  2. On the maneuvering area between aircraft and obstructions.
b. Expediting and maintaining an orderly flow of air traffic.

AIR TRAFFIC CONTROL SPECIALIST. A person authorized to provide air traffic control service. (See AIR TRAFFIC CONTROL.) (See FLIGHT SERVICE STATION.) (See ICAO term CONTROLLER.)

AIR TRAFFIC CONTROL SYSTEM COMMAND CENTER. An Air Traffic Tactical Operations facility responsible for monitoring and managing the flow of air traffic throughout the NAS, producing a safe, orderly, and expeditious flow of traffic while minimizing delays. The following functions are located at the ATCSCC:
a. Central Altitude Reservation Function (CARF). Responsible for coordinating, planning, and approving special user requirements under the Altitude Reservation (ALTRV) concept. (See ALTITUDE RESERVATION)
b. Airport Reservation Office (ARO). Responsible for approving IFR flights at designated high density traffic airports (John F. Kennedy, LaGuardia, and Ronald Reagan Washington National) during specified hours. (Refer to 14 CFR Part 93.) (Refer to AIRPORT/FACILITY DIRECTORY.)
c. U.S. Notice to Airmen (NOTAM) Office. Responsible for collecting, maintaining, and distributing NOTAMs for the U.S. civilian and military, as well as international aviation communities. (See NOTICE TO AIRMEN)
d. Weather Unit. Monitor all aspects of weather for the U.S. that might affect aviation including cloud cover, visibility, winds, precipitation, thunderstorms, icing, turbulence, and more. Provide forecasts based on observations and on discussions with meteorologists from various National Weather Service offices, FAA facilities, airlines, and private weather services.

AIR TRAFFIC SERVICE. A generic term meaning:
a. Flight Information Service.
b. Alerting Service.
c. Air Traffic Advisory Service.
d. Air Traffic Control Service:
  1. Area Control Service,
  2. Approach Control Service, or
  3. Airport Control Service.

AIR TRAFFIC SERVICE (ATS) ROUTES. The term "ATS route" is a generic term that includes "VOR Federal airways," "colored Federal airways," "alternate airways," "jet routes," "Military Training Routes," "named routes," and "RNAV routes." The term "ATS route" does not replace these more familiar route names, but serves only as an overall title when listing the types of routes that comprise the United States route structure.

AIRBORNE DELAY. Amount of delay to be encountered in airborne holding.

AIRCRAFT. Device(s) that are used or intended to be used for flight in the air, and when used in air traffic control terminology, may include the flight crew. (See ICAO term AIRCRAFT.)

AIRCRAFT [ICAO]. Any machine that can derive support in the atmosphere from the reactions of the air other than the reactions of the air against the earth's surface.

AIRCRAFT APPROACH CATEGORY. A grouping of aircraft based on a speed of 1.3 times the stall speed in the landing configuration at maximum gross landing weight. An aircraft must fit in only one category. If it is necessary to maneuver at speeds in excess of the upper limit of a speed range for a category, the minimums for the category for that speed must be used. For example, an aircraft which falls in Category A, but is circling to land at a speed in excess of 91 knots, must use the approach Category B minimums when circling to land. The categories are as follows:

a. Category A. Speed less than 91 knots.

b. Category B. Speed 91 knots or more but less than 121 knots.

c. Category C. Speed 121 knots or more but less than 141 knots.

d. Category D. Speed 141 knots or more but less than 166 knots.

e. Category E. Speed 166 knots or more.

(Refer to 14 CFR Part 97.)

AIRCRAFT CLASSES. For the purposes of Wake Turbulence Separation Minima, ATC classifies aircraft as Heavy, Large, and Small as follows:

a. Heavy. Aircraft capable of takeoff weights of more than 255,000 pounds whether or not they are operating at this weight during a particular phase of flight.

b. Large. Aircraft of more than 41,000 pounds, maximum certificated takeoff weight, up to 255,000 pounds.

c. Small. Aircraft of 41,000 pounds or less maximum certificated takeoff weight.

(Refer to AIM.)

AIRCRAFT CONFLICT. Predicted conflict, within URET, of two aircraft, or between aircraft and airspace. A Red alert is used for conflicts when the predicted minimum separation is 5 nautical miles or less. A Yellow alert is used when the predicted minimum separation is between 5 and approximately 12 nautical miles. A Blue alert is used for conflicts between an aircraft and predefined airspace. (See USER REQUEST EVALUATION TOOL.)

AIRCRAFT LIST (ACL). A view available with URET that lists aircraft currently in or predicted to be in a particular sector's airspace. The view contains textual flight data information in line format and may be sorted into various orders based on the specific needs of the sector team. (See USER REQUEST EVALUATION TOOL.)

AIRCRAFT SURGE LAUNCH AND RECOVERY. Procedures used at USAF bases to provide increased launch and recovery rates in instrument flight rules conditions. ASLAR is based on:

a. Reduced separation between aircraft which is based on time or distance. Standard arrival separation

applies between participants including multiple flights until the DRAG point. The DRAG point is a published location on an ASLAR approach where aircraft landing second in a formation slows to a predetermined airspeed. The DRAG point is the reference point at which MARSA applies as expanding elements effect separation within a flight or between subsequent participating flights.

b. ASLAR procedures shall be covered in a Letter of Agreement between the responsible USAF military ATC facility and the concerned Federal Aviation Administration facility. Initial Approach Fix spacing requirements are normally addressed as a minimum.

AIRMEN's METEOROLOGICAL INFORMATION. (See AIRMET.)

AIRMET. In-flight weather advisories issued only to amend the area forecast concerning weather phenomena which are of operational interest to all aircraft and potentially hazardous to aircraft having limited capability because of lack of equipment, instrumentation, or pilot qualifications. AIRMETs concern weather of less severity than that covered by SIGMETs or Convective SIGMETs. AIRMETs cover moderate icing, moderate turbulence, sustained winds of 30 knots or more at the surface, widespread areas of ceilings less than 1,000 feet and/or visibility less than 3 miles, and extensive mountain obscurement. (See AWW.) (See CONVECTIVE SIGMET.) (See CWA.) (See SIGMET.) (Refer to AIM.)

AIRPORT. An area on land or water that is used or intended to be used for the landing and takeoff of aircraft and includes its buildings and facilities, if any.

AIRPORT ADVISORY AREA. The area within ten miles of an airport without a control tower or where the tower is not in operation, and on which a Flight Service Station is located. (See LOCAL AIRPORT ADVISORY.) (Refer to AIM.)

AIRPORT ARRIVAL RATE (AAR). A dynamic input parameter specifying the number of arriving aircraft which an airport or airspace can accept from the ARTCC per hour. The AAR is used to calculate the desired interval between successive arrival aircraft.

AIRPORT DEPARTURE RATE (ADR). A dynamic parameter specifying the number of aircraft which can depart an airport and the airspace can accept per hour.

AIRPORT ELEVATION. The highest point of an airport's usable runways measured in feet from mean sea level. (See TOUCHDOWN ZONE ELEVATION.) (See ICAO term AERODROME ELEVATION.)

AIRPORT/FACILITY DIRECTORY. A publication designed primarily as a pilot's operational manual containing all airports, seaplane bases, and heliports open to the public including communications data, navigational facilities, and certain special notices and procedures. This publication is issued in seven volumes according to geographical area.

AIRPORT LIGHTING. Various lighting aids that may be installed on an airport. Types of airport lighting include:

a. Approach Light System (ALS). An airport lighting facility which provides visual guidance to landing aircraft by radiating light beams in a directional pattern by which the pilot aligns the aircraft with the extended centerline of the runway on his/her final approach for landing. Condenser-Discharge Sequential Flashing Lights/Sequenced Flashing Lights may be installed in conjunction with the ALS at some airports. Types of Approach Light Systems are:

1. ALSF-1. Approach Light System with Sequenced Flashing Lights in ILS Cat I configuration.
2. ALSF-2. Approach Light System with Sequenced Flashing Lights in ILS Cat-II configuration. The ALSF-2 may operate as an SSALR when weather conditions permit.
3. SSALF. Simplified Short Approach Light System with Sequenced Flashing Lights.
4. SSALR. Simplified Short Approach Light System with Runway Alignment Indicator Lights.
5. MALSF. Medium Intensity Approach Light System with Sequenced Flashing Lights.
6. MALSR. Medium Intensity Approach Light System with Runway Alignment Indicator Lights.
7. LDIN. Lead-in-light system. Consists of one or more series of flashing lights installed at or near ground level that provides positive visual guidance along an approach path, either curving or straight, where special problems exist with hazardous terrain, obstructions, or noise abatement procedures.
8. RAIL. Runway Alignment Indicator Lights. Sequenced Flashing Lights which are installed only in combination with other light systems.
9. ODALS. Omnidirectional Approach Lighting System consists of seven omnidirectional flashing lights located in the approach area of a non-precision runway. Five lights are located on the runway centerline extended with the first light located 300 feet from the threshold and extending at equal intervals up to 1,500 feet from the threshold. The other two lights are located, one on each side of the runway threshold, at a lateral distance of 40 feet from the runway edge, or 75 feet from the runway edge when installed on a runway equipped with a VASI. (Refer to FAAO 6850.2, VISUAL GUIDANCE LIGHTING SYSTEMS.)

b. Runway Lights/Runway Edge Lights—Lights having a prescribed angle of emission used to define the lateral limits of a runway. Runway lights are uniformly spaced at intervals of approximately 200 feet, and the intensity may be controlled or preset.

c. Touchdown Zone Lighting. Two rows of transverse light bars located symmetrically about the runway centerline normally at 100 foot intervals. The basic system extends 3,000 feet along the runway.

d. Runway Centerline Lighting. Flush centerline lights spaced at 50-foot intervals beginning 75 feet from the landing threshold and extending to within 75 feet of the opposite end of the runway.

e. Threshold Lights—Fixed green lights arranged symmetrically left and right of the runway centerline, identifying the runway threshold.

f. Runway End Identifier Lights (REIL). Two synchronized flashing lights, one on each side of the runway threshold, which provide rapid and positive identification of the approach end of a particular runway.

g. Visual Approach Slope Indicator (VASI). An airport lighting facility providing vertical visual approach slope guidance to aircraft during approach to landing by radiating a directional pattern of high intensity red and white focused light beams which indicate to the pilot that he/she is "on path" if he/she sees red/white, "above path" if white/white, and "below path" if red/red. Some airports serving large aircraft have three-bar VASIs which provide two visual glide paths to the same runway.

h. Precision Approach Path Indicator (PAPI). An airport lighting facility, similar to VASI, providing vertical approach slope guidance to aircraft during approach to landing. PAPIs consist of a single row of either two or four lights, normally installed on the left side of the runway, and have an effective visual range of about 5 miles during the day and up to 20 miles at night. PAPIs radiate a directional pattern of high intensity red and white focused light beams which indicate that the pilot is "on path" if the pilot sees an equal number of white lights and red lights, with white to the left of the red; "above path" if the pilot sees more white than red lights; and "below path" if the pilot sees more red than white lights.

i. Boundary Lights. Lights defining the perimeter of an airport or landing area.

(Refer to AIM.)

AIRPORT MARKING AIDS. Markings used on runway and taxiway surfaces to identify a specific runway, a runway threshold, a centerline, a hold line, etc. A runway should be marked in accordance with its present usage such as:

a. Visual.

b. Nonprecision instrument.

c. Precision instrument.

(Refer to AIM.)

AIRPORT MOVEMENT AREA SAFETY SYSTEM (AMASS). A software enhancement to ASDE radar which provides logic predicting the path of aircraft landing and/or departing, and aircraft and/or vehicular movements on runways. Visual and aural alarms are activated when logic projects a potential collision.

AIRPORT REFERENCE POINT (ARP). The approximate geometric center of all usable runway surfaces.

AIRPORT RESERVATION OFFICE. Office responsible for monitoring the operation of the high density rule. Receives and processes requests for IFR operations at high density traffic airports.

AIRPORT ROTATING BEACON. A visual NAVAID operated at many airports. At civil airports, alternating white and green flashes indicate the location of the airport. At military airports, the beacons flash alternately white and green, but are differentiated from civil beacons by dualpeaked (two quick) white flashes between the green flashes. (See INSTRUMENT FLIGHT RULES.) (See SPECIAL VFR OPERATIONS.) (See ICAO term AERODROME BEACON.) (Refer to AIM.)

AIRPORT SURFACE DETECTION EQUIPMENT. Radar equipment specifically designed to detect all principal features on the surface of an airport, including aircraft and vehicular traffic, and to present the entire image on a radar indicator console in the control tower. Used to augment visual observation by tower personnel of aircraft and/or vehicular movements on runways and taxiways.

AIRPORT SURVEILLANCE RADAR. Approach control radar used to detect and display an aircraft's position in the terminal area. ASR provides range and azimuth information but does not provide elevation data. Coverage of the ASR can extend up to 60 miles.

AIRPORT TAXI CHARTS. (See AERONAUTICAL CHART.)

AIRPORT TRAFFIC CONTROL SERVICE. A service provided by a control tower for aircraft operating on the movement area and in the vicinity of an airport. (See MOVEMENT AREA.) (See TOWER.) (See ICAO term AERODROME CONTROL SERVICE.)

AIRPORT TRAFFIC CONTROL TOWER. (See TOWER.)

AIRSPACE CONFLICT. Predicted conflict of an aircraft and active Special Activity Airspace (SAA).

AIRSPACE HIERARCHY. Within the airspace classes, there is a hierarchy and, in the event of an overlap of airspace: Class A preempts Class B, Class B preempts Class C, Class C preempts Class D, Class D preempts Class E, and Class E preempts Class G.

AIRSPEED. The speed of an aircraft relative to its surrounding air mass. The unqualified term "airspeed" means one of the following:

a. Indicated Airspeed. The speed shown on the aircraft airspeed indicator. This is the speed used in pilot/controller communications under the general term "airspeed." (Refer to 14 CFR Part 1.)

b. True Airspeed. The airspeed of an aircraft relative to undisturbed air. Used primarily in flight planning and en route portion of flight. When used in pilot/controller communications, it is referred to as "true airspeed" and not shortened to "airspeed."

AIRSTART. The starting of an aircraft engine while the aircraft is airborne, preceded by engine shutdown during training flights or by actual engine failure.

AIRWAY. A Class E airspace area established in the form of a corridor, the centerline of which is defined by radio navigational aids. (See FEDERAL AIRWAYS.) (See ICAO term AIRWAY.) (Refer to 14 CFR Part 71.) (Refer to AIM.)

AIRWAY [ICAO]. A control area or portion thereof established in the form of corridor equipped with radio navigational aids.

AIRWAY BEACON. Used to mark airway segments in remote mountain areas. The light flashes Morse Code to identify the beacon site. (Refer to AIM.)

AIT. (See AUTOMATED INFORMATION TRANSFER.)

ALERFA (Alert Phase) [ICAO]. A situation wherein apprehension exists as to the safety of an aircraft and its occupants.

ALERT. A notification to a position that there is an aircraft-to-aircraft or aircraft-to-airspace conflict, as detected by Automated Problem Detection (APD).

ALERT AREA. (See SPECIAL USE AIRSPACE.)

ALERT NOTICE. A request originated by a flight service station (FSS) or an air route traffic control center (ARTCC) for an extensive communication search for overdue, unreported, or missing aircraft.

ALERTING SERVICE. A service provided to notify appropriate organizations regarding aircraft in need of search and rescue aid and assist such organizations as required.

ALNOT. (See ALERT NOTICE.)

ALONG TRACK DISTANCE (LTD). The distance measured from a point-in-space by systems using area navigation reference capabilities that are not subject to slant range errors.

ALPHANUMERIC DISPLAY. Letters and numerals used to show identification, altitude, beacon code, and other information concerning a target on a radar display. (See AUTOMATED RADAR TERMINAL SYSTEMS.) (See NAS STAGE A.)

ALTERNATE AERODROME [ICAO]. An aerodrome to which an aircraft may proceed when it becomes either impossible or inadvisable to proceed to or to land at the aerodrome of intended landing.

Note: The aerodrome from which a flight departs may also be an en-route or a destination alternate aerodrome for the flight.

ALTERNATE AIRPORT. An airport at which an aircraft may land if a landing at the intended airport becomes inadvisable. (See ICAO term ALTERNATE AERODROME.)

ALTIMETER SETTING. The barometric pressure reading used to adjust a pressure altimeter for variations in existing atmospheric pressure or to the standard altimeter setting (29.92). (Refer to 14 CFR Part 91.) (Refer to AIM.)

ALTITUDE. The height of a level, point, or object measured in feet Above Ground Level (AGL) or from Mean Sea Level (MSL). (See FLIGHT LEVEL.)
a. MSL Altitude. Altitude expressed in feet measured from mean sea level.
b. AGL Altitude. Altitude expressed in feet measured above ground level.
c. Indicated Altitude. The altitude as shown by an altimeter. On a pressure or barometric altimeter it is altitude as shown uncorrected for instrument error and uncompensated for variation from standard atmospheric conditions.

(See ICAO term ALTITUDE.)

ALTITUDE [ICAO]. The vertical distance of a level, a point or an object considered as a point, measured from mean sea level (MSL).

ALTITUDE READOUT. An aircraft's altitude, transmitted via the Mode C transponder feature, that is visually displayed in 100-foot increments on a radar scope having readout capability. (See ALPHANUMERIC DISPLAY.) (See AUTOMATED RADAR TERMINAL SYSTEMS.) (See NAS STAGE A.) (Refer to AIM.)

ALTITUDE RESERVATION. Airspace utilization under prescribed conditions normally employed for the mass movement of aircraft or other special user requirements which cannot otherwise be accomplished. ALTRVs are approved by the appropriate FAA facility. (See AIR TRAFFIC CONTROL SYSTEM COMMAND CENTER.)

ALTITUDE RESTRICTION. An altitude or altitudes, stated in the order flown, which are to be maintained until reaching a specific point or time. Altitude restrictions may be issued by ATC due to traffic, terrain, or other airspace considerations.

ALTITUDE RESTRICTIONS ARE CANCELED. Adherence to previously imposed altitude restrictions is no longer required during a climb or descent.

ALTRV. (See ALTITUDE RESERVATION.)

AMASS. (See AIRPORT MOVEMENT AREA SAFETY SYSTEM.)

AMVER. (See AUTOMATED MUTUAL-ASSISTANCE VESSEL RESCUE SYSTEM.)

APB. (See AUTOMATED PROBLEM DETECTION BOUNDARY.)

APD. (See AUTOMATED PROBLEM DETECTION.)

APDIA. (See AUTOMATED PROBLEM DETECTION INHIBITED AREA.)

APPROACH CLEARANCE. Authorization by ATC for a pilot to conduct an instrument approach. The type of instrument approach for which a clearance and other pertinent information is provided in the approach clearance when required. (See CLEARED APPROACH.) (See INSTRUMENT APPROACH PROCEDURE.) (Refer to AIM.) (Refer to 14 CFR Part 91.)

APPROACH CONTROL FACILITY. A terminal ATC facility that provides approach control service in a terminal area. (See APPROACH CONTROL SERVICE.) (See RADAR APPROACH CONTROL FACILITY.)

APPROACH CONTROL SERVICE. Air traffic control service provided by an approach control facility for arriving and departing VFR/IFR aircraft and, on occasion, en route aircraft. At some airports not served by an approach control facility, the ARTCC provides limited approach control service. (See ICAO term APPROACH CONTROL SERVICE.) (Refer to AIM.)

APPROACH CONTROL SERVICE [ICAO]. Air traffic control service for arriving or departing controlled flights.

APPROACH GATE. An imaginary point used within ATC as a basis for vectoring aircraft to the final approach course. The gate will be established along the final approach course 1 mile from the final approach fix on the side away from the airport and will be no closer than 5 miles from the landing threshold.

APPROACH LIGHT SYSTEM. (See AIRPORT LIGHTING.)

APPROACH SEQUENCE. The order in which aircraft are positioned while on approach or awaiting approach clearance. (See LANDING SEQUENCE.) (See ICAO term APPROACH SEQUENCE.)

APPROACH SEQUENCE [ICAO]. The order in which two or more aircraft are cleared to approach to land at the aerodrome.

APPROACH SPEED. The recommended speed contained in aircraft manuals used by pilots when making an approach to landing. This speed will vary for different segments of an approach as well as for aircraft weight and configuration.

APPROPRIATE ATS AUTHORITY [ICAO]. The relevant authority designated by the State responsible for providing air traffic services in the airspace concerned. In the United States, the "appropriate ATS authority" is the Program Director for Air Traffic Planning and Procedures, ATP-1.

APPROPRIATE AUTHORITY.
  a. Regarding flight over the high seas: the relevant authority is the State of Registry.
  b. Regarding flight over other than the high seas: the relevant authority is the State having sovereignty over the territory being overflown.

APPROPRIATE OBSTACLE CLEARANCE MINIMUM ALTITUDE. Any of the following: (See Minimum En Route Altitude–MEA.) (See Minimum IFR Altitude–MIA.) (See Minimum Obstruction Clearance Altitude–MOCA.) (See Minimum Vectoring Altitude–MVA.)

APPROPRIATE TERRAIN CLEARANCE MINIMUM ALTITUDE. Any of the following: (See Minimum En Route Altitude–MEA.) (See Minimum IFR Altitude–MIA.) (See Minimum Obstruction Clearance Altitude–MOCA.) (See Minimum Vectoring Altitude–MVA.)

APRON. A defined area on an airport or heliport intended to accommodate aircraft for purposes of loading or unloading passengers or cargo, refueling, parking, or maintenance. With regard to seaplanes, a ramp is used for access to the apron from the water. (See ICAO term APRON.)

APRON [ICAO]. A defined area, on a land aerodrome, intended to accommodate aircraft for purposes of loading or unloading passengers, mail or cargo, refueling, parking or maintenance.

ARC. The track over the ground of an aircraft flying at a constant distance from a navigational aid by reference to distance measuring equipment (DME).

AREA CONTROL CENTER [ICAO]. An air traffic control facility primarily responsible for ATC services being provided IFR aircraft during the en route phase of flight. The U.S. equivalent facility is an air route traffic control center (ARTCC).

AREA NAVIGATION. Area Navigation (RNAV) provides enhanced navigational capability to the pilot. RNAV equipment can compute the airplane position, actual track and ground speed and then provide meaningful information relative to a route of flight selected by the pilot. Typical equipment will provide the pilot with distance, time, bearing and crosstrack error relative to the selected "TO" or "active" waypoint and the selected route. Several distinctly different navigational systems with different navigational performance characteristics are capable of providing area navigational functions. Present day RNAV includes INS, LORAN, VOR/DME, and GPS systems. Modern multi-sensor systems can integrate one or more of the above systems to provide a more accurate and reliable navigational system. Due to the different levels of performance, area navigational capabilities can satisfy different levels of required navigational performance (RNP). The major types of equipment are:
  a. VORTAC referenced or Course Line Computer (CLC) systems, which account for the greatest number of RNAV units in use. To function, the CLC must be within the service range of a VORTAC.
  b. OMEGA/VLF, although two separate systems, can be considered as one operationally. A long-range navigation system based upon Very Low Frequency radio signals transmitted from a total of 17 stations worldwide.
  c. Inertial (INS) systems, which are totally self. contained and require no information from external

references. They provide aircraft position and navigation information in response to signals resulting from inertial effects on components within the system.

d. MLS Area Navigation (MLS/RNAV), which provides area navigation with reference to an MLS ground facility.

e. LORAN-C is a long-range radio navigation system that uses ground waves transmitted at low frequency to provide user position information at ranges of up to 600 to 1,200 nautical miles at both en route and approach altitudes. The usable signal coverage areas are determined by the signal-to-noise ratio, the envelope-to-cycle difference, and the geometric relationship between the positions of the user and the transmitting stations.

f. GPS is a space-base radio positioning, navigation, and time-transfer system. The system provides highly accurate position and velocity information, and precise time, on a continuous global basis, to an unlimited number of properly equipped users. The system is unaffected by weather, and provides a worldwide common grid reference system.

(See ICAO term AREA NAVIGATION.)

AREA NAVIGATION [ICAO]. A method of navigation which permits aircraft operation on any desired flight path within the coverage of station-referenced navigation aids or within the limits of the capability of self-contained aids, or a combination of these.

AREA NAVIGATION (RNAV) APPROACH CONFIGURATION:

a. STANDARD T. An RNAV approach whose design allows direct flight to any one of three initial approach fixes (IAF) and eliminates the need for procedure turns. The standard design is to align the procedure on the extended centerline with the missed approach point (MAP) at the runway threshold, the final approach fix (FAF), and the initial approach/intermediate fix (IAF/IF). The other two IAFs will be established perpendicular to the IF.

b. MODIFIED T. An RNAV approach design for single or multiple runways where terrain or operational constraints do not allow for the standard T. The "T" may be modified by increasing or decreasing the angle from the corner IAF(s) to the IF or by eliminating one or both corner IAFs.

c. STANDARD I. An RNAV approach design for a single runway with both corner IAFs eliminated. Course reversal or radar vectoring may be required at busy terminals with multiple runways.

d. TERMINAL ARRIVAL AREA (TAA). The TAA is controlled airspace established in conjunction with the Standard or Modified T and I RNAV approach configurations. In the standard TAA, there are three areas: straight-in, left base, and right base. The arc boundaries of the three areas of the TAA are published portions of the approach and allow aircraft to transition from the en route structure direct to the nearest IAF. TAAs will also eliminate or reduce feeder routes, departure extensions, and procedure turns or course reversal.

1. STRAIGHT-IN AREA. A 30NM arc centered on the IF bounded by a straight line extending through the IF perpendicular to the intermediate course.

2. LEFT BASE AREA. A 30NM arc centered on the right corner IAF. The area shares a boundary with the straight-in area except that it extends out for 30NM from the IAF and is bounded on the other side by a line extending from the IF through the FAF to the arc.

3. RIGHT BASE AREA. A 30NM arc centered on the left corner IAF. The area shares a boundary with the straight-in area except that it extends out for 30NM from the IAF and is bounded on the other side by a line extending from the IF through the FAF to the arc.

ARINC. An acronym for Aeronautical Radio, Inc., a corporation largely owned by a group of airlines. ARINC is licensed by the FCC as an aeronautical station and contracted by the FAA to provide communications support for air traffic control and meteorological services in portions of international airspace.

ARMY AVIATION FLIGHT INFORMATION BULLETIN. A bulletin that provides air operation data covering Army, National Guard, and Army Reserve aviation activities.

ARO. (See AIRPORT RESERVATION OFFICE.)

ARRESTING SYSTEM. A safety device consisting of two major components, namely, engaging or catching devices and energy absorption devices for the purpose of arresting both tailhook and/or nontailhook-equipped aircraft. It is used to prevent aircraft from overrunning runways when the aircraft cannot be stopped after landing or during aborted takeoff. Arresting systems have various names; e.g., arresting gear, hook device, wire barrier cable. (See ABORT.) (Refer to AIM.)

ARRIVAL AIRCRAFT INTERVAL. An internally generated program in hundredths of minutes based upon the AAR. AAI is the desired optimum interval between successive arrival aircraft over the vertex.

ARRIVAL CENTER. The ARTCC having jurisdiction for the impacted airport.

ARRIVAL DELAY. A parameter which specifies a period of time in which no aircraft will be metered for arrival at the specified airport.

ARRIVAL SECTOR. An operational control sector containing one or more meter fixes.

ARRIVAL SECTOR ADVISORY LIST. An ordered list of data on arrivals displayed at the PVD/MDM of the sector which controls the meter fix.

ARRIVAL SEQUENCING PROGRAM. The automated program designed to assist in sequencing aircraft destined for the same airport.

ARRIVAL STREAM FILTER (ASF). An on/off filter that allows the conflict notification function to be inhibited for arrival streams into single or multiple airports to prevent nuisance alerts.

ARRIVAL TIME. The time an aircraft touches down on arrival.

ARSR. (See AIR ROUTE SURVEILLANCE RADAR.)

ARTCC. (See AIR ROUTE TRAFFIC CONTROL CENTER.)

ARTS. (See AUTOMATED RADAR TERMINAL SYSTEMS.)

ASDA. (See ACCELERATE-STOP DISTANCE AVAILABLE.)

ASDA [ICAO]. (See ICAO Term ACCELERATE-STOP DISTANCE AVAILABLE.)

ASDE. (See AIRPORT SURFACE DETECTION EQUIPMENT.)

ASF. (See ARRIVAL STREAM FILTER.)

ASLAR. (See AIRCRAFT SURGE LAUNCH AND RECOVERY.)

ASP. (See ARRIVAL SEQUENCING PROGRAM.)

ASR. (See AIRPORT SURVEILLANCE RADAR.)

ASR APPROACH. (See SURVEILLANCE APPROACH.)

ATC. (See AIR TRAFFIC CONTROL.)

ATC ADVISES. Used to prefix a message of noncontrol information when it is relayed to an aircraft by other than an air traffic controller. (See ADVISORY.)

ATC ASSIGNED AIRSPACE. Airspace of defined vertical/lateral limits, assigned by ATC, for the purpose of providing air traffic segregation between the specified activities being conducted within the assigned airspace and other IFR air traffic. (See SPECIAL USE AIRSPACE.)

ATC CLEARANCE. (See AIR TRAFFIC CLEARANCE.)

ATC CLEARS. Used to prefix an ATC clearance when it is relayed to an aircraft by other than an air traffic controller.

ATC INSTRUCTIONS. Directives issued by air traffic control for the purpose of requiring a pilot to take specific actions; e.g., "Turn left heading two five zero," "Go around," "Clear the runway." (Refer to 14 CFR Part 91.)

ATC PREFERRED ROUTE NOTIFICATION. URET notification to the appropriate controller of the need to determine if an ATC preferred route needs to be applied, based on destination airport. (See ROUTE ACTION NOTIFICATION.) (See USER REQUEST EVALUATION TOOL.)

ATC PREFERRED ROUTES. Preferred routes that are not automatically applied by Host.

ATC REQUESTS. Used to prefix an ATC request when it is relayed to an aircraft by other than an air traffic controller.

ATCAA. (See ATC ASSIGNED AIRSPACE.)

ATCRBS. (See RADAR.)

ATCSCC. (See AIR TRAFFIC CONTROL SYSTEM COMMAND CENTER.)

ATCT. (See TOWER.)

ATIS. (See AUTOMATIC TERMINAL INFORMATION SERVICE.)

ATIS [ICAO]. (See ICAO Term AUTOMATIC TERMINAL INFORMATION SERVICE.)

ATS ROUTE [ICAO]. A specified route designed for channeling the flow of traffic as necessary for the provision of air traffic services.

Note: The term "ATS Route" is used to mean variously, airway, advisory route, controlled or uncontrolled route, arrival or departure, etc.

ATTS. (See AUTOMATED TERMINAL TRACKING SYSTEM.)

AUTOLAND APPROACH. An autoland approach is a precision instrument approach to touchdown and, in some cases, through the landing rollout. An autoland approach is performed by the aircraft autopilot which is receiving position information and/or steering commands from onboard navigation equipment.

Note: Autoland and coupled approaches are flown in VFR and IFR. It is common for carriers to require their crews to fly coupled approaches and autoland approaches (if certified) when the weather conditions are less than approximately 4,000 RVR.

(See COUPLED APPROACH.)

AUTOMATED INFORMATION TRANSFER. A precoordinated process, specifically defined in facility directives, during which a transfer of altitude control and/or radar identification is accomplished without verbal coordination between controllers using information communicated in a full data block.

AUTOMATED MUTUAL-ASSISTANCE VESSEL RESCUE SYSTEM. A facility which can deliver, in a matter of minutes, a surface picture (SURPIC) of vessels in the area of a potential or actual search and rescue incident, including their predicted positions and their characteristics. (See FAAO 7110.65, Para 10-6-4, INFLIGHT CONTINGENCIES.)

AUTOMATED PROBLEM DETECTION (APD). An Automation Processing capability that compares trajectories in order to predict conflicts.

AUTOMATED PROBLEM DETECTION BOUND-ARY (APB). The adapted distance beyond a facilities boundary defining the airspace within which URET performs conflict detection. (See USER REQUEST EVALUATION TOOL.)

AUTOMATED PROBLEM DETECTION INHIB-ITED AREA (APDIA). Airspace surrounding a terminal area within which APD is inhibited for all flights within that airspace.

AUTOMATED RADAR TERMINAL SYSTEMS. The generic term for the ultimate in functional capability afforded by several automation systems. Each differs in functional capabilities and equipment. ARTS plus a suffix roman numeral denotes a specific system. A following letter indicates a major modification to that system. In general, an ARTS displays for the terminal controller aircraft identification, flight plan data, other flight associated information; e.g., altitude, speed, and aircraft position symbols in conjunction with his/her radar presentation. Normal radar co-exists with the alphanumeric display. In addition to enhancing visualization of the air traffic situation, ARTS facilitate intra/inter-facility transfer and coordination of flight information. These capabilities are enabled by specially designed computers and subsystems tailored to the radar and communications equipments and operational requirements of each automated facility. Modular design permits adoption of improvements in computer software and electronic technologies as they become available while retaining the characteristics unique to each system.

   a. ARTS II. A programmable nontracking, computer-aided display subsystem capable of modular expansion. ARTS II systems provide a level of automated air traffic control capability at terminals having low to medium activity. Flight identification and altitude may be associated with the display of secondary radar targets. The system has the capability of communicating with ARTCCs and other ARTS II, IIA, III, and IIIA facilities.

   b. ARTS IIA. A programmable radar-tracking computer subsystem capable of modular expansion. The ARTS IIA detects, tracks, and predicts secondary radar targets. The targets are displayed by means of computer-generated symbols, ground speed, and flight plan data. Although it does not track primary radar targets, they are displayed coincident with the secondary radar as well as the symbols and alphanumerics. The system has the capability of communicating with ARTCCs and other ARTS II, IIA, III, and IIIA facilities.

   c. ARTS III. The Beacon Tracking Level of the modular programmable automated radar terminal system in use at medium to high activity terminals. ARTS III detects, tracks, and predicts secondary radar-derived aircraft targets. These are displayed by means of computer-generated symbols and alphanumeric characters depicting flight identification, aircraft altitude, ground speed, and flight plan data. Although it does not track primary targets, they are displayed coincident with the secondary radar as well as the symbols and alphanumerics. The system has the capability of communicating with ARTCCs and other ARTS III facilities.

   d. ARTS IIIA. The Radar Tracking and Beacon Tracking Level (RT&BTL) of the modular, programmable automated radar terminal system. ARTS IIIA detects, tracks, and predicts primary as well as secondary radar-derived aircraft targets. This more sophisticated computer-driven system upgrades the existing ARTS III system by providing improved tracking, continuous data recording, and fail-soft capabilities.

AUTOMATED TERMINAL TRACKING SYSTEM (ATTS). ATTS is used to identify the numerous tracking systems including ARTS IIA, ARTS IIE, ARTS IIIA, ARTS IIIE, STARS, and M-EARTS.

AUTOMATED UNICOM. Provides completely automated weather, radio check capability and airport advisory information on an Automated UNICOM system. These systems offer a variety of features, typically selectable by microphone clicks, on the UNICOM frequency. Availability will be published in the Airport/Facility Directory and approach charts.

AUTOMATED WEATHER SYSTEM. Any of the

automated weather sensor platforms that collect weather data at airports and disseminate the weather information via radio and/or landline. The systems currently consist of the Automated Surface Observing System (ASOS), Automated Weather Sensor System (AWSS) and Automated Weather Observation System (AWOS).

AUTOMATIC ALTITUDE REPORT. (See ALTITUDE READOUT.)

AUTOMATIC ALTITUDE REPORTING. That function of a transponder which responds to Mode C interrogations by transmitting the aircraft's altitude in 100-foot increments.

AUTOMATIC CARRIER LANDING SYSTEM. U.S. Navy final approach equipment consisting of precision tracking radar coupled to a computer data link to provide continuous information to the aircraft, monitoring capability to the pilot, and a backup approach system.

AUTOMATIC DEPENDENT SURVEILLANCE (ADS) [ICAO]. A surveillance technique in which aircraft automatically provide, via a data link, data derived from on-board navigation and position fixing systems, including aircraft identification, four dimensional position and additional data as appropriate.

AUTOMATIC DEPENDENT SURVEILLANCE–BROADCAST (ADS–B). A surveillance system in which an aircraft or vehicle to be detected is fitted with cooperative equipment in the form of a data link transmitter. The aircraft or vehicle periodically broadcasts its GPS-derived position and other information such as velocity over the data link, which is received by a ground-based transmitter/receiver (transceiver) for processing and display at an air traffic control facility. (See GLOBAL POSITIONING SYSTEM.) (See GROUND-BASED TRANSCEIVER.)

AUTOMATIC DEPENDENT SURVEILLANCE–CONTRACT (ADS–C). A data link position reporting system, controlled by a ground station, that establishes contracts with an aircraft's avionics that occur automatically whenever specific events occur, or specific time intervals are reached.

AUTOMATIC DIRECTION FINDER. An aircraft radio navigation system which senses and indicates the direction to a L/MF nondirectional radio beacon (NDB) ground transmitter. Direction is indicated to the pilot as a magnetic bearing or as a relative bearing to the longitudinal axis of the aircraft depending on the type of indicator installed in the aircraft. In certain applications, such as military, ADF operations may be based on airborne and ground transmitters in the VHF/UHF frequency spectrum. (See BEARING.) (See NONDIRECTIONAL BEACON.)

AUTOMATIC TERMINAL INFORMATION SERVICE. The continuous broadcast of recorded noncontrol information in selected terminal areas. Its purpose is to improve controller effectiveness and to relieve frequency congestion by automating the repetitive transmission of essential but routine information; e.g., "Los Angeles information Alfa. One three zero zero Coordinated Universal Time. Weather, measured ceiling two thousand overcast, visibility three, haze, smoke, temperature seven one, dew point five seven, wind two five zero at five, altimeter two niner niner six. I-L-S Runway Two Five Left approach in use, Runway Two Five Right closed, advise you have Alfa." (See ICAO term AUTOMATIC TERMINAL INFORMATION SERVICE.) (Refer to AIM.)

AUTOMATIC TERMINAL INFORMATION SERVICE [ICAO]. The provision of current, routine information to arriving and departing aircraft by means of continuous and repetitive broadcasts throughout the day or a specified portion of the day.

AUTOROTATION. A rotorcraft flight condition in which the lifting rotor is driven entirely by action of the air when the rotorcraft is in motion.
a. Autorotative Landing/Touchdown Autorotation. Used by a pilot to indicate that the landing will be made without applying power to the rotor.
b. Low Level Autorotation. Commences at an altitude well below the traffic pattern, usually below 100 feet AGL and is used primarily for tactical military training.
c. 180 degrees Autorotation. Initiated from a downwind heading and is commenced well inside the normal traffic pattern. "Go around" may not be possible during the latter part of this maneuver.

AVAILABLE LANDING DISTANCE (ALD). The portion of a runway available for landing and roll-out for aircraft cleared for LAHSO. This distance is measured from the landing threshold to the hold-short point.

AVIATION WEATHER SERVICE. A service provided by the National Weather Service (NWS) and FAA which collects and disseminates pertinent weather information for pilots, aircraft operators, and ATC. Available aviation weather reports and forecasts are displayed at each NWS office and FAA FSS. (See EN ROUTE FLIGHT ADVISORY SERVICE.) (See

TRANSCRIBED WEATHER BROADCAST.) (See WEATHER ADVISORY.) (Refer to AIM.)

AWW. (See SEVERE WEATHER FORECAST ALERTS.)

AZIMUTH (MLS). A magnetic bearing extending from an MLS navigation facility.

Note: Azimuth bearings are described as magnetic and are referred to as "azimuth" in radio telephone communications.

B

BACK-TAXI. A term used by air traffic controllers to taxi an aircraft on the runway opposite to the traffic flow. The aircraft may be instructed to back-taxi to the beginning of the runway or at some point before reaching the runway end for the purpose of departure or to exit the runway.

BASE LEG. (See TRAFFIC PATTERN.)

BEACON. (See AERONAUTICAL BEACON.) (See AIRPORT ROTATING BEACON.) (See AIRWAY BEACON.) (See MARKER BEACON.) (See NON-DIRECTIONAL BEACON.) (See RADAR.)

BEARING. The horizontal direction to or from any point, usually measured clockwise from true north, magnetic north, or some other reference point through 360 degrees. (See NONDIRECTIONAL BEACON.)

BELOW MINIMUMS. Weather conditions below the minimums prescribed by regulation for the particular action involved; e.g., landing minimums, takeoff minimums.

BLAST FENCE. A barrier that is used to divert or dissipate jet or propeller blast.

BLIND SPEED. The rate of departure or closing of a target relative to the radar antenna at which cancellation of the primary radar target by moving target indicator (MTI) circuits in the radar equipment causes a reduction or complete loss of signal. (See ICAO term BLIND VELOCITY.)

BLIND SPOT. An area from which radio transmissions and/or radar echoes cannot be received. The term is also used to describe portions of the airport not visible from the control tower.

BLIND TRANSMISSION. (See TRANSMITTING IN THE BLIND.)

BLIND VELOCITY [ICAO]. The radial velocity of a moving target such that the target is not seen on primary radars fitted with certain forms of fixed echo suppression.

BLIND ZONE. (See BLIND SPOT.)

BLOCKED. Phraseology used to indicate that a radio transmission has been distorted or interrupted due to multiple simultaneous radio transmissions.

BOUNDARY LIGHTS. (See AIRPORT LIGHTING.)

BRAKING ACTION (GOOD, FAIR, POOR, OR NIL). A report of conditions on the airport movement area providing a pilot with a degree/quality of braking that he/she might expect. Braking action is reported in terms of good, fair, poor, or nil. (See RUNWAY CONDITION READING.)

BRAKING ACTION ADVISORIES. When tower controllers have received runway braking action reports which include the terms "poor" or "nil," or whenever weather conditions are conducive to deteriorating or rapidly changing runway braking conditions, the tower will include on the ATIS broadcast the statement, "BRAKING ACTION ADVISORIES ARE IN EFFECT." During the time Braking Action Advisories are in effect, ATC will issue the latest braking action report for the runway in use to each arriving and departing aircraft. Pilots should be prepared for deteriorating braking conditions and should request current runway condition information if not volunteered by controllers. Pilots should also be prepared to provide a descriptive runway condition report to controllers after landing.

BREAKOUT. A technique to direct aircraft out of the approach stream. In the context of close parallel operations, a breakout is used to direct threatened aircraft away from a deviating aircraft.

BROADCAST. Transmission of information for which an acknowledgement is not expected. (See ICAO term BROADCAST.)

BROADCAST [ICAO]. A transmission of information relating to air navigation that is not addressed to a specific station or stations.

C

CALCULATED LANDING TIME. A term that may be used in place of tentative or actual calculated landing time, whichever applies.

CALL FOR RELEASE. Wherein the overlying ARTCC requires a terminal facility to initiate verbal coordination to secure ARTCC approval for release of a departure into the en route environment.

CALL UP. Initial voice contact between a facility and

an aircraft, using the identification of the unit being called and the unit initiating the call. (Refer to AIM.)

CANADIAN MINIMUM NAVIGATION PERFORMANCE SPECIFICATION AIRSPACE. That portion of Canadian domestic airspace within which MNPS separation may be applied.

CARDINAL ALTITUDES. "Odd" or "Even" thousand-foot altitudes or flight levels; e.g., 5,000, 6,000, 7,000, FL 250, FL 260, FL 270. (See ALTITUDE.) (See FLIGHT LEVEL.)

CARDINAL FLIGHT LEVELS. (See CARDINAL ALTITUDES.)

CAT. (See CLEAR-AIR TURBULENCE.)

CATCH POINT. A fix/waypoint that serves as a transition point from the high altitude waypoint navigation structure to an arrival procedure (STAR) or the low altitude ground-based navigation structure.

CDT PROGRAMS. (See CONTROLLED DEPARTURE TIME PROGRAMS.)

CEILING. The heights above the earth's surface of the lowest layer of clouds or obscuring phenomena that is reported as "broken," "overcast," or "obscuration," and not classified as "thin" or "partial." (See ICAO term CEILING.)

CEILING [ICAO]. The height above the ground or water of the base of the lowest layer of cloud below 6,000 meters (20,000 feet) covering more than half the sky.

CENRAP. (See CENTER RADAR ARTS PRESENTATION/PROCESSING.)

CENRAP-PLUS. (See CENTER RADAR ARTS PRESENTATION/PROCESSING-PLUS.)

CENTER. (See AIR ROUTE TRAFFIC CONTROL CENTER.)

CENTER's AREA. The specified airspace within which an air route traffic control center (ARTCC) provides air traffic control and advisory service. (See AIR ROUTE TRAFFIC CONTROL CENTER.) (Refer to AIM.)

CENTER RADAR ARTS PRESENTATION/PROCESSING. A computer program developed to provide a back-up system for airport surveillance radar in the event of a failure or malfunction. The program uses air route traffic control center radar for the processing and presentation of data on the ARTS IIA or IIIA displays.

CENTER RADAR ARTS PRESENTATION/PRO-CESSING–PLUS. A computer program developed to provide a back-up system for airport surveillance radar in the event of a terminal secondary radar system failure. The program uses a combination of Air Route Traffic Control Center Radar and terminal airport surveillance radar primary targets displayed simultaneously for the processing and presentation of data on the ARTS IIA or IIIA displays.

CENTER TRACON AUTOMATION SYSTEM (CTAS). A computerized set of programs designed to aid Air Route Traffic Control Centers and TRACONs in the management and control of air traffic.

CENTER WEATHER ADVISORY. An unscheduled weather advisory issued by Center Weather Service Unit meteorologists for ATC use to alert pilots of existing or anticipated adverse weather conditions within the next 2 hours. A CWA may modify or redefine a SIGMET. (See AWW.) (See AIRMET.) (See CONVECTIVE SIGMET.) (See SIGMET.) (Refer to AIM.)

CENTRAL EAST PACIFIC. An organized route system between the U.S. West Coast and Hawaii.

CEP. (See CENTRAL EAST PACIFIC.)

CERAP. (See COMBINED CENTER-RAPCON.)

CERTIFIED TOWER RADAR DISPLAY (CTRD). A radar display that provides a presentation of primary, beacon radar videos, and alphanumeric data from an Air Traffic Control radar system, which is certified by the FAA to provide radar services. Examples include Digital Bright Radar Indicator Tower Equipment (DBRITE), Tower Display Workstation (TDW) and BRITE.

CFR. (See CALL FOR RELEASE.)

CHAFF. Thin, narrow metallic reflectors of various lengths and frequency responses, used to reflect radar energy. These reflectors when dropped from aircraft and allowed to drift downward result in large targets on the radar display.

CHARTED VFR FLYWAYS. Charted VFR Flyways are flight paths recommended for use to bypass areas heavily traversed by large turbine-powered aircraft. Pilot compliance with recommended flyways and associated altitudes is strictly voluntary. VFR Flyway Planning charts are published on the back of existing VFR Terminal Area charts.

CHARTED VISUAL FLIGHT PROCEDURE APPROACH. An approach conducted while operating on an instrument flight rules (IFR) flight plan which authorizes the pilot of an aircraft to proceed visually and clear of clouds to the airport via visual landmarks and other information depicted on a charted visual flight procedure. This approach must be authorized and under the control of the appropriate air traffic control facility. Weather minimums required are depicted on the chart.

CHASE. An aircraft flown in proximity to another aircraft normally to observe its performance during training or testing.

CHASE AIRCRAFT. (See CHASE.)

CIRCLE-TO-LAND MANEUVER. A maneuver initiated by the pilot to align the aircraft with a runway for landing when a straight-in landing from an instrument approach is not possible or is not desirable. At tower controlled airports, this maneuver is made only after ATC authorization has been obtained and the pilot has established required visual reference to the airport. (See CIRCLE TO RUNWAY.) (See LANDING MINIMUMS.) (Refer to AIM.)

CIRCLE TO RUNWAY (RUNWAY NUMBER). Used by ATC to inform the pilot that he/she must circle to land because the runway in use is other than the runway aligned with the instrument approach procedure. When the direction of the circling maneuver in relation to the airport/runway is required, the controller will state the direction (eight cardinal compass points) and specify a left or right downwind or base leg as appropriate; e.g., "Cleared VOR Runway Three Six Approach circle to Runway Two Two," or "Circle northwest of the airport for a right downwind to Runway Two Two." (See CIRCLE-TO-LAND MANEUVER.) (See LANDING MINIMUMS.) (Refer to AIM.)

CIRCLING APPROACH. (See CIRCLE-TO-LAND MANEUVER.)

CIRCLING MANEUVER. (See CIRCLE-TO-LAND MANEUVER.)

CIRCLING MINIMA. (See LANDING MINIMUMS.)

CLASS A AIRSPACE. (See CONTROLLED AIRSPACE.)

CLASS B AIRSPACE. (See CONTROLLED AIRSPACE.)

CLASS C AIRSPACE. (See CONTROLLED AIRSPACE.)

CLASS D AIRSPACE. (See CONTROLLED AIRSPACE.)

CLASS E AIRSPACE. (See CONTROLLED AIRSPACE.)

CLASS G AIRSPACE. That airspace not designated as Class A, B, C, D or E.

CLEAR AIR TURBULENCE (CAT). Turbulence encountered in air where no clouds are present. This term is commonly applied to high-level turbulence associated with wind shear. CAT is often encountered in the vicinity of the jet stream. (See WIND SHEAR.) (See JET STREAM.)

CLEAR OF THE RUNWAY.
a. A taxiing aircraft, which is approaching a runway, is clear of the runway when all parts of the aircraft are held short of the applicable holding position marking.
b. A pilot or controller may consider an aircraft, which is exiting or crossing a runway, to be clear of the runway when all parts of the aircraft are beyond the runway edge and there is no ATC restriction to its continued movement beyond the applicable holding position marking.
c. Pilots and controllers shall exercise good judgement to ensure that adequate separation exists between all aircraft on runways and taxiways at airports with inadequate runway edge lines or holding position markings.

CLEARANCE. (See AIR TRAFFIC CLEARANCE.)

CLEARANCE LIMIT. The fix, point, or location to which an aircraft is cleared when issued an air traffic clearance. (See ICAO term CLEARANCE LIMIT.)

CLEARANCE LIMIT [ICAO]. The point of which an aircraft is granted an air traffic control clearance.

CLEARANCE VOID IF NOT OFF BY (TIME). Used by ATC to advise an aircraft that the departure clearance is automatically canceled if takeoff is not made prior to a specified time. The pilot must obtain a new clearance or cancel his/her IFR flight plan if not off by the specified time. (See ICAO term CLEARANCE VOID TIME.)

CLEARANCE VOID TIME [ICAO]. A time specified by an air traffic control unit at which a clearance ceases to be valid unless the aircraft concerned has already taken action to comply therewith.

CLEARED APPROACH. ATC authorization for an aircraft to execute any standard or special instrument approach procedure for that airport. Normally, an aircraft will be cleared for a specific instrument approach procedure. (See CLEARED (Type of) APPROACH.) (See INSTRUMENT APPROACH PROCEDURE.) (Refer to 14 CFR Part 91.) (Refer to AIM.)

CLEARED (Type of) APPROACH. ATC authorization for an aircraft to execute a specific instrument approach procedure to an airport; e.g., "Cleared ILS

Runway Three Six Approach." (See APPROACH CLEARANCE.) (See INSTRUMENT APPROACH PROCEDURE.) (Refer to 14 CFR Part 91.) (Refer to AIM.)

CLEARED AS FILED. Means the aircraft is cleared to proceed in accordance with the route of flight filed in the flight plan. This clearance does not include the altitude, DP, or DP Transition. (See REQUEST FULL ROUTE CLEARANCE.) (Refer to AIM.)

CLEARED FOR TAKEOFF. ATC authorization for an aircraft to depart. It is predicated on known traffic and known physical airport conditions.

CLEARED FOR THE OPTION. ATC authorization for an aircraft to make a touch-and-go, low approach, missed approach, stop and go, or full stop landing at the discretion of the pilot. It is normally used in training so that an instructor can evaluate a student's performance under changing situations. (See OPTION APPROACH.) (Refer to AIM.)

CLEARED THROUGH. ATC authorization for an aircraft to make intermediate stops at specified airports without refiling a flight plan while en route to the clearance limit.

CLEARED TO LAND. ATC authorization for an aircraft to land. It is predicated on known traffic and known physical airport conditions.

CLEARWAY. An area beyond the takeoff runway under the control of airport authorities within which terrain or fixed obstacles may not extend above specified limits. These areas may be required for certain turbine-powered operations and the size and upward slope of the clearway will differ depending on when the aircraft was certificated. (Refer to 14 CFR Part 1.)

CLIMB TO VFR. ATC authorization for an aircraft to climb to VFR conditions within Class B, C, D, and E surface areas when the only weather limitation is restricted visibility. The aircraft must remain clear of clouds while climbing to VFR. (See SPECIAL VFR CONDITIONS.) (Refer to AIM.)

CLIMBOUT. That portion of flight operation between takeoff and the initial cruising altitude.

CLOSE PARALLEL RUNWAYS. Two parallel runways whose extended centerlines are separated by less than 4,300 feet, having a Precision Runway Monitoring (PRM) system that permits simultaneous independent ILS approaches.

CLOSED RUNWAY. A runway that is unusable for aircraft operations. Only the airport management/military operations office can close a runway.

CLOSED TRAFFIC. Successive operations involving takeoffs and landings or low approaches where the aircraft does not exit the traffic pattern.

CLOUD. A cloud is a visible accumulation of minute water droplets and/or ice particles in the atmosphere above the Earth's surface. Cloud differs from ground fog, fog, or ice fog only in that the latter are, by definition, in contact with the Earth's surface.

CLT. (See CALCULATED LANDING TIME.)

CLUTTER. In radar operations, clutter refers to the reception and visual display of radar returns caused by precipitation, chaff, terrain, numerous aircraft targets, or other phenomena. Such returns may limit or preclude ATC from providing services based on radar. (See CHAFF.) (See GROUND CLUTTER.) (See PRECIPITATION.) (See TARGET.) (See ICAO term RADAR CLUTTER.)

CMNPS. (See CANADIAN MINIMUM NAVIGATION PERFORMANCE SPECIFICATION AIRSPACE.)

COASTAL FIX. A navigation aid or intersection where an aircraft transitions between the domestic route structure and the oceanic route structure.

CODES. The number assigned to a particular multiple pulse reply signal transmitted by a transponder. (See DISCRETE CODE.)

COMBINED CENTER-RAPCON. An air traffic facility which combines the functions of an ARTCC and a radar approach control facility. (See AIR ROUTE TRAFFIC CONTROL CENTER.) (See RADAR APPROACH CONTROL FACILITY.)

COMMON POINT. A significant point over which two or more aircraft will report passing or have reported passing before proceeding on the same or diverging tracks. To establish/maintain longitudinal separation, a controller may determine a common point not originally in the aircraft's flight plan and then clear the aircraft to fly over the point. (See SIGNIFICANT POINT.)

COMMON PORTION. (See COMMON ROUTE.)

COMMON ROUTE. That segment of a North American Route between the inland navigation facility and the coastal fix.
or
COMMON ROUTE. Typically the portion of a RNAV STAR between the en route transition end point and the runway transition start point; however, the common route may only consist of a single point that joins the en route and runway transitions.

COMMON TRAFFIC ADVISORY FREQUENCY (CTAF). A frequency designed for the purpose of carrying out airport advisory practices while operating to or from an airport without an operating control tower. The CTAF may be a UNICOM, Multicom, FSS, or tower frequency and is identified in appropriate aeronautical publications. (Refer to AC 90-42, Traffic Advisory Practices at Airports Without Operating Control Towers.)

COMPASS LOCATOR. A low power, low or medium frequency (L/MF) radio beacon installed at the site of the outer or middle marker of an instrument landing system (ILS). It can be used for navigation at distances of approximately 15 miles or as authorized in the approach procedure.
a. Outer Compass Locator (LOM). A compass locator installed at the site of the outer marker of an instrument landing system. (See OUTER MARKER.)
b. Middle Compass Locator (LMM). A compass locator installed at the site of the middle marker of an instrument landing system. (See MIDDLE MARKER.)
(See ICAO term LOCATOR.)

COMPASS ROSE. A circle, graduated in degrees, printed on some charts or marked on the ground at an airport. It is used as a reference to either true or magnetic direction.

COMPOSITE FLIGHT PLAN. A flight plan which specifies VFR operation for one portion of flight and IFR for another portion. It is used primarily in military operations. (Refer to AIM.)

COMPOSITE ROUTE SYSTEM. An organized oceanic route structure, incorporating reduced lateral spacing between routes, in which composite separation is authorized.

COMPOSITE SEPARATION. A method of separating aircraft in a composite route system where, by management of route and altitude assignments, a combination of half the lateral minimum specified for the area concerned and half the vertical minimum is applied.

COMPULSORY REPORTING POINTS. Reporting points which must be reported to ATC. They are designated on aeronautical charts by solid triangles or filed in a flight plan as fixes selected to define direct routes. These points are geographical locations which are defined by navigation aids/fixes. Pilots should discontinue position reporting over compulsory reporting points when informed by ATC that their aircraft is in "radar contact."

CONFLICT ALERT. A function of certain air traffic control automated systems designed to alert radar controllers to existing or pending situations between tracked targets (known IFR or VFR aircraft) that require his/her immediate attention/action. (See MODE C INTRUDER ALERT.)

CONFLICT RESOLUTION. The resolution of potential conflictions between aircraft that are radar identified and in communication with ATC by ensuring that radar targets do not touch. Pertinent traffic advisories shall be issued when this procedure is applied.
Note: This procedure shall not be provided utilizing mosaic radar systems.

CONFORMANCE. The condition established when an aircraft's actual position is within the conformance region constructed around that aircraft at its position, according to the trajectory associated with the aircraft's Current Plan.

CONFORMANCE REGION. A volume, bounded laterally, vertically, and longitudinally, within which an aircraft must be at a given time in order to be in conformance with the Current Plan Trajectory for that aircraft. At a given time, the conformance region is determined by the simultaneous application of the lateral, vertical, and longitudinal conformance bounds for the aircraft at the position defined by time and aircraft's trajectory.

CONSOLAN. A low frequency, long-distance NAVAID used principally for transoceanic navigations.

CONTACT.
a. Establish communication with (followed by the name of the facility and, if appropriate, the frequency to be used).
b. A flight condition wherein the pilot ascertains the attitude of his/her aircraft and navigates by visual reference to the surface.
(See CONTACT APPROACH.) (See RADAR CONTACT.)

CONTACT APPROACH. An approach wherein an aircraft on an IFR flight plan, having an air traffic control authorization, operating clear of clouds with at least 1 mile flight visibility and a reasonable expectation of continuing to the destination airport in those conditions, may deviate from the instrument approach procedure and proceed to the destination airport by visual reference to the surface. This approach will only be authorized when requested by the pilot and the reported ground visibility at the destination airport is at least 1 statute mile. (Refer to AIM.)

CONTAMINATED RUNWAY. A runway is considered contaminated whenever standing water, ice, snow, slush, frost in any form, heavy rubber, or other substances are present. A runway is contaminated with respect to rubber deposits or other friction-degrading substances when the average friction value for any 500-foot segment of the runway within the ALD fails below the recommended minimum friction level and the average friction value in the adjacent 500-foot segments falls below the maintenance planning friction level.

CONTERMINOUS U.S. The 48 adjoining States and the District of Columbia.

CONTINENTAL UNITED STATES. The 49 States located on the continent of North America and the District of Columbia.

CONTINUE. When used as a control instruction should be followed by another word or words clarifying what is expected of the pilot. Example: "continue taxi", "continue descent", "continue inbound" etc.

CONTROL AREA [ICAO]. A controlled airspace extending upwards from a specified limit above the earth.

CONTROL SECTOR. An airspace area of defined horizontal and vertical dimensions for which a controller or group of controllers has air traffic control responsibility, normally within an air route traffic control center or an approach control facility. Sectors are established based on predominant traffic flows, altitude strata, and controller workload. Pilot. communications during operations within a sector are normally maintained on discrete frequencies assigned to the sector. (See DISCRETE FREQUENCY.)

CONTROL SLASH. A radar beacon slash representing the actual position of the associated aircraft. Normally, the control slash is the one closest to the interrogating radar beacon site. When ARTCC radar is operating in narrowband (digitized) mode, the control slash is converted to a target symbol.

CONTROLLED AIRSPACE. An airspace of defined dimensions within which air traffic control service is provided to IFR flights and to VFR flights in accordance with the airspace classification.

a. Controlled airspace is a generic term that covers Class A, Class B, Class C, Class D, and Class E airspace.

b. Controlled airspace is also that airspace within which all aircraft operators are subject to certain pilot qualifications, operating rules, and equipment requirements in 14 CFR Part 91 (for specific operating requirements, please refer to 14 CFR Part 91). For IFR operations in any class of controlled airspace, a pilot must file an IFR flight plan and receive an appropriate ATC clearance. Each Class B, Class C, and Class D airspace area designated for an airport contains at least one primary airport around which the airspace is designated (for specific designations and descriptions of the airspace classes, please refer to 14 CFR Part 71).

c. Controlled airspace in the United States is designated as follows:

1. CLASS A. Generally, that airspace from 18,000 feet MSL up to and including FL 600, including the airspace overlying the waters within 12 nautical miles of the coast of the 48 contiguous States and Alaska. Unless otherwise authorized, all persons must operate their aircraft under IFR.

2. CLASS B. Generally, that airspace from the surface to 10,000 feet MSL surrounding the nation's busiest airports in terms of airport operations or passenger enplanements. The configuration of each Class B airspace area is individually tailored and consists of a surface area and two or more layers (some Class B airspaces areas resemble upside-down wedding cakes), and is designed to contain all published instrument procedures once an aircraft enters the airspace. An ATC clearance is required for all aircraft to operate in the area, and all aircraft that are so cleared receive separation services within the airspace. The cloud clearance requirement for VFR operations is "clear of clouds."

3. CLASS C. Generally, that airspace from the surface to 4,000 feet above the airport elevation (charted in MSL) surrounding those airports that have an operational control tower, are serviced by a radar approach control, and that have a certain number of IFR operations or passenger enplanements. Although the configuration of each Class C area is individually tailored, the airspace usually consists of a surface area with a 5 nautical mile (NM) radius, a circle with a 10NM radius that extends no lower than 1,200 feet up to 4,000 feet above the airport elevation and an outer area that is not charted. Each person must establish two-way radio communications with the ATC facility providing air traffic services prior to entering the airspace and thereafter maintain those communications while within the airspace. VFR aircraft are only separated from IFR aircraft within the airspace. (See OUTER AREA.)

4. CLASS D. Generally, that airspace from the surface to 2,500 feet above the airport elevation (charted in MSL) surrounding those airports that have an operational control tower. The

configuration of each Class D airspace area is individually tailored and when instrument procedures are published, the airspace will normally be designed to contain the procedures. Arrival extensions for instrument approach procedures may be Class D or Class E airspace. Unless otherwise authorized, each person must establish two-way radio communications with the ATC facility providing air traffic services prior to entering the airspace and thereafter maintain those communications while in the airspace. No separation services are provided to VFR aircraft.

5. CLASS E. Generally, if the airspace is not Class A, Class B, Class C, or Class D, and it is controlled airspace, it is Class E airspace. Class E airspace extends upward from either the surface or a designated altitude to the overlying or adjacent controlled airspace. When designated as a surface area, the airspace will be configured to contain all instrument procedures. Also in this class are Federal airways, airspace beginning at either 700 or 1,200 feet AGL used to transition to/from the terminal or en route environment, en route domestic, and offshore airspace areas designated below 18,000 feet MSL. Unless designated at a lower altitude, Class E airspace begins at 14,500 MSL over the United States, including that airspace overlying the waters within 12 nautical miles of the coast of the 48 contiguous States and Alaska, up to, but not including 18,000 feet MSL, and the airspace above FL600.

CONTROLLED AIRSPACE [ICAO]. An airspace of defined dimensions within which air traffic control service is provided to IFR flights and to VFR flights in accordance with the airspace classification.

Note: Controlled airspace is a generic term which covers ATS airspace Classes A, B, C, D, and E.

CONTROLLED TIME OF ARRIVAL. Arrival time assigned during a Ground Delay Program. This time may be modified due to GDP adjustments or user options.

CONTROLLER. (See AIR TRAFFIC CONTROL SPECIALIST.)

CONTROLLER [ICAO]. A person authorized to provide air traffic control services.

CONTROLLER PILOT DATA LINK COMMUNICATIONS (CPDLC). A two-way digital very high frequency (VHF) air/ground communications system that conveys textual air traffic control messages between controllers and pilots.

CONVECTIVE SIGMET. A weather advisory concerning convective weather significant to the safety of all aircraft. Convective SIGMETs are issued for tornadoes, lines of thunderstorms, embedded thunderstorms of any intensity level, areas of thunderstorms greater than or equal to VIP level 4 with an area coverage of 4/10 (40%) or more, and hail 3/4 inch or greater. (See AIRMET.) (See AWW.) (See CWA.) (See SIGMET.) (Refer to AIM.)

CONVECTIVE SIGNIFICANT METEOROLOGICAL INFORMATION. (See CONVECTIVE SIGMET.)

COORDINATES. The intersection of lines of reference, usually expressed in degrees/minutes/seconds of latitude and longitude, used to determine position or location.

COORDINATION FIX. The fix in relation to which facilities will handoff, transfer control of an aircraft, or coordinate flight progress data. For terminal facilities, it may also serve as a clearance for arriving aircraft.

COPTER. (See HELICOPTER.)

CORRECTION. An error has been made in the transmission and the correct version follows.

COUPLED APPROACH. A coupled approach is an instrument approach performed by the aircraft autopilot which is receiving position information and/or steering commands from onboard navigation equipment. In general, coupled nonprecision approaches must be discontinued and flown manually at altitudes lower than 50 feet below the minimum descent altitude, and coupled precision approaches must be flown manually below 50 feet AGL.

Note: Coupled and autoland approaches are flown in VFR and IFR. It is common for carriers to require their crews to fly coupled approaches and autoland approaches (if certified) when the weather conditions are less than approximately 4,000 RVR. (See AUTOLAND APPROACH.)

COURSE.

a. The intended direction of flight in the horizontal plane measured in degrees from north.

b. The ILS localizer signal pattern usually specified as the front course or the back course.

c. The intended track along a straight, curved, or segmented MLS path.

(See BEARING.) (See INSTRUMENT LANDING SYSTEM.) (See MICROWAVE LANDING SYSTEM.) (See RADIAL.)

CPDLC. (See CONTROLLER PILOT DATA LINK COMMUNICATONS.)

CPL [ICAO]. (See ICAO term CURRENT FLIGHT PLAN.)

CRITICAL ENGINE. The engine which, upon failure, would most adversely affect the performance or handling qualities of an aircraft.

CROSS (FIX) AT (ALTITUDE). Used by ATC when a specific altitude restriction at a specified fix is required.

CROSS (FIX) AT OR ABOVE (ALTITUDE). Used by ATC when an altitude restriction at a specified fix is required. It does not prohibit the aircraft from crossing the fix at a higher altitude than specified; however, the higher altitude may not be one that will violate a succeeding altitude restriction or altitude assignment. (See ALTITUDE RESTRICTION.) (Refer to AIM.)

CROSS (FIX) AT OR BELOW (ALTITUDE). Used by ATC when a maximum crossing altitude at a specific fix is required. It does not prohibit the aircraft from crossing the fix at a lower altitude; however, it must be at or above the minimum IFR altitude. (See ALTITUDE RESTRICTION.) (See MINIMUM IFR ALTITUDES.) (Refer to 14 CFR Part 91.)

CROSSWIND.
a. When used concerning the traffic pattern, the word means "crosswind leg." (See TRAFFIC PATTERN.)
b. When used concerning wind conditions, the word means a wind not parallel to the runway or the path of an aircraft. (See CROSSWIND COMPONENT.)

CROSSWIND COMPONENT. The wind component measured in knots at 90 degrees to the longitudinal axis of the runway.

CRUISE. Used in an ATC clearance to authorize a pilot to conduct flight at any altitude from the minimum IFR altitude up to and including the altitude specified in the clearance. The pilot may level off at any intermediate altitude within this block of airspace. Climb/descent within the block is to be made at the discretion of the pilot. However, once the pilot starts descent and verbally reports leaving an altitude in the block, he/she may not return to that altitude without additional ATC clearance. Further, it is approval for the pilot to proceed to and make an approach at destination airport and can be used in conjunction with:
a. An airport clearance limit at locations with a standard/special instrument approach procedure. The CFRs require that if an instrument letdown to an airport is necessary, the pilot shall make the letdown in accordance with a standard/special

instrument approach procedure for that airport, or
b. An airport clearance limit at locations that are within/below/outside controlled airspace and without a standard/special instrument approach procedure. Such a clearance is NOT AUTHORIZATION for the pilot to descend under IFR conditions below the applicable minimum IFR altitude nor does it imply that ATC is exercising control over aircraft in Class G airspace; however, it provides a means for the aircraft to proceed to destination airport, descend, and land in accordance with applicable CFRs governing VFR flight operations. Also, this provides search and rescue protection until such time as the IFR flight plan is closed.
(See INSTRUMENT APPROACH PROCEDURE.)

CRUISE CLIMB. A climb technique employed by aircraft, usually at a constant power setting, resulting in an increase of altitude as the aircraft weight decreases.

CRUISING ALTITUDE. An altitude or flight level maintained during en route level flight. This is a constant altitude and should not be confused with a cruise clearance. (See ALTITUDE.) (See ICAO term CRUISING LEVEL.)

CRUISING LEVEL. (See CRUISING ALTITUDE.)

CRUISING LEVEL [ICAO]. A level maintained during a significant portion of a flight.

CT MESSAGE. An EDCT time generated by the ATCSCC to regulate traffic at arrival airports. Normally, a CT message is automatically transferred from the Traffic Management System computer to the NAS en route computer and appears as an EDCT. In the event of a communication failure between the TMS and the NAS, the CT message can be manually entered by the TMC at the en route facility.

CTA. (See CONTROLLED TIME OF ARRIVAL.) (See ICAO term CONTROL AREA.)

CTAF. (See COMMON TRAFFIC ADVISORY FREQUENCY.)

CTAS. (See CENTER TRACON AUTOMATION SYSTEM.)

CTRD. (See CERTIFIED TOWER RADAR DISPLAY.)

CURRENT FLIGHT PLAN [ICAO]. The flight plan, including changes, if any, brought about by subsequent clearances.

CURRENT PLAN. The ATC clearance the aircraft has received and is expected to fly.

CVFP APPROACH. (See CHARTED VISUAL

FLIGHT PROCEDURE APPROACH.)

CWA. (See CENTER WEATHER ADVISORY and WEATHER ADVISORY.)

D

D–ATIS. (See DIGITAL–AUTOMATIC TERMINAL INFORMATION SERVICE.)

DA [ICAO]. (See ICAO Term DECISION ALTITUDE/DECISION HEIGHT.)

DAIR. (See DIRECT ALTITUDE AND IDENTITY READOUT.)

DANGER AREA [ICAO]. An airspace of defined dimensions within which activities dangerous to the flight of aircraft may exist at specified times.

Note: The term "Danger Area" is not used in reference to areas within the United States or any of its possessions or territories.

DATA BLOCK. (See ALPHANUMERIC DISPLAY.)

DEAD RECKONING. Dead reckoning, as applied to flying, is the navigation of an airplane solely by means of computations based on airspeed, course, heading, wind direction, and speed, groundspeed, and elapsed time.

DECISION ALTITUDE/DECISION HEIGHT [ICAO]. A specified altitude or height (A/H) in the precision approach at which a missed approach must be initiated if the required visual reference to continue the approach has not been established.

Note 1: Decision altitude [DA] is referenced to mean sea level [MSL] and decision height [DH] is referenced to the threshold elevation.

Note 2: The required visual reference means that section of the visual aids or of the approach area which should have been in view for sufficient time for the pilot to have made an assessment of the aircraft position and rate of change of position, in relation to the desired flight path.

DECISION HEIGHT. With respect to the operation of aircraft, means the height at which a decision must be made during an ILS, MLS, or PAR instrument approach to either continue the approach or to execute a missed approach. (See ICAO term DECISION ALTITUDE/DECISION HEIGHT.)

DECODER. The device used to decipher signals received from ATCRBS transponders to effect their display as select codes. (See CODES.) (See RADAR.)

DEFENSE VISUAL FLIGHT RULES. Rules applicable to flights within an ADIZ conducted under the visual flight rules in 14 CFR Part 91. (See AIR DEFENSE IDENTIFICATION ZONE.) (Refer to 14 CFR Part 91.) (Refer to 14 CFR Part 99.)

DELAY ASSIGNMENT (DAS). Delays are distributed to aircraft based on the Ground Delay Program parameters. The delay assignment is calculated in 15-minute increments and appears as a table in ETMS.

DELAY INDEFINITE (REASON IF KNOWN) EXPECT FURTHER CLEARANCE (TIME). Used by ATC to inform a pilot when an accurate estimate of the delay time and the reason for the delay cannot immediately be determined; e.g., a disabled aircraft on the runway, terminal or center area saturation, weather below landing minimums, etc. (See EXPECT FURTHER CLEARANCE (TIME).)

DELAY TIME. The amount of time that the arrival must lose to cross the meter fix at the assigned meter fix time. This is the difference between ACLT and VTA.

DEPARTURE CENTER. The ARTCC having jurisdiction for the airspace that generates a flight to the impacted airport.

DEPARTURE CONTROL. A function of an approach control facility providing air traffic control service for departing IFR and, under certain conditions, VFR aircraft. (See APPROACH CONTROL FACILITY.) (Refer to AIM.)

DEPARTURE SEQUENCING PROGRAM. A program designed to assist in achieving a specified interval over a common point for departures.

DEPARTURE TIME. The time an aircraft becomes airborne.

DESCENT SPEED ADJUSTMENTS. Speed deceleration calculations made to determine an accurate VTA. These calculations start at the transition point and use arrival speed segments to the vertex.

DESIRED COURSE.
  a. True. A predetermined desired course direction to be followed (measured in degrees from true north).
  b. Magnetic. A predetermined desired course direction to be followed (measured in degrees from local magnetic north).

DESIRED TRACK. The planned or intended track between two waypoints. It is measured in degrees from either magnetic or true north. The instantaneous angle may change from point to point along the great circle track between waypoints.

DETRESFA (DISTRESS PHASE) [ICAO]. The code word used to designate an emergency phase wherein there is reasonable certainty that an aircraft and its occupants are threatened by grave and imminent danger or require immediate assistance.

DEVIATIONS.

a. A departure from a current clearance, such as an off course maneuver to avoid weather or turbulence.

b. Where specifically authorized in the CFRs and requested by the pilot, ATC may permit pilots to deviate from certain regulations.

(Refer to AIM.)

DF. (See DIRECTION FINDER.)

DF APPROACH PROCEDURE. Used under emergency conditions where another instrument approach procedure cannot be executed. DF guidance for an instrument approach is given by ATC facilities with DF capability. (See DF GUIDANCE.) (See DIRECTION FINDER.) (Refer to AIM.)

DF FIX. The geographical location of an aircraft obtained by one or more direction finders. (See DIRECTION FINDER.)

DF GUIDANCE. Headings provided to aircraft by facilities equipped with direction finding equipment. These headings, if followed, will lead the aircraft to a predetermined point such as the DF station or an airport. DF guidance is given to aircraft in distress or to other aircraft which request the service. Practice DF guidance is provided when workload permits. (See DIRECTION FINDER.) (See DF FIX.) (Refer to AIM.)

DF STEER. (See DF GUIDANCE.)

DH. (See DECISION HEIGHT.)

DH [ICAO]. (See ICAO Term DECISION ALTITUDE/ DECISION HEIGHT.)

DIGITAL–AUTOMATIC TERMINAL INFORMATION SERVICE (D–ATIS). The service provides text messages to aircraft, airlines, and other users outside the standard reception range of conventional ATIS via landline and data link communications to the cockpit. Also, the service provides a computer-synthesized voice message that can be transmitted to all aircraft within range of existing transmitters. The Terminal Data Link System (TDLS) D–ATIS application uses weather inputs from local automated weather sources or manually entered meteorological data together with preprogrammed menus to provide standard information to users. Airports with D–ATIS capability are listed in the Airport/Facility Directory.

DIRECT. Straight line flight between two navigational aids, fixes, points, or any combination thereof. When used by pilots in describing off-airway routes, points defining direct route segments become compulsory reporting points unless the aircraft is under radar contact.

DIRECT ALTITUDE AND IDENTITY READOUT. The DAIR System is a modification to the AN/TPX-42 Interrogator System. The Navy has two adaptations of the DAIR System-Carrier Air Traffic Control Direct Altitude and Identification Readout System for Aircraft Carriers and Radar Air Traffic Control Facility Direct Altitude and Identity Readout System for land-based terminal operations. The DAIR detects, tracks, and predicts secondary radar aircraft targets. Targets are displayed by means of computer-generated symbols and alphanumeric characters depicting flight identification, altitude, ground speed, and flight plan data. The DAIR System is capable of interfacing with ARTCCs.

DIRECTION FINDER. A radio receiver equipped with a directional sensing antenna used to take bearings on a radio transmitter. Specialized radio direction finders are used in aircraft as air navigation aids. Others are ground-based, primarily to obtain a "fix" on a pilot requesting orientation assistance or to locate downed aircraft. A location "fix" is established by the intersection of two or more bearing lines plotted on a navigational chart using either two separately located Direction Finders to obtain a fix on an aircraft or by a pilot plotting the bearing indications of his/her DF on two separately located ground-based transmitters, both of which can be identified on his/her chart. UDFs receive signals in the ultra high frequency radio broadcast band; VDFs in the very high frequency band; and UVDFs in both bands. ATC provides DF service at those air traffic control towers and flight service stations listed in the Airport/Facility Directory and the DOD FLIP IFR En Route Supplement. (See DF FIX.) (See DF GUIDANCE.)

DISCRETE BEACON CODE. (See DISCRETE CODE.)

DISCRETE CODE. As used in the Air Traffic Control Radar Beacon System (ATCRBS), any one of the 4096 selectable Mode 3/A aircraft transponder codes except those ending in zero zero; e.g., discrete codes: 0010, 1201, 2317, 7777; nondiscrete codes: 0100, 1200, 7700. Nondiscrete codes are normally reserved for radar facilities that are not equipped with discrete decoding capability and for other purposes such as emergencies (7700), VFR aircraft (1200), etc. (See RADAR.) (Refer to AIM.)

DISCRETE FREQUENCY. A separate radio frequency for use in direct pilot-controller communications in air traffic control which reduces frequency congestion by controlling the number of aircraft operating on a particular frequency at one time. Discrete frequencies are normally designated for each control sector in en route/terminal ATC facilities. Discrete frequencies are listed in the Airport/Facility Directory and the DOD FLIP IFR En Route Supplement. (See CONTROL SECTOR.)

DISPLACED THRESHOLD. A threshold that is located at a point on the runway other than the designated beginning of the runway. (See THRESHOLD.) (Refer to AIM.)

DISTANCE MEASURING EQUIPMENT. Equipment (airborne and ground) used to measure, in nautical miles, the slant range distance of an aircraft from the DME navigational aid. (See MICROWAVE LANDING SYSTEM.) (See TACAN.) (See VORTAC.)

DISTRESS. A condition of being threatened by serious and/or imminent danger and of requiring immediate assistance.

DIVE BRAKES. (See SPEED BRAKES.)

DIVERSE VECTOR AREA. In a radar environment, that area in which a prescribed departure route is not required as the only suitable route to avoid obstacles. The area in which random radar vectors below the MVA/MIA, established in accordance with the TERPS criteria for diverse departures, obstacles and terrain avoidance, may be issued to departing aircraft.

DIVERSION (DVRSN). Flights that are required to land at other than their original destination for reasons beyond the control of the pilot/company, e.g. periods of significant weather.

DME. (See DISTANCE MEASURING EQUIPMENT.)

DME FIX. A geographical position determined by reference to a navigational aid which provides distance and azimuth information. It is defined by a specific distance in nautical miles and a radial, azimuth, or course (i.e., localizer) in degrees magnetic from that aid. (See DISTANCE MEASURING EQUIPMENT.) (See FIX.) (See MICROWAVE LANDING SYSTEM.)

DME SEPARATION. Spacing of aircraft in terms of distances (nautical miles) determined by reference to distance measuring equipment (DME). (See DISTANCE MEASURING EQUIPMENT.)

DOD FLIP. Department of Defense Flight Information Publications used for flight planning, en route, and terminal operations. FLIP is produced by the National Imagery and Mapping Agency (NIMA) for world-wide use. United States Government Flight Information Publications (en route charts and instrument approach procedure charts) are incorporated in DOD FLIP for use in the National Airspace System (NAS).

DOMESTIC AIRSPACE. Airspace which overlies the continental land mass of the United States plus Hawaii and U.S. possessions. Domestic airspace extends to 12 miles offshore.

DOWNBURST. A strong downdraft which induces an outburst of damaging winds on or near the ground. Damaging winds, either straight or curved, are highly divergent. The sizes of downbursts vary from 1/2 mile or less to more than 10 miles. An intense downburst often causes widespread damage. Damaging winds, lasting 5 to 30 minutes, could reach speeds as high as 120 knots.

DOWNWIND LEG. (See TRAFFIC PATTERN.)

DP. (See INSTRUMENT DEPARTURE PROCEDURE.)

DRAG CHUTE. A parachute device installed on certain aircraft which is deployed on landing roll to assist in deceleration of the aircraft.

DSP. (See DEPARTURE SEQUENCING PROGRAM.)

DT. (See DELAY TIME.)

DUE REGARD. A phase of flight wherein an aircraft commander of a State-operated aircraft assumes responsibility to separate his/her aircraft from all other aircraft. (See also FAAO 7110.65, Para 1-2-1, WORD MEANINGS.)

DUTY RUNWAY. (See RUNWAY IN USE/ACTIVE RUNWAY/DUTY RUNWAY.)

DVA. (See DIVERSE VECTOR AREA.)

DVFR. (See DEFENSE VISUAL FLIGHT RULES.)

DVRSN. (See DIVERSION.)

DVFR FLIGHT PLAN. A flight plan filed for a VFR aircraft which intends to operate in airspace within which the ready identification, location, and control of aircraft are required in the interest of national security.

DYNAMIC. Continuous review, evaluation, and change to meet demands.

DYNAMIC RESTRICTIONS. Those restrictions imposed by the local facility on an "as needed" basis to manage unpredictable fluctuations in traffic demands.

E

EAS. (See EN ROUTE AUTOMATION SYSTEM.)

EDCT. (See EXPECT DEPARTURE CLEARANCE TIME.)

EFC. (See EXPECT FURTHER CLEARANCE (TIME).)

ELT. (See EMERGENCY LOCATOR TRANSMITTER.)

EMERGENCY. A distress or an urgency condition.

EMERGENCY LOCATOR TRANSMITTER. A radio transmitter attached to the aircraft structure which operates from its own power source on 121.5 MHz and 243.0 MHz. It aids in locating downed aircraft by radiating a downward sweeping audio tone, 2-4 times per second. It is designed to function without human action after an accident. (Refer to 14 CFR Part 91.) (Refer to AIM.)

E-MSAW. (See EN ROUTE MINIMUM SAFE ALTITUDE WARNING.)

EN ROUTE AIR TRAFFIC CONTROL SERVICES. Air traffic control service provided aircraft on IFR flight plans, generally by centers, when these aircraft are operating between departure and destination terminal areas. When equipment, capabilities, and controller workload permit, certain advisory/assistance services may be provided to VFR aircraft. (See AIR ROUTE TRAFFIC CONTROL CENTER.) (See NAS STAGE A.) (Refer to AIM.)

EN ROUTE AUTOMATION SYSTEM (EAS). The complex integrated environment consisting of situation display systems, surveillance systems and flight data processing, remote devices, decision support tools, and the related communications equipment that form the heart of the automated IFR air traffic control system. It interfaces with automated terminal systems and is used in the control of en route IFR aircraft. (Refer to AIM.)

EN ROUTE CHARTS. (See AERONAUTICAL CHART.)

EN ROUTE DESCENT. Descent from the en route cruising altitude which takes place along the route of flight.

EN ROUTE FLIGHT ADVISORY SERVICE. A service specifically designed to provide, upon pilot request, timely weather information pertinent to his/her type of flight, intended route of flight, and altitude. The FSS's providing this service are listed in the Airport/Facility Directory. (See FLIGHT WATCH.) (Refer to AIM.)

EN ROUTE HIGH ALTITUDE CHARTS. (See AERONAUTICAL CHART.)

EN ROUTE LOW ALTITUDE CHARTS. (See AERONAUTICAL CHART.)

EN ROUTE MINIMUM SAFE ALTITUDE WARNING. A function of the EAS that aids the controller by providing an alert when a tracked aircraft is below or predicted by the computer to go below a predetermined minimum IFR altitude (MIA).

EN ROUTE SPACING PROGRAM. A program designed to assist the exit sector in achieving the required in-trail spacing.

EN ROUTE TRANSITION.
  a. Conventional STARs/SIDs. The portion of a SID/STAR that connects to one or more en route airway/jet route.
  b. RNAV STARs/SIDs. The portion of a STAR preceding the common route or point, or for a SID the portion following, that is coded for a specific en route fix, airway or jet route.

EPS. (See ENGINEERED PERFORMANCE STANDARDS.)

ESP. (See EN ROUTE SPACING PROGRAM.)

ESTABLISHED. To be stable or fixed on a route, route segment, altitude, heading, etc.

ESTIMATED ELAPSED TIME [ICAO]. The estimated time required to proceed from one significant point to another. (See ICAO Term TOTAL ESTIMATED ELAPSED TIME.)

ESTIMATED OFF-BLOCK TIME [ICAO]. The estimated time at which the aircraft will commence movement associated with departure.

ESTIMATED POSITION ERROR (EPE). (See REQUIRED NAVIGATION PERFORMANCE.)

ESTIMATED TIME OF ARRIVAL. The time the flight is estimated to arrive at the gate (scheduled operators) or the actual runway on times for non-scheduled operators.

ESTIMATED TIME EN ROUTE. The estimated flying time from departure point to destination (lift-off to touchdown).

ETA. (See ESTIMATED TIME OF ARRIVAL.)

ETE. (See ESTIMATED TIME EN ROUTE.)

EXECUTE MISSED APPROACH. Instructions issued to a pilot making an instrument approach which means continue inbound to the missed approach point and execute the missed approach procedure as described on the Instrument Approach Procedure Chart or as previously assigned by ATC. The pilot may climb immediately to the altitude specified in the missed approach procedure upon making a missed approach. No turns should be initiated prior to reaching the missed approach point. When conducting an ASR or PAR approach, execute the assigned missed approach procedure immediately upon receiving instructions to "execute missed approach." (Refer to AIM.)

EXPECT (ALTITUDE) AT (TIME) or (FIX). Used under certain conditions to provide a pilot with an altitude to be used in the event of two-way communications failure. It also provides altitude information to assist the pilot in planning. (Refer to AIM.)

EXPECT DEPARTURE CLEARANCE TIME. The runway release time assigned to an aircraft in a ground delay program and shown on the flight progress strip as an EDCT. (See GROUND DELAY PROGRAM.)

EXPECT FURTHER CLEARANCE (TIME). The time a pilot can expect to receive clearance beyond a clearance limit.

EXPECT FURTHER CLEARANCE VIA (AIRWAYS, ROUTES OR FIXES). Used to inform a pilot of the routing he/she can expect if any part of the route beyond a short range clearance limit differs from that filed.

EXPEDITE. Used by ATC when prompt compliance is required to avoid the development of an imminent situation. Expedite climb/descent normally indicates to a pilot that the approximate best rate of climb/descent should be used without requiring an exceptional change in aircraft handling characteristics.

F

FAF. (See FINAL APPROACH FIX.)

FAST FILE. A system whereby a pilot files a flight plan via telephone that is tape recorded and then transcribed for transmission to the appropriate air traffic facility. Locations having a fast file capability are contained in the Airport/Facility Directory. (Refer to AIM.)

FAWP. Final Approach Waypoint

FCLT. (See FREEZE CALCULATED LANDING TIME.)

FEATHERED PROPELLER. A propeller whose blades have been rotated so that the leading and trailing edges are nearly parallel with the aircraft flight path to stop or minimize drag and engine rotation. Normally used to indicate shutdown of a reciprocating or turboprop engine due to malfunction.

FEDERAL AIRWAYS. (See LOW ALTITUDE AIRWAY STRUCTURE.)

FEEDER FIX. The fix depicted on Instrument Approach Procedure Charts which establishes the starting point of the feeder route.

FEEDER ROUTE. A route depicted on instrument approach procedure charts to designate routes for aircraft to proceed from the en route structure to the initial approach fix (IAF). (See INSTRUMENT APPROACH PROCEDURE.)

FERRY FLIGHT. A flight for the purpose of:
a. Returning an aircraft to base.
b. Delivering an aircraft from one location to another.
c. Moving an aircraft to and from a maintenance base. Ferry flights, under certain conditions, may be conducted under terms of a special flight permit.

FIELD ELEVATION. (See AIRPORT ELEVATION.)

FILED. Normally used in conjunction with flight plans, meaning a flight plan has been submitted to ATC.

FILED EN ROUTE DELAY. Any of the following preplanned delays at points/areas along the route of flight which require special flight plan filing and handling techniques.
a. Terminal Area Delay. A delay within a terminal area for touch-and-go, low approach, or other terminal area activity.
b. Special Use Airspace Delay. A delay within a Military Operations Area, Restricted Area, Warning Area, or ATC Assigned Airspace.
c. Aerial Refueling Delay. A delay within an Aerial Refueling Track or Anchor.

FILED FLIGHT PLAN. The flight plan as filed with an ATS unit by the pilot or his/her designated representative without any subsequent changes or clearances.

FINAL. Commonly used to mean that an aircraft is on the final approach course or is aligned with a landing area. (See FINAL APPROACH COURSE.) (See FINAL APPROACH-IFR.) (See SEGMENTS OF AN INSTRUMENT APPROACH PROCEDURE.)

FINAL APPROACH [ICAO]. That part of an instrument approach procedure which commences at the specified final approach fix or point, or where such a fix or point is not specified.
a. At the end of the last procedure turn, base turn or inbound turn of a racetrack procedure, if specified; or
b. At the point of interception of the last track specified in the approach procedure; and ends at a point

in the vicinity of an aerodrome from which:
1. A landing can be made; or
2. A missed approach procedure is initiated.

FINAL APPROACH COURSE. A bearing/radial/track of an instrument approach leading to a runway or an extended runway centerline all without regard to distance.

FINAL APPROACH FIX. The fix from which the final approach (IFR) to an airport is executed and which identifies the beginning of the final approach segment. It is designated on Government charts by the Maltese Cross symbol for nonprecision approaches and the lightning bolt symbol for precision approaches; or when ATC directs a lower-than. published glideslope/path intercept altitude, it is the resultant actual point of the glideslope/path intercept. (See FINAL APPROACH POINT.) (See GLIDESLOPE INTERCEPT ALTITUDE.) (See SEGMENTS OF AN INSTRUMENT APPROACH PROCEDURE.)

FINAL APPROACH—IFR. The flight path of an aircraft which is inbound to an airport on a final instrument approach course, beginning at the final approach fix or point and extending to the airport or the point where a circle-to-land maneuver or a missed approach is executed. (See FINAL APPROACH COURSE.) (See FINAL APPROACH FIX.) (See FINAL APPROACH POINT.) (See SEGMENTS OF AN INSTRUMENT APPROACH PROCEDURE.) (See ICAO term FINAL APPROACH.)

FINAL APPROACH POINT. The point, applicable only to a nonprecision approach with no depicted FAF (such as an on airport VOR), where the aircraft is established inbound on the final approach course from the procedure turn and where the final approach descent may be commenced. The FAP serves as the FAF and identifies the beginning of the final approach segment. (See FINAL APPROACH FIX.) (See SEGMENTS OF AN INSTRUMENT APPROACH PROCEDURE.)

FINAL APPROACH SEGMENT. (See SEGMENTS OF AN INSTRUMENT APPROACH PROCEDURE.)

FINAL APPROACH SEGMENT [ICAO]. That segment of an instrument approach procedure in which alignment and descent for landing are accomplished.

FINAL CONTROLLER. The controller providing information and final approach guidance during PAR and ASR approaches utilizing radar equipment. (See RADAR APPROACH.)

FINAL GUARD SERVICE. A value added service provided in conjunction with LAA/RAA only during periods of significant and fast changing weather conditions that may affect landing and takeoff operations.

FINAL MONITOR AID. A high resolution color display that is equipped with the controller alert system hardware/software which is used in the precision runway monitor (PRM) system. The display includes alert algorithms providing the target predictors, a color change alert when a target penetrates or is predicted to penetrate the no transgression zone (NTZ), a color change alert if the aircraft transponder becomes inoperative, synthesized voice alerts, digital mapping, and like features contained in the PRM system. (See RADAR APPROACH.)

FINAL MONITOR CONTROLLER. Air Traffic Control Specialist assigned to radar monitor the flight path of aircraft during simultaneous parallel and simultaneous close parallel ILS approach operations. Each runway is assigned a final monitor controller during simultaneous parallel and simultaneous close parallel ILS approaches. Final monitor controllers shall utilize the Precision Runway Monitor (PRM) system during simultaneous close parallel ILS approaches.

FIR. (See FLIGHT INFORMATION REGION.)

FIRST TIER CENTER. The ARTCC immediately adjacent to the impacted center.

FIX. A geographical position determined by visual reference to the surface, by reference to one or more radio NAVAIDs, by celestial plotting, or by another navigational device.

FIX BALANCING. A process whereby aircraft are evenly distributed over several available arrival fixes reducing delays and controller workload.

FLAG. A warning device incorporated in certain airborne navigation and flight instruments indicating that:
a. Instruments are inoperative or otherwise not operating satisfactorily, or
b. Signal strength or quality of the received signal falls below acceptable values.

FLAG ALARM. (See FLAG.)

FLAMEOUT. An emergency condition caused by a loss of engine power.

FLAMEOUT PATTERN. An approach normally conducted by a single-engine military aircraft experiencing loss or anticipating loss of engine power or control. The standard overhead approach starts at a relatively high altitude over a runway ("high key") followed by a continuous 180 degree turn to a high, wide position ("low key") followed by a continuous 180 degree turn final. The standard straight-in pattern starts at a point that results in a straight-in approach with a high rate of descent to the runway. Flameout approaches terminate in the type approach requested by the pilot (normally fullstop).

FLIGHT CHECK. A call-sign prefix used by FAA aircraft engaged in flight inspection/certification of navigational aids and flight procedures. The word "recorded" may be added as a suffix; e.g., "Flight Check 320 recorded" to indicate that an automated flight inspection is in progress in terminal areas. (See FLIGHT INSPECTION.) (Refer to AIM.)

FLIGHT FOLLOWING. (See TRAFFIC ADVISORIES.)

FLIGHT INFORMATION REGION. An airspace of defined dimensions within which Flight Information Service and Alerting Service are provided.
  a. Flight Information Service. A service provided for the purpose of giving advice and information useful for the safe and efficient conduct of flights.
  b. Alerting Service. A service provided to notify appropriate organizations regarding aircraft in need of search and rescue aid and to assist such organizations as required.

FLIGHT INFORMATION SERVICE. A service provided for the purpose of giving advice and information useful for the safe and efficient conduct of flights.

FLIGHT INSPECTION. Inflight investigation and evaluation of a navigational aid to determine whether it meets established tolerances. (See FLIGHT CHECK.) (See NAVIGATIONAL AID.)

FLIGHT LEVEL. A level of constant atmospheric pressure related to a reference datum of 29.92 inches of mercury. Each is stated in three digits that represent hundreds of feet. For example, flight level (FL) 250 represents a barometric altimeter indication of 25,000 feet; FL 255, an indication of 25,500 feet. (See ICAO term FLIGHT LEVEL.)

FLIGHT LEVEL [ICAO]. A surface of constant atmospheric pressure which is related to a specific pressure datum, 1013.2 hPa (1013.2 mb), and is separated from other such surfaces by specific pressure intervals.

Note 1: A pressure type altimeter calibrated in accordance with the standard atmosphere:
  a. When set to a QNH altimeter setting, will indicate altitude;
  b. When set to a QFE altimeter setting, will indicate height above the QFE reference datum; and
  c. When set to a pressure of 1013.2 hPa (1013.2 mb), may be used to indicate flight levels.

Note 2: The terms 'height' and 'altitude,' used in Note 1 above, indicate altimetric rather than geometric heights and altitudes.

FLIGHT LINE. A term used to describe the precise movement of a civil photogrammetric aircraft along a predetermined course(s) at a predetermined altitude during the actual photographic run.

FLIGHT MANAGEMENT SYSTEMS. A computer system that uses a large data base to allow routes to be preprogrammed and fed into the system by means of a data loader. The system is constantly updated with respect to position accuracy by reference to conventional navigation aids. The sophisticated program and its associated data base insures that the most appropriate aids are automatically selected during the information update cycle.

FLIGHT MANAGEMENT SYSTEM PROCEDURE. An arrival, departure, or approach procedure developed for use by aircraft with a slant (/) E or slant (/) F equipment suffix.

FLIGHT PATH. A line, course, or track along which an aircraft is flying or intended to be flown. (See COURSE.) (See TRACK.)

FLIGHT PLAN. Specified information relating to the intended flight of an aircraft that is filed orally or in writing with an FSS or an ATC facility. (See FAST FILE.) (See FILED.) (Refer to AIM.)

FLIGHT PLAN AREA. The geographical area assigned by regional air traffic divisions to a flight service station for the purpose of search and rescue for VFR aircraft, issuance of NOTAMs, pilot briefing, in-flight services, broadcast, emergency services, flight data processing, international operations, and aviation weather services. Three letter identifiers are assigned to every flight service station and are annotated in AFDs and FAAO 7350.7, LOCATION IDENTIFIERS, as tie-in facilities. (See FAST FILE.) (See FILED.) (Refer to AIM.)

FLIGHT RECORDER. A general term applied to any instrument or device that records information about the performance of an aircraft in flight or about conditions encountered in flight. Flight recorders may make records of airspeed, outside air temperature, vertical acceleration, engine RPM, manifold pressure, and other pertinent variables for a given flight. (See ICAO term FLIGHT RECORDER.)

FLIGHT RECORDER [ICAO]. Any type of recorder installed in the aircraft for the purpose of complementing accident/incident investigation.

Note: See Annex 6 Part I, for specifications relating to flight recorders.

FLIGHT SERVICE STATION. Air traffic facilities which provide pilot briefing, en route communications and VFR search and rescue services, assist lost aircraft and aircraft in emergency situations, relay ATC clearances, originate Notices to Airmen, broadcast aviation weather and NAS information, receive and process IFR flight plans, and monitor NAVAIDs. In addition, at selected locations, FSS's provide En Route Flight Advisory Service (Flight Watch), take weather observations, issue airport advisories, and advise Customs and Immigration of transborder flights. (Refer to AIM.)

FLIGHT STANDARDS DISTRICT OFFICE. An FAA field office serving an assigned geographical area and staffed with Flight Standards personnel who serve the aviation industry and the general public on matters relating to the certification and operation of air carrier and general aviation aircraft. Activities include general surveillance of operational safety, certification of airmen and aircraft, accident prevention, investigation, enforcement, etc.

FLIGHT TEST. A flight for the purpose of:
a. Investigating the operation/flight characteristics of an aircraft or aircraft component.
b. Evaluating an applicant for a pilot certificate or rating.

FLIGHT VISIBILITY. (See VISIBILITY.)

FLIGHT WATCH. A shortened term for use in air-ground contacts to identify the flight service station providing En Route Flight Advisory Service; e.g., "Oakland Flight Watch." (See EN ROUTE FLIGHT ADVISORY SERVICE.)

FLIP. (See DOD FLIP.)

FLY HEADING (DEGREES). Informs the pilot of the heading he/she should fly. The pilot may have to turn to, or continue on, a specific compass direction in order to comply with the instructions. The pilot is expected to turn in the shorter direction to the heading unless otherwise instructed by ATC.

FLY-BY WAYPOINT. A fly-by waypoint requires the use of turn anticipation to avoid overshoot of the next flight segment.

FLY-OVER WAYPOINT. A fly-over waypoint precludes any turn until the waypoint is overflown and is followed by an intercept maneuver of the next flight segment.

FMA. (See FINAL MONITOR AID.)

FMS. (See FLIGHT MANAGEMENT SYSTEM.)

FMSP. (See FLIGHT MANAGEMENT SYSTEM PROCEDURE.)

FORMATION FLIGHT. More than one aircraft which, by prior arrangement between the pilots, operate as a single aircraft with regard to navigation and position reporting. Separation between aircraft within the formation is the responsibility of the flight leader and the pilots of the other aircraft in the flight. This includes transition periods when aircraft within the formation are maneuvering to attain separation from each other to effect individual control and during join-up and breakaway.
a. A standard formation is one in which a proximity of no more than 1 mile laterally or longitudinally and within 100 feet vertically from the flight leader is maintained by each wingman.
b. Nonstandard formations are those operating under any of the following conditions:
1. When the flight leader has requested and ATC has approved other than standard formation dimensions.
2. When operating within an authorized altitude reservation (ALTRV) or under the provisions of a letter of agreement.
3. When the operations are conducted in airspace specifically designed for a special activity.
(See ALTITUDE RESERVATION.) (Refer to 14 CFR Part 91.)

FRC. (See REQUEST FULL ROUTE CLEARANCE.)

FREEZE/FROZEN. Terms used in referring to arrivals which have been assigned ACLTs and to the lists in which they are displayed.

FREEZE CALCULATED LANDING TIME. A dynamic parameter number of minutes prior to the meter fix calculated time of arrival for each aircraft when the TCLT is frozen and becomes an ACLT (i.e., the VTA is updated and consequently the TCLT is modified as appropriate until FCLT minutes prior to meter fix calculated time of arrival, at which time updating is suspended and an ACLT and a frozen meter fix crossing time (MFT) is assigned).

FREEZE HORIZON. The time or point at which an aircraft's STA becomes fixed and no longer fluctuates with each radar update. This setting insures a constant time for each aircraft, necessary for the metering controller to plan his/her delay technique. This setting can be either in distance from the meter fix or a prescribed flying time to the meter fix.

FREEZE SPEED PARAMETER. A speed adapted for each aircraft to determine fast and slow aircraft. Fast aircraft freeze on parameter FCLT and slow aircraft freeze on parameter MLDI.

FRICTION MEASUREMENT. A measurement of the friction characteristics of the runway pavement surface using continuous self-watering friction measurement equipment in accordance with the specifications, procedures and schedules contained in AC 150/5320-12, Measurement, Construction, and Maintenance of Skid Resistant Airport Pavement Surfaces.

FSDO. (See FLIGHT STANDARDS DISTRICT OFFICE.)

FSPD. (See FREEZE SPEED PARAMETER.)

FSS. (See FLIGHT SERVICE STATION.)

FUEL DUMPING. Airborne release of usable fuel. This does not include the dropping of fuel tanks. (See JETTISONING OF EXTERNAL STORES.)

FUEL REMAINING. A phrase used by either pilots or controllers when relating to the fuel remaining on board until actual fuel exhaustion. When transmitting such information in response to either a controller question or pilot initiated cautionary advisory to air traffic control, pilots will state the AP-PROXIMATE NUMBER OF MINUTES the flight can continue with the fuel remaining. All reserve fuel SHOULD BE INCLUDED in the time stated, as should an allowance for established fuel gauge system error.

FUEL SIPHONING. Unintentional release of fuel caused by overflow, puncture, loose cap, etc.

FUEL VENTING. (See FUEL SIPHONING.)

G

GATE HOLD PROCEDURES. Procedures at selected airports to hold aircraft at the gate or other ground location whenever departure delays exceed or are anticipated to exceed 15 minutes. The sequence for departure will be maintained in accordance with initial call-up unless modified by flow control restrictions. Pilots should monitor the ground control/clearance delivery frequency for engine start/taxi advisories or new proposed start/taxi time if the delay changes. (See FLOW CONTROL.)

GBT. (See GROUND-BASED TRANSCEIVER.)

GCA. (See GROUND CONTROLLED APPROACH.)

GENERAL AVIATION. That portion of civil aviation which encompasses all facets of aviation except air carriers holding a certificate of public convenience and necessity from the Civil Aeronautics Board and large aircraft commercial operators. (See ICAO term GENERAL AVIATION.)

GENERAL AVIATION [ICAO]. All civil aviation operations other than scheduled air services and nonscheduled air transport operations for remuneration or hire.

GEO MAP. The digitized map markings associated with the ASR-9 Radar System.

GLIDEPATH. (See GLIDESLOPE.)

GLIDEPATH [ICAO]. A descent profile determined for vertical guidance during a final approach.

GLIDEPATH INTERCEPT ALTITUDE. (See GLIDESLOPE INTERCEPT ALTITUDE.)

GLIDESLOPE. Provides vertical guidance for aircraft during approach and landing. The glideslope/glidepath is based on the following:
 a. Electronic components emitting signals which provide vertical guidance by reference to airborne instruments during instrument approaches such as ILS/MLS, or
 b. Visual ground aids, such as VASI, which provide vertical guidance for a VFR approach or for the visual portion of an instrument approach and landing.
 c. PAR. Used by ATC to inform an aircraft making a PAR approach of its vertical position (elevation) relative to the descent profile.
(See ICAO term GLIDEPATH.)

GLIDESLOPE INTERCEPT ALTITUDE. The minimum altitude to intercept the glideslope/path on a precision approach. The intersection of the published intercept altitude with the glideslope/path, designated on Government charts by the lightning bolt symbol, is the precision FAF; however, when the approach chart shows an alternative lower glideslope intercept altitude, and ATC directs a lower altitude, the resultant lower intercept position is then the FAF. (See FINAL APPROACH FIX.) (See SEGMENTS OF AN INSTRUMENT APPROACH PROCEDURE.)

GLOBAL POSITIONING SYSTEM (GPS). A space-base radio positioning, navigation, and time. transfer system. The system provides highly accurate position and velocity information, and precise time, on a continuous global basis, to an unlimited number of properly equipped users. The system is unaffected by weather, and provides a worldwide common grid reference system. The GPS concept is predicated upon accurate and continuous knowledge of the spatial position of each satellite in the system with respect to time and distance from a transmitting satellite to the user. The GPS receiver automatically selects appropriate signals from the satellites in view and translates these into three-dimensional position, velocity, and time. System accuracy for civil users is normally 100 meters horizontally.

GO AHEAD. Proceed with your message. Not to be used for any other purpose.

GO AROUND. Instructions for a pilot to abandon his/her approach to landing. Additional instructions may follow. Unless otherwise advised by ATC, a VFR aircraft or an aircraft conducting visual approach should overfly the runway while climbing to traffic pattern altitude and enter the traffic pattern via the crosswind leg. A pilot on an IFR flight plan making an instrument approach should execute the published missed approach procedure or proceed as instructed by ATC; e.g., "Go around" (additional instructions if required). (See LOW APPROACH.) (See MISSED APPROACH.)

GPD. (See GRAPHIC PLAN DISPLAY.)

GPS. (See GLOBAL POSITIONING SYSTEM.)

GRAPHIC PLAN DISPLAY (GPD). A view available with URET that provides a graphic display of aircraft, traffic, and notification of predicted conflicts. Graphic routes for Current Plans and Trial Plans are displayed upon controller request. (See USER REQUEST EVALUATION TOOL.)

GROUND-BASED TRANSCEIVER (GBT). The ground-based transmitter/receiver (transceiver) receives automatic dependent surveillance-broadcast messages, which are forwarded to an air traffic control facility for processing and display with other radar targets on the plan position indicator (radar display). (See AUTOMATIC DEPENDENT SURVEILLANCE-BROADCAST.)

GROUND CLUTTER. A pattern produced on the radar scope by ground returns which may degrade other radar returns in the affected area. The effect of ground clutter is minimized by the use of moving target indicator (MTI) circuits in the radar equipment resulting in a radar presentation which displays only targets which are in motion. (See CLUTTER.)

GROUND COMMUNICATION OUTLET (GCO). An unstaffed, remotely controlled, ground/ground communications facility. Pilots at uncontrolled airports may contact ATC and FSS via VHF to a telephone connection to obtain an instrument clearance or close a VFR or IFR flight plan. They may also get an updated weather briefing prior to takeoff. Pilots will use four "key clicks" on the VHF radio to contact the appropriate ATC facility or six "key clicks" to contact the FSS. The GCO system is intended to be used only on the ground.

GROUND CONTROLLED APPROACH. A radar approach system operated from the ground by air traffic control personnel transmitting instructions to the pilot by radio. The approach may be conducted with surveillance radar (ASR) only or with both surveillance and precision approach radar (PAR). Usage of the term "GCA" by pilots is discouraged except when referring to a GCA facility. Pilots should specifically request a "PAR" approach when a precision radar approach is desired or request an "ASR" or "surveillance" approach when a nonprecision radar approach is desired. (See RADAR APPROACH.)

GROUND DELAY PROGRAM (GDP). A traffic management process administered by the ATCSCC; when aircraft are held on the ground. The purpose of the program is to support the TM mission and limit airborne holding. It is a flexible program and may be implemented in various forms depending upon the needs of the AT system. Ground delay programs provide for equitable assignment of delays to all system users.

GROUND SPEED. The speed of an aircraft relative to the surface of the earth.

GROUND STOP. The GS is a process that requires aircraft that meet a specific criteria to remain on the ground. The criteria may be airport specific, airspace specific, or equipment specific; for example, all departures to San Francisco, or all departures entering Yorktown sector, or all Category I and II aircraft going to Charlotte. GS's normally occur with little or no warning.

GROUND VISIBILITY. (See VISIBILITY.)

H

HAA. (See HEIGHT ABOVE AIRPORT.)

HAL. (See HEIGHT ABOVE LANDING.)

HANDOFF. An action taken to transfer the radar identification of an aircraft from one controller to another if the aircraft will enter the receiving controller's airspace and radio communications with the aircraft will be transferred.

HAR. (See HIGH ALTITUDE REDESIGN.)

HAT. (See HEIGHT ABOVE TOUCHDOWN.)

HAVE NUMBERS. Used by pilots to inform ATC that they have received runway, wind, and altimeter information only.

HAZARDOUS INFLIGHT WEATHER ADVISORY SERVICE. Continuous recorded hazardous inflight weather forecasts broadcasted to airborne pilots over selected VOR outlets defined as an HIWAS BROADCAST AREA.

HAZARDOUS WEATHER INFORMATION. Summary of significant meteorological information (SIGMET/WS), convective significant meteorological information (convective SIGMET/WST), urgent pilot weather reports (urgent PIREP/UUA), center weather advisories (CWA), airmen's meteorological information (AIRMET/WA) and any other weather such as isolated thunderstorms that are rapidly developing and increasing in intensity, or low ceilings and visibilities that are becoming widespread which is considered significant and are not included in a current hazardous weather advisory.

HEAVY (AIRCRAFT). (See AIRCRAFT CLASSES.)

HEIGHT ABOVE AIRPORT. The height of the Minimum Descent Altitude above the published airport elevation. This is published in conjunction with circling minimums. (See MINIMUM DESCENT ALTITUDE.)

HEIGHT ABOVE LANDING. The height above a designated helicopter landing area used for helicopter instrument approach procedures. (Refer to 14 CFR Part 97.)

HEIGHT ABOVE TOUCHDOWN. The height of the Decision Height or Minimum Descent Altitude above the highest runway elevation in the touchdown zone (first 3,000 feet of the runway). HAT is published on instrument approach charts in conjunction with all straight-in minimums. (See DECISION HEIGHT.) (See MINIMUM DESCENT ALTITUDE.)

HELICOPTER. Rotorcraft that, for its horizontal motion, depends principally on its engine-driven rotors. (See ICAO term HELICOPTER.)

HELICOPTER [ICAO]. A heavier-than-air aircraft supported in flight chiefly by the reactions of the air on one or more power-driven rotors on substantially vertical axes.

HELIPAD. A small, designated area, usually with a prepared surface, on a heliport, airport, landing/takeoff area, apron/ramp, or movement area used for takeoff, landing, or parking of helicopters.

HELIPORT. An area of land, water, or structure used or intended to be used for the landing and takeoff of helicopters and includes its buildings and facilities if any.

HELIPORT REFERENCE POINT (HRP). The geographic center of a heliport.

HERTZ. The standard radio equivalent of frequency in cycles per second of an electromagnetic wave. Kilohertz (KHz) is a frequency of one thousand cycles per second. Megahertz (MHz) is a frequency of one million cycles per second.

HF. (See HIGH FREQUENCY.)

HF COMMUNICATIONS. (See HIGH FREQUENCY COMMUNICATIONS.)

HIGH ALTITUDE REDESIGN (HAR). A level of non-restrictive routing (NRR) service for aircraft that have all waypoints associated with the HAR program in their flight management systems or RNAV equipage.

HIGH FREQUENCY. The frequency band between 3 and 30 MHz. (See HIGH FREQUENCY COMMUNICATIONS.)

HIGH FREQUENCY COMMUNICATIONS. High radio frequencies (HF) between 3 and 30 MHz used for air-to-ground voice communication in overseas operations.

HIGH SPEED EXIT. (See HIGH SPEED TAXIWAY.)

HIGH SPEED TAXIWAY. A long radius taxiway designed and provided with lighting or marking to define the path of aircraft, traveling at high speed (up to 60 knots), from the runway center to a point on the center of a taxiway. Also referred to as long radius exit or turn-off taxiway. The high speed taxiway is designed to expedite aircraft turning off the runway after landing, thus reducing runway occupancy time.

HIGH SPEED TURNOFF. (See HIGH SPEED TAXIWAY.)

HIWAS. (See HAZARDOUS INFLIGHT WEATHER ADVISORY SERVICE.)

HIWAS AREA. (See HAZARDOUS INFLIGHT WEATHER ADVISORY SERVICE.)

HIWAS BROADCAST AREA. A geographical area of responsibility including one or more HIWAS outlet areas assigned to an AFSS/FSS for hazardous weather advisory broadcasting.

HIWAS OUTLET AREA. An area defined as a 150 NM radius of a HIWAS outlet, expanded as necessary to provide coverage.

HOLD FOR RELEASE. Used by ATC to delay an aircraft for traffic management reasons; i.e., weather, traffic volume, etc. Hold for release instructions (including departure delay information) are used to inform a pilot or a controller (either directly or through an authorized relay) that an IFR departure clearance is not valid until a release time or additional instructions have been received. (See ICAO term HOLDING POINT.)

HOLD PROCEDURE. A predetermined maneuver which keeps aircraft within a specified airspace while awaiting further clearance from air traffic control. Also used during ground operations to keep aircraft within a specified area or at a specified point while awaiting further clearance from air traffic control. (See HOLDING FIX.) (Refer to AIM.)

HOLDING FIX. A specified fix identifiable to a pilot by NAVAIDs or visual reference to the ground used as a reference point in establishing and maintaining the position of an aircraft while holding. (See FIX.) (See VISUAL HOLDING.) (Refer to AIM.)

HOLDING POINT [ICAO]. A specified location, identified by visual or other means, in the vicinity of which the position of an aircraft in flight is maintained in accordance with air traffic control clearances.

HOLDING PROCEDURE. (See HOLD PROCEDURE.)

HOLD-SHORT POINT. A point on the runway beyond which a landing aircraft with a LAHSO clearance is not authorized to proceed. This point may be located prior to an intersecting runway, taxiway, predetermined point, or approach/departure flight path.

HOLD-SHORT POSITION LIGHTS. Flashing in-pavement white lights located at specified hold-short points.

HOLD-SHORT POSITION MARKING. The painted runway marking located at the hold-short point on all LAHSO runways.

HOLD-SHORT POSITION SIGNS. Red and white holding position signs located alongside the hold-short point.

HOMING. Flight toward a NAVAID, without correcting for wind, by adjusting the aircraft heading to maintain a relative bearing of zero degrees. (See BEARING.) (See ICAO term HOMING.)

HOMING [ICAO]. The procedure of using the direction-finding equipment of one radio station with the emission of another radio station, where at least one of the stations is mobile, and whereby the mobile station proceeds continuously towards the other station.

HOVER CHECK. Used to describe when a helicopter/VTOL aircraft requires a stabilized hover to conduct a performance/power check prior to hover taxi, air taxi, or takeoff. Altitude of the hover will vary based on the purpose of the check.

HOVER TAXI. Used to describe a helicopter/VTOL aircraft movement conducted above the surface and in ground effect at airspeeds less than approximately 20 knots. The actual height may vary, and some helicopters may require hover taxi above 25 feet AGL to reduce ground effect turbulence or provide clearance for cargo slingloads. (See AIR TAXI.) (See HOVER CHECK.) (Refer to AIM.)

HOW DO YOU HEAR ME? A question relating to the quality of the transmission or to determine how well the transmission is being received.

HZ. (See HERTZ.)

I

I SAY AGAIN. The message will be repeated.

IAF. (See INITIAL APPROACH FIX.)

IAP. (See INSTRUMENT APPROACH PROCEDURE.)

IAWP. Initial Approach Waypoint

ICAO. (See ICAO Term INTERNATIONAL CIVIL AVIATION ORGANIZATION.)

ICING. The accumulation of airframe ice.
Types of icing are:
a. Rime Ice. Rough, milky, opaque ice formed by the instantaneous freezing of small supercooled water droplets.
b. Clear Ice. A glossy, clear, or translucent ice formed by the relatively slow freezing or large supercooled water droplets.
c. Mixed. A mixture of clear ice and rime ice.
Intensity of icing:
a. Trace. Ice becomes perceptible. Rate of accumulation is slightly greater than the rate of sublimation. Deicing/anti-icing equipment is not utilized unless encountered for an extended period of time (over 1 hour).

b. Light. The rate of accumulation may create a problem if flight is prolonged in this environment (over 1 hour). Occasional use of deicing/anti-icing equipment removes/prevents accumulation. It does not present a problem if the deicing/anti-icing equipment is used.

c. Moderate. The rate of accumulation is such that even short encounters become potentially hazardous and use of deicing/anti-icing equipment or flight diversion is necessary.

d. Severe. The rate of accumulation is such that deicing/anti-icing equipment fails to reduce or control the hazard. Immediate flight diversion is necessary.

IDENT. A request for a pilot to activate the aircraft transponder identification feature. This will help the controller to confirm an aircraft identity or to identify an aircraft. (Refer to AIM.)

IDENT FEATURE. The special feature in the Air Traffic Control Radar Beacon System (ATCRBS) equipment. It is used to immediately distinguish one displayed beacon target from other beacon targets. (See IDENT.)

IF. (See INTERMEDIATE FIX.)

IFIM. (See INTERNATIONAL FLIGHT INFORMATION MANUAL.)

IF NO TRANSMISSION RECEIVED FOR (TIME). Used by ATC in radar approaches to prefix procedures which should be followed by the pilot in event of lost communications. (See LOST COMMUNICATIONS.)

IFR. (See INSTRUMENT FLIGHT RULES.)

IFR AIRCRAFT. An aircraft conducting flight in accordance with instrument flight rules.

IFR CONDITIONS. Weather conditions below the minimum for flight under visual flight rules. (See INSTRUMENT METEOROLOGICAL CONDITIONS.)

IFR DEPARTURE PROCEDURE. (See IFR TAKEOFF MINIMUMS AND DEPARTURE PROCEDURES.) (Refer to AIM.)

IFR FLIGHT. (See IFR AIRCRAFT.)

IFR LANDING MINIMUMS. (See LANDING MINIMUMS.)

IFR MILITARY TRAINING ROUTES (IR). Routes used by the Department of Defense and associated Reserve and Air Guard units for the purpose of conducting low-altitude navigation and tactical training in both IFR and VFR weather conditions below 10,000 feet MSL at airspeeds in excess of 250 knots IAS.

IFR TAKEOFF MINIMUMS AND DEPARTURE PROCEDURES. Title 14 Code of Federal Regulations Part 91, prescribes standard takeoff rules for certain civil users. At some airports, obstructions or other factors require the establishment of nonstandard takeoff minimums, departure procedures, or both to assist pilots in avoiding obstacles during climb to the minimum en route altitude. Those airports are listed in FAA/DOD Instrument Approach Procedures (IAPs) Charts under a section entitled "IFR Takeoff Minimums and Departure Procedures." The FAA/DOD IAP chart legend illustrates the symbol used to alert the pilot to nonstandard takeoff minimums and departure procedures. When departing IFR from such airports or from any airports where there are no departure procedures, DPs, or ATC facilities available, pilots should advise ATC of any departure limitations. Controllers may query a pilot to determine acceptable departure directions, turns, or headings after takeoff. Pilots should be familiar with the departure procedures and must assure that their aircraft can meet or exceed any specified climb gradients.

IF/IAWP. Intermediate Fix/Initial Approach Waypoint. The waypoint where the final approach course of a T approach meets the crossbar of the T. When designated (in conjunction with a TAA) this waypoint will be used as an IAWP when approaching the airport from certain directions, and as an IFWP when beginning the approach from another IAWP.

IFWP. Intermediate Fix Waypoint

ILS. (See INSTRUMENT LANDING SYSTEM.)

ILS CATEGORIES.

1. ILS Category I. An ILS approach procedure which provides for approach to a height above touchdown of not less than 200 feet and with runway visual range of not less than 1,800 feet.

2. ILS Category II. An ILS approach procedure which provides for approach to a height above touchdown of not less than 100 feet and with runway visual range of not less than 1,200 feet.

3. ILS Category III:

   a. IIIA. An ILS approach procedure which provides for approach without a decision height minimum and with runway visual range of not less than 700 feet.

   b. IIIB. An ILS approach procedure which provides

for approach without a decision height minimum and with runway visual range of not less than 150 feet.

   c. IIIC. An ILS approach procedure which provides for approach without a decision height minimum and without runway visual range minimum.

ILS PRM APPROACH. An instrument landing system (ILS) approach conducted to parallel runways whose extended centerlines are separated by less than 4,300 feet and the parallel runways have a Precision Runway Monitoring (PRM) system that permits simultaneous independent ILS approaches.

IM. (See INNER MARKER.)

IMC. (See INSTRUMENT METEOROLOGICAL CONDITIONS.)

IMMEDIATELY. Used by ATC or pilots when such action compliance is required to avoid an imminent situation.

INCERFA (Uncertainty Phase) [ICAO]. A situation wherein uncertainty exists as to the safety of an aircraft and its occupants.

INCREASE SPEED TO (SPEED). (See SPEED ADJUSTMENT.)

INERTIAL NAVIGATION SYSTEM. An RNAV system which is a form of self-contained navigation. (See AREA NAVIGATION (RNAV.)

INFLIGHT REFUELING. (See AERIAL REFUELING.)

INFLIGHT WEATHER ADVISORY. (See WEATHER ADVISORY.)

INFORMATION REQUEST. A request originated by an FSS for information concerning an overdue VFR aircraft.

INITIAL APPROACH FIX. The fixes depicted on instrument approach procedure charts that identify the beginning of the initial approach segment(s). (See FIX.) (See SEGMENTS OF AN INSTRUMENT APPROACH PROCEDURE.)

INITIAL APPROACH SEGMENT. (See SEGMENTS OF AN INSTRUMENT APPROACH PROCEDURE.)

INITIAL APPROACH SEGMENT [ICAO]. That segment of an instrument approach procedure between the initial approach fix and the intermediate approach fix or, where applicable, the final approach fix or point.

INLAND NAVIGATION FACILITY. A navigation aid on a North American Route at which the common route and/or the noncommon route begins or ends.

INNER MARKER. A marker beacon used with an ILS (CAT II) precision approach located between the middle marker and the end of the ILS runway, transmitting a radiation pattern keyed at six dots per second and indicating to the pilot, both aurally and visually, that he/she is at the designated decision height (DH), normally 100 feet above the touchdown zone elevation, on the ILS CAT II approach. It also marks progress during a CAT III approach. (See INSTRUMENT LANDING SYSTEM.) (Refer to AIM.)

INNER MARKER BEACON. (See INNER MARKER.)

INREQ. (See INFORMATION REQUEST.)

INS. (See INERTIAL NAVIGATION SYSTEM.)

INSTRUMENT APPROACH. (See INSTRUMENT APPROACH PROCEDURE.)

INSTRUMENT APPROACH PROCEDURE. A series of predetermined maneuvers for the orderly transfer of an aircraft under instrument flight conditions from the beginning of the initial approach to a landing or to a point from which a landing may be made visually. It is prescribed and approved for a specific airport by competent authority. (See SEGMENTS OF AN INSTRUMENT APPROACH PROCEDURE.) (Refer to 14 CFR Part 91.) (Refer to AIM.)

   a. U.S. civil standard instrument approach procedures are approved by the FAA as prescribed under 14 CFR Part 97 and are available for public use.

   b. U.S. military standard instrument approach procedures are approved and published by the Department of Defense.

   c. Special instrument approach procedures are approved by the FAA for individual operators but are not published in 14 CFR Part 97 for public use.

(See ICAO term INSTRUMENT APPROACH PROCEDURE.)

INSTRUMENT APPROACH PROCEDURE [ICAO]. A series of predetermined maneuvers by reference to flight instruments with specified protection from obstacles from the initial approach fix, or where applicable, from the beginning of a defined arrival route to a point from which a landing can be completed and thereafter, if a landing is not completed, to a position at which holding or en route obstacle clearance criteria apply.

INSTRUMENT APPROACH PROCEDURES CHARTS. (See AERONAUTICAL CHART.)

INSTRUMENT DEPARTURE PROCEDURE (DP). A preplanned instrument flight rule (IFR) departure procedure published for pilot use, in graphic or textual format, that provides obstruction clearance from the terminal area to the appropriate en route structure. There are two types of DP, Obstacle Departure Procedure (ODP), printed either textually or graphically, and, Standard Instrument Departure (SID), which is always printed graphically. (See IFR TAKEOFF MINIMUMS AND DEPARTURE PROCEDURES.) (See OBSTACLE DEPARTURE PROCEDURES.) (See STANDARD INSTRUMENT DEPARTURES.) (Refer to AIM.)

INSTRUMENT FLIGHT RULES. Rules governing the procedures for conducting instrument flight. Also a term used by pilots and controllers to indicate type of flight plan. (See INSTRUMENT METEOROLOGICAL CONDITIONS.) (See VISUAL FLIGHT RULES.) (See VISUAL METEOROLOGICAL CONDITIONS.) (See ICAO term INSTRUMENT FLIGHT RULES.) (Refer to AIM.)

INSTRUMENT FLIGHT RULES [ICAO]. A set of rules governing the conduct of flight under instrument meteorological conditions.

INSTRUMENT LANDING SYSTEM. A precision instrument approach system which normally consists of the following electronic components and visual aids:
a. Localizer. (See LOCALIZER.)
b. Glideslope. (See GLIDESLOPE.)
c. Outer Marker. (See OUTER MARKER.)
d. Middle Marker. (See MIDDLE MARKER.)
e. Approach Lights. (See AIRPORT LIGHTING.)
(Refer to 14 CFR Part 91.) (Refer to AIM.)

INSTRUMENT METEOROLOGICAL CONDITIONS. Meteorological conditions expressed in terms of visibility, distance from cloud, and ceiling less than the minima specified for visual meteorological conditions. (See INSTRUMENT FLIGHT RULES.) (See VISUAL FLIGHT RULES.) (See VISUAL METEOROLOGICAL CONDITIONS.)

INSTRUMENT RUNWAY. A runway equipped with electronic and visual navigation aids for which a precision or nonprecision approach procedure having straight-in landing minimums has been approved. (See ICAO term INSTRUMENT RUNWAY.)

INSTRUMENT RUNWAY [ICAO]. One of the following types of runways intended for the operation of aircraft using instrument approach procedures:

a. Nonprecision Approach Runway—An instrument runway served by visual aids and a nonvisual aid providing at least directional guidance adequate for a straight-in approach.
b. Precision Approach Runway, Category I—An instrument runway served by ILS and visual aids intended for operations down to 60 m (200 feet) decision height and down to an RVR of the order of 800 m.
c. Precision Approach Runway, Category II—An instrument runway served by ILS and visual aids intended for operations down to 30 m (100 feet) decision height and down to an RVR of the order of 400 m.
d. Precision Approach Runway, Category III—An instrument runway served by ILS to and along the surface of the runway and:
   1. Intended for operations down to an RVR of the order of 200 m (no decision height being applicable) using visual aids during the final phase of landing;
   2. Intended for operations down to an RVR of the order of 50 m (no decision height being applicable) using visual aids for taxiing;
   3. Intended for operations without reliance on visual reference for landing or taxiing.

Note 1: See Annex 10 Volume I, Part I, Chapter 3, for related ILS specifications.

Note 2: Visual aids need not necessarily be matched to the scale of nonvisual aids provided. The criterion for the selection of visual aids is the conditions in which operations are intended to be conducted.

INTEGRITY. The ability of a system to provide timely warnings to users when the system should not be used for navigation.

INTERMEDIATE APPROACH SEGMENT. (See SEGMENTS OF AN INSTRUMENT APPROACH PROCEDURE.)

INTERMEDIATE APPROACH SEGMENT [ICAO]. That segment of an instrument approach procedure between either the intermediate approach fix and the final approach fix or point, or between the end of a reversal, race track or dead reckoning track procedure and the final approach fix or point, as appropriate.

INTERMEDIATE FIX. The fix that identifies the beginning of the intermediate approach segment of an instrument approach procedure. The fix is not normally identified on the instrument approach chart as an intermediate fix (IF). (See SEGMENTS OF AN INSTRUMENT APPROACH PROCEDURE.)

INTERMEDIATE LANDING. On the rare occasion that this option is requested, it should be approved. The departure center, however, must advise the ATC-SCC so that the appropriate delay is carried over and assigned at the intermediate airport. An intermediate landing airport within the arrival center will not be accepted without coordination with and the approval of the ATCSCC.

INTERNATIONAL AIRPORT. Relating to international flight, it means:
a. An airport of entry which has been designated by the Secretary of Treasury or Commissioner of Customs as an international airport for customs service.
b. A landing rights airport at which specific permission to land must be obtained from customs authorities in advance of contemplated use.
c. Airports designated under the Convention on International Civil Aviation as an airport for use by international commercial air transport and/or international general aviation.
(See ICAO term INTERNATIONAL AIRPORT.) (Refer to AIRPORT/FACILITY DIRECTORY.) (Refer to IFIM.)

INTERNATIONAL AIRPORT [ICAO]. Any airport designated by the Contracting State in whose territory it is situated as an airport of entry and departure for international air traffic, where the formalities incident to customs, immigration, public health, animal and plant quarantine and similar procedures are carried out.

INTERNATIONAL CIVIL AVIATION ORGANIZATION [ICAO]. A specialized agency of the United Nations whose objective is to develop the principles and techniques of international air navigation and to foster planning and development of international civil air transport.
a. Regions include:
  1. African-Indian Ocean Region
  2. Caribbean Region
  3. European Region
  4. Middle East/Asia Region
  5. North American Region
  6. North Atlantic Region
  7. Pacific Region
  8. South American Region

INTERNATIONAL FLIGHT INFORMATION MANUAL. A publication designed primarily as a pilot's preflight planning guide for flights into foreign airspace and for flights returning to the U.S. from foreign locations.

INTERROGATOR. The ground-based surveillance radar beacon transmitter-receiver, which normally scans in synchronism with a primary radar, transmitting discrete radio signals which repetitiously request all transponders on the mode being used to reply. The replies received are mixed with the primary radar returns and displayed on the same plan position indicator (radar scope). Also, applied to the airborne element of the TACAN/DME system. (See TRANSPONDER.) (Refer to AIM.)

INTERSECTING RUNWAYS. Two or more runways which cross or meet within their lengths. (See INTERSECTION.)

INTERSECTION.
a. A point defined by any combination of courses, radials, or bearings of two or more navigational aids.
b. Used to describe the point where two runways, a runway and a taxiway, or two taxiways cross or meet.

INTERSECTION DEPARTURE. A departure from any runway intersection except the end of the runway. (See INTERSECTION.)

INTERSECTION TAKEOFF. (See INTERSECTION DEPARTURE.)

IR. (See IFR MILITARY TRAINING ROUTES.)

J

JAMMING. Electronic or mechanical interference which may disrupt the display of aircraft on radar or the transmission/reception of radio communications/navigation.

JET BLAST. Jet engine exhaust (thrust stream turbulence). (See WAKE TURBULENCE.)

JET ROUTE. A route designed to serve aircraft operations from 18,000 feet MSL up to and including flight level 450. The routes are referred to as "J" routes with numbering to identify the designated route; e.g., J105. (See Class A AIRSPACE.) (Refer to 14 CFR Part 71.)

JET STREAM. A migrating stream of high-speed winds present at high altitudes.

JETTISONING OF EXTERNAL STORES. Airborne release of external stores; e.g., tiptanks, ordnance. (See FUEL DUMPING.) (Refer to 14 CFR Part 91.)

JOINT USE RESTRICTED AREA. (See RESTRICTED AREA.)

K

KNOWN TRAFFIC. With respect to ATC clearances, means aircraft whose altitude, position, and intentions are known to ATC.

L

LAA. (See LOCAL AIRPORT ADVISORY.)

LAAS. (See LOW ALTITUDE ALERT SYSTEM.)

LAHSO. An acronym for "Land and Hold Short Operation." These operations include landing and holding short of an intersecting runway, a taxiway, a predetermined point, or an approach/departure flightpath.

LAHSO–DRY. Land and hold short operations on runways that are dry.

LAHSO–WET. Land and hold short operations on runways that are wet (but not contaminated).

LAND AND HOLD SHORT OPERATIONS. Operations which include simultaneous takeoffs and landings and/or simultaneous landings when a landing aircraft is able and is instructed by the controller to hold-short of the intersecting runway/taxiway or designated hold-short point. Pilots are expected to promptly inform the controller if the hold short clearance cannot be accepted. (See PARALLEL RUNWAYS.) (Refer to AIM.)

LANDING AREA. Any locality either on land, water, or structures, including airports/heliports and intermediate landing fields, which is used, or intended to be used, for the landing and takeoff of aircraft whether or not facilities are provided for the shelter, servicing, or for receiving or discharging passengers or cargo. (See ICAO term LANDING AREA.)

LANDING AREA [ICAO]. That part of a movement area intended for the landing or take-off of aircraft.

LANDING DIRECTION INDICATOR. A device which visually indicates the direction in which landings and takeoffs should be made. (See TETRAHEDRON.) (Refer to AIM.)

LANDING DISTANCE AVAILABLE [ICAO]. The length of runway which is declared available and suitable for the ground run of an aeroplane landing.

LANDING MINIMUMS. The minimum visibility prescribed for landing a civil aircraft while using an instrument approach procedure. The minimum applies with other limitations set forth in 14 CFR Part 91 with respect to the Minimum Descent Altitude (MDA) or Decision Height (DH) prescribed in the instrument approach procedures as follows:

a. Straight-in landing minimums. A statement of MDA and visibility, or DH and visibility, required for a straight-in landing on a specified runway, or

b. Circling minimums. A statement of MDA and visibility required for the circle-to-land maneuver.

Note: Descent below the established MDA or DH is not authorized during an approach unless the aircraft is in a position from which a normal approach to the runway of intended landing can be made and adequate visual reference to required visual cues is maintained. (See CIRCLE-TO-LAND MANEUVER.) (See DECISION HEIGHT.) (See INSTRUMENT APPROACH PROCEDURE.) (See MINIMUM DESCENT ALTITUDE.) (See STRAIGHT-IN LANDING.) (See VISIBILITY.) (Refer to 14 CFR Part 91.)

LANDING ROLL. The distance from the point of touchdown to the point where the aircraft can be brought to a stop or exit the runway.

LANDING SEQUENCE. The order in which aircraft are positioned for landing. (See APPROACH SEQUENCE.)

LAST ASSIGNED ALTITUDE. The last altitude/flight level assigned by ATC and acknowledged by the pilot. (See MAINTAIN.) (Refer to 14 CFR Part 91.)

LATERAL NAVIGATION (LNAV). A function of area navigation (RNAV) equipment which calculates, displays, and provides lateral guidance to a profile or path.

LATERAL SEPARATION. The lateral spacing of aircraft at the same altitude by requiring operation on different routes or in different geographical locations. (See SEPARATION.)

LDA. (See LOCALIZER TYPE DIRECTIONAL AID.) (See ICAO Term LANDING DISTANCE AVAILABLE.)

LF. (See LOW FREQUENCY.)

LIGHTED AIRPORT. An airport where runway and obstruction lighting is available. (See AIRPORT LIGHTING.) (Refer to AIM.)

LIGHT GUN. A handheld directional light signaling device which emits a brilliant narrow beam of white, green, or red light as selected by the tower controller. The color and type of light transmitted can be used to approve or disapprove anticipated pilot actions where radio communication is not available. The light gun is used for controlling traffic operating in the vicinity of the airport and on the airport movement area. (Refer to AIM.)

LOCAL AIRPORT ADVISORY (LAA). A service provided by facilities, which are located on the landing airport, have a discrete ground-to-air communication frequency or the tower frequency when the tower is closed, automated weather reporting with voice broadcasting, and a continuous ASOS/AWOS data display, other continuous direct reading instruments, or manual observations available to the specialist. (See AIRPORT ADVISORY AREA.)

LOCAL TRAFFIC. Aircraft operating in the traffic pattern or within sight of the tower, or aircraft known to be departing or arriving from flight in local practice areas, or aircraft executing practice instrument approaches at the airport. (See TRAFFIC PATTERN.)

LOCALIZER. The component of an ILS which provides course guidance to the runway. (See INSTRUMENT LANDING SYSTEM.) (See ICAO term LOCALIZER COURSE.) (Refer to AIM.)

LOCALIZER COURSE [ICAO]. The locus of points, in any given horizontal plane, at which the DDM (difference in depth of modulation) is zero.

LOCALIZER OFFSET. An angular offset of the localizer from the runway extended centerline in a direction away from the no transgression zone (NTZ) that increases the normal operating zone (NOZ) width. An offset requires a 50 foot increase in DH and is not authorized for CAT II and CAT III approaches.

LOCALIZER TYPE DIRECTIONAL AID. A NAVAID used for nonprecision instrument approaches with utility and accuracy comparable to a localizer but which is not a part of a complete ILS and is not aligned with the runway. (Refer to AIM.)

LOCALIZER USABLE DISTANCE. The maximum distance from the localizer transmitter at a specified altitude, as verified by flight inspection, at which reliable course information is continuously received. (Refer to AIM.)

LOCATOR [ICAO]. An LM/MF NDB used as an aid to final approach.

Note: A locator usually has an average radius of rated coverage of between 18.5 and 46.3 km (10 and 25 0NM).

LONG RANGE NAVIGATION. (See LORAN.)

LONGITUDINAL SEPARATION. The longitudinal spacing of aircraft at the same altitude by a minimum distance expressed in units of time or miles. (See SEPARATION.) (Refer to AIM.)

LORAN. An electronic navigational system by which hyperbolic lines of position are determined by measuring the difference in the time of reception of synchronized pulse signals from two fixed transmitters. Loran A operates in the 1750-1950 KHz frequency band. Loran C and D operate in the 100–110 KHz frequency band. (Refer to AIM.)

LOST COMMUNICATIONS. Loss of the ability to communicate by radio. Aircraft are sometimes referred to as NORDO (No Radio). Standard pilot procedures are specified in 14 CFR Part 91. Radar controllers issue procedures for pilots to follow in the event of lost communications during a radar approach when weather reports indicate that an aircraft will likely encounter IFR weather conditions during the approach. (Refer to 14 CFR Part 91.) (Refer AIM.)

LOW ALTITUDE AIRWAY STRUCTURE. The network of airways serving aircraft operations up to but not including 18,000 feet MSL. (See AIRWAY.) (Refer to AIM.)

LOW ALTITUDE ALERT, CHECK YOUR ALTITUDE IMMEDIATELY. (See SAFETY ALERT.)

LOW ALTITUDE ALERT SYSTEM. An automated function of the TPX-42 that alerts the controller when a Mode C transponder equipped aircraft on an IFR flight plan is below a predetermined minimum safe altitude. If requested by the pilot, Low Altitude Alert System monitoring is also available to VFR Mode C transponder equipped aircraft.

LOW APPROACH. An approach over an airport or runway following an instrument approach or a VFR approach including the go-around maneuver where the pilot intentionally does not make contact with the runway. (Refer to AIM.)

LOW FREQUENCY. The frequency band between 30 and 300 KHz. (Refer to AIM.)

LPV. A type of approach with vertical guidance (APV) based on WAAS, published on RNAV (GPS) approach charts. This procedure takes advantage of the precise lateral guidance available from WAAS. The minima is published as a decision altitude (DA).

M

M-EARTS. (See MICRO-EN ROUTE AUTOMATED RADAR TRACKING SYSTEM.)

MAA. (See MAXIMUM AUTHORIZED ALTITUDE.)

MACH NUMBER. The ratio of true airspeed to the speed of sound; e.g., MACH .82, MACH 1.6. (See AIRSPEED.)

MACH TECHNIQUE [ICAO]. Describes a control technique used by air traffic control whereby turbojet aircraft operating successively along suitable routes are cleared to maintain appropriate MACH numbers for a relevant portion of the en route phase of flight. The principle objective is to achieve improved utilization of the airspace and to ensure that separation between successive aircraft does not decrease below the established minima.

MAHWP. Missed Approach Holding Waypoint

MAINTAIN.
a. Concerning altitude/flight level, the term means to remain at the altitude/flight level specified. The phrase "climb and" or "descend and" normally precedes "maintain" and the altitude assignment; e.g., "descend and maintain 5,000."
b. Concerning other ATC instructions, the term is used in its literal sense; e.g., maintain VFR.

MAINTENANCE PLANNING FRICTION LEVEL. The friction level specified in AC 150/5320-12, Measurement, Construction, and Maintenance of Skid Resistant Airport Pavement Surfaces, which represents the friction value below which the runway pavement surface remains acceptable for any category or class of aircraft operations but which is beginning to show signs of deterioration. This value will vary depending on the particular friction measurement equipment used.

MAKE SHORT APPROACH. Used by ATC to inform a pilot to alter his/her traffic pattern so as to make a short final approach. (See TRAFFIC PATTERN.)

MAN PORTABLE AIR DEFENSE SYSTEMS (MANPADS). MANPADS are lightweight, shoulder-launched, missile systems used to bring down aircraft and create mass casualties. The potential for MANPADS use against airborne aircraft is real and requires familiarity with the subject. Terrorists choose MANPADS because the weapons are low cost, highly mobile, require minimal set-up time, and are easy to use and maintain. Although the weapons have limited range, and their accuracy is affected by poor visibility and adverse weather, they can be fired from anywhere on land or from boats where there is unrestricted visibility to the target.

MANDATORY ALTITUDE. An altitude depicted on an instrument Approach Procedure Chart requiring the aircraft to maintain altitude at the depicted value.

MANPADS. (See MAN PORTABLE AIR DEFENSE SYSTEMS.)

MAP. (See MISSED APPROACH POINT.)

MARKER BEACON. An electronic navigation facility transmitting a 75 MHz vertical fan or boneshaped radiation pattern. Marker beacons are identified by their modulation frequency and keying code, and when received by compatible airborne equipment, indicate to the pilot, both aurally and visually, that he/she is passing over the facility. (See INNER MARKER.) (See MIDDLE MARKER.) (See OUTER MARKER.) (Refer to AIM.)

MARSA. (See MILITARY AUTHORITY ASSUMES RESPONSIBILITY FOR SEPARATION OF AIRCRAFT.)

MAWP. Missed Approach Waypoint

MAXIMUM AUTHORIZED ALTITUDE. A published altitude representing the maximum usable altitude or flight level for an airspace structure or route segment. It is the highest altitude on a Federal airway, jet route, area navigation low or high route, or other direct route for which an MEA is designated in 14 CFR Part 95 at which adequate reception of navigation aid signals is assured.

MAYDAY. The international radiotelephony distress signal. When repeated three times, it indicates imminent and grave danger and that immediate assistance is requested. (See PAN-PAN.) (Refer to AIM.)

MCA. (See MINIMUM CROSSING ALTITUDE.)

MDA. (See MINIMUM DESCENT ALTITUDE.)

MEA. (See MINIMUM EN ROUTE IFR ALTITUDE.)

METEOROLOGICAL IMPACT STATEMENT. An unscheduled planning forecast describing conditions expected to begin within 4 to 12 hours which may impact the flow of air traffic in a specific center's (ARTCC) area.

METER FIX ARC. A semicircle, equidistant from a meter fix, usually in low altitude relatively close to the meter fix, used to help CTAS/HOST calculate a meter time, and determine appropriate sector meter list assignments for aircraft not on an established arrival route or assigned a meter fix.

METER FIX TIME/SLOT TIME. A calculated time to depart the meter fix in order to cross the vertex at the ACLT. This time reflects descent speed adjustment and any applicable time that must be absorbed prior to crossing the meter fix.

METER LIST. (See ARRIVAL SECTOR ADVISORY LIST.)

METER LIST DISPLAY INTERVAL. A dynamic parameter which controls the number of minutes prior to the flight plan calculated time of arrival at the meter fix for each aircraft, at which time the TCLT is frozen and becomes an ACLT; i.e., the VTA is updated and consequently the TCLT modified as appropriate until frozen at which time updating is suspended and an ACLT is assigned. When frozen, the flight entry is inserted into the arrival sector's meter list for display on the sector PVD/MDM. MLDI is used if filed true airspeed is less than or equal to freeze speed parameters (FSPD).

METERING. A method of time-regulating arrival traffic flow into a terminal area so as not to exceed a predetermined terminal acceptance rate.

METERING AIRPORTS. Airports adapted for metering and for which optimum flight paths are defined. A maximum of 15 airports may be adapted.

METERING FIX. A fix along an established route from over which aircraft will be metered prior to entering terminal airspace. Normally, this fix should be established at a distance from the airport which will facilitate a profile descent 10,000 feet above airport elevation (AAE) or above.

METERING POSITION(S). Adapted PVDs/MDMs and associated "D" positions eligible for display of a metering position list. A maximum of four PVDs/MDMs may be adapted.

METERING POSITION LIST. An ordered list of data on arrivals for a selected metering airport displayed on a metering position PVD/MDM.

MFT. (See METER FIX TIME/SLOT TIME.)

MHA. (See MINIMUM HOLDING ALTITUDE.)

MIA. (See MINIMUM IFR ALTITUDES.)

MICROBURST. A small downburst with outbursts of damaging winds extending 2.5 miles or less. In spite of its small horizontal scale, an intense microburst could induce wind speeds as high as 150 knots (Refer to AIM.)

MICRO-EN ROUTE AUTOMATED RADAR TRACKING SYSTEM (MEARTS). An automated radar and radar beacon tracking system capable of employing both short-range (ASR) and long-range (ARSR) radars. This microcomputer driven system provides improved tracking, continuous data recording, and use of full digital radar displays.

MICROWAVE LANDING SYSTEM. A precision instrument approach system operating in the microwave spectrum which normally consists of the following components:
a. Azimuth Station.
b. Elevation Station.
c. Precision Distance Measuring Equipment.
(See MLS CATEGORIES.)

MID RVR. (See VISIBILITY.)

MIDDLE COMPASS LOCATOR. (See COMPASS LOCATOR.)

MIDDLE MARKER. A marker beacon that defines a point along the glideslope of an ILS normally located at or near the point of decision height (ILS Category I). It is keyed to transmit alternate dots and dashes, with the alternate dots and dashes keyed at the rate of 95 dot/dash combinations per minute on a 1300 Hz tone, which is received aurally and visually by compatible airborne equipment. (See INSTRUMENT LANDING SYSTEM.) (See MARKER BEACON.) (Refer to AIM.)

MILES-IN-TRAIL. A specified distance between aircraft, normally, in the same stratum associated with the same destination or route of flight.

MILITARY AUTHORITY ASSUMES RESPONSIBILITY FOR SEPARATION OF AIRCRAFT. A condition whereby the military services involved assume responsibility for separation between participating military aircraft in the ATC system. It is used only for required IFR operations which are specified in letters of agreement or other appropriate FAA or military documents.

MILITARY LANDING ZONE. A landing strip used exclusively by the military for training. A military landing zone does not carry a runway designation.

MILITARY OPERATIONS AREA. (See SPECIAL USE AIRSPACE.)

MILITARY TRAINING ROUTES. Airspace of defined vertical and lateral dimensions established for the conduct of military flight training at airspeeds in excess of 250 knots IAS. (See IFR MILITARY TRAINING ROUTES.) (See VFR MILITARY TRAINING ROUTES.)

MINIMA. (See MINIMUMS.)

MINIMUM CROSSING ALTITUDE. The lowest altitude at certain fixes at which an aircraft must cross when proceeding in the direction of a higher minimum en route IFR altitude (MEA). (See MINIMUM EN ROUTE IFR ALTITUDE.)

MINIMUM DESCENT ALTITUDE. The lowest altitude, expressed in feet above mean sea level, to which descent is authorized on final approach or during circle-to-land maneuvering in execution of a standard instrument approach procedure where no electronic glideslope is provided. (See NONPRECISION APPROACH PROCEDURE.)

MINIMUM EN ROUTE IFR ALTITUDE. The lowest published altitude between radio fixes which assures acceptable navigational signal coverage and meets obstacle clearance requirements between those fixes. The MEA prescribed for a Federal airway or segment thereof, area navigation low or high route, or other direct route applies to the entire width of the airway, segment, or route between the radio fixes defining the airway, segment, or route. (Refer to 14 CFR Part 91.) (Refer to 14 CFR Part 95.) (Refer to AIM.)

MINIMUM FRICTION LEVEL. The friction level specified in AC 150/5320-12, Measurement, Construction, and Maintenance of Skid Resistant Airport Pavement Surfaces, that represents the minimum recommended wet pavement surface friction value for any turbojet aircraft engaged in LAHSO. This value will vary with the particular friction measurement equipment used.

MINIMUM FUEL. Indicates that an aircraft's fuel supply has reached a state where, upon reaching the destination, it can accept little or no delay. This is not an emergency situation but merely indicates an emergency situation is possible should any undue delay occur. (Refer to AIM.)

MINIMUM HOLDING ALTITUDE. The lowest altitude prescribed for a holding pattern which assures navigational signal coverage, communications, and meets obstacle clearance requirements.

MINIMUM IFR ALTITUDES. Minimum altitudes for IFR operations as prescribed in 14 CFR Part 91. These altitudes are published on aeronautical charts and prescribed in 14 CFR Part 95 for airways and routes, and in 14 CFR Part 97 for standard instrument approach procedures. If no applicable minimum altitude is prescribed in 14 CFR Part 95 or 14 CFR Part 97, the following minimum IFR altitude applies:
a. In designated mountainous areas, 2,000 feet above the highest obstacle within a horizontal distance of 4 nautical miles from the course to be flown; or
b. Other than mountainous areas, 1,000 feet above the highest obstacle within a horizontal distance of 4 nautical miles from the course to be flown; or
c. As otherwise authorized by the Administrator or assigned by ATC.

(See MINIMUM CROSSING ALTITUDE.) (See MINIMUM EN ROUTE IFR ALTITUDE.) (See MINIMUM OBSTRUCTION CLEARANCE ALTITUDE.) (See MINIMUM SAFE ALTITUDE.) (See MINIMUM VECTORING ALTITUDE.) (Refer to 14 CFR Part 91.)

MINIMUM NAVIGATION PERFORMANCE SPECIFICATION. A set of standards which require aircraft to have a minimum navigation performance capability in order to operate in MNPS designated airspace. In addition, aircraft must be certified by their State of Registry for MNPS operation.

MINIMUM NAVIGATION PERFORMANCE SPECIFICATION AIRSPACE. Designated airspace in which MNPS procedures are applied between MNPS certified and equipped aircraft. Under certain conditions, non-MNPS aircraft can operate in MNPSA. However, standard oceanic separation minima is provided between the non-MNPS aircraft and other traffic. Currently, the only designated MNPSA is described as follows:
a. Between FL 285 and FL 420;
b. Between latitudes 27°N and the North Pole;
c. In the east, the eastern boundaries of the CTAs Santa Maria Oceanic, Shanwick Oceanic, and Reykjavik;
d. In the west, the western boundaries of CTAs Reykjavik and Gander Oceanic and New York Oceanic excluding the area west of 60°W and south of 38°30'N.

MINIMUM OBSTRUCTION CLEARANCE ALTITUDE. The lowest published altitude in effect between radio fixes on VOR airways, off-airway routes, or route segments which meets obstacle clearance requirements for the entire route segment and which assures acceptable navigational signal coverage only within 25 statute (22 nautical) miles of a VOR. (Refer to 14 CFR Part 91.) (Refer to 14 CFR Part 95.)

MINIMUM RECEPTION ALTITUDE. The lowest altitude at which an intersection can be determined. (Refer to 14 CFR Part 95.)

MINIMUM SAFE ALTITUDE.
a. The minimum altitude specified in 14 CFR Part 91 for various aircraft operations.
b. Altitudes depicted on approach charts which provide at least 1,000 feet of obstacle clearance for emergency use within a specified distance from the navigation facility upon which a procedure is predicated. These altitudes will be identified as Minimum Sector Altitudes or Emergency Safe Altitudes and are established as follows:
   1. Minimum Sector Altitudes. Altitudes depicted

on approach charts which provide at least 1,000 feet of obstacle clearance within a 25-mile radius of the navigation facility upon which the procedure is predicated. Sectors depicted on approach charts must be at least 90 degrees in scope. These altitudes are for emergency use only and do not necessarily assure acceptable navigational signal coverage. (See ICAO term Minimum Sector Altitude.)

2. Emergency Safe Altitudes. Altitudes depicted on approach charts which provide at least 1,000 feet of obstacle clearance in nonmountainous areas and 2,000 feet of obstacle clearance in designated mountainous areas within a 100-mile radius of the navigation facility upon which the procedure is predicated and normally used only in military procedures. These altitudes are identified on published procedures as "Emergency Safe Altitudes."

MINIMUM SAFE ALTITUDE WARNING. A function of the ARTS III computer that aids the controller by alerting him/her when a tracked Mode C equipped aircraft is below or is predicted by the computer to go below a predetermined minimum safe altitude. (Refer to AIM.)

MINIMUM SECTOR ALTITUDE [ICAO]. The lowest altitude which may be used under emergency conditions which will provide a minimum clearance of 300 m (1,000 feet) above all obstacles located in an area contained within a sector of a circle of 46 km (25 NM) radius centered on a radio aid to navigation.

MINIMUMS. Weather condition requirements established for a particular operation or type of operation; e.g., IFR takeoff or landing, alternate airport for IFR flight plans, VFR flight, etc. (See IFR CONDITIONS.) (See IFR TAKEOFF MINIMUMS AND DEPARTURE PROCEDURES.) (See LANDING MINIMUMS.) (See VFR CONDITIONS.) (Refer to 14 CFR Part 91.) (Refer to AIM.)

MINIMUM VECTORING ALTITUDE. The lowest MSL altitude at which an IFR aircraft will be vectored by a radar controller, except as otherwise authorized for radar approaches, departures, and missed approaches. The altitude meets IFR obstacle clearance criteria. It may be lower than the published MEA along an airway or J-route segment. It may be utilized for radar vectoring only upon the controller's determination that an adequate radar return is being received from the aircraft being controlled. Charts depicting minimum vectoring altitudes are normally available only to the controllers and not to pilots. (Refer to AIM.)

MINUTES-IN-TRAIL. A specified interval between aircraft expressed in time. This method would more likely be utilized regardless of altitude.

MIS. (See METEOROLOGICAL IMPACT STATEMENT.)

MISSED APPROACH.
a. A maneuver conducted by a pilot when an instrument approach cannot be completed to a landing. The route of flight and altitude are shown on instrument approach procedure charts. A pilot executing a missed approach prior to the Missed Approach Point (MAP) must continue along the final approach to the MAP.
b. A term used by the pilot to inform ATC that he/she is executing the missed approach.
c. At locations where ATC radar service is provided, the pilot should conform to radar vectors when provided by ATC in lieu of the published missed approach procedure.
(See MISSED APPROACH POINT.) (Refer to AIM.)

MISSED APPROACH POINT. A point prescribed in each instrument approach procedure at which a missed approach procedure shall be executed if the required visual reference does not exist. (See MISSED APPROACH.) (See SEGMENTS OF AN INSTRUMENT APPROACH PROCEDURE.)

MISSED APPROACH PROCEDURE [ICAO]. The procedure to be followed if the approach cannot be continued.

MISSED APPROACH SEGMENT. (See SEGMENTS OF AN INSTRUMENT APPROACH PROCEDURE.)

MLDI. (See METER LIST DISPLAY INTERVAL.)

MLS. (See MICROWAVE LANDING SYSTEM.)

MLS CATEGORIES.
a. MLS Category I. An MLS approach procedure which provides for an approach to a height above touchdown of not less than 200 feet and a runway visual range of not less than 1,800 feet.
b. MLS Category II. Undefined until data gathering/analysis completion.
c. MLS Category III. Undefined until data gathering/analysis completion.

MM. (See MIDDLE MARKER.)

MNPS. (See MINIMUM NAVIGATION PERFORMANCE SPECIFICATION.)

MNPSA. (See MINIMUM NAVIGATION PERFORMANCE–SPECIFICATION AIRSPACE.)

MOA. (See MILITARY OPERATIONS AREA.)

MOCA. (See MINIMUM OBSTRUCTION CLEARANCE ALTITUDE.)

MODE. The letter or number assigned to a specific pulse spacing of radio signals transmitted or received by ground interrogator or airborne transponder components of the Air Traffic Control Radar Beacon System (ATCRBS). Mode A (military Mode 3) and Mode C (altitude reporting) are used in air traffic control. (See INTERROGATOR.) (See RADAR.) (See TRANSPONDER.) (See ICAO term MODE.) (Refer to AIM.)

MODE (SSR MODE) [ICAO]. The letter or number assigned to a specific pulse spacing of the interrogation signals transmitted by an interrogator. There are 4 modes, A, B, C and D specified in Annex 10, corresponding to four different interrogation pulse spacings.

MODE C INTRUDER ALERT. A function of certain air traffic control automated systems designed to alert radar controllers to existing or pending situations between a tracked target (known IFR or VFR aircraft) and an untracked target (unknown IFR or VFR aircraft) that requires immediate attention/action. (See CONFLICT ALERT.)

MONITOR. (When used with communication transfer) listen on a specific frequency and stand by for instructions. Under normal circumstances do not establish communications.

MONITOR ALERT (MA). A function of the ETMS that provides traffic management personnel with a tool for predicting potential capacity problems in individual operational sectors. The MA is an indication that traffic management personnel need to analyze a particular sector for actual activity and to determine the required action(s), if any, needed to control the demand.

MONITOR ALERT PARAMETER (MAP). The number designated for use in monitor alert processing by the ETMS. The MAP is designated for each operational sector for increments of 15 minutes.

MOVEMENT AREA. The runways, taxiways, and other areas of an airport/heliport which are utilized for taxiing/hover taxiing, air taxiing, takeoff, and landing of aircraft, exclusive of loading ramps and parking areas. At those airports/heliports with a tower, specific approval for entry onto the movement area must be obtained from ATC. (See ICAO term MOVEMENT AREA.)

MOVEMENT AREA [ICAO]. That part of an aerodrome to be used for the takeoff, landing and taxiing of aircraft, consisting of the maneuvering area and the apron(s).

MOVING TARGET INDICATOR. An electronic device which will permit radar scope presentation only from targets which are in motion. A partial remedy for ground clutter.

MRA. (See MINIMUM RECEPTION ALTITUDE.)

MSA. (See MINIMUM SAFE ALTITUDE.)

MSAW. (See MINIMUM SAFE ALTITUDE WARNING.)

MTI. (See MOVING TARGET INDICATOR.)

MTR. (See MILITARY TRAINING ROUTES.)

MULTICOM. A mobile service not open to public correspondence used to provide communications essential to conduct the activities being performed by or directed from private aircraft.

MULTIPLE RUNWAYS. The utilization of a dedicated arrival runway(s) for departures and a dedicated departure runway(s) for arrivals when feasible to reduce delays and enhance capacity.

MVA. (See MINIMUM VECTORING ALTITUDE.)

N

NAS. (See NATIONAL AIRSPACE SYSTEM.)

NATIONAL AIRSPACE SYSTEM. The common network of U.S. airspace; air navigation facilities, equipment and services, airports or landing areas; aeronautical charts, information and services; rules, regulations and procedures, technical information, and manpower and material. Included are system components shared jointly with the military.

NATIONAL BEACON CODE ALLOCATION PLAN AIRSPACE. Airspace over United States territory located within the North American continent between Canada and Mexico, including adjacent territorial waters outward to about boundaries of oceanic control areas (CTA)/Flight Information Regions (FIR). (See FLIGHT INFORMATION REGION.)

NATIONAL FLIGHT DATA CENTER. A facility in Washington D.C., established by FAA to operate a central aeronautical information service for the collection, validation, and dissemination of aeronautical data in support of the activities of government, industry, and the aviation community. The information is published in the National Flight Data Digest. (See NATIONAL FLIGHT DATA DIGEST.)

NATIONAL FLIGHT DATA DIGEST. A daily (except weekends and Federal holidays) publication of flight information appropriate to aeronautical charts, aeronautical publications, Notices to Airmen, or other media serving the purpose of providing operational flight data essential to safe and efficient aircraft operations.

NATIONAL SEARCH AND RESCUE PLAN. An interagency agreement which provides for the effective utilization of all available facilities in all types of search and rescue missions.

NAVAID. (See NAVIGATIONAL AID.)

NAVAID CLASSES. VOR, VORTAC, and TACAN aids are classed according to their operational use. The three classes of NAVAIDs are:
a. T. Terminal.
b. L. Low altitude.
c. h. High altitude.

Note: The normal service range for T, L, and H class aids is found in the AIM. Certain operational requirements make it necessary to use some of these aids at greater service ranges than specified. Extended range is made possible through flight inspection determinations. Some aids also have lesser service range due to location, terrain, frequency protection, etc. Restrictions to service range are listed in Airport/Facility Directory.

NAVIGABLE AIRSPACE. Airspace at and above the minimum flight altitudes prescribed in the CFRs including airspace needed for safe takeoff and landing. (Refer to 14 CFR Part 91.)

NAVIGATION REFERENCE SYSTEM (NRS). The NRS is a system of waypoints developed for use within the United States for flight planning and navigation without reference to ground based navigational aids. The NRS waypoints are located in a grid pattern along defined latitude and longitude lines. The initial use of the NRS will be in the high altitude environment in conjunction with the High Altitude Redesign initiative. The NRS waypoints are intended for use by aircraft capable of point-to-point navigation.

NAVIGATIONAL AID. Any visual or electronic device airborne or on the surface which provides point-to-point guidance information or position data to aircraft in flight. (See AIR NAVIGATION FACILITY.)

NBCAP AIRSPACE. (See NATIONAL BEACON CODE ALLOCATION PLAN AIRSPACE.)

NDB. (See NONDIRECTIONAL BEACON.)

NEGATIVE. "No," or "permission not granted," or "that is not correct."

NEGATIVE CONTACT. Used by pilots to inform ATC that:
a. Previously issued traffic is not in sight. It may be followed by the pilot's request for the controller to provide assistance in avoiding the traffic.
b. They were unable to contact ATC on a particular frequency.

NFDC. (See NATIONAL FLIGHT DATA CENTER.)

NFDD. (See NATIONAL FLIGHT DATA DIGEST.)

NIGHT. The time between the end of evening civil twilight and the beginning of morning civil twilight, as published in the American Air Almanac, converted to local time. (See ICAO term NIGHT.)

NIGHT [ICAO]. The hours between the end of evening civil twilight and the beginning of morning civil twilight or such other period between sunset and sunrise as may be specified by the appropriate authority.

Note: Civil twilight ends in the evening when the center of the sun's disk is 6 degrees below the horizon and begins in the morning when the center of the sun's disk is 6 degrees below the horizon.

NO GYRO APPROACH. A radar approach/vector provided in case of a malfunctioning gyro-compass or directional gyro. Instead of providing the pilot with headings to be flown, the controller observes the radar track and issues control instructions "turn right/left" or "stop turn" as appropriate. (Refer to AIM.)

NO GYRO VECTOR. (See NO GYRO APPROACH.)

NO TRANSGRESSION ZONE (NTZ). The NTZ is a 2,000 foot wide zone, located equidistant between parallel runway final approach courses in which flight is not allowed.

NONAPPROACH CONTROL TOWER. Authorizes aircraft to land or takeoff at the airport controlled by the tower or to transit the Class D airspace. The primary function of a nonapproach control tower is the sequencing of aircraft in the traffic pattern and on the landing area. Nonapproach control towers also separate aircraft operating under instrument flight rules clearances from approach controls and centers. They provide ground control services to aircraft, vehicles, personnel, and equipment on the airport movement area.

NONCOMMON ROUTE/PORTION. That segment of a North American Route between the inland navigation facility and a designated North American terminal.

NONCOMPOSITE SEPARATION. Separation in accordance with minima other than the composite separation minimum specified for the area concerned.

NONDIRECTIONAL BEACON. An L/MF or UHF radio beacon transmitting nondirectional signals whereby the pilot of an aircraft equipped with direction finding equipment can determine his/her bearing to or from the radio beacon and "home" on or track to or from the station. When the radio beacon is installed in conjunction with the Instrument Landing System marker, it is normally called a Compass Locator. (See AUTOMATIC DIRECTION FINDER.) (See COMPASS LOCATOR.)

NONMOVEMENT AREAS. Taxiways and apron (ramp) areas not under the control of air traffic.

NONPRECISION APPROACH. (See NONPRECISION APPROACH PROCEDURE.)

NONPRECISION APPROACH PROCEDURE. A standard instrument approach procedure in which no electronic glideslope is provided; e.g., VOR, TACAN, NDB, LOC, ASR, LDA, or SDF approaches.

NONRADAR. Precedes other terms and generally means without the use of radar, such as:

a. Nonradar Approach. Used to describe instrument approaches for which course guidance on final approach is not provided by ground-based precision or surveillance radar. Radar vectors to the final approach course may or may not be provided by ATC. Examples of nonradar approaches are VOR, NDB, TACAN, and ILS/MLS approaches. (See FINAL APPROACH COURSE.) (See FINAL APPROACH-IFR.) (See INSTRUMENT APPROACH PROCEDURE.) (See RADAR APPROACH.)

b. Nonradar Approach Control. An ATC facility providing approach control service without the use of radar. (See APPROACH CONTROL FACILITY.) (See APPROACH CONTROL SERVICE.)

c. Nonradar Arrival. An aircraft arriving at an airport without radar service or at an airport served by a radar facility and radar contact has not been established or has been terminated due to a lack of radar service to the airport. (See RADAR ARRIVAL.) (See RADAR SERVICE.)

d. Nonradar Route. A flight path or route over which the pilot is performing his/her own navigation. The pilot may be receiving radar separation, radar

monitoring, or other ATC services while on a nonradar route. (See RADAR ROUTE.)

e. Nonradar Separation. The spacing of aircraft in accordance with established minima without the use of radar; e.g., vertical, lateral, or longitudinal separation. (See RADAR SEPARATION.) (See ICAO term NONRADAR SEPARATION.)

NONRADAR SEPARATION [ICAO]. The separation used when aircraft position information is derived from sources other than radar.

NON-RESTRICTIVE ROUTING (NRR). Portions of a proposed route of flight where a user can flight plan the most advantageous flight path with no requirement to make reference to ground-based NAVAIDs.

NOPAC. (See NORTH PACIFIC.)

NORDO. (See LOST COMMUNICATIONS.)

NORMAL OPERATING ZONE (NOZ). The NOZ is the operating zone within which aircraft flight remains during normal independent simultaneous parallel ILS approaches.

NORTH AMERICAN ROUTE. A numerically coded route preplanned over existing airway and route systems to and from specific coastal fixes serving the North Atlantic. North American Routes consist of the following:

a. Common Route/Portion. That segment of a North American Route between the inland navigation facility and the coastal fix.

b. Noncommon Route/Portion. That segment of a North American Route between the inland navigation facility and a designated North American terminal.

c. Inland Navigation Facility. A navigation aid on a North American Route at which the common route and/or the noncommon route begins or ends.

d. Coastal Fix. A navigation aid or intersection where an aircraft transitions between the domestic route structure and the oceanic route structure.

NORTH AMERICAN ROUTE PROGRAM (NRP). The NRP is a set of rules and procedures which are designed to increase the flexibility of user flight planning within published guidelines.

NORTH MARK. A beacon data block sent by the host computer to be displayed by the ARTS on a 360 degree bearing at a locally selected radar azimuth and distance. The North Mark is used to ensure correct range/azimuth orientation during periods of CENRAP.

NORTH PACIFIC. An organized route system between the Alaskan west coast and Japan.

NOTAM. (See NOTICE TO AIRMEN.)

NOTAM [ICAO]. A notice containing information concerning the establishment, condition or change in any aeronautical facility, service, procedure or hazard, the timely knowledge of which is essential to personnel concerned with flight operations.
a. I Distribution. Distribution by means of telecommunication.
b. II Distribution. Distribution by means other than telecommunications.

NOTICE TO AIRMEN. A notice containing information (not known sufficiently in advance to publicize by other means) concerning the establishment, condition, or change in any component (facility, service, or procedure of, or hazard in the National Airspace System) the timely knowledge of which is essential to personnel concerned with flight operations.
a. NOTAM(D). A NOTAM given (in addition to local dissemination) distant dissemination beyond the area of responsibility of the Flight Service Station. These NOTAMs will be stored and available until canceled.
b. NOTAM(L). A NOTAM given local dissemination by voice and other means, such as telautograph and telephone, to satisfy local user requirements.
c. FDC NOTAM. A NOTAM regulatory in nature, transmitted by USNOF and given system wide dissemination.
(See ICAO term NOTAM.)

NOTICES TO AIRMEN PUBLICATION. A publication issued every 28 days, designed primarily for the pilot, which contains current NOTAM information considered essential to the safety of flight as well as supplemental data to other aeronautical publications. The contraction NTAP is used in NOTAM text. (See NOTICE TO AIRMEN.)

NRR. (See NON-RESTRICTIVE ROUTING.)

NRS. (See NAVIGATION REFERENCE SYSTEM.)

NTAP. (See NOTICES TO AIRMEN PUBLICATION.)

NUMEROUS TARGETS VICINITY (LOCATION). A traffic advisory issued by ATC to advise pilots that targets on the radar scope are too numerous to issue individually. (See TRAFFIC ADVISORIES.)

O

OBSTACLE. An existing object, object of natural growth, or terrain at a fixed geographical location or which may be expected at a fixed location within a prescribed area with reference to which vertical clearance is or must be provided during flight operation.

OBSTACLE DEPARTURE PROCEDURE (ODP). A preplanned instrument flight rule (IFR) departure procedure printed for pilot use in textual or graphic form to provide obstruction clearance via the least onerous route from the terminal area to the appropriate en route structure. ODPs are recommended for obstruction clearance and may be flown without ATC clearance unless an alternate departure procedure (SID or radar vector) has been specifically assigned by ATC. (See IFR TAKEOFF MINIMUMS AND DEPARTURE PROCEDURES.) (See STANDARD INSTRUMENT DEPARTURES.) (Refer to AIM.)

OBSTACLE FREE ZONE. The OFZ is a three dimensional volume of airspace which protects for the transition of aircraft to and from the runway. The OFZ clearing standard precludes taxiing and parked airplanes and object penetrations, except for frangible NAVAID locations that are fixed by function. Additionally, vehicles, equipment, and personnel may be authorized by air traffic control to enter the area using the provisions of FAAO 7110.65, Para 3-1-5, VEHICLES/EQUIPMENT/PERSONNEL ON RUNWAYS. The runway OFZ and when applicable, the inner-approach OFZ, and the inner-transitional OFZ, comprise the OFZ.
a. Runway OFZ. The runway OFZ is a defined volume of airspace centered above the runway. The runway OFZ is the airspace above a surface whose elevation at any point is the same as the elevation of the nearest point on the runway centerline. The runway OFZ extends 200 feet beyond each end of the runway. The width is as follows:
1. For runways serving large airplanes, the greater of: (a) 400 feet, or (b) 180 feet, plus the wingspan of the most demanding airplane, plus 20 feet per 1,000 feet of airport elevation.
2. For runways serving only small airplanes:
(a) 300 feet for precision instrument runways.
(b) 250 feet for other runways serving small airplanes with approach speeds of 50 knots, or more.
(c) 120 feet for other runways serving small airplanes with approach speeds of less than 50 knots.
b. Inner-approach OFZ. The inner-approach OFZ

is a defined volume of airspace centered on the approach area. The inner-approach OFZ applies only to runways with an approach lighting system. The inner-approach OFZ begins 200 feet from the runway threshold at the same elevation as the runway threshold and extends 200 feet beyond the last light unit in the approach lighting system. The width of the inner-approach OFZ is the same as the runway OFZ and rises at a slope of 50 (horizontal) to 1 (vertical) from the beginning.

c. Inner-transitional OFZ. The inner transitional surface OFZ is a defined volume of airspace along the sides of the runway and inner-approach OFZ and applies only to precision instrument runways. The inner-transitional surface OFZ slopes 3 (horizontal) to 1 (vertical) out from the edges of the runway OFZ and inner-approach OFZ to a height of 150 feet above the established airport elevation.

(Refer to AC 150/5300-13, Chapter 3.) (Refer to FAAO 7110.65, Para 3-1-5, VEHICLES/EQUIPMENT/PERSONNEL ON RUNWAYS.)

OBSTRUCTION. Any object/obstacle exceeding the obstruction standards specified by 14 CFR Part 77, Subpart C.

OBSTRUCTION LIGHT. A light or one of a group of lights, usually red or white, frequently mounted on a surface structure or natural terrain to warn pilots of the presence of an obstruction.

OCEANIC AIRSPACE. Airspace over the oceans of the world, considered international airspace, where oceanic separation and procedures per the International Civil Aviation Organization are applied. Responsibility for the provisions of air traffic control service in this airspace is delegated to various countries, based generally upon geographic proximity and the availability of the required resources.

OCEANIC DISPLAY AND PLANNING SYSTEM. An automated digital display system which provides flight data processing, conflict probe, and situation display for oceanic air traffic control.

OCEANIC NAVIGATIONAL ERROR REPORT. A report filed when an aircraft exiting oceanic airspace has been observed by radar to be off course. ONER reporting parameters and procedures are contained in FAAO 7110.82, Monitoring of Navigational Performance In Oceanic Areas.

OCEANIC PUBLISHED ROUTE. A route established in international airspace and charted or described in flight information publications, such as Route Charts, DOD Enroute Charts, Chart Supplements, NOTAMs, and Track Messages.

OCEANIC TRANSITION ROUTE. An ATS route established for the purpose of transitioning aircraft to/from an organized track system.

ODAPS. (See OCEANIC DISPLAY AND PLANNING SYSTEM.)

ODP. (See OBSTACLE DEPARTURE PROCEDURE.)

OFF COURSE. A term used to describe a situation where an aircraft has reported a position fix or is observed on radar at a point not on the ATC-approved route of flight.

OFF-ROUTE VECTOR. A vector by ATC which takes an aircraft off a previously assigned route. Altitudes assigned by ATC during such vectors provide required obstacle clearance.

OFFSET PARALLEL RUNWAYS. Staggered runways having centerlines which are parallel.

OFFSHORE/CONTROL AIRSPACE AREA. That portion of airspace between the U.S. 12 NM limit and the oceanic CTA/FIR boundary within which air traffic control is exercised. These areas are established to provide air traffic control services. Offshore/Control Airspace Areas may be classified as either Class A airspace or Class E airspace.

OFT. (See OUTER FIX TIME.)

OM. (See OUTER MARKER.)

OMEGA. An RNAV system designed for long-range navigation based upon ground-based electronic navigational aid signals.

ON COURSE.
a. Used to indicate that an aircraft is established on the route centerline.
b. Used by ATC to advise a pilot making a radar approach that his/her aircraft is lined up on the final approach course.

(See ON-COURSE INDICATION.)

ON-COURSE INDICATION. An indication on an instrument, which provides the pilot a visual means of determining that the aircraft is located on the centerline of a given navigational track, or an indication on a radar scope that an aircraft is on a given track.

ONE-MINUTE WEATHER. The most recent one minute updated weather broadcast received by a pilot from an uncontrolled airport ASOS/AWOS.

ONER. (See OCEANIC NAVIGATIONAL ERROR REPORT.)

OPERATIONAL. (See DUE REGARD.)

OPPOSITE DIRECTION AIRCRAFT. Aircraft are operating in opposite directions when:

a. They are following the same track in reciprocal directions; or

b. Their tracks are parallel and the aircraft are flying in reciprocal directions; or

c. Their tracks intersect at an angle of more than 135°.

OPTION APPROACH. An approach requested and conducted by a pilot which will result in either a touch-and-go, missed approach, low approach, stop. and-go, or full stop landing. (See CLEARED FOR THE OPTION.) (Refer to AIM.)

ORGANIZED TRACK SYSTEM. A series of ATS routes which are fixed and charted; i.e., CEP, NOPAC, or flexible and described by NOTAM; i.e., NAT TRACK MESSAGE.

OROCA. An off-route altitude which provides obstruction clearance with a 1,000 foot buffer in non-mountainous terrain areas and a 2,000 foot buffer in designated mountainous areas within the United States. This altitude may not provide signal coverage from ground-based navigational aids, air traffic control radar, or communications coverage.

OTR. (See OCEANIC TRANSITION ROUTE.)

OTS. (See ORGANIZED TRACK SYSTEM.)

OUT. The conversation is ended and no response is expected.

OUTER AREA (associated with Class C airspace). Nonregulatory airspace surrounding designated Class C airspace airports wherein ATC provides radar vectoring and sequencing on a full-time basis for all IFR and participating VFR aircraft. The service provided in the outer area is called Class C service which includes: IFR/IFR-standard IFR separation; IFR/VFR-traffic advisories and conflict resolution; and VFR/VFR-traffic advisories and, as appropriate, safety alerts. The normal radius will be 20 nautical miles with some variations based on site-specific requirements. The outer area extends outward from the primary Class C airspace airport and extends from the lower limits of radar/radio coverage up to the ceiling of the approach control's delegated airspace excluding the Class C charted area and other airspace as appropriate. (See CONFLICT RESOLUTION.) (See CONTROLLED AIRSPACE.)

OUTER COMPASS LOCATOR. (See COMPASS LOCATOR.)

OUTER FIX. A general term used within ATC to describe fixes in the terminal area, other than the final approach fix. Aircraft are normally cleared to these fixes by an Air Route Traffic Control Center or an Approach Control Facility. Aircraft are normally cleared from these fixes to the final approach fix or final approach course.

or

OUTER FIX. An adapted fix along the converted route of flight, prior to the meter fix, for which crossing times are calculated and displayed in the metering position list.

OUTER FIX ARC. A semicircle, usually about a 50–70 mile radius from a meter fix, usually in high altitude, which is used by CTAS/HOST to calculate outer fix times and determine appropriate sector meter list assignments for aircraft on an established arrival route that will traverse the arc.

OUTER FIX TIME. A calculated time to depart the outer fix in order to cross the vertex at the ACLT. The time reflects descent speed adjustments and any applicable delay time that must be absorbed prior to crossing the meter fix.

OUTER MARKER. A marker beacon at or near the glideslope intercept altitude of an ILS approach. It is keyed to transmit two dashes per second on a 400 Hz tone, which is received aurally and visually by compatible airborne equipment. The OM is normally located four to seven miles from the runway threshold on the extended centerline of the runway. (See INSTRUMENT LANDING SYSTEM.) (See MARKER BEACON.) (Refer to AIM.)

OVER. My transmission is ended; I expect a response.

OVERHEAD MANEUVER. A series of predetermined maneuvers prescribed for aircraft (often in formation) for entry into the visual flight rules (VFR) traffic pattern and to proceed to a landing. An overhead maneuver is not an instrument flight rules (IFR) approach procedure. An aircraft executing an overhead maneuver is considered VFR and the IFR flight plan is cancelled when the aircraft reaches the "initial point" on the initial approach portion of the maneuver. The pattern usually specifies the following:

a. The radio contact required of the pilot.

b. The speed to be maintained.

c. An initial approach 3 to 5 miles in length.

d. An elliptical pattern consisting of two 180 degree turns.

e. A break point at which the first 180 degree turn is started.

f. The direction of turns.

g. Altitude (at least 500 feet above the conventional pattern).

h. A "Roll-out" on final approach not less than 1/4 mile from the landing threshold and not less than 300 feet above the ground.

OVERLYING CENTER. The ARTCC facility that is responsible for arrival/departure operations at a specific terminal.

P

P TIME. (See PROPOSED DEPARTURE TIME.)

P-ACP. (See PREARRANGED COORDINATION PROCEDURES.)

PAN-PAN. The international radio-telephony urgency signal. When repeated three times, indicates uncertainty or alert followed by the nature of the urgency. (See MAYDAY.) (Refer to AIM.)

PAR. (See PRECISION APPROACH RADAR.)

PAR [ICAO]. (See ICAO Term PRECISION APPROACH RADAR.)

PARALLEL ILS APPROACHES. Approaches to parallel runways by IFR aircraft which, when established inbound toward the airport on the adjacent final approach courses, are radar-separated by at least 2 miles. (See FINAL APPROACH COURSE.) (See SIMULTANEOUS ILS APPROACHES.)

PARALLEL MLS APPROACHES. (See PARALLEL ILS APPROACHES.)

PARALLEL OFFSET ROUTE. A parallel track to the left or right of the designated or established airway/route. Normally associated with Area Navigation (RNAV) operations. (See AREA NAVIGATION.)

PARALLEL RUNWAYS. Two or more runways at the same airport whose centerlines are parallel. In addition to runway number, parallel runways are designated as L (left) and R (right) or, if three parallel runways exist, L (left), C (center), and R (right).

PBCT. (See PROPOSED BOUNDARY CROSSING TIME.)

PDC. (See PRE-DEPARTURE CLEARANCE.)

PERMANENT ECHO. Radar signals reflected from fixed objects on the earth's surface; e.g., buildings, towers, terrain. Permanent echoes are distinguished from "ground clutter" by being definable locations rather than large areas. Under certain conditions they may be used to check radar alignment.

PHOTO RECONNAISSANCE. Military activity that requires locating individual photo targets and navigating to the targets at a preplanned angle and altitude. The activity normally requires a lateral route width of 16 NM and altitude range of 1,500 feet to 10,000 feet AGL.

PIDP. (See PROGRAMMABLE INDICATOR DATA PROCESSOR.)

PILOT BRIEFING. A service provided by the FSS to assist pilots in flight planning. Briefing items may include weather information, NOTAMs, military activities, flow control information, and other items as requested. (Refer to AIM.)

PILOT IN COMMAND. The pilot responsible for the operation and safety of an aircraft during flight time. (Refer to 14 CFR Part 91.)

PILOT WEATHER REPORT. A report of meteorological phenomena encountered by aircraft in flight. (Refer to AIM.)

PILOT'S DISCRETION. When used in conjunction with altitude assignments, means that ATC has offered the pilot the option of starting climb or descent whenever he/she wishes and conducting the climb or descent at any rate he/she wishes. He/she may temporarily level off at any intermediate altitude. However, once he/she has vacated an altitude, he/she may not return to that altitude.

PIREP. (See PILOT WEATHER REPORT.)

PITCH POINT. A fix/waypoint that serves as a transition point from a departure procedure or the low altitude ground-based navigation structure into the high altitude waypoint system.

PLANS DISPLAY. A display available in URET that provides detailed flight plan and predicted conflict information in textual format for requested Current Plans and all Trial Plans. (See USER REQUEST EVALUATION TOOL.)

POINT OUT. (See RADAR POINT OUT.)

POINT-TO-POINT (PTP). A level of NRR service for aircraft that is based on traditional waypoints in their FMS's or RNAV equipage.

POLAR TRACK STRUCTURE. A system of organized routes between Iceland and Alaska which overlie Canadian MNPS Airspace.

POSITION AND HOLD. Used by ATC to inform a pilot to taxi onto the departure runway in takeoff position and hold. It is not authorization for takeoff. It is used when takeoff clearance cannot immediately be issued because of traffic or other reasons. (See CLEARED FOR TAKEOFF.)

POSITION REPORT. A report over a known location as transmitted by an aircraft to ATC. (Refer to AIM.)

POSITION SYMBOL. A computer-generated indication shown on a radar display to indicate the mode of tracking.

POSITIVE CONTROL. The separation of all air traffic within designated airspace by air traffic control.

PRACTICE INSTRUMENT APPROACH. An instrument approach procedure conducted by a VFR or an IFR aircraft for the purpose of pilot training or proficiency demonstrations.

PRE-DEPARTURE CLEARANCE. An application with the Terminal Data Link System (TDLS) that provides clearance information to subscribers, through a service provider, in text to the cockpit or gate printer.

PREARRANGED COORDINATION. A standardized procedure which permits an air traffic controller to enter the airspace assigned to another air traffic controller without verbal coordination. The procedures are defined in a facility directive which ensures standard separation between aircraft.

PREARRANGED COORDINATION PROCEDURES. A facility's standardized procedure that describes the process by which one controller shall allow an aircraft to penetrate or transit another controller's airspace in a manner that assures standard separation without individual coordination for each aircraft.

PRECIPITATION. Any or all forms of water particles (rain, sleet, hail, or snow) that fall from the atmosphere and reach the surface.

PRECISION APPROACH. (See PRECISION APPROACH PROCEDURE.)

PRECISION APPROACH PROCEDURE. A standard instrument approach procedure in which an electronic glideslope/glidepath is provided; e.g., ILS, MLS, and PAR. (See INSTRUMENT LANDING SYSTEM.) (See MICROWAVE LANDING SYSTEM.) (See PRECISION APPROACH RADAR.)

PRECISION APPROACH RADAR. Radar equipment in some ATC facilities operated by the FAA and/or the military services at joint-use civil/military locations and separate military installations to detect and display azimuth, elevation, and range of aircraft on the final approach course to a runway. This equipment may be used to monitor certain nonradar approaches, but is primarily used to conduct a precision instrument approach (PAR) wherein the controller issues guidance instructions to the pilot based on the aircraft's position in relation to the final approach course (azimuth), the glidepath (elevation), and the distance (range) from the touchdown point on the runway as displayed on the radar scope.

Note: The abbreviation "PAR" is also used to denote preferential arrival routes in ARTCC computers.
(See GLIDEPATH.) (See PAR.) (See PREFERENTIAL ROUTES.) (See ICAO term PRECISION APPROACH RADAR.) (Refer to AIM.)

PRECISION APPROACH RADAR [ICAO]. Primary radar equipment used to determine the position of an aircraft during final approach, in terms of lateral and vertical deviations relative to a nominal approach path, and in range relative to touchdown.

Note: Precision approach radars are designed to enable pilots of aircraft to be given guidance by radio communication during the final stages of the approach to land.

PRECISION RUNWAY MONITOR (PRM). Provides air traffic controllers with high precision secondary surveillance data for aircraft on final approach to parallel runways that have extended centerlines separated by less than 4,300 feet. High resolution color monitoring displays (FMA) are required to present surveillance track data to controllers along with detailed maps depicting approaches and no transgression zone.

PREFERENTIAL ROUTES. Preferential routes (PDRs, PARs, and PDARs) are adapted in ARTCC computers to accomplish inter/intrafacility controller coordination and to assure that flight data is posted at the proper control positions. Locations having a need for these specific inbound and outbound routes normally publish such routes in local facility bulletins, and their use by pilots minimizes flight plan route amendments. When the workload or traffic situation permits, controllers normally provide radar vectors or assign requested routes to minimize circuitous routing. Preferential routes are usually confined to one ARTCC's area and are referred to by the following names or acronyms:

a. Preferential Departure Route (PDR). A specific departure route from an airport or terminal area to an en route point where there is no further need for flow control. It may be included in an Instrument Departure Procedure (DP) or a Preferred IFR Route.

b. Preferential Arrival Route (PAR). A specific arrival route from an appropriate en route point to an airport or terminal area. It may be included in a Standard Terminal Arrival (STAR) or a Preferred IFR Route. The abbreviation "PAR" is used primarily within the ARTCC and should not be confused with the abbreviation for Precision Approach Radar.

c. Preferential Departure and Arrival Route (PDAR). A route between two terminals which are within or immediately adjacent to one ARTCC's area. PDARs are not synonymous with Preferred IFR Routes but may be listed as such as they do accomplish essentially the same purpose.

(See NAS STAGE A.) (See PREFERRED IFR ROUTES.)

PREFERRED IFR ROUTES. Routes established between busier airports to increase system efficiency and capacity. They normally extend through one or more ARTCC areas and are designed to achieve balanced traffic flows among high density terminals. IFR clearances are issued on the basis of these routes except when severe weather avoidance procedures or other factors dictate otherwise. Preferred IFR Routes are listed in the Airport/Facility Directory. If a flight is planned to or from an area having such routes but the departure or arrival point is not listed in the Airport/Facility Directory, pilots may use that part of a Preferred IFR Route which is appropriate for the departure or arrival point that is listed. Preferred IFR Routes are correlated with DPs and STARs and may be defined by airways, jet routes, direct routes between NAVAIDs, Waypoints, NAVAID radials/DME, or any combinations thereof. (See CENTER's AREA.) (See INSTRUMENT DEPARTURE PROCEDURE.) (See PREFERENTIAL ROUTES.) (See STANDARD TERMINAL ARRIVAL.) (Refer to AIRPORT/FACILITY DIRECTORY.) (Refer to NOTICES TO AIRMEN PUBLICATION.)

PRE-FLIGHT PILOT BRIEFING. (See PILOT BRIEFING.)

PREVAILING VISIBILITY. (See VISIBILITY.)

PRM. (See ILS PRM APPROACH.) (See PRECISION RUNWAY MONITOR.)

PROCEDURE TURN. The maneuver prescribed when it is necessary to reverse direction to establish an aircraft on the intermediate approach segment or final approach course. The outbound course, direction of turn, distance within which the turn must be completed, and minimum altitude are specified in the procedure. However, unless otherwise restricted, the point at which the turn may be commenced and the type and rate of turn are left to the discretion of the pilot. (See ICAO term PROCEDURE TURN.)

PROCEDURE TURN [ICAO]. A maneuver in which a turn is made away from a designated track followed by a turn in the opposite direction to permit the aircraft to intercept and proceed along the reciprocal of the designated track.

Note 1: Procedure turns are designated "left" or "right" according to the direction of the initial turn.

Note 2: Procedure turns may be designated as being made either in level flight or while descending, according to the circumstances of each individual approach procedure.

PROCEDURE TURN INBOUND. That point of a procedure turn maneuver where course reversal has been completed and an aircraft is established inbound on the intermediate approach segment or final approach course. A report of "procedure turn inbound" is normally used by ATC as a position report for separation purposes. (See FINAL APPROACH COURSE.) (See PROCEDURE TURN.) (See SEGMENTS OF AN INSTRUMENT APPROACH PROCEDURE.)

PROFILE DESCENT. An uninterrupted descent (except where level flight is required for speed adjustment; e.g., 250 knots at 10,000 feet MSL) from cruising altitude/level to interception of a glideslope or to a minimum altitude specified for the initial or intermediate approach segment of a nonprecision instrument approach. The profile descent normally terminates at the approach gate or where the glideslope or other appropriate minimum altitude is intercepted.

PROGRAMMABLE INDICATOR DATA PROCESSOR. The PIDP is a modification to the AN/TPX-42 interrogator system currently installed in fixed RAPCONs. The PIDP detects, tracks, and predicts secondary radar aircraft targets. These are displayed by means of computer-generated symbols and alphanumeric characters depicting flight identification, aircraft altitude, ground speed, and flight plan data. Although primary radar targets are not tracked, they are displayed coincident with the secondary radar targets as well as with the other symbols and alphanumerics. The system has the capability of interfacing with ARTCCs.

PROGRESS REPORT. (See POSITION REPORT.)

PROGRESSIVE TAXI. Precise taxi instructions given to a pilot unfamiliar with the airport or issued in stages as the aircraft proceeds along the taxi route.

PROHIBITED AREA. (See SPECIAL USE AIRSPACE.) (See ICAO term PROHIBITED AREA.)

PROHIBITED AREA [ICAO]. An airspace of defined dimensions, above the land areas or territorial waters of a State, within which the flight of aircraft is prohibited.

PROPOSED BOUNDARY CROSSING TIME. Each center has a PBCT parameter for each internal airport. Proposed internal flight plans are transmitted to the adjacent center if the flight time along the proposed route from the departure airport to the center boundary is less than or equal to the value of PBCT or if airport adaptation specifies transmission regardless of PBCT.

PROPOSED DEPARTURE TIME. The time that the aircraft expects to become airborne.

PROTECTED AIRSPACE. The airspace on either side of an oceanic route/track that is equal to one-half the lateral separation minimum except where reduction of protected airspace has been authorized.

PT. (See PROCEDURE TURN.)

PTP. (See POINT-TO-POINT.)

PTS. (See POLAR TRACK STRUCTURE.)

PUBLISHED ROUTE. A route for which an IFR altitude has been established and published; e.g., Federal Airways, Jet Routes, Area Navigation Routes, Specified Direct Routes.

Q

QUEUING. (See STAGING/QUEUING.)

QNE. The barometric pressure used for the standard altimeter setting (29.92 inches Hg.).

QNH. The barometric pressure as reported by a particular station.

Q ROUTE. "Q" is the designator assigned to published RNAV routes used by the United States.

QUADRANT. A quarter part of a circle, centered on a NAVAID, oriented clockwise from magnetic north as follows: NE quadrant 000-089, SE quadrant 090-179, SW quadrant 180-269, NW quadrant 270-359.

QUICK LOOK. A feature of the EAS and ARTS which provides the controller the capability to display full data blocks of tracked aircraft from other control positions.

R

RADAR. A device which, by measuring the time interval between transmission and reception of radio pulses and correlating the angular orientation of the radiated antenna beam or beams in azimuth and/or elevation, provides information on range, azimuth, and/or elevation of objects in the path of the transmitted pulses.
  a. Primary Radar. A radar system in which a minute portion of a radio pulse transmitted from a site is reflected by an object and then received back at that site for processing and display at an air traffic control facility.
  b. Secondary Radar/Radar Beacon (ATCRBS). A radar system in which the object to be detected is fitted with cooperative equipment in the form of a radio receiver/transmitter (transponder). Radar pulses transmitted from the searching transmitter/receiver (interrogator) site are received in the cooperative equipment and used to trigger a distinctive transmission from the transponder. This reply transmission, rather than a reflected signal, is then received back at the transmitter/receiver site for processing and display at an air traffic control facility.
(See INTERROGATOR.) (See TRANSPONDER.) (See ICAO term RADAR.) (Refer to AIM.)

RADAR [ICAO]. A radio detection device which provides information on range, azimuth and/or elevation of objects.
  a. Primary Radar. Radar system which uses reflected radio signals.
  b. Secondary Radar. Radar system wherein a radio signal transmitted from a radar station initiates the transmission of a radio signal from another station.

RADAR ADVISORY. The provision of advice and information based on radar observations. (See ADVISORY SERVICE.)

RADAR ALTIMETER. (See RADIO ALTIMETER.)

RADAR APPROACH. An instrument approach procedure which utilizes Precision Approach Radar (PAR) or Airport Surveillance Radar (ASR). (See AIRPORT SURVEILLANCE RADAR.) (See INSTRUMENT APPROACH PROCEDURE.) (See PRECISION APPROACH RADAR.) (See SURVEILLANCE APPROACH.) (See ICAO term RADAR APPROACH.) (Refer to AIM.)

RADAR APPROACH [ICAO]. An approach, executed by an aircraft, under the direction of a radar controller.

RADAR APPROACH CONTROL FACILITY. A terminal ATC facility that uses radar and nonradar capabilities to provide approach control services to aircraft arriving, departing, or transiting airspace controlled by the facility. (See APPROACH CONTROL SERVICE.)
  a. Provides radar ATC services to aircraft operating in the vicinity of one or more civil and/or military airports in a terminal area. The facility may provide services of a ground controlled approach (GCA); i.e., ASR and PAR approaches. A radar approach control facility may be operated by FAA, USAF, US Army, USN, USMC, or jointly by FAA and a military service. Specific facility nomenclatures are used for administrative purposes only and are related to the physical location of the facility and the operating service generally as follows:
  1. Army Radar Approach Control (ARAC) (Army).
  2. Radar Air Traffic Control Facility (RATCF) (Navy/FAA).

3. Radar Approach Control (RAPCON) (Air Force/FAA).

4. Terminal Radar Approach Control (TRACON) (FAA).

5. Air Traffic Control Tower (ATCT) (FAA). (Only those towers delegated approach control authority).

RADAR ARRIVAL. An aircraft arriving at an airport served by a radar facility and in radar contact with the facility. (See NONRADAR.)

RADAR BEACON. (See RADAR.)

RADAR CLUTTER [ICAO]. The visual indication on a radar display of unwanted signals.

RADAR CONTACT.

a. Used by ATC to inform an aircraft that it is identified on the radar display and radar flight following will be provided until radar identification is terminated. Radar service may also be provided within the limits of necessity and capability. When a pilot is informed of "radar contact," he/she automatically discontinues reporting over compulsory reporting points. (See RADAR CONTACT LOST.) (See RADAR FLIGHT FOLLOWING.) (See RADAR SERVICE.) (See RADAR SERVICE TERMINATED.) (Refer to AIM.)

b. The term used to inform the controller that the aircraft is identified and approval is granted for the aircraft to enter the receiving controllers airspace. (See ICAO term RADAR CONTACT.)

RADAR CONTACT [ICAO]. The situation which exists when the radar blip or radar position symbol of a particular aircraft is seen and identified on a radar display.

RADAR CONTACT LOST. Used by ATC to inform a pilot that radar data used to determine the aircraft's position is no longer being received, or is no longer reliable and radar service is no longer being provided. The loss may be attributed to several factors including the aircraft merging with weather or ground clutter, the aircraft operating below radar line of sight coverage, the aircraft entering an area of poor radar return, failure of the aircraft transponder, or failure of the ground radar equipment. (See CLUTTER.) (See RADAR CONTACT.)

RADAR ENVIRONMENT. An area in which radar service may be provided. (See ADDITIONAL SERVICES.) (See RADAR CONTACT.) (See RADAR SERVICE.) (See TRAFFIC ADVISORIES.)

RADAR FLIGHT FOLLOWING. The observation of the progress of radar identified aircraft, whose primary navigation is being provided by the pilot,

wherein the controller retains and correlates the aircraft identity with the appropriate target or target symbol displayed on the radar scope. (See RADAR CONTACT.) (See RADAR SERVICE.) (Refer to AIM.)

RADAR IDENTIFICATION. The process of ascertaining that an observed radar target is the radar return from a particular aircraft. (See RADAR CONTACT.) (See RADAR SERVICE.) (See ICAO term RADAR IDENTIFICATION.)

RADAR IDENTIFICATION [ICAO]. The process of correlating a particular radar blip or radar position symbol with a specific aircraft.

RADAR IDENTIFIED AIRCRAFT. An aircraft, the position of which has been correlated with an observed target or symbol on the radar display. (See RADAR CONTACT.) (See RADAR CONTACT LOST.)

RADAR MONITORING. (See RADAR SERVICE.)

RADAR NAVIGATIONAL GUIDANCE. (See RADAR SERVICE.)

RADAR POINT OUT. An action taken by a controller to transfer the radar identification of an aircraft to another controller if the aircraft will or may enter the airspace or protected airspace of another controller and radio communications will not be transferred.

RADAR REQUIRED. A term displayed on charts and approach plates and included in FDC NOTAMs to alert pilots that segments of either an instrument approach procedure or a route are not navigable because of either the absence or unusability of a NAVAID. The pilot can expect to be provided radar navigational guidance while transiting segments labeled with this term. (See RADAR ROUTE.) (See RADAR SERVICE.)

RADAR ROUTE. A flight path or route over which an aircraft is vectored. Navigational guidance and altitude assignments are provided by ATC. (See FLIGHT PATH.) (See ROUTE.)

RADAR SEPARATION. (See RADAR SERVICE.)

RADAR SERVICE. A term which encompasses one or more of the following services based on the use of radar which can be provided by a controller to a pilot of a radar identified aircraft.

a. Radar Monitoring. The radar flight-following of aircraft, whose primary navigation is being performed by the pilot, to observe and note deviations from its authorized flight path, airway, or route. When being applied specifically to radar monitoring of instrument approaches; i.e., with precision approach radar (PAR) or radar monitoring of simultaneous ILS/MLS approaches, it includes advice and instructions whenever an aircraft nears or exceeds the prescribed PAR safety limit or simultaneous ILS/MLS no transgression zone. (See ADDITIONAL SERVICES.) (See TRAFFIC ADVISORIES.)

    b. Radar Navigational Guidance. Vectoring aircraft to provide course guidance.

    c. Radar Separation. Radar spacing of aircraft in accordance with established minima.

(See ICAO term RADAR SERVICE.)

RADAR SERVICE [ICAO]. Term used to indicate a service provided directly by means of radar.

    a. Monitoring. The use of radar for the purpose of providing aircraft with information and advice relative to significant deviations from nominal flight path.

    b. Separation. The separation used when aircraft position information is derived from radar sources.

RADAR SERVICE TERMINATED. Used by ATC to inform a pilot that he/she will no longer be provided any of the services that could be received while in radar contact. Radar service is automatically terminated, and the pilot is not advised in the following cases:

    a. An aircraft cancels its IFR flight plan, except within Class B airspace, Class C airspace, a TRSA, or where Basic Radar service is provided.

    b. An aircraft conducting an instrument, visual, or contact approach has landed or has been instructed to change to advisory frequency.

    c. An arriving VFR aircraft, receiving radar service to a tower-controlled airport within Class B airspace, Class C airspace, a TRSA, or where sequencing service is provided, has landed; or to all other airports, is instructed to change to tower or advisory frequency.

    d. An aircraft completes a radar approach.

RADAR SURVEILLANCE. The radar observation of a given geographical area for the purpose of performing some radar function.

RADAR TRAFFIC ADVISORIES. Advisories issued to alert pilots to known or observed radar traffic which may affect the intended route of flight of their aircraft. (See TRAFFIC ADVISORIES.)

RADAR TRAFFIC INFORMATION SERVICE. (See TRAFFIC ADVISORIES.)

RADAR VECTORING [ICAO]. Provision of navigational guidance to aircraft in the form of specific headings, based on the use of radar.

RADAR WEATHER ECHO INTENSITY LEVELS.
Existing radar systems cannot detect turbulence. However, there is a direct correlation between the degree of turbulence and other weather features associated with thunderstorms and the radar weather echo intensity. The National Weather Service has categorized radar weather echo intensity for precipitation into six levels. These levels are sometimes expressed during communications as "VIP LEVEL" 1 through 6 (derived from the component of the radar that produces the information. Video Integrator and Processor). The following list gives the "VIP LEVELS" in relation to the precipitation intensity within a thunderstorm:

    a. Level 1. WEAK
    b. Level 2. MODERATE
    c. Level 3. STRONG
    d. Level 4. VERY STRONG
    e. Level 5. INTENSE
    f. Level 6. EXTREME

(Refer to AC 00-45, Aviation Weather Services.)

RADIAL. A magnetic bearing extending from a VOR/VORTAC/TACAN navigation facility.

RADIO.

    a. A device used for communication.

    b. Used to refer to a flight service station; e.g., "Seattle Radio" is used to call Seattle FSS.

RADIO ALTIMETER. Aircraft equipment which makes use of the reflection of radio waves from the ground to determine the height of the aircraft above the surface.

RADIO BEACON. (See NONDIRECTIONAL BEACON.)

RADIO DETECTION AND RANGING. (See RADAR.)

RADIO MAGNETIC INDICATOR. An aircraft navigational instrument coupled with a gyro compass or similar compass that indicates the direction of a selected NAVAID and indicates bearing with respect to the heading of the aircraft.

RAMP. (See APRON.)

RANDOM ALTITUDE. An altitude inappropriate for direction of flight and/or not in accordance with FAAO 7110.65, Para 4-5-1, VERTICAL SEPARATION MINIMA.

RANDOM ROUTE. Any route not established or charted/published or not otherwise available to all users.

RC. (See ROAD RECONNAISSANCE.)

RCAG. (See REMOTE COMMUNICATIONS AIR/GROUND FACILITY.)

RCC. (See RESCUE COORDINATION CENTER.)

RCO. (See REMOTE COMMUNICATIONS OUTLET.)

RCR. (See RUNWAY CONDITION READING.)

READ BACK. Repeat my message back to me.

RECEIVER AUTONOMOUS INTEGRITY MONITORING (RAIM). A technique whereby a civil GNSS receiver/processor determines the integrity of the GNSS navigation signals without reference to sensors or non-DoD integrity systems other than the receiver itself. This determination is achieved by a consistency check among redundant pseudorange measurements.

RECEIVING CONTROLLER. A controller/facility receiving control of an aircraft from another controller/facility.

RECEIVING FACILITY. (See RECEIVING CONTROLLER.)

RECONFORMANCE. The automated process of bringing an aircraft's Current Plan Trajectory into conformance with its track.

REDUCE SPEED TO (SPEED). (See SPEED ADJUSTMENT.)

REIL. (See RUNWAY END IDENTIFIER LIGHTS.)

RELEASE TIME. A departure time restriction issued to a pilot by ATC (either directly or through an authorized relay) when necessary to separate a departing aircraft from other traffic. (See ICAO term RELEASE TIME.)

RELEASE TIME [ICAO]. Time prior to which an aircraft should be given further clearance or prior to which it should not proceed in case of radio failure.

REMOTE AIRPORT ADVISORY (RAA). A remote service which may be provided by facilities, which are not located on the landing airport, but have a discrete ground-to-air communication frequency or tower frequency when the tower is closed, automated weather reporting with voice available to the pilot at the landing airport, and a continuous ASOS/AWOS data display, other direct reading instruments, or manual observation is available to the AFSS specialist.

REMOTE AIRPORT INFORMATION SERVICE (RAIS). A temporary service provided by facilities, which are not located on the landing airport, but have communication capability and automated weather reporting available to the pilot at the landing airport.

REMOTE COMMUNICATIONS AIR/GROUND FACILITY. An unmanned VHF/UHF transmitter/receiver facility which is used to expand ARTCC air/ground communications coverage and to facilitate direct contact between pilots and controllers. RCAG facilities are sometimes not equipped with emergency frequencies 121.5 MHz and 243.0 MHz. (Refer to AIM.)

REMOTE COMMUNICATIONS OUTLET. An unmanned communications facility remotely controlled by air traffic personnel. RCOs serve FSS's. RTRs serve terminal ATC facilities. An RCO or RTR may be UHF or VHF and will extend the communication range of the air traffic facility. There are several classes of RCOs and RTRs. The class is determined by the number of transmitters or receivers. Classes A through G are used primarily for air/ground purposes. RCO and RTR class O facilities are nonprotected outlets subject to undetected and prolonged outages. RCO (O's) and RTR (O's) were established for the express purpose of providing ground-to-ground communications between air traffic control specialists and pilots located at a satellite airport for delivering en route clearances, issuing departure authorizations, and acknowledging instrument flight rules cancellations or departure/landing times. As a secondary function, they may be used for advisory purposes whenever the aircraft is below the coverage of the primary air/ground frequency.

REMOTE TRANSMITTER/RECEIVER. (See REMOTE COMMUNICATIONS OUTLET.)

REPORT. Used to instruct pilots to advise ATC of specified information; e.g., "Report passing Hamilton VOR."

REPORTING POINT. A geographical location in relation to which the position of an aircraft is reported. (See COMPULSORY REPORTING POINTS.) (See ICAO term REPORTING POINT.) (Refer to AIM.)

REPORTING POINT [ICAO]. A specified geographical location in relation to which the position of an aircraft can be reported.

REQUEST FULL ROUTE CLEARANCE. Used by pilots to request that the entire route of flight be read verbatim in an ATC clearance. Such request should be made to preclude receiving an ATC clearance based on the original filed flight plan when a filed IFR flight plan has been revised by the pilot, company, or operations prior to departure.

REQUIRED NAVIGATION PERFORMANCE (RNP). A statement of the navigational performance necessary for operation within a defined airspace. The following terms are commonly associated with RNP:

a. Required Navigation Performance Level or Type (RNP-X). A value, in nautical miles (NM), from the intended horizontal position within which an aircraft would be at least 95-percent of the total flying time.

b. Required Navigation Performance (RNP) Airspace. A generic term designating airspace, route (s), leg (s), operation (s), or procedure (s) where minimum required navigational performance (RNP) have been established.

c. Actual Navigation Performance (ANP). A measure of the current estimated navigational performance. Also referred to as Estimated Position Error (EPE).

d. Estimated Position Error (EPE). A measure of the current estimated navigational performance. Also referred to as Actual Navigation Performance (ANP).

e. Lateral Navigation (LNAV). A function of area navigation (RNAV) equipment which calculates, displays, and provides lateral guidance to a profile or path.

f. Vertical Navigation (VNAV). A function of area navigation (RNAV) equipment which calculates, displays, and provides vertical guidance to a profile or path.

RESCUE COORDINATION CENTER. A search and rescue (SAR) facility equipped and manned to coordinate and control SAR operations in an area designated by the SAR plan. The U.S. Coast Guard and the U.S. Air Force have responsibility for the operation of RCCs. (See ICAO term RESCUE CO-ORDINATION CENTRE.)

RESCUE CO-ORDINATION CENTRE [ICAO]. A unit responsible for promoting efficient organization of search and rescue service and for coordinating the conduct of search and rescue operations within a search and rescue region.

RESOLUTION ADVISORY. A display indication given to the pilot by the traffic alert and collision avoidance systems (TCAS II) recommending a maneuver to increase vertical separation relative to an intruding aircraft. Positive, negative, and vertical speed limit (VSL) advisories constitute the resolution advisories. A resolution advisory is also classified as corrective or preventive.

RESTRICTED AREA. (See SPECIAL USE AIR-SPACE.) (See ICAO term RESTRICTED AREA.)

RESTRICTED AREA [ICAO]. An airspace of defined dimensions, above the land areas or territorial waters of a State, within which the flight of aircraft is restricted in accordance with certain specified conditions.

RESUME NORMAL SPEED. Used by ATC to advise a pilot that previously issued speed control restrictions are deleted. An instruction to "resume normal speed" does not delete speed restrictions that are applicable to published procedures of upcoming segments of flight, unless specifically stated by ATC. This does not relieve the pilot of those speed restrictions which are applicable to 14 CFR Section 91.117.

RESUME OWN NAVIGATION. Used by ATC to advise a pilot to resume his/her own navigational responsibility. It is issued after completion of a radar vector or when radar contact is lost while the aircraft is being radar vectored. (See RADAR CONTACT LOST.) (See RADAR SERVICE TERMINATED.)

RMI. (See RADIO MAGNETIC INDICATOR.)

RNAV. (See AREA NAVIGATION.) (See ICAO Term AREA NAVIGATION.)

RNAV APPROACH. An instrument approach procedure which relies on aircraft area navigation equipment for navigational guidance. (See AREA NAVIGATION.) (See INSTRUMENT AP-PROACH PROCEDURE.)

ROAD RECONNAISSANCE. Military activity requiring navigation along roads, railroads, and rivers. Reconnaissance route/route segments are seldom along a straight line and normally require a lateral route width of 10 NM to 30 NM and an altitude range of 500 feet to 10,000 feet AGL.

ROGER. I have received all of your last transmission. It should not be used to answer a question requiring a yes or a no answer. (See AFFIRMATIVE.) (See NEGATIVE.)

ROLLOUT RVR. (See VISIBILITY.)

ROUTE. A defined path, consisting of one or more courses in a horizontal plane, which aircraft traverse over the surface of the earth. (See AIRWAY.) (See JET ROUTE.) (See PUBLISHED ROUTE.) (See UNPUBLISHED ROUTE.)

ROUTE ACTION NOTIFICATION. URET notification that a PAR/PDR/PDAR has been applied to the flight plan. (See ATC PREFERRED ROUTE NOTIFICATION.) (See USER REQUEST EVAL-UATION TOOL.)

ROUTE SEGMENT. As used in Air Traffic Control, a part of a route that can be defined by two navigational fixes, two NAVAIDs, or a fix and a NAVAID. (See FIX.) (See ROUTE.) (See ICAO term ROUTE SEGMENT.)

ROUTE SEGMENT [ICAO]. A portion of a route to be flown, as defined by two consecutive significant points specified in a flight plan.

RSA. (See RUNWAY SAFETY AREA.)

RTR. (See REMOTE TRANSMITTER/RECEIVER.)

RUNWAY. A defined rectangular area on a land airport prepared for the landing and takeoff run of aircraft along its length. Runways are normally numbered in relation to their magnetic direction rounded off to the nearest 10 degrees; e.g., Runway 1, Runway 25. (See PARALLEL RUNWAYS.) (See ICAO term RUNWAY.)

RUNWAY [ICAO]. A defined rectangular area on a land aerodrome prepared for the landing and take-off of aircraft.

RUNWAY CENTERLINE LIGHTING. (See AIRPORT LIGHTING.)

RUNWAY CONDITION READING. Numerical decelerometer readings relayed by air traffic controllers at USAF and certain civil bases for use by the pilot in determining runway braking action. These readings are routinely relayed only to USAF and Air National Guard Aircraft. (See BRAKING ACTION.)

RUNWAY END IDENTIFIER LIGHTS. (See AIRPORT LIGHTING.)

RUNWAY GRADIENT. The average slope, measured in percent, between two ends or points on a runway. Runway gradient is depicted on government aerodrome sketches when total runway gradient exceeds 0.3%.

RUNWAY HEADING. The magnetic direction that corresponds with the runway centerline extended, not the painted runway number. When cleared to "fly or maintain runway heading," pilots are expected to fly or maintain the heading that corresponds with the extended centerline of the departure runway. Drift correction shall not be applied; e.g., Runway 4, actual magnetic heading of the runway centerline 044, fly 044.

RUNWAY IN USE/ACTIVE RUNWAY/DUTY RUNWAY. Any runway or runways currently being used for takeoff or landing. When multiple runways are used, they are all considered active runways. In the metering sense, a selectable adapted item which specifies the landing runway configuration or direction of traffic flow. The adapted optimum flight plan from each transition fix to the vertex is determined by the runway configuration for arrival metering processing purposes.

RUNWAY LIGHTS. (See AIRPORT LIGHTING.)

RUNWAY MARKINGS. (See AIRPORT MARKING AIDS.)

RUNWAY OVERRUN. In military aviation exclusively, a stabilized or paved area beyond the end of a runway, of the same width as the runway plus shoulders, centered on the extended runway centerline.

RUNWAY PROFILE DESCENT. An instrument flight rules (IFR) air traffic control arrival procedure to a runway published for pilot use in graphic and/or textual form and may be associated with a STAR. Runway Profile Descents provide routing and may depict crossing altitudes, speed restrictions, and headings to be flown from the en route structure to the point where the pilot will receive clearance for and execute an instrument approach procedure. A Runway Profile Descent may apply to more than one runway if so stated on the chart. (Refer to AIM.)

RUNWAY SAFETY AREA. A defined surface surrounding the runway prepared, or suitable, for reducing the risk of damage to airplanes in the event of an undershoot, overshoot, or excursion from the runway. The dimensions of the RSA vary and can be determined by using the criteria contained within AC 150/5300-13, Airport Design, Chapter 3. Figure 3-1 in AC 150/5300-13 depicts the RSA. The design standards dictate that the RSA shall be:
a. Cleared, graded, and have no potentially hazardous ruts, humps, depressions, or other surface variations;
b. Drained by grading or storm sewers to prevent water accumulation;
c. Capable, under dry conditions, of supporting snow removal equipment, aircraft rescue and firefighting equipment, and the occasional passage of aircraft without causing structural damage to the aircraft; and,
d. Free of objects, except for objects that need to be located in the runway safety area because of their function. These objects shall be constructed on low impact resistant supports (frangible mounted structures) to the lowest practical height with the frangible point no higher than 3 inches above grade.
(Refer to AC 150/5300-13, Airport Design, Chapter 3.)

RUNWAY TRANSITION.
a. Conventional STARs/SIDs. The portion of a STAR/SID that serves a particular runway or runways at an airport.
b. RNAV STARs/SIDs. Defines a path(s) from the common route to the final point(s) on a STAR. For a SID, the common route that serves a particular runway or runways at an airport.

RUNWAY USE PROGRAM. A noise abatement runway selection plan designed to enhance noise abatement efforts with regard to airport communities for arriving and departing aircraft. These plans are developed into runway use programs and apply to all turbojet aircraft 12,500 pounds or heavier; turbojet aircraft less than 12,500 pounds are included only if the airport proprietor determines that the aircraft creates a noise problem. Runway use programs are coordinated with FAA offices, and safety criteria used in these programs are developed by the Office of Flight Operations. Runway use programs are administered by the Air Traffic Service as "Formal" or "Informal" programs.

a. Formal Runway Use Program. An approved noise abatement program which is defined and acknowledged in a Letter of Understanding between Flight Operations, Air Traffic Service, the airport proprietor, and the users. Once established, participation in the program is mandatory for aircraft operators and pilots as provided for in 14 CFR Section 91.129.

b. Informal Runway Use Program. An approved noise abatement program which does not require a Letter of Understanding, and participation in the program is voluntary for aircraft operators/pilots.

RUNWAY VISIBILITY VALUE. (See VISIBILITY.)

RUNWAY VISUAL RANGE. (See VISIBILITY.)

S

SAA. (See SPECIAL ACTIVITY AIRSPACE.)

SAFETY ALERT. A safety alert issued by ATC to aircraft under their control if ATC is aware the aircraft is at an altitude which, in the controller's judgment, places the aircraft in unsafe proximity to terrain, obstructions, or other aircraft. The controller may discontinue the issuance of further alerts if the pilot advises he/she is taking action to correct the situation or has the other aircraft in sight.

a. Terrain/Obstruction Alert. A safety alert issued by ATC to aircraft under their control if ATC is aware the aircraft is at an altitude which, in the controller's judgment, places the aircraft in unsafe proximity to terrain/obstructions; e.g., "Low Altitude Alert, check your altitude immediately."

b. Aircraft Conflict Alert. A safety alert issued by ATC to aircraft under their control if ATC is aware of an aircraft that is not under their control at an altitude which, in the controller's judgment, places both aircraft in unsafe proximity to each other.

With the alert, ATC will offer the pilot an alternate course of action when feasible; e.g., "Traffic Alert, advise you turn right heading zero niner zero or climb to eight thousand immediately."

Note: The issuance of a safety alert is contingent upon the capability of the controller to have an awareness of an unsafe condition. The course of action provided will be predicated on other traffic under ATC control. Once the alert is issued, it is solely the pilot's prerogative to determine what course of action, if any, he/she will take.

SAIL BACK. A maneuver during high wind conditions (usually with power off) where float plane movement is controlled by water rudders/opening and closing cabin doors.

SAME DIRECTION AIRCRAFT. Aircraft are operating in the same direction when:

a. They are following the same track in the same direction; or

b. Their tracks are parallel and the aircraft are flying in the same direction; or

c. Their tracks intersect at an angle of less than 45 degrees.

SAR. (See SEARCH AND RESCUE.)

SAY AGAIN. Used to request a repeat of the last transmission. Usually specifies transmission or portion thereof not understood or received; e.g., "Say again all after ABRAM VOR."

SAY ALTITUDE. Used by ATC to ascertain an aircraft's specific altitude/flight level. When the aircraft is climbing or descending, the pilot should state the indicated altitude rounded to the nearest 100 feet.

SAY HEADING. Used by ATC to request an aircraft heading. The pilot should state the actual heading of the aircraft.

SCHEDULED TIME OF ARRIVAL (STA). A STA is the desired time that an aircraft should cross a certain point (landing or metering fix). It takes other traffic and airspace configuration into account. A STA time shows the results of the TMA scheduler that has calculated an arrival time according to parameters such as optimized spacing, aircraft performance, and weather.

SDF. (See SIMPLIFIED DIRECTIONAL FACILITY.)

SEA LANE. A designated portion of water outlined by visual surface markers for and intended to be used by aircraft designed to operate on water.

SEARCH AND RESCUE. A service which seeks missing aircraft and assists those found to be in need of assistance. It is a cooperative effort using the facilities and services of available Federal, state and local agencies. The U.S. Coast Guard is responsible for coordination of search and rescue for the Maritime Region, and the U.S. Air Force is responsible for search and rescue for the Inland Region. Information pertinent to search and rescue should be passed through any air traffic facility or be transmitted directly to the Rescue Coordination Center by telephone. (See FLIGHT SERVICE STATION.) (See RESCUE COORDINATION CENTER.) (Refer to AIM.)

SEARCH AND RESCUE FACILITY. A facility responsible for maintaining and operating a search and rescue (SAR) service to render aid to persons and property in distress. It is any SAR unit, station, NET, or other operational activity which can be usefully employed during an SAR Mission; e.g., a Civil Air Patrol Wing, or a Coast Guard Station. (See SEARCH AND RESCUE.)

SECTIONAL AERONAUTICAL CHARTS. (See AERONAUTICAL CHART.)

SECTOR LIST DROP INTERVAL. A parameter number of minutes after the meter fix time when arrival aircraft will be deleted from the arrival sector list.

SEE AND AVOID. When weather conditions permit, pilots operating IFR or VFR are required to observe and maneuver to avoid other aircraft. Right-of-way rules are contained in 14 CFR Part 91.

SEGMENTED CIRCLE. A system of visual indicators designed to provide traffic pattern information at airports without operating control towers. (Refer to AIM.)

SEGMENTS OF AN INSTRUMENT APPROACH PROCEDURE. An instrument approach procedure may have as many as four separate segments depending on how the approach procedure is structured.

a. Initial Approach. The segment between the initial approach fix and the intermediate fix or the point where the aircraft is established on the intermediate course or final approach course. (See ICAO term INITIAL APPROACH SEGMENT.)

b. Intermediate Approach. The segment between the intermediate fix or point and the final approach fix. (See ICAO term INTERMEDIATE APPROACH SEGMENT.)

c. Final Approach. The segment between the final approach fix or point and the runway, airport, or missed approach point. (See ICAO term FINAL APPROACH SEGMENT.)

d. Missed Approach. The segment between the missed approach point or the point of arrival at decision height and the missed approach fix at the prescribed altitude. (Refer to 14 CFR Part 97.)

(See ICAO term MISSED APPROACH PROCEDURE.)

SEPARATION. In air traffic control, the spacing of aircraft to achieve their safe and orderly movement in flight and while landing and taking off. (See SEPARATION MINIMA.) (See ICAO term SEPARATION.)

SEPARATION [ICAO]. Spacing between aircraft, levels or tracks.

SEPARATION MINIMA. The minimum longitudinal, lateral, or vertical distances by which aircraft are spaced through the application of air traffic control procedures. (See SEPARATION.)

SERVICE. A generic term that designates functions or assistance available from or rendered by air traffic control. For example, Class C service would denote the ATC services provided within a Class C airspace area.

SEVERE WEATHER AVOIDANCE PLAN. An approved plan to minimize the affect of severe weather on traffic flows in impacted terminal and/or ARTCC areas. SWAP is normally implemented to provide the least disruption to the ATC system when flight through portions of airspace is difficult or impossible due to severe weather.

SEVERE WEATHER FORECAST ALERTS. Preliminary messages issued in order to alert users that a Severe Weather Watch Bulletin (WW) is being issued. These messages define areas of possible severe thunderstorms or tornado activity. The messages are unscheduled and issued as required by the National Severe Storm Forecast Center at Kansas City, Missouri. (See AIRMET.) (See CONVECTIVE SIGMET.) (See CWA.) (See SIGMET.)

SFA. (See SINGLE FREQUENCY APPROACH.)

SFO. (See SIMULATED FLAMEOUT.)

SHF. (See SUPER HIGH FREQUENCY.)

SHORT RANGE CLEARANCE. A clearance issued to a departing IFR flight which authorizes IFR flight to a specific fix short of the destination while air traffic control facilities are coordinating and obtaining the complete clearance.

SHORT TAKEOFF AND LANDING AIRCRAFT. An aircraft which, at some weight within its approvedoperating weight, is capable of operating from a STOL runway in compliance with the applicable STOL characteristics, airworthiness, operations, noise, and pollution standards. (See VERTICAL TAKEOFF AND LANDING AIRCRAFT.)

SIAP. (See STANDARD INSTRUMENT AP-PROACH PROCEDURE.)

SID. (See STANDARD INSTRUMENT DEPAR-TURE.)

SIDESTEP MANEUVER. A visual maneuver accomplished by a pilot at the completion of an instrument approach to permit a straight-in landing on a parallel runway not more than 1,200 feet to either side of the runway to which the instrument approach was conducted. (Refer to AIM.)

SIGMET. A weather advisory issued concerning weather significant to the safety of all aircraft. SIGMET advisories cover severe and extreme turbulence, severe icing, and widespread dust or sandstorms that reduce visibility to less than 3 miles. (See AIRMET.) (See AWW.) (See CONVECTIVE SIGMET.) (See CWA.) (See ICAO term SIGMET INFORMA-TION.) (Refer to AIM.)

SIGMET INFORMATION [ICAO]. Information issued by a meteorological watch office concerning the occurrence or expected occurrence of specified en-route weather phenomena which may affect the safety of aircraft operations.

SIGNIFICANT METEOROLOGICAL INFORMA-TION. (See SIGMET.)

SIGNIFICANT POINT. A point, whether a named intersection, a NAVAID, a fix derived from a NAVAID(s), or geographical coordinate expressed in degrees of latitude and longitude, which is established for the purpose of providing separation, as a reporting point, or to delineate a route of flight.

SIMPLIFIED DIRECTIONAL FACILITY.
A NAVAID used for nonprecision instrument approaches. The final approach course is similar to that of an ILS localizer except that the SDF course may be offset from the runway, generally not more than 3 degrees, and the course may be wider than the localizer, resulting in a lower degree of accuracy. (Refer to AIM.)

SIMULATED FLAMEOUT. A practice approach by a jet aircraft (normally military) at idle thrust to a runway. The approach may start at a runway (high key) and may continue on a relatively high and wide downwind leg with a continuous turn to final. It terminates in landing or low approach. The purpose of this approach is to simulate a flameout. (See FLAMEOUT.)

SIMULTANEOUS ILS APPROACHES. An approach system permitting simultaneous ILS/MLS approaches to airports having parallel runways separated by at least 4,300 feet between centerlines. Integral parts of a total system are ILS/MLS, radar, communications, ATC procedures, and appropriate airborne equipment. (See PARALLEL RUNWAYS.) (Refer to AIM.)

SIMULTANEOUS MLS APPROACHES. (See SI-MULTANEOUS ILS APPROACHES.)

SINGLE DIRECTION ROUTES. Preferred IFR Routes which are sometimes depicted on high altitude en route charts and which are normally flown in one direction only. (See PREFERRED IFR ROUTES.) (Refer to AIRPORT/FACILITY DIRECTORY.)

SINGLE FREQUENCY APPROACH. A service provided under a letter of agreement to military single-piloted turbojet aircraft which permits use of a single UHF frequency during approach for landing. Pilots will not normally be required to change frequency from the beginning of the approach to touchdown except that pilots conducting an en route descent are required to change frequency when control is transferred from the air route traffic control center to the terminal facility. The abbreviation "SFA" in the DOD FLIP IFR Supplement under "Communications" indicates this service is available at an aerodrome.

SINGLE-PILOTED AIRCRAFT. A military turbojet aircraft possessing one set of flight controls, tandem cockpits, or two sets of flight controls but operated by one pilot is considered single-piloted by ATC when determining the appropriate air traffic service to be applied. (See SINGLE FREQUENCY AP-PROACH.)

SKYSPOTTER. A pilot who has received specialized training in observing and reporting inflight weather phenomena.

SLASH. A radar beacon reply displayed as an elongated target.

SLDI. (See SECTOR LIST DROP INTERVAL.)

SLOT TIME. (See METER FIX TIME/SLOT TIME.)

SLOW TAXI. To taxi a float plane at low power or low RPM.

SN. (See SYSTEM STRATEGIC NAVIGATION.)

SPEAK SLOWER. Used in verbal communications as a request to reduce speech rate.

SPECIAL ACTIVITY AIRSPACE (SAA). Any airspace with defined dimensions within the National Airspace System wherein limitations may be imposed upon aircraft operations. This airspace may be restricted areas, prohibited areas, military operations areas, air ATC assigned airspace, and any other designated airspace areas. The dimensions of this airspace are programmed into URET and can be designated as either active or inactive by screen entry. Aircraft trajectories are constantly tested against the dimensions of active areas and alerts issued to the applicable sectors when violations are predicted. (See USER REQUEST EVALUATION TOOL.)

SPECIAL EMERGENCY. A condition of air piracy or other hostile act by a person(s) aboard an aircraft which threatens the safety of the aircraft or its passengers.

SPECIAL INSTRUMENT APPROACH PROCEDURE. (See INSTRUMENT APPROACH PROCEDURE.)

SPECIAL USE AIRSPACE. Airspace of defined dimensions identified by an area on the surface of the earth wherein activities must be confined because of their nature and/or wherein limitations may be imposed upon aircraft operations that are not a part of those activities. Types of special use airspace are:

a. Alert Area. Airspace which may contain a high volume of pilot training activities or an unusual type of aerial activity, neither of which is hazardous to aircraft. Alert Areas are depicted on aeronautical charts for the information of nonparticipating pilots. All activities within an Alert Area are conducted in accordance with Federal Aviation Regulations, and pilots of participating aircraft as well as pilots transiting the area are equally responsible for collision avoidance.

b. Controlled Firing Area. Airspace wherein activities are conducted under conditions so controlled as to eliminate hazards to nonparticipating aircraft and to ensure the safety of persons and property on the ground.

c. Military Operations Area (MOA). A MOA is airspace established outside of Class A airspace area to separate or segregate certain nonhazardous military activities from IFR traffic and to identify for VFR traffic where these activities are conducted. (Refer to AIM.)

d. Prohibited Area. Airspace designated under 14 CFR Part 73 within which no person may operate an aircraft without the permission of the using agency. (Refer to AIM.) (Refer to En Route Charts.)

e. Restricted Area. Airspace designated under 14 CFR Part 73, within which the flight of aircraft, while not wholly prohibited, is subject to restriction. Most restricted areas are designated joint use and IFR/VFR operations in the area may be authorized by the controlling ATC facility when it is not being utilized by the using agency. Restricted areas are depicted on en route charts. Where joint use is authorized, the name of the ATC controlling facility is also shown. (Refer to 14 CFR Part 73.) (Refer to AIM.)

f. Warning Area. A warning area is airspace of defined dimensions extending from 3 nautical miles outward from the coast of the United States, that contains activity that may be hazardous to nonparticipating aircraft. The purpose of such warning area is to warn nonparticipating pilots of the potential danger. A warning area may be located over domestic or international waters or both.

SPECIAL VFR CONDITIONS. Meteorological conditions that are less than those required for basic VFR flight in Class B, C, D, or E surface areas and in which some aircraft are permitted flight under visual flight rules. (See SPECIAL VFR OPERATIONS.) (Refer to 14 CFR Part 91.)

SPECIAL VFR FLIGHT [ICAO]. A VFR flight cleared by air traffic control to operate within Class B, C, D, and E surface areas in meteorological conditions below VMC.

SPECIAL VFR OPERATIONS. Aircraft operating in accordance with clearances within Class B, C, D, and E surface areas in weather conditions less than the basic VFR weather minima. Such operations must be requested by the pilot and approved by ATC. (See SPECIAL VFR CONDITIONS.) (See ICAO term SPECIAL VFR FLIGHT.)

SPEED. (See AIRSPEED.) (See GROUND SPEED.)

SPEED ADJUSTMENT. An ATC procedure used to request pilots to adjust aircraft speed to a specific value for the purpose of providing desired spacing. Pilots are expected to maintain a speed of plus or minus 10 knots or 0.02 Mach number of the specified speed. Examples of speed adjustments are:

a. "Increase/reduce speed to Mach point (number.)"

b. "Increase/reduce speed to (speed in knots)" or "Increase/reduce speed (number of knots) knots."

SPEED BRAKES. Moveable aerodynamic devices on aircraft that reduce airspeed during descent and landing.

SPEED SEGMENTS. Portions of the arrival route between the transition point and the vertex along the optimum flight path for which speeds and altitudes are specified. There is one set of arrival speed segments adapted from each transition point to each vertex. Each set may contain up to six segments.

SQUAWK (Mode, Code, Function). Activate specific modes/codes/functions on the aircraft transponder; e.g., "Squawk three/alpha, two one zero five, low." (See TRANSPONDER.)

STA. (See SCHEDULED TIME OF ARRIVAL.)

STAGING/QUEUING. The placement, integration, and segregation of departure aircraft in designated movement areas of an airport by departure fix, EDCT, and/or restriction.

STAND BY. Means the controller or pilot must pause for a few seconds, usually to attend to other duties of a higher priority. Also means to wait as in "stand by for clearance." The caller should reestablish contact if a delay is lengthy. "Stand by" is not an approval or denial.

STANDARD INSTRUMENT APPROACH PROCEDURE (SIAP). (See INSTRUMENT APPROACH PROCEDURE.)

STANDARD INSTRUMENT DEPARTURE (SID). A preplanned instrument flight rule (IFR) air traffic control (ATC) departure procedure printed for pilot/controller use in graphic form to provide obstacle clearance and a transition from the terminal area to the appropriate en route structure. SIDs are primarily designed for system enhancement to expedite traffic flow and to reduce pilot/controller workload. ATC clearance must always be received prior to flying a SID. (See IFR TAKEOFF MINIMUMS AND DEPARTURE PROCEDURES.) (See OBSTACLE DEPARTURE PROCEDURE.) (Refer to AIM.)

STANDARD RATE TURN. A turn of three degrees per second.

STANDARD TERMINAL ARRIVAL. A preplanned instrument flight rule (IFR) air traffic control arrival procedure published for pilot use in graphic and/or textual form. STARs provide transition from the en route structure to an outer fix or an instrument approach fix/arrival waypoint in the terminal area.

STANDARD TERMINAL ARRIVAL CHARTS. (See AERONAUTICAL CHART.)

STAR. (See STANDARD TERMINAL ARRIVAL.)

STATE AIRCRAFT. Aircraft used in military, customs and police service, in the exclusive service of any government, or of any political subdivision, thereof including the government of any state, territory, or possession of the United States or the District of Columbia, but not including any government-owned aircraft engaged in carrying persons or property for commercial purposes.

STATIC RESTRICTIONS. Those restrictions that are usually not subject to change, fixed, in place, and/or published.

STATIONARY RESERVATIONS. Altitude reservations which encompass activities in a fixed area. Stationary reservations may include activities, such as special tests of weapons systems or equipment, certain U.S. Navy carrier, fleet, and anti-submarine operations, rocket, missile and drone operations, and certain aerial refueling or similar operations.

STEP TAXI. To taxi a float plane at full power or high RPM.

STEP TURN. A maneuver used to put a float plane in a planing configuration prior to entering an active sea lane for takeoff. The STEP TURN maneuver should only be used upon pilot request.

STEPDOWN FIX. A fix permitting additional descent within a segment of an instrument approach procedure by identifying a point at which a controlling obstacle has been safely overflown.

STEREO ROUTE. A routinely used route of flight established by users and ARTCCs identified by a coded name; e.g., ALPHA 2. These routes minimize flight plan handling and communications.

STOL AIRCRAFT. (See SHORT TAKEOFF AND LANDING AIRCRAFT.)

STOP ALTITUDE SQUAWK. Used by ATC to inform an aircraft to turn-off the automatic altitude reporting feature of its transponder. It is issued when the verbally reported altitude varies 300 feet or more from the automatic altitude report. (See ALTITUDE READOUT.) (See TRANSPONDER.)

STOP AND GO. A procedure wherein an aircraft will land, make a complete stop on the runway, and then commence a takeoff from that point. (See LOW APPROACH.) (See OPTION APPROACH.)

STOP BURST. (See STOP STREAM.)

STOP BUZZER. (See STOP STREAM.)

STOP SQUAWK (Mode or Code). Used by ATC to tell the pilot to turn specified functions of the aircraft transponder off. (See STOP ALTITUDE SQUAWK.) (See TRANSPONDER.)

STOP STREAM. Used by ATC to request a pilot to suspend electronic attack activity. (See JAMMING.)

STOPOVER FLIGHT PLAN. A flight plan format which permits in a single submission the filing of a sequence of flight plans through interim full-stop destinations to a final destination.

STOPWAY. An area beyond the takeoff runway no

less wide than the runway and centered upon the extended centerline of the runway, able to support the airplane during an aborted takeoff, without causing structural damage to the airplane, and designated by the airport authorities for use in decelerating the airplane during an aborted takeoff.

STRAIGHT-IN APPROACH IFR. An instrument approach wherein final approach is begun without first having executed a procedure turn, not necessarily completed with a straight-in landing or made to straight-in landing minimums. (See LANDING MINIMUMS.) (See STRAIGHT-IN APPROACH VFR.) (See STRAIGHT-IN LANDING.)

STRAIGHT-IN APPROACH VFR. Entry into the traffic pattern by interception of the extended runway centerline (final approach course) without executing any other portion of the traffic pattern. (See TRAFFIC PATTERN.)

STRAIGHT-IN LANDING. A landing made on a runway aligned within 30° of the final approach course following completion of an instrument approach. (See STRAIGHT-IN APPROACH IFR.)

STRAIGHT-IN LANDING MINIMUMS. (See LANDING MINIMUMS.)

STRAIGHT-IN MINIMUMS. (See STRAIGHT-IN LANDING MINIMUMS.)

STRATEGIC PLANNING. Planning whereby solutions are sought to resolve potential conflicts.

SUBSTITUTE ROUTE. A route assigned to pilots when any part of an airway or route is unusable because of NAVAID status. These routes consist of:
a. Substitute routes which are shown on U.S. Government charts.
b. Routes defined by ATC as specific NAVAID radials or courses.
c. Routes defined by ATC as direct to or between NAVAIDs.

SUNSET AND SUNRISE. The mean solar times of sunset and sunrise as published in the Nautical Almanac, converted to local standard time for the locality concerned. Within Alaska, the end of evening civil twilight and the beginning of morning civil twilight, as defined for each locality.

SUPER HIGH FREQUENCY. The frequency band between 3 and 30 gigahertz (GHz). The elevation and azimuth stations of the microwave landing system operate from 5031 MHz to 5091 MHz in this spectrum.

SUPPLEMENTAL WEATHER SERVICE LOCATION. Airport facilities staffed with contract personnel who take weather observations and provide current local weather to pilots via telephone or radio. (All other services are provided by the parent FSS.)

SUPPS. Refers to ICAO Document 7030 Regional Supplementary Procedures. SUPPS contain procedures for each ICAO Region which are unique to that Region and are not covered in the worldwide provisions identified in the ICAO Air Navigation Plan. Procedures contained in Chapter 8 are based in part on those published in SUPPS.

SURFACE AREA. The airspace contained by the lateral boundary of the Class B, C, D, or E airspace designated for an airport that begins at the surface and extends upward.

SURPIC. A description of surface vessels in the area of a Search and Rescue incident including their predicted positions and their characteristics. (Refer to FAAO 7110.65, Para 10-6-4, INFLIGHT CONTINGENCIES.)

SURVEILLANCE APPROACH. An instrument approach wherein the air traffic controller issues instructions, for pilot compliance, based on aircraft position in relation to the final approach course (azimuth), and the distance (range) from the end of the runway as displayed on the controller's radar scope. The controller will provide recommended altitudes on final approach if requested by the pilot. (Refer to AIM.)

SWAP. (See SEVERE WEATHER AVOIDANCE PLAN.)

SWSL. (See SUPPLEMENTAL WEATHER SERVICE LOCATION.)

SYSTEM STRATEGIC NAVIGATION. Military activity accomplished by navigating along a preplanned route using internal aircraft systems to maintain a desired track. This activity normally requires a lateral route width of 10 NM and altitude range of 1,000 feet to 6,000 feet AGL with some route segments that permit terrain following.

T

TACAN. (See TACTICAL AIR NAVIGATION.)

TACAN-ONLY AIRCRAFT. An aircraft, normally military, possessing TACAN with DME but no VOR navigational system capability. Clearances must specify TACAN or VORTAC fixes and approaches.

TACTICAL AIR NAVIGATION. An ultra-high frequency electronic rho-theta air navigation aid which provides suitably equipped aircraft a continuous indication of bearing and distance to the TACAN station. (See VORTAC.) (Refer to AIM.)

TAILWIND. Any wind more than 90 degrees to the longitudinal axis of the runway. The magnetic direction of the runway shall be used as the basis for determining the longitudinal axis.

TAKEOFF AREA. (See LANDING AREA.)

TAKE-OFF DISTANCE AVAILABLE [ICAO]. The length of the take-off run available plus the length of the clearway, if provided.

TAKE-OFF RUN AVAILABLE [ICAO]. The length of runway declared available and suitable for the ground run of an aeroplane take-off.

TARGET. The indication shown on a radar display resulting from a primary radar return or a radar beacon reply. (See RADAR.) (See TARGET SYMBOL.) (See ICAO term TARGET.)

TARGET [ICAO]. In radar:
a. Generally, any discrete object which reflects or retransmits energy back to the radar equipment.
b. Specifically, an object of radar search or surveillance.

TARGET RESOLUTION. A process to ensure that correlated radar targets do not touch. Target resolution shall be applied as follows:
a. Between the edges of two primary targets or the edges of the ASR-9 primary target symbol.
b. Between the end of the beacon control slash and the edge of a primary target.
c. Between the ends of two beacon control slashes.

Note 1: MANDATORY TRAFFIC ADVISORIES AND SAFETY ALERTS SHALL BE ISSUED WHEN THIS PROCEDURE IS USED.

Note 2: This procedure shall not be provided utilizing mosaic radar systems.

TARGET SYMBOL. A computer-generated indication shown on a radar display resulting from a primary radar return or a radar beacon reply.

TAXI. The movement of an airplane under its own power on the surface of an airport (14 CFR Section 135.100 [Note]). Also, it describes the surface movement of helicopters equipped with wheels. (See AIR TAXI.) (See HOVER TAXI.) (Refer to 14 CFR Section 135.100.) (Refer to AIM.)

TAXI PATTERNS. Patterns established to illustrate the desired flow of ground traffic for the different runways or airport areas available for use.

TCAS. (See TRAFFIC ALERT AND COLLISION AVOIDANCE SYSTEM.)

TCH. (See THRESHOLD CROSSING HEIGHT.)

TCLT. (See TENTATIVE CALCULATED LANDING TIME.)

TDLS. (See TERMINAL DATA LINK SYSTEM.)

TDZE. (See TOUCHDOWN ZONE ELEVATION.)

TELEPHONE INFORMATION BRIEFING SERVICE. A continuous telephone recording of meteorological and/or aeronautical information. (Refer to AIM.)

TENTATIVE CALCULATED LANDING TIME. A projected time calculated for adapted vertex for each arrival aircraft based upon runway configuration, airport acceptance rate, airport arrival delay period, and other metered arrival aircraft. This time is either the VTA of the aircraft or the TCLT/ACLT of the previous aircraft plus the AAI, whichever is later. This time will be updated in response to an aircraft's progress and its current relationship to other arrivals.

TERMINAL AREA. A general term used to describe airspace in which approach control service or airport traffic control service is provided.

TERMINAL AREA FACILITY. A facility providing air traffic control service for arriving and departing IFR, VFR, Special VFR, and on occasion en route aircraft. (See APPROACH CONTROL FACILITY.) (See TOWER.)

TERMINAL DATA LINK SYSTEM (TDLS). A system that provides Digital Automatic Terminal Information Service (D–ATIS) both on a specified radio frequency and also, for subscribers, in a text message via data link to the cockpit or to a gate printer. TDLS also provides Pre-Departure Clearance (PDC), at selected airports, to subscribers, through a service provider, in text to the cockpit or to a gate printer. In addition, TDLS will emulate the Flight Data Input/Output (FDIO) information within the control tower.

TERMINAL RADAR SERVICE AREA. Airspace surrounding designated airports wherein ATC provides radar vectoring, sequencing, and separation on a full-time basis for all IFR and participating VFR aircraft. The AIM contains an explanation of TRSA. TRSAs are depicted on VFR aeronautical charts. Pilot participation is urged but is not mandatory.

TERMINAL VFR RADAR SERVICE. A national program instituted to extend the terminal radar services provided instrument flight rules (IFR) aircraft to visual flight rules (VFR) aircraft. The program is divided into four types service referred to as basic radar service, terminal radar service area (TRSA) service, Class B service and Class C service. The type of service provided at a particular location is contained in the Airport/Facility Directory.

a. Basic Radar Service. These services are provided for VFR aircraft by all commissioned terminal radar facilities. Basic radar service includes safety alerts, traffic advisories, limited radar vectoring when requested by the pilot, and sequencing at locations where procedures have been established for this purpose and/or when covered by a letter of agreement. The purpose of this service is to adjust the flow of arriving IFR and VFR aircraft into the traffic pattern in a safe and orderly manner and to provide traffic advisories to departing VFR aircraft.

b. TRSA Service. This service provides, in addition to basic radar service, sequencing of all IFR and participating VFR aircraft to the primary airport and separation between all participating VFR aircraft. The purpose of this service is to provide separation between all participating VFR aircraft and all IFR aircraft operating within the area defined as a TRSA.

c. Class C Service. This service provides, in addition to basic radar service, approved separation between IFR and VFR aircraft, and sequencing of VFR aircraft, and sequencing of VFR arrivals to the primary airport.

d. Class B Service. This service provides, in addition to basic radar service, approved separation of aircraft based on IFR, VFR, and/or weight, and sequencing of VFR arrivals to the primary airport(s).

(See CONTROLLED AIRSPACE.) (See TERMINAL RADAR SERVICE AREA.) (Refer to AIM.) (Refer to AIRPORT/FACILITY DIRECTORY.)

TERMINAL-VERY HIGH FREQUENCY OMNI-DIRECTIONAL RANGE STATION. A very high frequency terminal omnirange station located on or near an airport and used as an approach aid. (See NAVIGATIONAL AID.) (See VOR.)

TERRAIN FOLLOWING. The flight of a military aircraft maintaining a constant AGL altitude above the terrain or the highest obstruction. The altitude of the aircraft will constantly change with the varying terrain and/or obstruction.

TETRAHEDRON. A device normally located on uncontrolled airports and used as a landing direction indicator. The small end of a tetrahedron points in the direction of landing. At controlled airports, the tetrahedron, if installed, should be disregarded because tower instructions supersede the indicator. (See SEGMENTED CIRCLE.) (Refer to AIM.)

TF. (See TERRAIN FOLLOWING.)

THAT IS CORRECT. The understanding you have is right.

360 OVERHEAD. (See OVERHEAD MANEUVER.)

THRESHOLD. The beginning of that portion of the runway usable for landing. (See AIRPORT LIGHTING.) (See DISPLACED THRESHOLD.)

THRESHOLD CROSSING HEIGHT. The theoretical height above the runway threshold at which the aircraft's glideslope antenna would be if the aircraft maintains the trajectory established by the mean ILS glideslope or MLS glidepath. (See GLIDESLOPE.) (See THRESHOLD.)

THRESHOLD LIGHTS. (See AIRPORT LIGHTING.)

TIBS. (See TELEPHONE INFORMATION BRIEFING SERVICE.)

TIME GROUP. Four digits representing the hour and minutes from the Coordinated Universal Time (UTC) clock. FAA uses UTC for all operations. The term "ZULU" may be used to denote UTC. The word "local" or the time zone equivalent shall be used to denote local when local time is given during radio and telephone communications. When written, a time zone designator is used to indicate local time; e.g. "0205M" (Mountain). The local time may be based on the 24-hour clock system. The day begins at 0000 and ends at 2359.

TMA. (See TRAFFIC MANAGEMENT ADVISOR.)

TMPA. (See TRAFFIC MANAGEMENT PROGRAM ALERT.)

TMU. (See TRAFFIC MANAGEMENT UNIT.)

TODA [ICAO]. (See ICAO Term TAKE-OFF DISTANCE AVAILABLE.)

TORA [ICAO]. (See ICAO Term TAKE-OFF RUN AVAILABLE.)

TORCHING. The burning of fuel at the end of an exhaust pipe or stack of a reciprocating aircraft engine, the result of an excessive richness in the fuel air mixture.

TOTAL ESTIMATED ELAPSED TIME [ICAO]. For IFR flights, the estimated time required from take-off to arrive over that designated point, defined by reference to navigation aids, from which it is intended that an instrument approach procedure will be commenced, or, if no navigation aid is associated with the destination aerodrome, to arrive over the destination aerodrome. For VFR flights, the estimated time required from take-off to arrive over the destination aerodrome. (See ICAO term ESTIMATED ELAPSED TIME.)

TOUCH-AND-GO. An operation by an aircraft that lands and departs on a runway without stopping or exiting the runway.

TOUCH-AND-GO LANDING. (See TOUCH-AND-GO.)

TOUCHDOWN.
a. The point at which an aircraft first makes contact with the landing surface.
b. Concerning a precision radar approach (PAR), it is the point where the glide path intercepts the landing surface.

(See ICAO term TOUCHDOWN.)

TOUCHDOWN [ICAO]. The point where the nominal glide path intercepts the runway.

Note: Touchdown as defined above is only a datum and is not necessarily the actual point at which the aircraft will touch the runway.

TOUCHDOWN RVR. (See VISIBILITY.)

TOUCHDOWN ZONE. The first 3,000 feet of the runway beginning at the threshold. The area is used for determination of Touchdown Zone Elevation in the development of straight-in landing minimums for instrument approaches. (See ICAO term TOUCHDOWN ZONE.)

TOUCHDOWN ZONE [ICAO]. The portion of a runway, beyond the threshold, where it is intended landing aircraft first contact the runway.

TOUCHDOWN ZONE ELEVATION. The highest elevation in the first 3,000 feet of the landing surface. TDZE is indicated on the instrument approach procedure chart when straight-in landing minimums are authorized. (See TOUCHDOWN ZONE.)

TOUCHDOWN ZONE LIGHTING. (See AIRPORT LIGHTING.)

TOWER. A terminal facility that uses air/ground communications, visual signaling, and other devices to provide ATC services to aircraft operating in the vicinity of an airport or on the movement area. Authorizes aircraft to land or takeoff at the airport controlled by the tower or to transit the Class D airspace area regardless of flight plan or weather conditions (IFR or VFR). A tower may also provide approach control services (radar or nonradar). (See AIRPORT TRAFFIC CONTROL SERVICE.) (See APPROACH CONTROL FACILITY.) (See APPROACH CONTROL SERVICE.) (See MOVEMENT AREA.) (See TOWER EN ROUTE CONTROL SERVICE.) (See ICAO term AERODROME CONTROL TOWER.) (Refer to AIM.)

TOWER EN ROUTE CONTROL SERVICE. The control of IFR en route traffic within delegated airspace between two or more adjacent approach control facilities. This service is designed to expedite traffic and reduce control and pilot communication requirements.

TOWER TO TOWER. (See TOWER EN ROUTE CONTROL SERVICE.)

TPX-42. A numeric beacon decoder equipment/system. It is designed to be added to terminal radar systems for beacon decoding. It provides rapid target identification, reinforcement of the primary radar target, and altitude information from Mode C. (See AUTOMATED RADAR TERMINAL SYSTEMS.) (See TRANSPONDER.)

TRACEABLE PRESSURE STANDARD. The facility station pressure instrument, with certification/calibration traceable to the National Institute of Standards and Technology. Traceable pressure standards may be mercurial barometers, commissioned ASOS or dual transducer AWOS, or portable pressure standards or DASI.

TRACK. The actual flight path of an aircraft over the surface of the earth. (See COURSE.) (See FLIGHT PATH.) (See ROUTE.) (See ICAO term TRACK.)

TRACK [ICAO]. The projection on the earth's surface of the path of an aircraft, the direction of which path at any point is usually expressed in degrees from North (True, Magnetic, or Grid).

TRAFFIC.
a. A term used by a controller to transfer radar identification of an aircraft to another controller for the purpose of coordinating separation action. Traffic is normally issued:
1. In response to a handoff or point out,
2. In anticipation of a handoff or point out, or
3. In conjunction with a request for control of an aircraft.
b. A term used by ATC to refer to one or more aircraft.

TRAFFIC ADVISORIES. Advisories issued to alert pilots to other known or observed air traffic which may be in such proximity to the position or intended route of flight of their aircraft to warrant their attention. Such advisories may be based on:

a. Visual observation.

b. Observation of radar identified and nonidentified aircraft targets on an ATC radar display, or

c. Verbal reports from pilots or other facilities.

Note 1: The word "traffic" followed by additional information, if known, is used to provide such advisories; e.g., "Traffic, 2 o'clock, one zero miles, southbound, eight thousand."

Note 2: Traffic advisory service will be provided to the extent possible depending on higher priority duties of the controller or other limitations; e.g., radar limitations, volume of traffic, frequency congestion, or controller workload. Radar/nonradar traffic advisories do not relieve the pilot of his/her responsibility to see and avoid other aircraft. Pilots are cautioned that there are many times when the controller is not able to give traffic advisories concerning all traffic in the aircraft's proximity; in other words, when a pilot requests or is receiving traffic advisories, he/she should not assume that all traffic will be issued.

(Refer to AIM.)

TRAFFIC ALERT (aircraft call sign), TURN (left/right) IMMEDIATELY, (climb/descend) AND MAINTAIN (altitude). (See SAFETY ALERT.)

TRAFFIC ALERT AND COLLISION AVOIDANCE SYSTEM. An airborne collision avoidance system based on radar beacon signals which operates independent of ground-based equipment. TCAS-I generates traffic advisories only. TCAS-II generates traffic advisories, and resolution (collision avoidance) advisories in the vertical plane.

TRAFFIC INFORMATION. (See TRAFFIC ADVISORIES.)

TRAFFIC IN SIGHT. Used by pilots to inform a controller that previously issued traffic is in sight. (See NEGATIVE CONTACT.) (See TRAFFIC ADVISORIES.)

TRAFFIC MANAGEMENT ADVISOR (TMA). A computerized tool which assists Traffic Management Coordinators to efficiently schedule arrival traffic to a metered airport, by calculating meter fix times and delays then sending that information to the sector controllers.

TRAFFIC MANAGEMENT PROGRAM ALERT. A term used in a Notice to Airmen (NOTAM) issued in conjunction with a special traffic management program to alert pilots to the existence of the program and to refer them to either the Notices to Airmen publication or a special traffic management program advisory message for program details. The contraction TMPA is used in NOTAM text.

TRAFFIC MANAGEMENT UNIT. The entity in ARTCCs and designated terminals directly involved in the active management of facility traffic. Usually under the direct supervision of an assistant manager for traffic management.

TRAFFIC NO FACTOR. Indicates that the traffic described in a previously issued traffic advisory is no factor.

TRAFFIC NO LONGER OBSERVED. Indicates that the traffic described in a previously issued traffic advisory is no longer depicted on radar, but may still be a factor.

TRAFFIC PATTERN. The traffic flow that is prescribed for aircraft landing at, taxiing on, or taking off from an airport. The components of a typical traffic pattern are upwind leg, crosswind leg, downwind leg, base leg, and final approach.

a. Upwind Leg. A flight path parallel to the landing runway in the direction of landing.

b. Crosswind Leg. A flight path at right angles to the landing runway off its upwind end.

c. Downwind Leg. A flight path parallel to the landing runway in the direction opposite to landing. The downwind leg normally extends between the crosswind leg and the base leg.

d. Base Leg. A flight path at right angles to the landing runway off its approach end. The base leg normally extends from the downwind leg to the intersection of the extended runway centerline.

e. Final Approach. A flight path in the direction of landing along the extended runway centerline. The final approach normally extends from the base leg to the runway. An aircraft making a straight-in approach VFR is also considered to be on final approach.

(See STRAIGHT-IN APPROACH VFR.) (See TAXI PATTERNS.) (See ICAO term AERODROME TRAFFIC CIRCUIT.) (Refer to 14 CFR Part 91.) (Refer to AIM.)

TRAFFIC SITUATION DISPLAY (TSD). TSD is a computer system that receives radar track data from all 20 CONUS ARTCCs, organizes this data into a mosaic display, and presents it on a computer screen. The display allows the traffic management coordinator multiple methods of selection and highlighting of individual aircraft or groups of aircraft. The user has the option of superimposing these aircraft positions over any number of background displays. These background options include ARTCC boundaries, any stratum of en route sector boundaries, fixes, airways, military and other special use airspace, airports, and geopolitical boundaries. By using the TSD, a coordinator can monitor any number of traffic situations or the entire systemwide traffic flows.

TRAJECTORY. A URET representation of the path an aircraft is predicted to fly based upon a Current Plan or Trial Plan. (See USER REQUEST EVALUATION TOOL.)

TRAJECTORY MODELING. The automated process of calculating a trajectory.

TRANSCRIBED WEATHER BROADCAST. A continuous recording of meteorological and aeronautical information that is broadcast on L/MF and VOR facilities for pilots. (Refer to AIM.)

TRANSFER OF CONTROL. That action whereby the responsibility for the separation of an aircraft is transferred from one controller to another. (See ICAO term TRANSFER OF CONTROL.)

TRANSFER OF CONTROL [ICAO]. Transfer of responsibility for providing air traffic control service.

TRANSFERRING CONTROLLER. A controller/facility transferring control of an aircraft to another controller/facility. (See ICAO term TRANSFERRING UNIT/CONTROLLER.)

TRANSFERRING FACILITY. (See TRANSFERRING CONTROLLER.)

TRANSFERRING UNIT/CONTROLLER [ICAO]. Air traffic control unit/air traffic controller in the process of transferring the responsibility for providing air traffic control service to an aircraft to the next air traffic control unit/air traffic controller along the route of flight.

Note: See definition of accepting unit/controller.

TRANSITION.
a. The general term that describes the change from one phase of flight or flight condition to another; e.g., transition from en route flight to the approach or transition from instrument flight to visual flight.
b. A published procedure (DP Transition) used to connect the basic DP to one of several en route airways/jet routes, or a published procedure (STAR Transition) used to connect one of several en route airways/jet routes to the basic STAR. (Refer to DP/STAR Charts.)

TRANSITION POINT. A point at an adapted number of miles from the vertex at which an arrival aircraft would normally commence descent from its en route altitude. This is the first fix adapted on the arrival speed segments.

TRANSITION WAYPOINT. The waypoint that defines the beginning of a runway or en route transition on an RNAV SID or STAR.

TRANSITIONAL AIRSPACE. That portion of controlled airspace wherein aircraft change from one phase of flight or flight condition to another.

TRANSMISSOMETER. An apparatus used to determine visibility by measuring the transmission of light through the atmosphere. It is the measurement source for determining runway visual range (RVR) and runway visibility value (RVV). (See VISIBILITY.)

TRANSMITTING IN THE BLIND. A transmission from one station to other stations in circumstances where two-way communication cannot be established, but where it is believed that the called stations may be able to receive the transmission.

TRANSPONDER. The airborne radar beacon receiver/transmitter portion of the Air Traffic Control Radar Beacon System (ATCRBS) which automatically receives radio signals from interrogators on the ground, and selectively replies with a specific reply pulse or pulse group only to those interrogations being received on the mode to which it is set to respond. (See INTERROGATOR.) (See ICAO term TRANSPONDER.) (Refer to AIM.)

TRANSPONDER [ICAO]. A receiver/transmitter which will generate a reply signal upon proper interrogation; the interrogation and reply being on different frequencies.

TRANSPONDER CODES. (See CODES.)

TRIAL PLAN. A proposed amendment which utilizes automation to analyze and display potential conflicts along the predicted trajectory of the selected aircraft.

TRSA. (See TERMINAL RADAR SERVICE AREA.)

TSD. (See TRAFFIC SITUATION DISPLAY.)

TURBOJET AIRCRAFT. An aircraft having a jet engine in which the energy of the jet operates a turbine which in turn operates the air compressor.

TURBOPROP AIRCRAFT. An aircraft having a jet engine in which the energy of the jet operates a turbine which drives the propeller.

TURN ANTICIPATION. (maneuver anticipation).

TVOR. (See TERMINAL-VERY HIGH FREQUENCY OMNIDIRECTIONAL RANGE STATION.)

TWEB. (See TRANSCRIBED WEATHER BROADCAST.)

TWO-WAY RADIO COMMUNICATIONS FAILURE. (See LOST COMMUNICATIONS.)

U

UDF. (See DIRECTION FINDER.)

UHF. (See ULTRAHIGH FREQUENCY.)

ULTRAHIGH FREQUENCY. The frequency band between 300 and 3,000 MHz. The bank of radio frequencies used for military air/ground voice communications. In some instances this may go as low as 225 MHz and still be referred to as UHF.

ULTRALIGHT VEHICLE. An aeronautical vehicle operated for sport or recreational purposes which does not require FAA registration, an airworthiness certificate, nor pilot certification. They are primarily single occupant vehicles, although some two-place vehicles are authorized for training purposes. Operation of an ultralight vehicle in certain airspace requires authorization from ATC. (Refer to 14 CFR Part 103.)

UNABLE. Indicates inability to comply with a specific instruction, request, or clearance.

UNDER THE HOOD. Indicates that the pilot is using a hood to restrict visibility outside the cockpit while simulating instrument flight. An appropriately rated pilot is required in the other control seat while this operation is being conducted. (Refer to 14 CFR Part 91.)

UNFROZEN. The Scheduled Time of Arrival (STA) tags, which are still being rescheduled by traffic management advisor (TMA) calculations. The aircraft will remain unfrozen until the time the corresponding estimated time of arrival (ETA) tag passes the preset freeze horizon for that aircraft's stream class. At this point the automatic rescheduling will stop, and the STA becomes "frozen."

UNICOM. A nongovernment communication facility which may provide airport information at certain airports. Locations and frequencies of UNICOMs are shown on aeronautical charts and publications. (See AIRPORT/FACILITY DIRECTORY.) (Refer to AIM.)

UNPUBLISHED ROUTE. A route for which no minimum altitude is published or charted for pilot use. It may include a direct route between NAVAIDs, a radial, a radar vector, or a final approach course beyond the segments of an instrument approach procedure. (See PUBLISHED ROUTE.) (See ROUTE.)

UNRELIABLE (GPS/WAAS). An advisory to pilots indicating the expected level of service of the GPS and/or WAAS may not be available. Pilots must then determine the adequacy of the signal for desired use.

UPWIND LEG. (See TRAFFIC PATTERN.)

URET. (See USER REQUEST EVALUATION TOOL.)

URGENCY. A condition of being concerned about safety and of requiring timely but not immediate assistance; a potential distress condition. (See ICAO term URGENCY.)

URGENCY [ICAO]. A condition concerning the safety of an aircraft or other vehicle, or of person on board or in sight, but which does not require immediate assistance.

USAFIB. (See ARMY AVIATION FLIGHT INFORMATION BULLETIN.)

USER REQUEST EVALUATION TOOL (URET). User Request Evaluation Tool is an automated tool provided at each Radar Associate position in selected En Route facilities. This tool utilizes flight and radar data to determine present and future trajectories for all active and proposal aircraft and provides enhanced, automated flight data management.

UVDF. (See DIRECTION FINDER.)

V

VASI. (See VISUAL APPROACH SLOPE INDICATOR.)

VDF. (See DIRECTION FINDER.)

VDP. (See VISUAL DESCENT POINT.)

VECTOR. A heading issued to an aircraft to provide navigational guidance by radar. (See ICAO term RADAR VECTORING.)

VERIFY. Request confirmation of information; e.g., "verify assigned altitude."

VERIFY SPECIFIC DIRECTION OF TAKEOFF (OR TURNS AFTER TAKEOFF). Used by ATC to ascertain an aircraft's direction of takeoff and/or direction of turn after takeoff. It is normally used for IFR departures from an airport not having a control tower. When direct communication with the pilot is not possible, the request and information may be relayed through an FSS, dispatcher, or by other means. (See IFR TAKEOFF MINIMUMS AND DEPARTURE PROCEDURES.)

VERTEX. The last fix adapted on the arrival speed segments. Normally, it will be the outer marker of the runway in use. However, it may be the actual threshold or other suitable common point on the approach path for the particular runway configuration.

VERTEX TIME OF ARRIVAL. A calculated time of aircraft arrival over the adapted vertex for the runway configuration in use. The time is calculated via the optimum flight path using adapted speed segments.

VERTICAL NAVIGATION (VNAV). A function of area navigation (RNAV) equipment which calculates, displays, and provides vertical guidance to a profile or path.

VERTICAL SEPARATION. Separation established by assignment of different altitudes or flight levels. (See SEPARATION.) (See ICAO term VERTICAL SEPARATION.)

VERTICAL SEPARATION [ICAO]. Separation between aircraft expressed in units of vertical distance.

VERTICAL TAKEOFF AND LANDING AIRCRAFT. Aircraft capable of vertical climbs and/or descents and of using very short runways or small areas for takeoff and landings. These aircraft include, but are not limited to, helicopters. (See SHORT TAKEOFF AND LANDING AIRCRAFT.)

VERY HIGH FREQUENCY. The frequency band between 30 and 300 MHz. Portions of this band, 108 to 118 MHz, are used for certain NAVAIDs; 118 to 136 MHz are used for civil air/ground voice communications. Other frequencies in this band are used for purposes not related to air traffic control.

VERY HIGH FREQUENCY OMNIDIRECTIONAL RANGE STATION. (See VOR.)

VERY LOW FREQUENCY. The frequency band between 3 and 30 KHz.

VFR. (See VISUAL FLIGHT RULES.)

VFR AIRCRAFT. An aircraft conducting flight in accordance with visual flight rules. (See VISUAL FLIGHT RULES.)

VFR CONDITIONS. Weather conditions equal to or better than the minimum for flight under visual flight rules. The term may be used as an ATC clearance/instruction only when:
   a. An IFR aircraft requests a climb/descent in VFR conditions.
   b. The clearance will result in noise abatement benefits where part of the IFR departure route does not conform to an FAA approved noise abatement route or altitude.
   c. A pilot has requested a practice instrument approach and is not on an IFR flight plan.

Note: All pilots receiving this authorization must comply with the VFR visibility and distance from cloud criteria in 14 CFR Part 91. Use of the term does not relieve controllers of their responsibility to separate

aircraft in Class B and Class C airspace or TRSAs as required by FAAO 7110.65. When used as an ATC clearance/instruction, the term may be abbreviated "VFR;" e.g., "MAINTAIN VFR," "CLIMB/DESCEND VFR," etc.

VFR FLIGHT. (See VFR AIRCRAFT.)

VFR MILITARY TRAINING ROUTES. Routes used by the Department of Defense and associated Reserve and Air Guard units for the purpose of conducting low-altitude navigation and tactical training under VFR below 10,000 feet MSL at airspeeds in excess of 250 knots IAS.

VFR NOT RECOMMENDED. An advisory provided by a flight service station to a pilot during a preflight or inflight weather briefing that flight under visual flight rules is not recommended. To be given when the current and/or forecast weather conditions are at or below VFR minimums. It does not abrogate the pilot's authority to make his/her own decision.

VFR-ON-TOP. ATC authorization for an IFR aircraft to operate in VFR conditions at any appropriate VFR altitude (as specified in 14 CFR and as restricted by ATC). A pilot receiving this authorization must comply with the VFR visibility, distance from cloud criteria, and the minimum IFR altitudes specified in 14 CFR Part 91. The use of this term does not relieve controllers of their responsibility to separate aircraft in Class B and Class C airspace or TRSAs as required by FAAO 7110.65.

VFR TERMINAL AREA CHARTS. (See AERONAUTICAL CHART.)

VFR WAYPOINT. (See WAYPOINT.)

VHF. (See VERY HIGH FREQUENCY.)

VHF OMNIDIRECTIONAL RANGE/TACTICAL AIR NAVIGATION. (See VORTAC.)

VIDEO MAP. An electronically displayed map on the radar display that may depict data such as airports, heliports, runway centerline extensions, hospital emergency landing areas, NAVAIDs and fixes, reporting points, airway/route centerlines, boundaries, handoff points, special use tracks, obstructions, prominent geographic features, map alignment indicators, range accuracy marks, minimum vectoring altitudes.

VISIBILITY. The ability, as determined by atmospheric conditions and expressed in units of distance, to see and identify prominent unlighted objects by day and prominent lighted objects by night. Visibility is reported as statute miles, hundreds of feet or meters. (Refer to 14 CFR Part 91.) (Refer to AIM.)

a. Flight Visibility. The average forward horizontal distance, from the cockpit of an aircraft in flight, at which prominent unlighted objects may be seen and identified by day and prominent lighted objects may be seen and identified by night.

b. Ground Visibility. Prevailing horizontal visibility near the earth's surface as reported by the United States National Weather Service or an accredited observer.

c. Prevailing Visibility. The greatest horizontal visibility equaled or exceeded throughout at least half the horizon circle which need not necessarily be continuous.

d. Runway Visibility Value (RVV). The visibility determined for a particular runway by a transmissometer. A meter provides a continuous indication of the visibility (reported in miles or fractions of miles) for the runway. RVV is used in lieu of prevailing visibility in determining minimums for a particular runway.

e. Runway Visual Range (RVR). An instrumentally derived value, based on standard calibrations, that represents the horizontal distance a pilot will see down the runway from the approach end. It is based on the sighting of either high intensity runway lights or on the visual contrast of other targets whichever yields the greater visual range. RVR, in contrast to prevailing or runway visibility, is based on what a pilot in a moving aircraft should see looking down the runway. RVR is horizontal visual range, not slant visual range. It is based on the measurement of a transmissometer made near the touchdown point of the instrument runway and is reported in hundreds of feet. RVR is used in lieu of RVV and/or prevailing visibility in determining minimums for a particular runway.

1. Touchdown RVR. The RVR visibility readout values obtained from RVR equipment serving the runway touchdown zone.

2. Mid-RVR. The RVR readout values obtained from RVR equipment located midfield of the runway.

3. Rollout RVR. The RVR readout values obtained from RVR equipment located nearest the rollout end of the runway.

(See ICAO term VISIBILITY.)

VISIBILITY [ICAO]. The ability, as determined by atmospheric conditions and expressed in units of distance, to see and identify prominent unlighted objects by day and prominent lighted objects by night.

a. Flight Visibility—The visibility forward from the cockpit of an aircraft in flight.

b. Ground Visibility—The visibility at an aerodrome as reported by an accredited observer.

c. Runway Visual Range [RVR]—The range over which the pilot of an aircraft on the centerline of a runway can see the runway surface markings or the lights delineating the runway or identifying its centerline.

VISUAL APPROACH. An approach conducted on an instrument flight rules (IFR) flight plan which authorizes the pilot to proceed visually and clear of clouds to the airport. The pilot must, at all times, have either the airport or the preceding aircraft in sight. This approach must be authorized and under the control of the appropriate air traffic control facility. Reported weather at the airport must be ceiling at or above 1,000 feet and visibility of 3 miles or greater. (See ICAO term VISUAL APPROACH.)

VISUAL APPROACH [ICAO]. An approach by an IFR flight when either part or all of an instrument approach procedure is not completed and the approach is executed in visual reference to terrain.

VISUAL APPROACH SLOPE INDICATOR. (See AIRPORT LIGHTING.)

VISUAL DESCENT POINT. A defined point on the final approach course of a nonprecision straight-in approach procedure from which normal descent from the MDA to the runway touchdown point may be commenced, provided the approach threshold of that runway, or approach lights, or other markings identifiable with the approach end of that runway are clearly visible to the pilot.

VISUAL FLIGHT RULES. Rules that govern the procedures for conducting flight under visual conditions. The term "VFR" is also used in the United States to indicate weather conditions that are equal to or greater than minimum VFR requirements. In addition, it is used by pilots and controllers to indicate type of flight plan. (See INSTRUMENT FLIGHT RULES.) (See INSTRUMENT METEOROLOGICAL CONDITIONS.) (See VISUAL METEOROLOGICAL CONDITIONS.) (Refer to 14 CFR Part 91.) (Refer to AIM.)

VISUAL HOLDING. The holding of aircraft at selected, prominent geographical fixes which can be easily recognized from the air. (See HOLDING FIX.)

VISUAL METEOROLOGICAL CONDITIONS. Meteorological conditions expressed in terms of visibility, distance from cloud, and ceiling equal to or better than specified minima. (See INSTRUMENT FLIGHT RULES.) (See INSTRUMENT METEO-

ROLOGICAL CONDITIONS.) (See VISUAL FLIGHT RULES.)

VISUAL SEPARATION. A means employed by ATC to separate aircraft in terminal areas and en route airspace in the NAS. There are two ways to effect this separation:

a. The tower controller sees the aircraft involved and issues instructions, as necessary, to ensure that the aircraft avoid each other.

b. A pilot sees the other aircraft involved and upon instructions from the controller provides his/her own separation by maneuvering his/her aircraft as necessary to avoid it. This may involve following another aircraft or keeping it in sight until it is no longer a factor.

(See SEE AND AVOID.) (Refer to 14 CFR Part 91.)

VLF. (See VERY LOW FREQUENCY.)

VMC. (See VISUAL METEOROLOGICAL CONDITIONS.)

VOICE SWITCHING AND CONTROL SYSTEM. The VSCS is a computer controlled switching system that provides air traffic controllers with all voice circuits (air to ground and ground to ground) necessary for air traffic control. (See VOICE SWITCHING AND CONTROL SYSTEM.) (Refer to AIM.)

VOR. A ground-based electronic navigation aid transmitting very high frequency navigation signals, 360 degrees in azimuth, oriented from magnetic north. Used as the basis for navigation in the National Airspace System. The VOR periodically identifies itself by Morse Code and may have an additional voice identification feature. Voice features may be used by ATC or FSS for transmitting instructions/information to pilots. (See NAVIGATIONAL AID.) (Refer to AIM.)

VOR TEST SIGNAL. (See VOT.)

VORTAC. A navigation aid providing VOR azimuth, TACAN azimuth, and TACAN distance measuring equipment (DME) at one site. (See DISTANCE MEASURING EQUIPMENT.) (See NAVIGATIONAL AID.) (See TACAN.) (See VOR.) (Refer to AIM.)

VORTICES. Circular patterns of air created by the movement of an airfoil through the air when generating lift. As an airfoil moves through the atmosphere in sustained flight, an area of area of low pressure is created above it. The air flowing from the high pressure area to the low pressure area around and about the tips of the airfoil tends to roll up into two rapidly rotating vortices, cylindrical in shape. These vortices are the most predominant parts of aircraft wake turbulence and their rotational force is dependent upon the wing loading, gross weight, and speed of the generating aircraft. The vortices from medium to heavy aircraft can be of extremely high velocity and hazardous to smaller aircraft. (See AIRCRAFT CLASSES.) (See WAKE TURBULENCE.) (Refer to AIM.)

VOT. A ground facility which emits a test signal to check VOR receiver accuracy. Some VOTs are available to the user while airborne, and others are limited to ground use only. (See AIRPORT/FACILITY DIRECTORY.) (Refer to 14 CFR Part 91.) (Refer to AIM.)

VR. (See VFR MILITARY TRAINING ROUTES.)

VSCS. (See VOICE SWITCHING AND CONTROL SYSTEM.)

VTA. (See VERTEX TIME OF ARRIVAL.)

VTOL AIRCRAFT. (See VERTICAL TAKEOFF AND LANDING AIRCRAFT.)

W

WA. (See AIRMET.) (See WEATHER ADVISORY.)

WAAS. (See WIDE-AREA AUGMENTATION SYSTEM.)

WAKE TURBULENCE. Phenomena resulting from the passage of an aircraft through the atmosphere. The term includes vortices, thrust stream turbulence, jet blast, jet wash, propeller wash, and rotor wash both on the ground and in the air. (See AIRCRAFT CLASSES.) (See JET BLAST.) (See VORTICES.) (Refer to AIM.)

WARNING AREA. (See SPECIAL USE AIRSPACE.)

WAYPOINT. A predetermined geographical position used for route/instrument approach definition, progress reports, published VFR routes, visual reporting points or points for transitioning and/or circumnavigating controlled and/or special use airspace, that is defined relative to a VORTAC station or in terms of latitude/longitude coordinates.

WEATHER ADVISORY. In aviation weather forecast practice, an expression of hazardous weather conditions not predicted in the area forecast, as they affect the operation of air traffic and as prepared by the NWS. (See AIRMET.) (See SIGMET.)

WHEN ABLE. When used in conjunction with ATC instructions, gives the pilot the latitude to delay compliance until a condition or event has been reconciled. Unlike "pilot discretion," when instructions are prefaced "when able," the pilot is expected to seek the first opportunity to comply. Once a maneuver has been initiated, the pilot is expected to continue until the specifications of the instructions have been met. "When able," should not be used when expeditious compliance is required.

WIDE-AREA AUGMENTATION SYSTEM (WAAS). The WAAS is a satellite navigation system consisting of the equipment and software which augments the GPS Standard Positioning Service (SPS). The WAAS provides enhanced integrity, accuracy, availability, and continuity over and above GPS SPS. The differential correction function provides improved accuracy required for precision approach.

WILCO. I have received your message, understand it, and will comply with it.

WIND GRID DISPLAY. A display that presents the latest forecasted wind data overlaid on a map of the ARTCC area. Wind data is automatically entered and updated periodically by transmissions from the National Weather Service. Winds at specific altitudes, along with temperatures and air pressure can be viewed.

WIND SHEAR. A change in wind speed and/or wind direction in a short distance resulting in a tearing or shearing effect. It can exist in a horizontal or vertical direction and occasionally in both.

WING TIP VORTICES. (See VORTICES.)

WORDS TWICE.
a. As a request: "Communication is difficult. Please say every phrase twice."
b. As information: "Since communications are difficult, every phrase in this message will be spoken twice."

WORLD AERONAUTICAL CHARTS. (See AERONAUTICAL CHART.)

WS. (See SIGMET.) (See WEATHER ADVISORY.)

WST. (See CONVECTIVE SIGMET.) (See WEATHER ADVISORY.)